From Peasant to Patriarch

From Peasant to Patriarch

Account of the Birth, Upbringing, and Life of His Holiness Nikon, Patriarch of Moscow and All Russia

Written by His Cleric Ioann Shusherin

Translated and Annotated by
Kevin Kain and Katia Levintova

LEXINGTON BOOKS

A division of
ROWMAN & LITTLEFIELD PUBLISHERS, INC.
Lanham • Boulder • New York • Toronto • Plymouth, UK

LEXINGTON BOOKS

A division of Rowman & Littlefield Publishers, Inc.
A wholly owned subsidary of The Rowman & Littlefield Publishing Group, Inc.
4501 Forbes Boulevard, Suite 200
Lanham, MD 20706

Estover Road
Plymouth PL6 7PY
United Kingdom

British Library Cataloguing in Publication Information Available

Library of Congress Cataloging-in-Publication Data

The hardback edition of this book was previously cataloged by the Library of Congress as
follows:

Shusherin, Ivan Kornil'evich, ca. 1630–1690.
 [Izviestie o rozhdenii i vospitanii i o zhitii sviatieishago Nikona, Patriarkha
Moskovskago i vseia Rossii. English]
 From peasant to patriarch : account of the birth, upbringing, and life of His Holiness
Nikon, Patriarch of Moscow and All Russia / written by Ioann Shusherin ; translated and
annotated by Kevin Kain and Katia Levintova.
   p. cm.
 Includes bibliographical references and index.
 1. Nikon, Patriarch of Moscow and of Russia, 1605–1681. 2. Russkaia pravoslavnaia
tserkov'—Bishops—Biography. 3. Orthodox Eastern Church—Russia—Bishops—
Biography. I. Kain, Kevin, 1966–II. Levintova, Katia, 1970–III. Title.
 BX597.N5S4913 2007
 281.9092—dc22   2007006866

 ISBN-13: 978-0-7391-1579-4 (cloth : alk. paper)
 ISBN-10: 0-7391-1579-0 (cloth : alk. paper)
 ISBN-13: 978-0-7391-1580-0 (pbk. : alk. paper)
 ISBN-10: 0-7391-1580-4 (pbk. : alk. paper)

Printed in the United States of America

⊗™ The paper used in this publication meets the minimum requirements of American
National Standard for Information Sciences—Permanence of Paper for Printed Library
Materials, ANSI/NISO Z39.48–1992.

To Misha, Tatiana, Mikhail, and our families

Contents

Acknowledgements

First we want to thank the scholars of Russian history who supported our efforts to translate this important document. We are especially grateful to Galina Mitrofanovna Zelenskaia who not only encouraged this book, but generously shared her own research findings and alerted us to the latest Russian scholarship on patriarch Nikon. Staff of the New Jerusalem Monastery Museum, especially its director, Nataliia Alekseevna Abakumova immensely aided our research efforts at that repository. We wish to thank John Norman for the inspiration and training in Russian cultural history that provided the foundation upon which this project grew. His generous help throughout our graduate careers and extremely helpful comments on parts of this book are also appreciated. In the process of bringing Shusherin's narrative to an English-speaking audience, we had strong support from many American and Russian scholars who encouraged our efforts, especially Georg Michels, Nadieszda Kizenko, Susan MacCaffrey, Irina Vassil'evna Pozdeeva, and Leonid Iosifovich Borodkin. Marina Osipenko set an important example of commitment to research that we tried to emulate in this and other projects.

We are also indebted to Kristin Szylvian and Michael Chiarappa who provided insights from the perspective of non-Russian specialists. Ashlyn Kuersten's expert advice is also much appreciated. Jim Butterfield, Emily Hauptmann, Judith Stone, Vyacheslav Karpov, and James Palmitessa set examples of academic rigor and integrity that we try to follow in this and other projects. We are better scholars because of our graduate mentors.

We gratefully thank the anonymous reviewer of the original manuscript whose careful reading made this book stronger by offering insightful suggestions in terms of content and style and providing bibliographical references. All the shortcomings that remain are ours and ours alone.

Much of the research for the annotations to this book was conducted during two consecutive associateships at the Summer Research Lab on Russia and Eastern Europe held at the University of Illinois, Urbana-Champaign (2005, 2006). We would also like to thank the Faculty Senate and the library staff of

Texas A&M University-Texarkana, especially Teri Stover and Melba Surman, for procuring several published primary sources and rare Russian books essential for this project.

This book would not be possible without the selfless dedication of Tatiana Chekalina and Mikhail Levintov who ensured that we had time and energy to complete this project and who provided useful advice when it was most needed.

Introduction

Nikita Minov (1605–1681), better known as Nikon, patriarch of Moscow and all Russia, is one of the most complex, controversial, and important figures in Russian history. Capable of both pious acts of humility and daring political maneuvers, Nikon led a life of extremes. Born into a peasant family, Nikon rose through the ranks of the church hierarchy, earning the admiration of *tsar* Aleksei Mikhailovich to become the head of the Russian Orthodox Church (1652), the second most powerful figure in the Muscovite state. As patriarch, Nikon imposed comprehensive religious reforms, fought to preserve traditional church prerogatives, and founded three monasteries—the Iverskii Monastery (1654), the Cross Monastery (1656), and the Resurrection, also known as New Jerusalem, Monastery (1657).

Nikon's fall from grace was no less dramatic. In July 1658, the patriarch withdrew from Moscow and devoted himself primarily to his monastery building program. Nikon's intransigence in resisting demands to relinquish the patriarchal title and prerogatives generated powerful opposition, culminating in an organized campaign to remove him. In December 1666, following more than five years of official investigations of his activities, the patriarch was tried before a state-sanctioned council of the church synod composed of Russian churchmen and headed by two ecumenical Orthodox patriarchs. Found guilty of charges ranging from abandoning his flock to treason, Nikon was removed from the patriarchal throne, reduced to the rank of "simple monk" and sentenced to exile in a remote northern monastery.

After nearly twenty years of imprisonment Nikon's fortune took another drastic turn when a royal order recalled him from exile. The reprieve however came too late and the ailing patriarch died on August 17, 1681 en route to his Resurrection Monastery. By the decree of *tsar* Fedor Alekseevich, son and heir to Aleksei Mikhailovich, Nikon was buried and commemorated with appropriate patriarchal honors at the Resurrection Monastery. Full rehabilitation followed in 1682, when four ecumenical Orthodox patriarchs formally absolved the patriarch of the most damning charges and issued permission to commemorate him as all other Moscow patriarchs.

Nikon's life is well documented. Contemporary Russian and foreign commentators often discussed the patriarch and Nikon himself left multiple autobiographical records. But only a single source, Ioann Shusherin's *Account of Birth, Life, and Upbringing of His Holiness Nikon, Patriarch of Moscow and All Russia* (1681–1686), comes close to immortalizing the vicissitudes of Nikon's life in its entirety. Written by the patriarch's trusted servant, the biography appeared in hundreds of handwritten copies in the late seventeenth and eighteenth centuries, making the *Account* "the most circulated work in the repertoire of the late Russian handwritten book culture."[1] Numerous manuscripts of the biography differ in minor details, but generally fall into four redactions: Iverskii, New Jerusalem, Solovetskii, and Rumiantsev.[2]

Shusherin's work first appeared in print in 1784, when O. P. Kozodavlev published the Iverskii version under the title *Zhitie of His Holiness Patriarch Nikon Written by a Certain Cleric Close to Him,* suggesting a hagiographical treatment of Nikon's life.[3] It was reprinted in 1817 and 1909.[4] Notwithstanding the changes in the title, the Kozodavlev editions were published as exact copies of the Iverskii manuscript, without corrections, editorial work, or annotations to appeal to scholars and educated readers interested in Russian "antiquities" [*drevnosti*].[i] Printed on poor quality paper these early publications became bibliographical rarities by the mid-nineteenth century and were regarded as inaccessible, despite their authenticity.[5]

When Leonid Kavelin, archimandrite of the Resurrection Monastery (1869–1877), published the *Account* in 1871 it was a welcome improvement over the existing editions. The archimandrite not only compared the four existing manuscript versions, reconciling the discrepancies among them, but established a standard for publishing Shusherin's work, recognized as the most thoroughly researched. Kavelin's critical edition was reprinted in 1906, 1908, and after a lengthy hiatus, again in 1997 and 2004.[6] The current text is a translation of Kavelin's original edition of the *Account*.

More than the sheer numbers of copies and editions, Shusherin's work which discussed one of the most fascinating figures of national history emerged as a Russian cultural phenomenon. The *Account* became central to the study of Nikon, galvanizing both favorable and critical assessments of the patriarch, his character, and role in Russian history. But it is not a mere biography; it deals

---

[i] The first time important terms are introduced, the Russian originals are given in italics following their English translations. When the italicized Russian terms appear in parentheses, their detailed descriptions can be found in the Glossary. When the Russian term cannot be adequately translated or does not have an appropriate English equivalent, it is given in italics throughout the text and is also explained in the Glossary and, where necessary, in footnotes. In the cases when there was an accepted English equivalent of the Russian term which did not require further explanation, or when the meaning of a term was clarified in the text itself, the Russian italicized terms were given in brackets. The Russian terms in brackets are provided for immediate clarification and are not included in the Glossary.

with issues that ignite a number of philosophical and cultural discussions, including the relationship between the church, state and society, the consequences of social change and reforms, the nature of dissent and opposition, and the construction of Russian national identity. Shusherin's book, like Nikon himself, remains relevant today because it touches upon enduring themes of Russian history and culture.

Shusherin's biography is a seminal piece in the enduring polemics which although originating in the seventeenth century with Nikon's liturgical reforms, continues throughout Russian history. At the heart of the disagreement are questions about the legitimacy of the Russian Church, whose rituals and practices owe much to Nikon and which is often referred to as the "Nikonian Church." In the West, more scholarly attention has gone to the dissenting side and its main champions, especially archpriest Avvakum Petrov. But in Russia, the debate is much more intense with Nikon and his side receiving no less consideration. The *Account* which shows Nikon through the eyes of his disciple-assistant Shusherin reflects the arguments of the patriarch's seventeenth-century supporters and lays the foundation for future evaluation of Nikon, both adulatory and critical.

The *Account* also functions as a social commentary on seventeenth-century Russian life from a domestic, not a foreign perspective. Shusherin brings into his narrative all levels of Muscovite society, including the royal family, nobility, clergy, military, peasants, beggars, miscreants, and rebels. The biography likewise highlights the remarkable ethnic and religious diversity of a Russian state populated by Germans, Tartars, Jews, Greeks, Muslims, and others. Shusherin of course perpetuates common ethnic and gender stereotypes, but one of the most memorable and praised characters in the *Account* is Tatiana Mikhailovna (d. 1706), the sister of *tsar* Aleksei Mikhailovich. From the text we also learn about Muscovy's military campaigns, popular revolts, judicial system, art and architecture, dress, daily life (diet, work, and travel), popular belief, observance of religious festivals and holy days, funeral rites, education, and health issues. The author even enlightens readers on the consumption patterns and prestige goods of seventeenth-century Russia, which included Chinese silk, Italian wines, and furs.

Shusherin's text, notwithstanding its status in Russia, both pre-revolutionary and contemporary, is relatively unknown to English-speaking audiences.[7] Introducing Shusherin's work to English readers for the first time, this book goes beyond the previous editions by including glossaries and extensive annotations, which contain references to primary source and contemporary research findings. The parallel texts, many of which are translated for the first time, highlight the documentary and not simply the literary or sociological value of Shusherin's *Account* and frame the narrative in a new way, giving it added utility.

This translated and annotated edition of the *Account* is not intended to provide definitive answers to questions about Nikon's personality and motivations, his role in Russian history, or his lasting impact, nor do we seek to rehabilitate the patriarch. Even if we take Shusherin's story at face value, Nikon's personality and deeds are still controversial since the author himself did not portray the patriarch as flawless or beyond reproach. Rather, the current book serves to complement and expand the existing English-language scholarship on seventeenth-century Russia and its most important personalities and events. It also raises questions about the long accepted claims, especially the arguments that Nikon's patriarchate is best understood through the prism of his liturgical reforms and that patriarch's dethronement in 1666 determined his entire legacy. The *Account* indeed complicates what may otherwise appear as simple and clear-cut oppositions of official vs. dissenting, church vs. state, or progress vs. tradition often employed in conventional discussions of seventeenth-century Russia. Already this critical evidentiary piece further supports recent research findings which cast doubt on the extent and intensity of the original opposition to Nikon's religious reforms.[8] Shusherin's narrative too suggests that while there was comparatively little resistance to the patriarch's innovations, his monastery building program attracted much more attention in its day. It is our hope then that the current text will spark new analyses and reevaluation of existing scholarship on Nikon.

Ioann Shusherin and His Relationship with Patriarch Nikon

Much of what we know about Shusherin is found in his narrative about Nikon's life. From the text we learn that Ioann Kornil'ev Shusherin (Ripatov) was born in Novgorod the Great, most likely in the late 1630s, and educated in Nikon's household while the latter was metropolitan of Novgorod (1649–1652). When Nikon was elected patriarch, Shusherin went to Moscow with him and served as a sub-deacon. He also became Nikon's personal attendant and assistant, entrusted with delicate, even clandestine matters, including the smuggling of Nikon's letters critical of *tsar* Aleksei Mikhailovich to the patriarchs of Constantinople and Jerusalem.[9]

Shusherin's service to Nikon placed him in a dangerous position. In October 1666, the sub-deacon was charged with conspiracy for making a secret trip to Moscow during the previous year.[10] According to Shusherin, at that time Nikon warned him that he could be arrested for his loyalty. This indeed happened on November 30, 1666 when Shusherin, serving in the highly symbolic position as the patriarch's cross bearer, was taken into the *tsar's* custody. Two days later Aleksei Mikhailovich noted that he had the sub-deacon arrested "because for nine years he brought various messages to Nikon and caused many quarrels."[11]

Shusherin's account of his interrogation by the *tsar* is perhaps the strongest proof of his devotion to Nikon. In the author's own words, when the *tsar* demanded a confession under the threat of imprisonment, "strengthened by Holy God who gave me courage, I said that I knew nothing."[12] Displeasing the *tsar* with such intransigence, the sub-deacon was held in the chancery of secret affairs for eleven days, imprisoned in Moscow for three years, and then exiled to Novgorod the Great for ten years. Shusherin never saw Nikon alive again.

After the death of Aleksei Mikhailovich, Shusherin's fate was reversed by *tsarevna* Tatiana Mikhailovna, sister of the late *tsar* and one of Nikon's strongest allies in the royal family. When Shusherin returned from the exile to the capital city in 1679, he "enjoyed the grace of her highness more than others of the same rank" and served at the vestry of the *tsarevnas'* church. He composed most, if not all, of his *Account* upon return from exile.

The biographer not only immortalized his mentor in a literary and historical masterpiece, but continued Nikon's life work. The rehabilitated sub-deacon took a leading role supervising the completion of the main Church of the Resurrection Monastery. Indeed, Shusherin explained that he "cared tirelessly about all the monastery's needs because he had the intention of being buried near his mentor, in the holy Resurrection Monastery after his life would end." In 1693, in reward for his dedication and service, Shusherin was laid to rest next to patriarch Nikon in the monastery's Church of John the Baptist.

Sources of Shusherin's Account

Shusherin, writing in the third person, explained that he "described all the events from the very beginning and in great detail, witnessing some of what he has written and hearing some from his holiness and the rest from the brothers living with his holiness the patriarch who told [the author] about the life of his holiness in exile, where he endured calamities and deprivation until his death." Indeed, the biographer shows passion and admiration for his subject that is unlikely to have come from a disinterested third party or the official documents.

Contrary to his assertions however Shusherin based his work on much more than his personal experiences and the oral testimonials of Nikon and others close to the patriarch. It is clear that the author incorporated several of Nikon's own writings. It also appears that his close proximity to the royal family gave Shusherin access to official documents, including state decrees and Nikon's correspondence with Aleksei Mikhailovich. The biographer directly referenced specific documents and often wove extended quotations into his narrative. He even appended Russian translations of the patriarchal decrees which posthumously rehabilitated Nikon.[13] The annotations to this book contain translations of the many primary sources Shusherin mentioned in his text. The notes also include references to documents with which Shusherin was not familiar or which he omitted deliberately. In some cases, these sources clarify the author's statements; in others, they contradict his version of events.

Shusherin's use of sources is critical in understanding what makes his *Account* different from both the majority of the seventeenth-century records used to condemn Nikon at his trial and the patriarch's own writings at the time. The seventeenth-century documents are valid and authentic, but the atmosphere in which they were created and the intent with which they were to be used, of course, cast a long shadow on their treatment of Nikon. They include testimonials by individuals openly hostile to the patriarch who sought to remove him from the patriarchal throne. But even the numerous eyewitness accounts of Nikon's departure from the patriarchal seat in July 1658 provided by more neutral witnesses were extracted two years later, after the official proceedings to dislodge Nikon had begun.

Perhaps the most damning contemporary sources are the testimonies of openly anti-Nikon foreign clergymen, Paisius Ligarides, metropolitan of Gaza, and, to a lesser degree, Paul of Aleppo, son of the patriarch of Antioch, both of whom actively participated in the patriarch's dethronement. In a work tellingly titled "History of the Condemnation of the Patriarch Nikon" Ligarides marshals a host of important historical evidence as long as it supports the guilty verdict. Although working with eyewitness accounts and official documents, Ligarides painted such a negative picture of Nikon that *tsar* Aleksei Mikhailovich, to whom the book was dedicated, rejected it. Aleppo's somewhat more balanced narrative, "The Travels of Macarius of Antioch" (1670), is often interrupted with negative asides inserted after the patriarch's trial.[14]

Nikon's own writings at that time were affected by the same circumstances. He responded to the charges, both official and unofficial, in two significant works, *Replies of the Humble Nikon, by the Mercy of God Patriarch Against the Questions of Boyar Simeon Streshnev and the Answers of the Metropolitan of Gaza Paisius Ligarides* (1663) and his letter to Dionysius, patriarch of Constantinople (1665).[15] Although Shusherin was well aware of Nikon's *Replies* and the letter to Dionysius, he chose to avoid them and their often acerbic tone. During his exile too, the embattled patriarch was constantly under attack and often implicated himself; many of his responses to official charges were recorded by jailers looking for proofs of alleged transgressions.

Given the appeal and authority of the anti-Nikon sources, the patriarch's persistent treatment in historical scholarship as a power-hungry, morally corrupt, and ambitious statesman at odds with secular and ecclesiastical leadership is hardly surprising. But the official attitudes towards Nikon changed during the reign of Fedor Alekseevich, ultimately resulting in the patriarch's recall from exile and posthumous rehabilitation. This explains why Shusherin is able (and perhaps even eager) to leave out many of the negative, albeit historically accurate, details offered by the patriarch's opponents. And it is the sources created in this new atmosphere that Shusherin prefers over the documents which precipitated and justified patriarch's trial and exile. His story does not end with Nikon's defeat; on the contrary, he describes patriarch's final triumph. Shusherin's Nikon is radically different from the enduring image left by Ligarides and others or even by the patriarch himself.

Historical Context of the Account: Russian Church-State Relationship

The seventeenth century in Russia is widely recognized as a century in flux, torn between adherence to old piety, customs, and laws, often informal and not standardized, and the establishment of new rules and the codification of contemporary practices beyond simple informal enforcement. Following the Time of Troubles (1598–1613) and decades of foreign invasion, the Russian state was resurgent, rapidly expanding and deepening its power. These changes were not unlike the transformations which took place in Europe; indeed they were a part of larger European processes of centralization, legalization, confessionalization, and secularization. The state's encroachment into religious practices and economic activities increased the power of the Russian tsardom to new, unprecedented levels. Territorial expansion too necessitated strengthening of state power and regulation. The re-codification of Russian law, manifest in the Law Code [*Ulozhenie*] of 1649, legalized serfdom and established secular hegemony over spheres traditionally under church authority.

The reform, or rather secularization of the church's judicial and economic practices was one of the major consequences of the 1649 Law Code. For the first time, clergy and inhabitants of church properties, excluding those living on the patriarch's land holdings, were subject to the jurisdiction of the newly formed Monasterial Chancellery (*monastyrskii prikaz*) headed by secular judges. Moreover, the Code prohibited clerics, with the exception of the patriarch, from acquiring new properties. Nikon, an active defender of church prerogatives vis-à-vis the state, used these exemptions, actively acquiring properties to increase the power of his monasteries and thus the extent of his patriarchal authority and wealth.[16]

Shusherin however describes a different, somewhat idealized church-state relationship in which both institutions act in harmony, mutually reinforcing each other. The author, himself a cleric, frequently draws attention to the important role of the church and religious authority in providing societal discipline, moral order, and enlightenment of the population, administering penance, and legitimizing the state. The state in turn acts as the patron of the church, defending it against internal and foreign enemies and funding the construction and beautification of religious buildings and monasteries. The church and state, working together, ward off dissent, both political and religious. In short, Shusherin puts forward a textbook example of the seventeenth-century Russian take on the Byzantine doctrine of the state-church symphony.

The author also demonstrates the continued reliance of both the Russian church and the state on the authority of foreign Orthodox patriarchs. Throughout the narrative, we see Aleksei Mikhailovich and Nikon seeking the ecumenical patriarchs' seal of approval for the most contentious internal matters. Shusherin emphasizes the patriarchs' involvement in the reform of the Russian Church as well as Nikon's trial, condemnation, and posthumous rehabilitation.

Beyond the general discussion of the relationship between the state and church, a central theme of the *Account* is Nikon's relationship with *tsar* Aleksei Mikhailovich and his family. Nikon emerges as the autocrat's trusted ally and adviser, dispensing justice, putting down popular rebellions, and even serving as the head of the state in the *tsar's* absence from the capital. On another level, Shusherin stresses the close personal friendship between the patriarch and the *tsar*. We see Nikon serving as the godfather of Aleksei Mikhailovich's children, twice delivering the royal family from the plague, and praying for the deceased royals. The *tsar* reciprocates this loyalty by favoring Nikon and granting him titles, privileges, and properties. The author repeatedly mentions that Nikon and Aleksei Mikhailovich "love each other." The intimacy of this relationship is conveyed by extensive use of private dialogues and the actual personal correspondence between the patriarch and the *tsar*. It was ultimately Shusherin's portrayal of the congeniality and friendship between Nikon and Aleksei Mikhailovich that made the *Account* relevant in the enduring national discussions about the ideal balance between the state and church.

While explaining that conflicts between Nikon and Aleksei Mikhailovich did in fact occur, Shusherin often glances over them, omitting discussion of their causes. When tensions arise in the text, the author usually attributes them to a third party instigated by Satan stating, for example, that the discords between the *tsar* and the patriarch were "ignited by the evil people who were emblazoned by the enemy." Indeed, Shusherin often presents a much more congenial relationship between the *tsar* and the patriarch than Nikon himself did, a point made clear in the annotations to the text.

But in fact the patriarch did have a very dramatic fall from the *tsar's* grace. Arguably, the most poignant events of Nikon's biography involve the nearly eight years of self-imposed seclusion at the Resurrection Monastery (1658–1666), investigations of the official charges, clerical trial, condemnation, and exile. Shusherin, for whom the trial meant the end of the personal relationship with his mentor, spends as many pages describing its drama as he does discussing Nikon's entire patriarchate. The author clearly tries to discount the various charges raised against Nikon before and during the trial. Monastic deacon Feodosii, royal table attendant Roman Bobarykin, foreigners, Jewish converts, *boyar* Nikita Ziuzin and others are introduced to take the blame.

As in other sections of the narrative, Shusherin's account of the actual proceedings against Nikon centers on the patriarch's relationship with Aleksei Mikhailovich, including the private conversations between the patriarch and the *tsar* that allegedly took place during the trial, but were not recorded in the official transcripts. And whether or not it was true, Aleksei Mikhailovich is portrayed as innocently playing along the anti-Nikon party at his court, never deliberately trying to hurt his former friend. At times, Aleksei Mikhailovich's anguish is almost palpable. The *tsar's* exit mid-way through the trial obviously signals the end of this conflict. Later in the narrative, Shusherin catalogues the gifts and letters that the *tsar* sent to Nikon in exile in search of reconciliation.

The dramatic treatment of the confrontation between Nikon and Aleksei Mikhalovich during the patriarch's trial also underscores the moral limitations of the *tsar's* authority. At the height of the drama when the *boyars* face the dilemma of complying with the *tsar's* request and perjuring themselves or defying the royal behest, they choose the latter. In the divine economy of salvation in seventeenth-century Russia the secular state appears to play second fiddle to the moral authority of the church. Indeed, according to Shusherin, the humiliated *tsar* "comes to his senses" and privately seeks reconciliation with the patriarch, but the wheels of the judicial machinery are already set in motion. And even though Nikon may come across as the loser at the end of the trial, Shusherin establishes him as the long-term winner and the *tsar* as scoring a pyrrhic victory. The biographer even dutifully mentions that the church hierarchs privately continued to call Nikon "patriarch" long after his official demotion.

Historical Context: Moscow as the New Jerusalem, Nikon and His Monastery Building Program

The choice of the Resurrection New Jerusalem Monastery as another organizing principle of the *Account* is hardly accidental. The new Russian state required a compelling national idea. In the mid-seventeenth century during the reign of *tsar* Aleksei Mikhailovich and the patriarchate of Nikon the notions of Moscow as the Third Rome and Moscow as the New Jerusalem became the main staple of political and religious discourse. Both doctrines, which had deep roots in Russian political and religious thought, re-emerged as particularly attractive national ideas for several reasons. With most of the Orthodox world under Turkish control, the hierarchs of the Eastern Church recognized Russia, the strongest and wealthiest Orthodox state, as the bastion of the true faith and her *tsar* as its protector. In acknowledgement of Russia's new status, they frequented its capital, sought favors and military support from its *tsar,* and transferred relics from the Holy Land to this "Noah's ark" of Orthodoxy for safekeeping.[17]

Nikon did more than any of his contemporaries to promote the conception of Moscow as the New Jerusalem. The patriarch facilitated the translation of the relics from the Holy Land to Moscow, collected and redistributed the relics of Russian national saints and celebrated Russian holy men and their miracle-working capacities reinforcing the image of his people as the "chosen" ones. Nikon's vision of a Russian Holy Land came to full fruition in the three monasteries he founded. In theological writings about the monasteries Nikon unveils a plan to make the new foundations important centers of Orthodox piety and pilgrimage on par with the Holy Land and thus transfer religious authority and legitimacy to Russia.[18]

Engendering two critical issues of the seventeenth century—the church-state relationship and the new Russian national idea—Nikon's Resurrection New Jerusalem Monastery is of particular importance. It represents the patriarch's most ambitious and complete plan to create a new, Russian Holy Land. Located approximately fifty kilometers northeast of Moscow, the monastery survives to this day. In keeping with Nikon's vision, the surrounding areas were given names from the Holy Land; its toponomy included the Mount of Olives, the Garden of Gethsemane, and the River Jordan. The monastery's main sanctuary, the Church of the Resurrection, was modeled after the Church of the Holy Sepulcher in Jerusalem and contained replicas of Golgotha and Christ's tomb. While Nikon followed the basic lines or, to use his term, "prototype" of the original church, the New Jerusalem church was built and decorated in a distinctly Russian style and included altars dedicated to national saints.[19] The monastery is central to Shusherin's biography of the patriarch; indeed, the author sees it as the *modus vivendi* of the entire narrative:

> This pious man wrote this tale about the birth, upbringing, and entire life of his holiness patriarch Nikon, about the founding of the Resurrection Monastery and its great church, how they were founded and completed, and about the demise and burial of his holiness the patriarch. . . . All this he has written to glorify and honor the holy name of God and for the pleasure of readers and listeners so that the future

brothers of the Resurrection Monastery, also called New Jerusalem, and the entire Christian fold would learn about these events and so that the name of his holiness Nikon, patriarch of Moscow and all Russia, and the founder of the monastery, would be remembered to the end of the world.

The Resurrection Monastery is also crucial to understanding the patriarch's condemnation and removal from the patriarchal throne as well as his subsequent rehabilitation. Shusherin explains that between his departure from Moscow and the trial, Nikon busied himself primarily with the construction of the monastery. But this project proved to be a source of contention. Although initially praised by Aleksei Mikhailovich, who named it "New Jerusalem," the monastery was mentioned in several serious charges against Nikon raised in the 1660s. Indeed, the accusations of usurping the authority of the patriarch of Jerusalem and inappropriately using the name "New Jerusalem" which allegedly detracted from the significance of the Old City of Jerusalem were central to Nikon's removal from the patriarchal throne in 1666.[20] Condemning Nikon on these charges, the ecumenical patriarchs struck a major blow not only against the monastery, but against the national idea itself.

Yet the monastery's fall from grace, much like Nikon's, proved to be relatively short-lived. Shusherin explicitly states that *tsar* Fedor Alekseevich freed Nikon from exile and posthumously commemorated him as patriarch out of admiration for the New Jerusalem Monastery. From this perspective, the decision to recall Nikon signaled not only the rehabilitation of the patriarch, but his monastery and the concept of Moscow as the New Jerusalem. Tellingly, the *Account* ends not with Nikon's burial, but with the consecration of the monastery's main sanctuary in 1685.

In the epilogue, the author finally reveals the core objective of his entire narrative. The concluding section connects the contemporary Romanovs with the monastery. In a key passage the biographer explains: "With faith in our Lord and Savior and with love for the holy monastery, by the diligence of their majesties [Ioann Alekseevich and Piotr Alekseevich], they soon completed the building of the great stone church which patriarch Nikon founded in honor and glory of Christ our God and in praise of the Russian state." By placing the Resurrection Monastery within the traditional framework of Moscow as the New Jerusalem and by portraying the Romanov dynasty as its unwavering patron, Shusherin captured Nikon's vision of the flattering relationship that the ruling dynasty would be hard pressed to reject and that resurfaced in force in the nineteenth century.

Nikon and Russian Monasticism in the Seventeenth Century

Shusherin places monasticism at the center of life in seventeenth-century Russia and gives us vivid descriptions of existing monastic conditions. Indeed, he directly references more than twenty monasteries and several Moscow monastery lodges. Guiding the reader through Nikon's biography, the author offers rare glimpses into the lived experiences of seventeenth-century Russian monks, their diet, work habits, prayer regimes, monastic discipline, and interaction with secular society both within and beyond the walls of monasteries. Especially interesting are the commentaries on the persistence of popular belief even among the clergy, who are occasionally seen practicing magic and concocting hexes.

In devoting significant portions of his narrative to the monasteries, the author reflects yet another aspect of reform undertaken by his patron. Championing monasticism, Nikon strengthened the church's power base and patriarchal prerogatives by heightening the status of monasteries in the fabric of Muscovite society. Obligingly, Shusherin depicts monasteries not only as spiritual centers and refuges for the monks and those fleeing the earthly life, but also as full participants in the life of the realm. Indeed, they provide shelter for soldiers heading to or returning from battle, a place of respite for travelers, a safe haven in times of epidemics, and a royal residence outside the capital city. Another important function of monasteries that is given substantial, albeit less idealized, treatment is their role as prisons, a place of detention for both church hierarchs and the regular clergy.

Monasticism as a focal point of the narrative also helps Shusherin to immortalize Nikon as a humble monk. The patriarch's virtues shine most often in the monastic setting and not in the center of political power. Nikon labors together with the monastery brethren to secure their sustenance, be it gardening, fishing, or raking hay; he also shares royal food donations with them, even when he himself suffers from deprivation in exile. The patriarch is often shown participating in monastery chores and sharing responsibilities, firing and carrying bricks, constructing fences, and draining wetlands. It seems that he is most comfortable in daily monastic activities; when things go wrong, Nikon retires to his monasteries, busing himself in their construction and improvement. A paragon of monastic humbleness, generosity, and fairness, he also emerges as someone to whom ordinary monks could easily relate. He is a familiar and close figure, not a distant and haughty hierarch. This is what Shusherin wants his audience to remember about Nikon and what the author sees as the most powerful lesson for his readers, especially contemporary and future monks.

The biographer's emphasis also illuminates the status of the monastic hierarchy in the politics of the seventeenth-century Russian realm. Throughout the *Account*, we see archimandrites and abbots playing central roles in affairs outside their monasteries. They double as social reformers, royal emissaries, interrogators, state witnesses, wardens, and even acting commanders of state troops.

Historical Context: Seventeenth-Century Artistic Transformation

The century which witnessed the strengthening of the state, paradoxically also saw a growing appreciation for the personal among the Muscovite elite. Instead of abstract notions of power, tsardom, and state, Aleksei Mikhailovich, the sovereign ruler of Russia, was described not only in terms of state might and tradition, but as a person. Epithets "most serene," "most meek," and "pious," associated with the second Romanov epitomized his own, not standard royal virtues.[21]

This new significance of the individual was most visible in art, especially the realistic Western style portraits of the Muscovite ruling class that exploded in the mid-seventeenth century.[22] The *Tituliarnik* (1672), an illustrated book of royal genealogy, included pictures of Aleksei Mikhailovich and his *boyars* in their likeness. As patriarch, Nikon too established a reputation for commissioning Western painters to create life-like portraits of himself. Other important new forms of personalized art were developing genres of biography and autobiography.

Traditional Muscovite hagiographies or *zhitii* were reserved for saints whose individuality "was so reduced to the typical that the writings have practically no value as historical evidence."[23] However, once standardized as a genre, eventually hagiographies became differentiated, consisting of several sub-types, and not exclusively reserved for saints. People of immaculate Christian living or even people with lives open to intense debate were immortalized in literary works, which included some formulaic elements of *zhitie* and select biographic details necessary for the inspiration and persuasion of their audience. Nowhere was the transformation more evident than in the *Tale of Boiarynia Morozova*, a seventeenth-century Old Believer narrative, which "provides a compelling example of this [individualization of personality] through its frequent inclusion of homely incidents and snatches of conversation that bring alive Morozova and her milieu."[24]

Shusherin's work is a prime example of the transformation of hagiographical literature of the late Muscovite period into historical and biographical narrative. It does contain some hagiographical *topoi*. For example, Nikon's charity, erudition, early signs of exceptionality, strength of religious conviction, asceticism, and the incorruptibility of his body after death are cited as proofs of the state of blessedness. But the *Account* goes well beyond the formula to present realistic, and not always flattering scenes from Nikon's life. The patriarch is shown as a fallible man prone to occasional bouts of anger; he is sarcastic and witty, even unforgiving, a far cry from a perfect subjects of traditional hagiographies. The validation of popular beliefs and practices, including magic and sorcery, also subverts customary hagiographical conventions. Nikon's rise to power is portrayed, at least obliquely, as fulfilling the prophecies of a fortune-telling Muslim Tartar, a remark which is made early in the narrative and which appears to give Nikon a destiny very different from traditional Christian vocation. The biographer even omits well-known details which do clearly fit the hagiographical mold. Contrary to the common claim that Shusherin portrayed the patriarch as a "saint," the author did not include a host of materials, especially Nikon's visions and healings, which could have been employed in the construction of a hagiographic narrative.[25] Defying easy characterization, the *Account* is a hybrid literary form, a semi-hagiography which can just as easily be called a semi-biography. Nikon emerges as an emblematic figure of the century which saw a growing artistic recognition of the personal and realistic as opposed to the formulaic, collective, and standardized.

Shusherin's narrative style too is anything but conventional. In creating atmospheric settings of Nikon's trial, his trip to exile, imminent demise, and the state funeral, the author shows propensity for the theatrical and dramatic. In describing the larger-than-life confrontations between Nikon and his opponents, Shusherin however not only dramatizes them, but with a dexterous hand paints a very personal picture full of touching *mis-en-scenes* and human passion. And even though these vignettes might appear authentic, in all probability Shusherin uses them more as literary devices, and not as verbatim records of actual encounters. We see Nikon the man in the personal details that the biographer interjects, a feeling very different from the intended effect of classical hagiographies.

Historical Context: The Reform of the Russian Church in the Seventeenth Century

Two discrete, but inherently related processes affected the Russian Orthodox Church in the mid-seventeenth century—the secularization of church judicial and economic interests manifest in the new Law Code of 1649 and the standardization of the church texts, dogmas, rites, and rituals imposed during the so-called "Nikonian reforms." The second set of reforms, initiated between 1654 and 1666, included the revision of liturgical books and ritualistic changes ranging from the most basic daily practices, such as the making of the sign of the cross, to the Palm Sunday procession in which the patriarch symbolically reenacted Christ's entry into Jerusalem.[26] Ironically, the same synod council of 1666–1667 that first tried and condemned Nikon, also confirmed the Nikonian reforms.[27]

The reform of the Russian Church formulated and imposed during Nikon's patriarchate is clearly one of the most well-known and most controversial aspects of his life, if not all Russian history. Just as important as the changes themselves are the social tensions they produced over time. Those who rejected the Nikonian changes in favor of existing traditions and practices became known as schismatics [*raskolniki*] or Old Believers [*staroobriadtsy*]. Initially championed by a handful of religious zealots, including archpriests Avvakum Petrov and Ioann Neronov and deacon Fedor Ivanov, the Old Belief eventually developed into a complex movement, differentiated into several not necessarily cooperative concords.

The early Old Believer fathers considered the Nikonian reforms heretical innovations that undercut rather than improved traditional Russian piety and compromised the salvation of the faithful. The state's support for the practices that the early dissenters considered anti-Christian made the Nikonian reforms even more unacceptable, appearing to confirm apocalyptic ideas about the imminent coming of the Antichrist and the end of the world. Ultimately however it was Nikon and not the state who generated the most animus among the Old Believers. Because the 1666–1667 council of the synod not only confirmed the Nikonian reforms but condemned many previous rituals as heresies, practicing Old Believers were subsequently persecuted and treated as state criminals. Official persecution continued to varying degrees until April 17, 1905, when *tsar* Nicholas II promulgated his edict on religious toleration. The schism however persists to this day.[28]

The *Account*'s discussion of the reforms focuses almost exclusively on the revision of church books in 1654–1655. More specifically, the author's explanation of the book reform faithfully follows the official version which Nikon presented in the Church Service Book (*Sluzhebnik*) of 1655, a point emphasized in the annotations. The only ritualistic change mentioned explicitly in the *Account* is Nikon's introduction of the new monophonic church singing (*edinoglasnoe narechnoe penie*). No reference is made to what is usually considered the most symbolic change in church rituals, namely the making of the sign of the cross with three, as opposed to two, fingers.

Shusherin does not shy away from recording resistance to Nikon's textual reforms, but surprisingly, it is not the opposition that the modern reader might expect. It also appears that the author is quick to dismiss the dissent as an isolated episode which was dealt a decisive blow:

> At that time [1658–1666], the number of schismatics who followed the heretical monk Kapiton increased. They criticized his holiness Nikon for correcting the Divine Scripture, called him the Antichrist and other insulting names which cannot even be copied on paper. The pious *tsar*, caring about the holy church, ordered to look for the schismatics everywhere, to destroy their secret asylums, and to execute or to imprison them for not submitting to God's holy church.

The sub-deacon must have felt assured that the state support for the Nikonian reforms and the *tsar's* swift punitive action were sufficient for quelling the discontent. He singled out dissenting monk Kapiton, who in fact opposed the church authority long before the Nikonian reforms, as a leader of the resistance, suggesting that with Kapiton out of the picture the confrontation was over. From Shusherin's perspective, which was perhaps the reality of seventeenth-century Russia, the Old Believer fathers Avvakum and Fedor were not recognized threats, a point discussed in the annotations. But history has proven Nikon's disciple wrong on both counts. What he had described as a still-born opposition led by Kapiton was actually the beginning of a different and still ongoing dispute over Nikon and his reforms. And the dissident movement which traces its origins to Avvakum and Fedor would soon call into question Shusherin's biography.

Reactions to the Account: The Old Believers

Shusherin's *Account* was destined to stir powerful sentiments among the patriarch's most vocal opposition, the Old Believers. Their efforts to co-opt, counter, and compete with Shusherin's work demonstrate the power of his narrative. In the 1730s, an anonymous author from the Vyg community of Old Believers directly challenged Shusherin by penning the *Account About the Birth, Education, Life, and Death of Nikon Former Patriarch of Moscow and All Russia Collected From Many True Persons Who Lived During the Days of Our Fathers*, the earliest known reaction to Nikon's biography. This story closely imitated Shusherin's original, adopting its biographical framework, content, and most obviously, its title. The competing narrative however also draws on earlier Old Believer tales about Nikon, including deacon Fedor's *Authentic Testimony About the Marked by God Wolf and Predator Who Is Pastor in Sheep's Skin and Forerunner of the Antichrist* (late 1660s) and the *Life of Kornilii of Vyg* (1723–1727). Like Shusherin, the dissenting author worked with intimate portrayals of Nikon; eyewitness testimonials attributed to those living with and serving the patriarch play a central role in the Old Believer *Account*. Recording stories which were allegedly left out of the official accusations and proceedings against Nikon, the Old Believer authors, much like Shusherin himself, set out to present an authoritative personal vision of the "real" Nikon. But the Old Believer biography transformed what Shusherin presented as Nikon's most pious deeds into heresies and acts of depravity and sensationalized points raised, but not clarified in the original *Account*.[29]

The reactions to Shusherin's *Account* persisted well beyond the early eighteenth century making them one of the most dynamic genres of Old Believer literature. Indeed, over the course of the imperial period they became more complex and fantastic. Late nineteenth-century illustrated redactions of the *History about Patriarch Nikon, Eliminator of the Ancient Orthodox Faith*, which infused modern historical scholarship, art, and even historical fiction into the original Old Believer *Account*, stand as the most sophisticated responses to Shusherin's book. The very title *History* also implied a greater sense of credibility that the Old Believer authors hoped to command for their cultural product.[30]

The Old Believer tales about Nikon became so powerful in the nineteenth century that the patriarch's supporters in the official church felt compelled to refute them. Defending and promoting Shusherin's version of Nikon's life meant not only protecting the patriarch's legacy, but also the broader themes articulated in the *Account,* in particular the legitimacy of the Russian church and state. The persistent Old Believer attacks on Shusherin's work actually increased the cultural standing of the *Account*, making it a major point of contention in an ongoing struggle to control the patriarch's image and legacy.

The Account and the Nineteenth-Century Historical Scholarship

It was nineteenth-century historians and clergymen who tried to reclaim Nikon as a positive historical figure and a symbol of the dignity and legitimacy of the Russian Orthodox Church. The modern image of Nikon and our understanding of his legacy can be traced to the dialogue of two clearly demarcated historical schools, Shusherin's supporters and detractors. But historians also changed the status of the *Account* itself, ensuring its staying power.

At this time, two interrelated processes affected scholarly perceptions of Nikon and Shusherin's biography. First, new disciplines of archeography, archeology, and ethnography facilitated a more systematic study of the past and introduced new types of historical evidence, especially pre-Petrine literature, art and material culture. For the first time seventeenth-century religious and artistic artifacts were recognized as important sources of historical information. The painted portraits Nikon commissioned of himself as well as objects belonging to or worn by the patriarch were upheld as proof of Nikon's character. The same logic revolutionized Russian historical scholarship, making it "scientific." Scholars no longer treated Shusherin's text exclusively as religious literature, but as a historical source in its own right. Moreover, it was now imperative to compare the *Account* with other types of empirical evidence. And the archival sources that became the staple of "scientific history" were used to either support or refute the biographer's contentions.

The second process solidified important symbolic relationships between Nikon, the Romanov dynasty, and the Russian national idea embodied in the New Jerusalem Monastery. Numerous publications about Nikon and historical descriptions of the monasteries he founded, especially the New Jerusalem, appeared at this time.[31] Following the emphasis of Shusherin's *Account*, early nineteenth-century historians presented the New Jerusalem Monastery as proof of past collaboration between the *tsar* and the patriarch. As the monastery's status and its symbolic significance in Russia grew, so did Shusherin's biography. But Shusherin's fundamental claim about the congenial relationship between Aleksei Mikhailovich and Nikon and between the church and state in general could also be called into question by using the new historical methods.

Indeed such challenges soon appeared. In the mid-nineteenth century, positive interpretations of Nikon were assailed not only by the Old Believers, but by Russia's most renowned historian, S. M. Solov'ev. The publication of the eleventh volume of his *History of the Russian State* (1861) demarcates a watershed in historical scholarship on Nikon. Adhering to the conventions of "scientific history" and the program of the "statist school," the historian favored seventeenth-century archival documents and eye-witness testimonies recorded by servants of the state, particularly Paisius Ligarides, over Shusherin's narrative. Solov'ev not only dismissed Shusherin's interpretation of Nikon's personality and character in general as biased, but flatly rejected the biographer's claims about the patriarch's altruism and his friendship with Aleksei Mikhailovich as largely unsupported. Instead, the historian argued that Nikon's primary motives were power lust and personal aggrandizement and that the patriarch was a threat to the Russian state.[32]

Solov'ev was not the first to recognize the weaknesses of Shusherin's *Account*, but he commanded such great authority in the scholarly community that his revision of Nikon's role in Russian history galvanized a pro-Nikon camp which quickly rallied in support of both Nikon and Shusherin.[33] Led by N. I. Subbotin, a member of the Moscow Ecclesiastical Academy and a staunch opponent of the Old Believers, the pro-Nikon movement turned the tables on Solov'ev accusing him of biased source selection and refuting his representations of Nikon's character and relationship with the *tsar*.[34] Insisting on the *Account's* validity, Subbotin explained that "supporters of Nikon, forming their opinion of him on the tales of Shusherin, must regrettably say that the historian, who looked at those tales with excessive mistrust, mercilessly dispels the greatness of the great patriarch."[35] Indeed, Subbotin drew a sharp line between adherents to Shusherin's *Account* and his critics:

Following Shusherin's tale and unwittingly submitting to the power of the character and acumen of patriarch Nikon to which testify both his indefatigable activities in different areas of church and secular administration and his quick elevation through the steps of the hierarchical ladder, some extol him with praises and stop in wonderment in front of the greatness of, at the very least, this extremely noteworthy historical personality; others, on the contrary, paying attention exclusively to the dark sides of his character heap reproaches on him accusing him of many things of which he could hardly be accused and are ready to see in him the dark figure of Aleksei Mikhailovich's reign.[36]

Seen from this perspective, Solov'ev's *History* undercut the practice of using the friendship between Nikon and Aleksei Mikhailovich to illustrate the strong positive alliance between the Russian state and church. Moreover, the statist historian appeared to give credence to Old Believer critiques of the patriarch and the official church, an irony not lost on Subbotin, whose purpose was after all to "weaken the schism" and "reunite the schismatics with the Orthodox Church."[37]

Other pro-Nikon scholars, most notably archimandrite Leonid Kavelin and N. Gibbenet, were also critical of Solov'ev. They agreed that the publication and objective study of primary sources concerning Nikon's life would supply the "historical facts" about the patriarch needed to refute both Solov'ev's contentions and the "lies" perpetuated by "schismatics."[38] Kavelin's publication of the *Account* (1871) was intended to reassert control over Nikon's legacy and commemoration. Already in the "Introduction," the archimandrite engaged in the polemics with Solov'ev and his adherents.

Some modern writers, who, it appears, take the destruction of historical personalities as a special accomplishment, call Shusherin's work 'biased' without any proof and on this basis are ready to exclude it entirely from the sources assessing the patriarch. But for us, the judgments of the contemporaries, from whom we received not a single reproach of a "bias," are more valuable. On the contrary, the spread of this work [the *Account*] all over Russia in numerous redactions testifies that the attention of the Russian people towards it is justified. . . . And if one does not always agree with its conclusions and inferences, one should not, I repeat, be suspicious of the factual side of this tale.[39]

The historical debates about Shusherin's *Account* spread beyond the Russian borders, when Englishman William Palmer offered a European (and distinctly liberal) take on the historical controversies surrounding Nikon in his monumental *The Patriarch and the Tsar* (1871–1876).[40] Palmer's interest in Nikon was motivated by an even larger discourse on what he considered the subjugation or "captivity" of the Russian Church by the autocracy. For the English scholar, all that was wrong with the state-church relationship in Russia could be traced directly to Nikon's persecution. Palmer, like Subbotin and Kavelin, was intent on refuting both the Old Believers and Solov'ev by analyzing primary sources about the patriarch. From this perspective, Palmer lauded the *Account* explaining that Shusherin "writes as if he were writing the life of a saint; and the anecdotes and sayings related by him bear such marks of character that the reader feels brought into personal contact with the patriarch himself." But Palmer was also highly critical of Shusherin. He believed that "whether from fear, or from some other cause, Shusherin says merely that the enemy sowed discord between the *tsar* and blessed Nikon, without a word of the occasion or nature of their difference."[41] This is apparently why the Englishman, who did more than anyone else in Russia or abroad to publish Nikon-related original documents, did not include the *Account* in his multi-volume compilation.

Historians continued to debate the merits of Shusherin's narrative, but by the end of the nineteenth century it was generally acknowledged that the *Account*, although not without critical flaws, was nonetheless replete with important historical details and frank in its description of the patriarch and his character.[42]

The historical literature on Nikon which owed much to Shusherin's *Account* continued to expand beyond the confines of academic debates. The Russian Orthodox Church and the Ministry of Public Education published pro-Nikon scholarship to inoculate peasants, school children, and "simple people" against Old Believer propaganda about the patriarch and distributed new publications to the areas believed to be most susceptible dissent.[43] During the late imperial period the *Account* also inspired both popular biographies and fiction about the patriarch, but it fell into relative obscurity soon thereafter.[44] Unlike the biographies and autobiographies of early Old Believers, Shusherin's *Account* received little attention in the Soviet period, although it was used by Soviet anti-religious propagandists to suggest that the relationship between Aleksei Mikhailovich and Nikon proved that the church and state often worked in concert to exploit the masses.[45]

Shusherin's Account and Nikon's Place in the Contemporary Russia

Nikon remains an enduring part of public discourse because the central issues of his patriarchate, especially the relationship between church, state, and society and the Russian national idea re-emerged as important national discussions following the collapse of the Soviet Union. Shusherin's *Account*, where these themes are clearly articulated, enjoys renewed appeal. Tellingly, Aleksei II, the current patriarch of Moscow and all Russia, stressed the relevance of Nikon and the church-state relationship of his day for those living in the twenty-first century. Citing the personalities of the patriarch and *tsar* Aleksei Mikhailovich, Aleksei II urged contemporary Russians to draw inferences from the "living examples" offered by the seventeenth century.[46] Doing just that, the current patriarch himself concluded that although "the existing differences in the nature of church and state prevent them from merging into one whole . . . they can and should work together for the benefit of the people."[47]

Even more importantly, Shusherin's biography appears to have established a model through which to judge Nikon and perpetuate his commemoration. A recent exhibition "*Tsar* Aleksei Mikhailovich and Patriarch Nikon" followed closely the fabric of Shusherin's narrative, including noteworthy omissions and emphases:

[C]hronologically, the exhibition covers thirty years of the relationship between the *tsar* and the head of the Russian Church (1630–1660), paying particular attention to the period of 1640–1650, "the period of friendship," which is the most important in the history of their complex relationship. This time represents the embodiment of the idea of a 'wise pair' which includes harmonious balance between the authority of the *tsar* and the authority of the patriarch. . . . The period chosen by the authors of the exhibition does not discuss the events of the church schism however it talks about Nikon's church reforms. . . . Some exhibits tell about the construction of the new monasteries which Nikon built with the assistance of the *tsar*.[48]

Today, as in the past, Nikon continues to fascinate all levels of Russian society. The four hundredth anniversary of his birth (2005) was celebrated with the grandeur worthy of a national icon. The patriarch has become the subject of scholarly conferences and seminars and has been profiled in several exhibits at the Russian State Historical Museum, the Moscow Kremlin, the New Jerusalem Monastery, and Nizhnii Novgorod. *Nikonovskie Chteniia* is a contemporary publication dedicated to the analysis of various aspects of Nikon's life and actions. Recently, the patriarch's own writings and classic historical works about the patriarch have been republished.[49] New artistic representations of the patriarch in all genres, including icons, portraits, historical paintings, drawings, posters, calendars, and postcards abound. Nikon also remains a lighting rod for contemporary Old Believer writers and hierarchs; their writings provide a different interpretation which promotes debate about the patriarch no less than Shusherin's *Account*.[50] At this point it appears that the interest in Nikon which began with his seventeenth-century biography will not subside any time soon.

Notes

1. N. Iu. Bubnov and A. V. Lavrent'ev, "Ioann Kornil'ev Shusherin-Ripatov," in D. M. Bulanin and A. A. Turilov, eds. *Slovar' knizhnikov i knizhnosti drevnei Rusi (XVII vek),* Issue 3, Pt. 2 (St. Petersburg, 1993), 70.

2. The names of the four redactions of the *Account* are derived from the manuscript collections in which they were held. The variation in wording among the redactions is insignificant. We note these slight differences in the footnotes throughout the main text.

3. *Zhitie sviateishago patriarkha Nikona, pisannoe nekotorym byvshim pri nem klirikom* (St. Petersburg, 1784).

4. *Zhitie sviateishago patriarkha Nikona, pisannoe nekotorym byvshim pri nem klirikom* (St. Petersburg, 1817); and "Zhitie sviateishago patriarkha Nikona, pisannoe nekotorym byvshim pri nem klirikom," *Russkii Arkhiv* 9 (1909): 109–144.

5. See archimandrite Apollos, *Nachertanie zhitiia i deianii Nikona, patriarkha moskovskago i vseia Rusi. Sochinenie Novospasskago pervoklassnago stavropigial'nago monastyria* (Moscow, 1846), iii–iv; and archimandrite Leonid Kavelin, *Izvestie o rozhdenii i vospitanii i o zhitii sviateishago Nikona patriarkha moskovskago i vseia Rossii, napisannoe klirikom ego Ioannom Shusherinym* (Moscow, 1871), iii.

6. See *Izvestie o rozhdenii i vospitanii i o zhitii sviateishago Nikona patriarkha moskovskago i vseia Rossii, napisannoe klirikom ego Ioannom Shusherinym* (Moscow, 1906); *Izvestie o rozhdenii i vospitanii i o zhitii sviateishago Nikona patriarkha moskovskago i vseia Rossii, napisannoe klirikom ego Ioannom Shusherinym* (Moscow, 1908); *Povest' o rozhdenii i vospitanii i o zhitii sviateishego Nikona patriarkha moskovskogo i vseia Rossii* (Moscow, 1997); and V. V. Shmidt, *Patriarkh Nikon. Trudy* (Moscow, 2004), 19–75.

7. The *Account* was translated into German more than two hundred years ago. See J. Bachmeister, *Beytrage zur lebensgeschichte des Patriarchen Nikon* (Riga, 1788).

8. G. Michels, *At War with the Church* (Stanford, 1999).

9. See S. M. Solov'ev, *Istoriia Rossii s drevneishikh vremen, 1613–1657*, Bk. 5, Vol. 11 [St. Petersburg, 1860] (reprint Moscow, 2001), 328–331; W. Palmer, *The Patriarch and the Tsar*, Vol. 3 (London, 1873), 379–381; N. Gibbenet, *Istoricheskoe issledovanie dela patriarkha Nikona*, Pt. 2 (St. Petersburg, 1884), 267–274, especially 268; and metropolitan Makarii (Bulgakov), *Istoriia Russkoi tserkvi*, Bk. 7, Vol. 12 [St. Petersburg, 1883] (reprint Moscow, 1996), 256.

10. Gibbenet, *Istoricheskoe issledovanie*, Pt. 2, 297–298.

11. Ibid., 1043.

12. Here and thereafter the unattributed direct quotes are from Shusherin's *Account*.

13. Kavelin omitted the documents appended in Shusherin's original because they already appeared in other collections of published primary documents. See *Sobranie gosudarstvennykh gramot i dogovorov* (*SGGD*), Vol. 4 (Moscow: 1828), Nos. 135–140, 417–432.

14. These accounts are translated and published as Paisius Ligarides, "History of the Condemnation of the Patriarch Nicon," in W. Palmer, *The Patriarch and the Tsar*, Vol. 3 (London, 1873); and Paul of Aleppo, "Testimonies Concerning the Patriarch Nicon, the Tsar, and the Boyars from the Travels of Patriarch Macarius of Antioch," in W. Palmer, *The Patriarch and the Tsar*, Vol. 2 (London, 1873).

15. An English translation of Nikon's *Replies* is published in W. Palmer, *The Patriarch and the Tsar*, Vol. 1 (London, 1871). For Russian publications of the same document, see G. Vernadsky and A. A. Tumins, eds. *Patriarch Nikon on Church and State, Nikon's Refutation* (The Hague, 1982); and Schmidt, 197–469. An English translation of Nikon's *Letter to Dionysius* is published in W. Palmer, *The Patriarch and the Tsar*, Vol. 3 (London, 1873). The missive was originally published in *Zapiski otdelenia russkoi i slavianskoi arkheologiii Imperatorskago russkago arkheograficheskago obshchestva*, Vol. 2 (St. Petersburg, 1861), 510–530. For commentary on the larger significance of the *Letter*, see E. Matthes-Hohlfeld, *Der Brief des Moskauer Patriarchen Nikon an Dionysios Patriarch Konstantinopel (1665)* (Amsterdam, 1970).

16. On the extent of Nikon's holdings and power *vis-à-vis* the state, see N. F. Kapterev, *Patriarch Nikon i tsar' Aleksei Mikhailovich*, Vol. 2 (Sergiev Posad, 1912), especially 164–177.

17. On the conception of Russia as the New Israel, see D. B. Rowland's classic "Moscow—The Third Rome or the New Israel?" *The Russian Review* 55 (October 1996): 591–614; L. Lebedev, *Moskva Patriarshaia* (Moscow, 1995), 285–332; and G. M. Zelenskaia, *Sviatyni Novogo Ierusalima* (Moscow, 2003), 370–376.

18. Nikon explained the significance of the monasteries in his *Rai Myslennyi* (1659); *Gramota o Krestnom monastyre* (1656); and *Replies* (1663). See Nikon, *Rai Myslennyi*, V. S. Belenko, ed. (St. Petersburg, 1999); 27–33 and 62–65; Nikon, "Gramota o Krestnom monastyre," in archimandrite Lavrentii, *Kratkoe izvestie o Krestnom onezhskom arkhangel'skoi eparkhii monastyre* (Moscow, 1805), 1–22; and Nikon, "Replies," 67–89. See also M. A. Il'in, *Kamennaia letopis' Moskovskoi Rusi* (Moscow, 1966), 93–105; K.

A. Shchedrina, "Nekotorye istoriko-bogoslovskie aspekty monastyrskogo stroitel'stva patriarkha Nikona," in G. M. Zelenskaia, ed. *Nikonovskie chteniia v muzee 'Novyi Ierusalim.' Sbornik statei*. (Moscow, 2002), 15–22; and N. F. Kapterev, *Patriarch Nikon i tsar Aleksei Mikhailovich*, Vol. 2, 164–177.

19. See Zelenskaia, *Sviatyni Novogo Ierusalima*, 8–28; Lebedev, 136–155, 306–331; Il'in, 177–202; Rowland, 609–612; and W. C. Brumfield, *A History of Russian Architecture* (New York, 1993), 166–167. For a seventeenth-century eyewitness description of the "holy places" at the Resurrection Monastery, see Nicholaas Witsen, *Moscovische Reyes 1664–1665 Journal En Aentekeningen*, Th. J. G Locher and P. de Buck, eds. (Amsterdam, 1966), 280–281.

20. See Nikon, "Replies," 68; Ligarides, 158, 165; and Gibbenet, *Istoricheskoe issledovanie*, Pt. 2, 349, 367–368, 1059–1060, and 1093–1094.

21. R. Wortman makes this point most forcefully: "Aleksei's piety was presented not as a feature of an abstract image of *tsar*, but as a distinctive personal quality demonstrating spiritual and therefore political preeminence." R. Wortman, *Scenarios of Power. Myth and Ceremony in Russian Monarchy*, Vol. 1 (Princeton, 1995), 33. See also V. M. Zhivov, "Religious Reform and the Emergence of the Individual in Russian Seventeenth-Century Literature," in S. H. Baron and N. S. Kollmann, eds., *Religion and Culture in Early Modern Russia and Ukraine* (DeKalb, 1997), 184-198.

22. J. Cracraft, *The Petrine Revolution in Russian Imagery* (Chicago, 1997), 82–131.

23. D. S. Mirsky, *A History of Russian Literature*, F. J. Whitfield, ed. (New York, 1949), 18.

24. M. Ziolkowski, *Tale of Boiarynia Morozova: A Seventeenth-Century Religious Life* (New York, 2000), 12–13. Other important examples of transitional hagiographies include *The Life of Archpriest Avvakum by Himself* (1672–1673) and *The Life of Yuliania Lazarevsky* (1600–1625?). Both tales are published in S. A. Zenkovsky, ed. *Medieval Russia's Epics, Chronicles and Tales* (New York, 1974), 391–448.

25. See the annotations in the main text for examples of Nikon's own descriptions of divinely inspired visions. On Nikon's healings, see S. A. Belokurov, *Dela sviateishago Nikona patriarkha, pache zhe rechi dela vrachebnye. Materialy dlia russkoi istorii* (Moscow, 1888). For examples of scholars who stress the hagiographical nature of Shusherin's work, see Palmer, *The Patriarch and the Tsar*, Vol.1, xii; M. V. Zyzykin, *Patriarkh Nikon. Ego gosudarstvennye i kanonicheskie idei*, Pt. 3 (Warsaw, 1938), 316; and P. M. Meyendorff, *Russia, Ritual & Reform* (Crestwood, 1991), 82.

26. For useful studies of the reforms and their content, see Meyendorff; and M. Flier, "Court Ceremony in an Age of Reform. Patriarch Nikon and the Palm Sunday Ritual," in S. H. Baron and N. S. Kollmann, eds., *Religion and Culture in Early Modern Russia and Ukraine* (DeKalb, 1997).

27. Many informal practices that Nikon introduced and for which he was criticized at the 1666–1667 council continued after his removed from the patriarchal throne. For instance, Nikon's successor, patriarch Ioakim also used the title "great sovereign" in self-address, although Nikon was condemned for the same practice during the council.

28. For classic Russian works on the church schism, see V. V. Andreev, *Raskol i ego znachenie v narodnoi russkoi istorii* (St. Petersburg, 1870); P. S. Smirnov, *Vnutrennie voprosy v raskole v XVII veka* (St. Petersburg, 1898); and N. F. Kapterev, *Patriarch Nikon i ego protivniki* (Sergiev Posad, 1913). For path-breaking recent works, see R. O. Crummey, *Old Believers in the World of the Antichrist* (Madison, 1970); Michels, *At War with the Church*; R. R. Robson, *Old Believers in Modern Russia* (DeKalb, 1995); and I. K. Paert, *Old Believers, Religious Dissent and Gender in Russia, 1760–1850* (Manchester, 2003).

22 *Introduction*

29. The Old Believer *Account* is published in A. K. Borozdin, *Protopop Avvakum: ocherk iz istorii umstvennoi zhizni russkago obshchestva v XVII veke* (St. Petersburg, 1900), No. 33, 145–167; and V. N. Peretz, *Slukhi i tolki o patriarkhe Nikone v literaturnoi obrabotke pisatelei XVII-XVIII vv.* (St. Petersburg, 1900), 177–190. Deacon Fedor's *Authentic Testimonies* is published in L. V. Titova, "Skazanie o patriarkhe Nikone—publitsisticheskii traktat pustozerskikh uznikov," in *Istoriia russkoi dukhuvnoi kul'tury v rukopisnom nasledii XVI–XX vv.,* E. K. Romodanovskaia, ed. (Novosibirsk, 1998), 232–237. Thé tales about Nikon recorded in the *Life of Kornilii of Vyg* are published in Peretz, 144, 147, 149–151, and 162–169. For an overview of the Old Believer tales about patriarch Nikon, see N. Iu. Bubnov, "Skazaniia i povesti o patriarkhe Nikone," in *Russkaia knizhnost': Voprosy istochnikovedeniia i paleografii* (XVII v.), Pt. 3 (P–S) (St. Petersburg, 1998), 459–462; and D. N. Breshchinskii, "Zhitie Korniliia Vygovskogo kak literaturnyi pamiatnik i ego literaturnye sviazi na Vygu," in *Trudy otdela drevnerusskoi literatury Akademii Nauk SSSR,* Vol. XXXIII (Leningrad, 1979), especially 137–141. For comparative analysis of the Old Believer *Account* and Shusherin's work, see K. M. Kain, "Patriarch Nikon's Image in Russian History and Culture" (Ph.D. Diss, Western Michigan University, 2004), 290–316.

30. N. Iu. Bubnov, "Litsevye rukopisi staroobriadcheskoi knigopisnoi masterskoi vologodskikh krest'ian Kalikinykh," in *Staroobriadchestvo: Istoriia i sovremennost', mestnye traditsii, russkiie i zarubezhnye sviazi* (Ulan-Ude, 2001), 314–320. For comparative analysis of the Old Believer *History about Patriarch Nikon* and Shusherin's work, see Kain, 322–405.

31. For biographies of Nikon, see Apollos, *Nachertanie zhitiia i deianii Nikona;* and idem., *Kratkoe nachertanie zhizni i deianii Nikona, patriarkha moskovskago i vseia Rusi, s portretom ego,* 2nd ed. (Moscow, 1836). More than thirty books and articles devoted to the New Jerusalem Monastery appeared over the course of the nineteenth century alone. See, for example, M. Dmitreevskii, *Puteshestvie v Novyi Ierusalim ili kratkoe istoricheskoe, khronologicheskoe i topograficheskoe opisanie stavropigial'nago Voskresenskago monastyria* (Moscow, 1808); A. N. Murav'ev, *Puteshestvie po sviatym mestam russkim* (St. Petersburg, 1836); *Kratkoe istoricheskoe opisanie stavropigial'nago Voskresenskago, Novyi Ierusalim imenuemago, monastyria* (Moscow, 1852); *Opisanie sobornago khrama Voskreseniia Khristova, postroennago po Ierusalimskomu obraztsu sv. patriarkhom Nikonom v Voskresenskom, Novyi Ierusalim imenuemom, monastyre* (Moscow, 1870); E. Gorchakova, *Poezdka v Novyi Ierusalim, Savvino-Storozhevskii monastyr' i gorod Dmitrov* (Moscow, 1886). The publications devoted to Nikon's other monasteries include archimandrite Lavrentii, *Kratkoe izvestie o Krestnom onezhskom arkhangel'skoi eparkhii monastyre*; archimandrite Piotr, *Opisanie pervoklassnago Iverskago Bogoroditskago monastyria Novgorodskoi eparkhii* (St. Petersburg, 1850); archimandrite Varlaam, *Istoriko-arkheologicheskoe opisanie drevnostei i redkikh veshchei, nakhodiashchikhsia v Kirillo-Belozerskom monastyre* (Moscow, 1859); and A. N. Murav'ev, *Russkaia Fivaida na severe* [St. Petersburg, 1855] (reprint Moscow, 1998).

32. Solov'ev, Vol. 10, 204–206, 211–212.

33. For example, in his biography of Nikon, archimandrite Apollos explained that "Ivan Shusherin, who shared [Nikon's] fate, on occasion raises suspicion of biases. Moreover, he was unaware of many circumstances hidden from his contemporaries and revealed in charters and other written sources of the seventeenth century." Apollos, *Nachertanie zhitiia i deianii Nikona,* iii–iv.

34. See N. I. Subbotin, *Delo patriarkha Nikona. Istoricheskoe issledovanie po povodu XI T. "Istorii Rossii," prof. Solov'eva* (Moscow, 1862), especially 1–8 and 169–177.

35. Ibid., 3.

36. Ibid., 2.

37. Subbotin founded the Brotherhood of St. Peter (1872) and its journal *Bratskoe slovo* (1875–1876) with the intention of eliminating the Old Belief. On the Brotherhood's goals, see I. Shevelkin, "Slovo v den' torzhestvennago otkrytiia . . . bratstva sviatago Petra mitropolita," in *Dushepoleznoe Chtenie*, Pt. 1 (Moscow, 1873), 13–57.

38. Subbotin, 2–7; and N. Gibbenet, *Istoricheskoe issledovanie dela patriarkha Nikona*, Pt. 1, i–iv. See also P. Nikolaevskii, *Zhizn' patriarkha Nikona v ssylke i zakluchenii posle osuzhdeniia ego na Moskovskom sobore 1666 goda* (St. Petersburg, 1666), especially 141; and S. Mikhailovskii, *Zhizn' sviateishago Nikona patriarkha vserossiiskago* (Moscow, 1878), 5–12.

39. Kavelin, *Izvestie*, vii. Kavelin's publication of a previously ignored source pertaining to the patriarch's trial, *D'iakon Lugovskoi po Tatishchevu pisatel' xvii veka i ego sochinenie o sude nad patriarkhom Nikonom* (St. Petersburg, 1885), was likewise intended as a corrective for Solov'ev's work. Kavelin continued his efforts to defend the patriarch at the newly organized "Museum Dedicated to the Memory of His Holiness Patriarch Nikon" at the Resurrection Monastery inaugurated on September 15, 1874.

40. W. Palmer, *The Patriarch and the Tsar*, 6 Vols. (London, 1871–1876).

41. Palmer, *The Patriarch and the Tsar*, Vol. 1, xii.

42. For surveys of the literature on patriarch Nikon produced in the nineteenth and early twentieth centuries, see V. S. Ikonnikov, *Novye materialy i trudy o patriarkhe Nikone* (Kiev, 1888); and Zyzykin, 295–365. Both authors comment on Shusherin's work as well. See Ikonnikov, 60–61; and Zyzykin, 316. See also Makarii, *Istoriia*, Vol. 12, 338; and S. V. Lobachev, *Patriarkh Nikon* (St. Petersburg, 2003), 269.

43. See, for example, N. Sergeev, *Kratkoe zhizneopisanie sviateishago patriarkha Nikona* (Viatka, 1888); N. A. Sergeevskii, *Sviateishii vserossiiskii patriarkh Nikon. Ego zhizn', deiatel'nost', zatochenie i konchina* (Moscow, 1894); Postoiannaia komissiia po ustroistvu narodnykh chtenii pri Ministerstve Narodnago Prosveshcheniia, *Novyi Ierusalim (Voskresenskii monastyr')* (St. Petersburg, 1887); *Sviateishii patriarkh vserossiiskii Nikon* (Moscow, 1904); *Zhizn' sviateishago Nikona patriarkha vserossiiskago* (Moscow, 1907); *Sviateishii Nikon—patriarkh vserossiiskii i osnovannyi im Voskresenskii monastyr'* (Moscow, 1909); and V. N. Fal'kovskii, *Konchina patriarkha Nikona* (Kiev, 1913).

44. The popular biographies include A. S. Suvorin, *Zamechatel'nye liudi: patriarkh Nikon, Ermak—pokoritel' Sibiri, boyarin Artamon Sergeevich Matveev* (St. Petersburg, 1874); A. A. Bychkov, *Patriarkh Nikon. Biograficheskii ocherk* (St. Petersburg, 1891); S. F. Chiretskii, *Patriarkh Nikon, ego zhizn' i deiatel'nost'. Biograficheskii ocherk* (St. Petersburg, 1908); S. I. Grechushkin, *Iz russkoi istorii. Patriarkh Nikon* (Moscow, 1910). The fictional works include D. L. Mordovtsev, *Velikii raskol* (St. Petersburg, 1881); M. A. Filippov, *Patriarkh Nikon* (Moscow, 1885); A. S. Suvorin, *Patriarkh Nikon* (St. Petersburg, 1893); A. Lindt, *Nikon i Avvakum* (Moscow, 1906); V. Altaev, *V debriakh Mordvy. Detstvo patriarkha Nikona* (Moscow, 1912); and P. Bunina, *Nikon i velikii raskol* (Moscow, 1912).

45. See *Gosudarstvennyi khudozhestvenno-istoricheskii kraevoi muzei v g. Voskresenske, Moskovskoi gubernii. Putevoditel' po muzeiu* (Voskresensk, 1925), 14; *Gosudarstvennyi khudozhestvenno-istoricheskii kraevoi muzei v g. Voskresenske, Moskovskoi gubernii. Kratkii putevoditel'* (Moscow, 1928), 19–21; and N. A. Sheerson, *Antireligioznaia propaganda v kraevedcheskikh muzeiakh* (Istra, 1930).

46. Patriarch Aleksei II, "Vstupitel'noe slovo," in E. M. Iukhimenko, ed. *Patriarkh Nikon. Oblacheniia, lichnye veshchi, avtografy, vklady, portrety*, 7–11.

47. Ibid., 11.

48. See I. A. Bobrovnitskaia, "Tsar' Aleksei Mikhailovich i patriarch Nikon. 'Premudraia dvoitsa'," in *Tsar Aleksei Mikhailovich i patriarkh Nikon* (Moscow, 2005), 8–9.

49. Several of the republished classics are cited above. See the most recent publications in notes 6, 8, 9, 18, and 31.

50. A. A. Bezgodov, "Liutaia godina," in *Kalendar' Drevlepravoslavnoi pomorskoi tserkvi na 2002 god* (Moscow, 2002), 65–71; T. Konstantinova, "N. F. Kapterev o patriarkhe Nikone i tsare Aleksee Mikhailoviche," in *Kalendar' Drevlepravoslavnoi pomorskoi tserkvi na 2004 god* (Moscow, 2004), 71–75; "Skazanie o zhitii i stradanii sviatago sviashchennomuchennika i ispovednika Pavla, episkopa Kolomenskago," in *Tserkovnyi Kalendar' na 2002 god* (Moscow 2002), 107–114; and entries devoted to Nikon in *Istoriia Russkoi pravoslavnoi staroobriadcheskoi tserkvi* (Moscow, 2003), 3–13.

Account of the Birth, Upbringing, and Life of His Holiness Nikon, Patriarch of Moscow and All Russia Written by His Cleric Ioann Shusherin[i]

In the year 7113 (1605) from the creation of the world, in the month of May, in a village called Vel'demanovo, near Nizhnii Novgorod, his holiness the patriarch (*patriarkh*) was born from ordinary, but pious parents. His father was called Mina and his mother Mariama. The infant was named Nikita in honor of the reverend Nikita, the miracle-worker of Per'iaslavl', who is commemorated by the holy church on May 24.[1]

After Nikita's birth, his mother did not live long, leaving the young boy for eternal life. After the death of Nikita's mother, a woman called Kseniia, seeing his loneliness and young age, took pity on the orphan and started to care for him by taking his mother's place. His father remarried however, and the stepmother was very wicked to Nikita.

The stepmother brought her own children to the house and fed them well, but Nikita was given only bread. Once, starving, he decided to go to the cellar and take food which his stepmother was feeding her children, but the stepmother noticed him going to the cellar and hit him hard between the shoulder blades as only a stepmother, not a natural mother, would do. After this blow, the boy fell into the cellar and almost died.

One winter morning, freezing Nikita climbed into the furnace to warm himself and fell asleep. The stepmother, who hated her stepson, saw him there and decided to burn him; she put firewood into the furnace and ignited it. Awakened by fire and smoke, the boy, who was frightened to death, cried out very loudly, asking to be saved from an inevitable death. His grandmother heard the screams, took the burning firewood [out of the furnace] at once, and saved the boy from a heinous death. The grandmother was very merciful to the orphan. When Nikita's father left the house, the stepmother, taking advantage of his absence, would

---

[i] This is a translation of the 1871 redaction of Shusherin's work, compiled by Leonid Kavelin, archimandrite of the New Jerusalem Monastery. In cases when there was a discrepancy between this and earlier redactions, Kavelin noted the differences, citing additions or omissions. His notes are included in this text as footnotes.

insult Nikita in various ways, frequently beating him until he bled; he was beaten as only stepchildren and not one's own progeny get beaten.

When the father returned home and saw his son beaten, pitying Nikita very much, he would chastise his wife and sometimes even beat her. However he failed to rein in his wife's hatred and only further inflamed it, for the stepmother told her husband many hateful stories about Nikita. This woman had so much spite towards the boy that she, a curse be upon her, decided to get rid of him not by bloodshed, but by poison. After she devised this plan, she did not postpone its realization. She ground arsenic and put it into Nikita's food and, pretending to be guided by maternal love, urged the boy to taste and enjoy the dish. Unsuspecting the insidious plan which could have led to heinous death, Nikita started to eat. But God saved him. When the boy felt a strange tickling in his throat, he started to drink water and, thanks to the protection of God and abundant drinking, escaped the pernicious poison.

Some time later, according to Nikita's wish, or rather according to God's will, Nikita's father sent him to learn how to read and write the Holy Scripture. By the grace of God and the actions of the Holy Spirit, the boy easily learned to read holy books, but after he left his teacher and returned to his father's house, he began to quickly forget the Holy Scripture. Realizing that, Nikita decided immediately to take a little money from his father's house so he could settle in a monastery and continue studying the Holy Scripture. He did so [in the 1620s] and went to the monastery of the reverend Makarii Zheltovodskii[2] to see a God-inspired elder (*starets*). After coming to the elder, Nikita donated money as a contribution to the holy monastery so that the abbot (*igumen*) and the brethren would bless him to stay in the monastery, live with clergy, and learn the Holy Scripture.

The elder took the money and went to the abbot and the brethren to tell them about the boy and his contribution and to plead with the abbot and the brethren to allow Nikita to live in the monastery.

The abbot and the brethren accepted the money and blessed Nikita to stay in the monastery and live with the choir (*kliroshanie*). After Nikita's wish was granted, he thanked God and started to visit the church regularly, trying to always come at the beginning of the service. Knowing that he was a child, the boy feared that his sleep could be too sound and that he might miss the beginning of the service. So, in the summer, he slept near the bell which called the brethren to attend the service. This is how intent he was on singing at the divine service even at an early age. And so he lived in that monastery studiously learning the Holy Scripture.

One day, the boys, blessed by the abbot, went on a walk to a different monastery and took Nikita with them. On the way, they happened to stop at the house of a Tartar,[3] known to Nikita's companions, who, although a Muslim, always cheerfully extended hospitality to traveling Christians and gave them shelter according to the Christian custom. This time he also greeted the boys benevolently and convinced them to spend the night in his house because evening was already upon them. Nikita's companions, knowing that the Tartar could tell fortunes and predict the future, for example, whether or not a person will be rich or poor and what his rank will be, begged the host to tell each of them their fortune.

He did not refuse and, following their wish, with the help of his craft told each about his future life and rank. When it was Nikita's turn, the Tartar, looking back and forth between the boy and his fortune-telling book, suddenly became astounded, started to quickly rotate the fortune-telling book and asked the boy about his lineage. Nikita replied that he was a commoner. Hearing this, the Tartar said: "Nikita, how can you walk so carelessly? Be careful and cautious because you will become a great sovereign of the Russian tsardom." This prophesy did come true but it will be told later. Hearing those strange words, the boy Nikita became surprised and did not believe the Tartar.

Having spent the night, the boys continued their intended journey and upon its completion returned to the monastery of the reverend Makarii. Life resumed its normal course, as before. Nikita went to church with great diligence and studied the Holy Scripture.

Soon Nikita's father learned where Nikita lived and sent his friend to the monastery to convince the boy to return home. In the case Nikita refused, his father asked to tell him the following words: "Your father Mina, very weak from great sorrow, is dying, and your grandmother is ill from the old age and will also meet her end soon."

The messenger tried to convince Nikita to return to his father's house the best he could, but did not succeed, and finally told the boy: "Do you, Nikita, know that your father and grandmother are almost near death, your father from missing you and your grandmother from old age? If you do not hurry, it is unlikely that you will ever see them alive." When Nikita heard this, he started to cry out of love for his father and grandmother; he left the monastery of the reverend Makarii at once to go to his father's house, wishing to see them alive. When he arrived however, he found them alive and well. Even though his father lied to Nikita about his and grandmother's imminent demise, his words did come true. Soon after Nikita's arrival home, both his father and grandmother fell ill and left for eternal life after preparing themselves for the journey as befits Christians.

Having buried the bodies of his father and grandmother with appropriate honors and having remembered them with prayers, as befits the Christian custom, Nikita again set out for the monastery, but his relatives started to convince him to enter lawful matrimony. That was God's will. Nikita surrendered to the wishes of his relatives and got married [in 1626]. Shortly thereafter, wishing to enjoy serving the church, Nikita went to search for a position. Soon he found what he was looking for. One village needed a clergyman for its church. Both its priests and parishioners lovingly accepted Nikita. There, he settled with his wife, lived for several years, and was ordained as the church's priest.

ভ

Shortly thereafter [in 1627] Nikita, together with his family, moved to the ruling city of Moscow. There, after several years, he realized the vanity and instability of this world and, wishing to achieve salvation, started to convince his wife to follow this path. With God's help he succeeded in his persuasion. His wife decided to serve God and not the world. She chose the Alekseevskii Convent[4] in the ruling city of Moscow to pursue a God-pleasing life.

Having thanked God for His help, Nikita built his wife a cell, donated the necessary contribution for her, and left her with the means to purchase clothes and food. He himself decided to go to the Isle of Anzer that lay in the White Sea near the Solovetskii Isle. Nikita lived with his wife for ten years before their separation; they had three children all of whom died in infancy. And after his decision was made, he immediately went to the aforesaid isle. Having reached it [in 1636], Nikita was tonsured and received the monastic name Nikon. He was mentored by the God-inspired elder Eleazar who was in charge of the isle's hermitage (*skit*).[5]

At this time, the Anzer hermitage where the fathers lived had the following structure. The cells stood two *poprishches*[i] from each other and the church. At that point of time, the island was inhabited by twelve brothers, each living in his own cell. They had the following prayer rule (*molitvennoe pravilo*). On Saturday evening all the brothers assembled in the church and sang the evening prayers (*vechernia* and *povecher'e*) and then, without a break, they sang the morning prayers (*utrenia*) with all twenty proper psalms (*kafismas*) of the Book of Psalms (*Psaltyr'*); after the tenth proper psalm, they read and interpreted the Sunday Gospel. During the reading of the Book of Psalms, the brothers were seated because they spent the whole night singing and reading without sleep. When morning came, the brothers did not leave to go to their cells, but instead served the holy liturgy (*liturgiia*), after which they bade each other farewell and asked each other to pray. Then, they returned to their cells and did not see each other until the next week. Their food came mostly from the *tsar's* generosity. Each brother received about three *chetvert's* of flour a year.[ii] Occasionally, fishermen would share fish with them and the brothers themselves also grew vegetables on the isle. Living on Anzer, Nikon, blessed by elder Eleazar, fasted and lived in great moderation. His prayer rule was very strict. In addition to the prayers, proper psalms, and canons (*kanon*), common to all the brethren, he also read the Book of Psalms daily and made one thousand prostrations a day. Nikon slept very little.

The devil, the hater of all good, seeing Nikon's diligence in the service of God, tempted him in his cell. When Nikon wanted to rest a little from his labors, the evil spirits immediately came to his cell, suffocating and maliciously tormenting him with various frightening visions. Feeling the strength of the devil's wrath against him, Nikon added prayers against the assault by the evil spirits to his prayer rule. He sprinkled holy water in his cell daily and so was able to defeat these enemies of the virtuous life and rest from his labors without being tormented.

Nikon's wife lived in the Alekseevskii Convent without taking the veil. Instigated by the enemy to forego her vow to become a nun, she decided to return to secular vanity and remarry. Having received a letter from his relatives in the ruling city of Moscow, in which they wrote about all this, Nikon was greatly

---

[i] About three kilometers.
[ii] About six hundred and twenty kilograms.

saddened and his soul was filled with sorrow. He started to pray to Almighty God and Our Lord to save his former wife so that she would abandon her ill intent and become a nun. He also wrote to his relatives asking them to persuade his wife to follow her previous vow and to take the veil.

Merciful God, who did not refuse the prayers of His servant Nikon, strengthened the relatives' persuasion so that the woman decided to follow her previous vows and purged the thoughts about returning to the world from her heart. Soon thereafter she became a nun of the Alekseevskii Convent. After learning about this, Nikon thanked God because He did not neglect his petitions. Nikon continued his faithful service to Him as a cleric in the Anzer hermitage of the Solovetskii Monastery.[6]

Once [in 1638] God-pleasing elder Eleazar decided to go to Moscow to solicit donations to build a stone church in the hermitage. He took monastic priest (*ieromonakh*) Nikon with him.

Upon arriving in the ruling city of Moscow where many noble and pious people had heard about the virtuous life of the Anzer brethren, the monks petitioned Mikhail Fedorovich, the pious great sovereign, *tsar* and grand prince of all Russias, the pious *boyars*, and other virtuous people of various ranks for contributions to build the church. They collected five hundred *rubles* for the construction of the church and after returning to Anzer, hid the money in the vestry (*riznitsa*) where it lay for two or three years. Monastic priest Nikon, fearing the assault of robbers who, if knowing about the money, could not only steal it, but also kill the brethren, advised the head of the hermitage, elder Eleazar, to either start the construction of the church or to store the money in the Solovetskii Monastery, so that the money would not provoke robbers to attack the hermitage. But elder Eleazar did not like this advice and took a disliking to Nikon, very much saddening the monastic priest.[7] Once Nikon had a dream; he saw a vessel brimming with seeds. Next to the vessel stood a man who told Nikon: "The vessel which measures your labors is full." Nikon, wishing to turn around, dropped the vessel and spilled all the seeds. Then he started collecting the seeds and putting them back in the same vessel, but when he collected all the seeds, the vessel was not as full as before. After this dream, seeing that the elder's fury was not subsiding, but instead increasing daily, and that peace could not reign in his heart, Nikon decided not to upset the elder. [In 1639], together with a peasant, Nikon set sail in a small boat for the mainland. At sea, they were caught in a storm, lost their way, and almost drowned, but in the end their boat was tossed ashore on the Isle of Kii. Having thanked God for deliverance from drowning, Nikon erected a wooden cross on the island and took an oath to build the Cross Monastery, with God's will and help, at the place where he erected the cross.[8] Today, thanks to the wishes and diligence of Nikon, the generosity of the *tsar*, and the personal means of Nikon himself, the monastery is magnificently built and is worthy of wonderment. Monastic priest Nikon lived on the Isle of Anzer for three years; he stayed on the Isle of Kii until the weather permitted the continuation of his sailing. Having set sail from the Isle of Kii, they headed directly to the mouth of the Onega River, located ten *poprishches* from the island.[i] Having reached the

---

[i] About fifteen kilometers.

Onega River, Nikon remunerated the peasant and started walking along the river.

Following this path, he depleted his food supply and starved for ten days. Having reached a village on the opposite bank of the river, Nikon called upon its people, begging to be transported to the village. None of the wealthy peasants living there wanted to carry the starving monk across, only a poor widow who heard the traveler's call took pity upon him and ordered her son to convey him to the other side. Once on the opposite side of the river, Nikon could not pay for his transport and simply bowed and said: "God Himself will pay you for the love you showed me." Hoping to find a person to feed him and give him shelter, Nikon went to the village, but no one in this wealthy village took him in and he returned to the widow who already took pity on him once. Seeing that no one would show him mercy or give him food, the woman lovingly invited Nikon into her house. Even though there was a famine and she herself did not have bread, she fed him whatever God gave her. Wishing to thank the widow, Nikon said: "If God wills it and I am alive, I will certainly repay you for your mercy." This promise was fulfilled later.

When the Cross Monastery was built on the Isle of Kii,[i] the most pious great sovereign Aleksei Mikhailovich, *tsar* and grand prince of all Great, Little, and White Russias, gave the village where the widow lived, as well as many other villages, to the new monastery.[9] For her mercy, the widow and her children were forever exempted by his holiness the patriarch from all taxes.[ii]

After spending the night at the widow's, monastic priest Nikon went to the Kozheezerskii Monastery where he asked the abbot and brethren to accept him. This monastery did not accept anyone without a donation and the monastic priest, who did not have anything to offer, had to give up his last possessions, two books, the Church Slavonic Liturgy (*Poluustav*) and the Book of Canons (*Kanonik*) that he copied himself. After they accepted the books, he was invited to stay with them in the monastery where he started to live and serve the liturgy. Some time later Nikon desired to live in solitude and asked the abbot and the brethren to bless him so that he could seclude himself on an island of his choice where he would build a cell and follow his previous prayer rule.

The abbot and the brethren, seeing his ardor in prayer, fulfilled his request and, having blessed him, released him from the monastery. Having arrived on the chosen island, he build a cell with his own hands and started to live there according to the rules of the Anzer hermitage; the island was located on the same lake as the Kozheezerskii Monastery. Living on the island, he fished after prayer because the lake around the island was abundant in fish and the nearest dwelling was forty *poprishches* away.[iii] When he lived on the island, the abbot of the Kozheezerskii Monastery left for an eternal life and the brethren, seeing

---

[i] Shusherin describes the founding of the Cross Monastery later in the text.

[ii] The concluding sentence regarding the exemption of the widow and her family from taxes does not appear in other manuscripts or in the 1784 and 1871 printed editions. This conclusion is included only in the New Jerusalem handwritten version of Shusherin's *Account*.

[iii] About sixty kilometers.

the God-given intelligence and the virtuous life of monastic priest Nikon, diligently asked him to have mercy on them for the love of Christ, to leave his seclusion, and become the abbot of the monastery. He refused at first, but in the end the brethren succeeded in their begging. Having left the island,[i] monastic priest Nikon went to Novgorod the Great where [in 1642/3] the most reverend Affonii, metropolitan (*mitropolit*) of Novgorod and Velikie Luki, appointed him abbot of the Kozheezerskii Monastery.[10] After returning from Novgorod to the monastery, Nikon continued to labor. He often caught fish for the brethren which he himself served during the meals.

Three years of his life in the monastery passed and during the reign of pious and Christ-loving Aleksei Mikhailovich, the great sovereign, *tsar* and grand prince of all Great, Little, and White Russias, he had to go to the ruling city of Moscow on account of the monastery's needs.[11] When abbot Nikon lived in the ruling city of Moscow and attended to the monastery's affairs, the sovereign heard about him and his holiness patriarch Iosif[12] appointed Nikon to be archimandrite (*arkhimandrit*) of the New Savior [*Novospasskii*] Monastery.[13] Living at the New Savior Monastery and continuing to labor, archimandrite Nikon diligently shepherded Christ's flock entrusted to him; he also governed the monastery aptly. For this the sovereign took a strong liking to him and, wishing to enjoy God-inspired conversations with the archimandrite, ordered him to visit every Friday during the morning prayers at the *tsar's* court. Following the great sovereign's orders, he came to the palace for the morning prayers every Friday and was able to help many aggrieved widows and orphans through his petitions.

Seeing archimandrite's attention to truth, the pious *tsar* ordered him to bring the petitions (*chelobitnaia*) of the aggrieved directly to him, the great sovereign, for the *tsar* liked to do justice. This order became known in the ruling city and many people started to come to the New Savior Monastery to see the archimandrite and ask for his merciful protection. Some waited for him on Fridays and gave their petitions right before he went to the *tsar*. Archimandrite Nikon was willing to help all the aggrieved and deprived, especially widows and helpless orphans. He passed on all the petitions to the *tsar* with diligent pleas for protection.

The great sovereign always listened to these petitions after morning prayer, right there in the church and would then order to write his merciful resolutions on them and give those resolutions to the archimandrite. And so Nikon, a benefactor to all, lived in the New Savior Monastery for three years [1646–1649].

ⱭⱭ

After three years [on March 19, 1649], upon the wishes of the great sovereign, his holiness Iosif, patriarch of Moscow and all Russia,[14] appointed archimandrite Nikon, known for his virtuous life, to be the metropolitan of Novgorod the Great to replace metropolitan Affonii who lived a holy life, but was very old and suf-

---

[i] In the printed Iverskii redaction of Shusherin's *Account*, there is an additional detail inserted here. "The brothers wrote a handwritten petition about monastic priest Nikon which they gave him. After accepting the petition he went to Novgorod the Great."

fered from a loss of memory.[15] Metropolitan Affonii himself asked the sovereign and his holiness the patriarch to be retired. Immediately after his arrival in Novgorod, his eminence metropolitan Nikon visited metropolitan Affonii who lived at the the Monastery of the Savior at Khutyn' [*Spassko-Khutynskii*][16] to ask for the old man's blessing. But Affonii told him: "You should bless me," and they argued about who should bless whom at length. Finally, Affonii said: "Bless me, patriarch." The metropolitan responded: "No, holy father, I am not the patriarch but the sinful metropolitan Nikon." Affonii replied: "But you will be the patriarch and so bless me." And only then, after receiving the blessing, Affonii blessed Nikon.[17]

Heading the metropolitanate of Novgorod, his eminence metropolitan Nikon, not only retained his kind character, but tried to diligently solve every problem so as to glorify God. He paid particular attention to justice in the courts. The metropolitan himself judged the most serious allegations and conflicts, arrived at very just decisions and was able to reconcile opponents with great mercy.[18] He was very generous with donations, especially in the years when God sent famine to this land. The metropolitan ordered to feed the starving and the destitute along with everyone else who came, in one of the chambers of his house called the cellar. On some days, up to one hundred people were fed there; at other times there were two hundred, or even three hundred people. A man of holy life, named Vasilii, who after baptism received the name Vavila, but was nicknamed "Barefoot" because he went barefoot in both winter and summer, served in the refectory (*trapeznaia*). He had the following habit. After sitting down all the destitute for the meal, as his eminence metropolitan Nikon ordered, Vavila checked whether or not the destitute had crosses around their necks and if someone did not have a cross, he would give them his own. He then would plead with them to always wear and look at Christ's cross as a sign of salvation, remembering Christ's great and perfect love for us and serving Him who suffered for us with our entire hearts and minds.

Each Sunday, by the metropolitan's orders, donations were given from his treasury. The old received two *den'gas*, the middle-aged—one *den'ga*, and children and infants received half a *den'ga*.[i] Each morning, all who came would receive bread, two pounds each. All these donations were given on the metropolitan's orders from the accounts of the hierarchal household. In addition to this, his eminence Nikon always carried a ruble or two of his personal money to give to the poor. Sometimes he would give each a *grivna*, sometimes a *poltina*[ii] or even more, depending on need.

His eminence the metropolitan opened four new shelters for orphans and the poor in Novgorod and secured food for the shelters from the great sovereign. He himself donated to both the old and the new shelters as well as the prisons. During visits to the prisons he asked the prisoners about their crimes as the great sovereign ordered him. Having considered the crime and taken into account penitence, his eminence the metropolitan released some from jail, helping especially the weak and those unjustly condemned by the strong and the powerful,

---

[i] The equivalent of one *kopek*, half a *kopek*, and a quarter *kopek* respectively.
[ii] Ten and fifty *kopeks* respectively.

because he cared greatly for the truth. On the sovereign's orders, he supervised the city officials so that they did not abuse, impoverish, or levy taxes on the residents of Novgorod. Having heard about this, the great sovereign was very pleased that during his reign God kindly sent him a clergyman so benevolent to the people. This is why the great sovereign often wrote letters full of amazing wisdom and love to his eminence Nikon in Novgorod and wished that his eminence the metropolitan was always in the ruling city to please the great sovereign with instructive and sweet conversation. His eminence Nikon could not fulfill this wish because of his numerous obligations to care for the flock of Christ's sheep entrusted to him. Even so, every winter the sovereign summoned his eminence Nikon to the ruling city and ordered him to stay in Moscow at length because his eminence the metropolitan was quite skillful in interpreting the Holy Scripture and had the God-given gift of eloquence. His speech was enlightening and pleasing to listeners, but frightening to those who did not submit to God and the holy church. In short, at this time, there was no hierarch (*arkhierei*) equal to his eminence in eloquence or anything else. His eminence the metropolitan frequently conducted the divine liturgy on Sundays and holy days and delivered homilies to his flock. Many people came from remote parishes to listen to his eminence's sweet homilies during the liturgies. They listened with attention and love to the metropolitan's wonderful sermons and the beautiful church singing because he was the first to introduce Kievan and Greek chants (*raspevy*) in the cathedral [of Novgorod the Great].[19] His eminence Nikon took care of adorning the churches and providing the clergy with proper attire, for he desired the clergy to have ample food supply and clothes so that the people would respect and revere their shepherds.[20] His eminence Nikon paid attention to these matters as no one else.[i]

Seeing the metropolitan of Novgorod's care in glorifying the name of God and in following the Holy Commandments, and being impressed by his eminence's diligence, the great sovereign grew increasingly fond of his eminence and did not refuse any of his requests.[21]

The pious sovereign, a great adherent to piety, knew that the singing and the reading at the churches were not practiced according to the ancient canons of the holy church. Instead of one, several people read simultaneously and without any regard for uniformity, competing with each other in speed and not paying attention to the meaning of the readings. The *tsar* was greatly saddened by such misbalance. Upon the advice and blessing of his spiritual father (*dukhovnyi otets*), Stefan Vonifat'ev, archpriest (*protopop*) of the Church of Annunciation [*Blagoveshchen'e*] of the Holiest Mother of God at the *tsar's* court, the sovereign began to introduce monophonic singing (*edinoglasnoe narechnoe penie*).[ii]

---

[i] The Iverskii redaction contains another line: "[H]e instilled in them a love of singing. He succeeded in staffing the choirs with magnificent singers with wonderful voices. They sang soulfully, not like a soulless organ. Nowhere else could one find such singing, only at metropolitan Nikon's."

[ii] In monophonic (*edinoglasnoe*) singing, a singular text is read or sung at any particular time. In contrast, in polyphonic (*mnogoglasnoe*) singing, as the name suggests, several texts may be read simultaneously. *Narechnoe* singing is also different from *khomovoe* singing. In the former, the soft and hard signs at the end of nouns and verbs are omitted.

His eminence metropolitan Nikon helped and assisted the sovereign in this God-pleasing affair, but his holiness patriarch Iosif resisted the good deed out of habit and did not wish to replace the wrong old practices with the new, correct ones.[22]

This is why when his eminence the metropolitan was in Moscow, the pious *tsar* always ordered Nikon to conduct the services wherever the sovereign was present, either at the *tsar's* court or at other churches where religious holy days were celebrated.

☙

When his eminence Nikon was the metropolitan of Novgorod and prince Fedor Andreevich Khilkov served as its governor and military commander (*voevoda*), powerful rebellions shook Novgorod and Pskov.[23]

In Novgorod the Great it happened in the following way. A man nicknamed the "Wolf,"[24] inspired by the devil, visited the houses of the German merchants for the sake of unjust profiteering and asked them in German: "How much would you pay me if I revealed a secret plan by the Novgorodians that concerns you?" Having collected German silver coins (*Joachimstalers* or *yefimki*) for his wickedness, he told the Germans: "Did you hear that people are unhappy with *boyar* Boris Ivanovich Morozov[25] and call him a traitor?" At that time, the people were indeed displeased with the *boyars*. "Soon they will kill you for being his friends and spies and will raid your houses. If you wish to escape death, flee without delay!" After hearing this, the Germans believed the "Wolf," for indeed there was a strong popular resentment of Boris Morozov. They promptly prepared for the journey, left Novgorod the Great with their merchandise, and set out for Germany, some on their own horses, others on hired ones.

The ill-intentioned "Wolf," not satisfied with his malicious lie for which he was already paid by the Germans, had an even more wicked design. He ran into the town hall (*zemskaia izba*) and the trading rows where he told many people that the Germans were friends of the traitorous *boyar* Boris Morozov, that they visited the *boyar* in Moscow to conspire for treason, received a generous reward from him, and set out for Germany. But now they were here, in Novgorod the Great.

The "Wolf" also suggested that the Novgorodians should serve the great sovereign and the entire Moscow tsardom by capturing all Germans, taking their money and condemning them as traitors and turncoats.

Listening to the malefactor's libelous and revolt-instigating speeches, enraged crowds started to pursue the Germans, captured them and started, as it usually happens during revolts, to beat them senseless with whatever happened to be available and rob them of their possessions. Thanks to the protection of noble and rich Novgorodians, who did not wish to see the death of the foreign merchants, the Germans were saved from heinous death. The noble Novgorodians

---

In the latter, the listener can hardly understand the words because the syllables are repeated randomly and soft and hard signs at the end of verbs and nouns are substituted with the letter "o."

told the rebels: "If you kill the Germans, who will testify against the traitorous *boyar* Boris Morozov? Better place them under guard in prison." The people listened to them and brought the Germans to prison, then proceeded to rob the houses of the merchants and the rich.

The governor and military commander, prince Fedor Andreevich Khilkov, seeing the uprising, sent his chancellery secretaries (*d'iaks*) and the heads of *strel'tsy* regiments (*streletskie golovy*) to quell the rebellion, but the rebels did not listen and almost killed them. The fury of the mutineers reached the point that they decided to kill the governor himself and together with the *strel'tsy* and cossacks went to the governor's house in the Kremlin,[i] saying: "All these traitors are friends of *boyar* Boris Morozov. They ordered to carry the bread, meat, and fish abroad so that we would have shortages and high prices."

[On March 16, 1650], having learned about this plan, the governor fled to the house of his eminence metropolitan Nikon, using the fortress wall as an escape route. The metropolitan received him with love, hid him in his inner chamber, and ordered the servants to lock the gates of the metropolitan's St. Sophia residence.[26]

When [on March 17, 1650] the agitated people who besieged the governor's house with wild screams and outrageous actions learned that the governor had fled to his eminence the metropolitan, someone yelled: "Let us go there and kill the traitor!" The crowd went to the St. Sophia residence, some with sticks, others with stones. At the same time, by the rebels' orders, two bells constantly rung, one in the big city tower, the other in the Cathedral of St. Nicholas, the miracle-worker, near the town hall and the custom chamber (*tamozhennaia izba*), the center of the revolt. Having come to the metropolitan's house, the insurgents started to mercilessly beat the servants, asking them about the whereabouts of the cell in which the governor was hiding. But even after heavy beatings, the servants said that they did not know where the governor was. Then the rebels, wishing to find the *boyar*, started to batter the gate of the St. Sophia residence with a heavy log.

His eminence Nikon, hearing the heavy thuds on the gates and wishing to save the governor from an untimely violent death by giving his own soul for the *boyar*, hid him in a secret place, and, entrusting himself to God's will, went out to the rebellious and furious crowd with words of admonition from the Holy Scripture.

Hearing words designed to lessen their rage but which did not agree with the goal of the revolt, the rebels furiously yelled: "Here is the protector and concealer of the traitors," and like beasts they jumped at his eminence Nikon, some with sticks, others with stones. He however simply said: "Father, forgive them; they know not what they are doing."[ii] God, our Lord, not wishing the death of the metropolitan at that time, put compassion in the hearts of some of the rebels. Seeing the metropolitan dragged on the ground and barely alive, they surrounded his eminence Nikon and did not allow him to be killed. Some thought

---

[i] In Muscovite Russia, a stone fortress in the heart of a town, the seat of military, religious, and administrative power was called the Kremlin.

[ii] See Lk. 23:34.

that his eminence the metropolitan was already dead and, overcome by fear, started to leave one by one until they all left.

The servants raised his eminence the metropolitan from the ground and carried him to his chambers. With his whole soul, he, not at all afraid of being killed if it would pacify the revolt and save innocent souls from death, forgot about the heavy beating inflicted on him. He immediately ordered to ring the large cathedral bell as if calling for a prayer and sent messengers to the monasteries to summon the archimandrites and abbots without delay. That was around the third hour of daylight.[i] And at this time his eminence Nikon was at confession.

When everyone assembled in the Cathedral of St. Sophia, the wisdom of God, his eminence the metropolitan, together with the council of clergy, went to the Cathedral of the Holy Sign on the trading side, carrying holy icons and the holy cross. The metropolitan walked with great difficulty, coughing up blood, and could barely conduct the holy liturgy in the Cathedral of the Holy Sign, during which he took holy communion to give him the strength to pacify the rebellion. He lay down in a sleigh in pain and exhaustion and ordered to be carried openly to the town hall and the customs chamber, the rebels' place of assembly.

When his eminence Nikon was brought there, he started to speak without the slightest fear: "You already heard the truthful words that I was not ashamed to tell you and now I will tell you even more; my sinful soul is ready to die because I had the honor of partaking in the source of eternity, the body and blood of Christ, my God. I, sinful, came to you as befits the shepherd, wishing to save your souls from the wolves stirring you up. And if you know any crime or treason that I committed against the *tsar* or the Russian tsardom, announce these crimes and then kill me." Hearing these words, the masterminds and the most insidious instigators of the unlawful assembly were overcome with fear and shame and started to leave one by one and soon everyone had returned to their homes.[27]

His eminence the metropolitan, seeing God's help in this matter, ordered to be carried to the Cathedral of St. Sophia, the wisdom of God, and there publicly cursed the names of all the instigators of the rebellion and then returned to his residence. The rebels, wishing to hide their evil deeds, wrote a petition to the great sovereign in Moscow on behalf of the entire population of Novgorod the Great, as if they stirred the rebellion for the benefit of the sovereign and Moscow tsardom.[28] Many thousands of Novgorodians signed this petition to the sovereign of Moscow. The rebels forced people of various ranks to sign blank sheets of paper and threatened those who did not want to sign with death. To this end they put an executioner's block and an axe nearby. They were especially forceful in regards to the clergy. The rebels elected their own governor, Ioann Zheglov, the butler of his eminence the metropolitan, who at that time was in jail chained by the neck, for a crime he committed. The rebels freed him, appointed him governor in a town hall, and assigned officials to him.[29] The mutineers put guards around Novgorod the Great and at all the roads to Moscow, so as to stop messengers with letters from his eminence the metropolitan and the governor

---

[i] Approximately nine o'clock in the morning.

from getting to the great sovereign.[30] Knowing their crime, the rebels started to think about seceding from the great sovereign and subjecting themselves to the power of the Polish or Swedish kings.

His eminence the metropolitan, still hiding the governor in his chambers, wrote about all these events and immediately sent the letter with a messenger who knew secret paths.[31] The messenger soon arrived in Moscow and gave the letter to the great sovereign.

The great sovereign responded at once and sent a decree (*gramota*) with the same messenger. The *tsar's* missive started as follows. "To the new passion-bearer, confessor, and martyr, his eminence metropolitan Nikon." The decree also contained many other praises and thanks.[32] The *tsar* sent a letter to the town hall with the same messenger. The letter was addressed to the entire town; in it the *tsar* wrote that the townsfolk must repent for their evil deeds and ask his eminence the metropolitan for mercy and forgiveness for their great sin against him, if they did not want to be condemned to death; they were also to surrender the main instigators. If his eminence the metropolitan kindly agreed to forgive them, then the great sovereign would likewise show them his mercy and forgive them. But, if the Novgorodians did not do these things, they would soon be put to death. Even before the sovereign's decree and the letter reached Novgorod, right after his eminence Nikon cursed the rebels, the best of them started to come to the cathedral to beg his eminence the metropolitan for forgiveness and the removal of his curse. So when the great sovereign's missives were read, all the town's inhabitants, from young to old, were overcome with fear of the death sentence. They could only find solace in the great sovereign's entrusting the whole affair to his eminence the metropolitan, because on the petition of his eminence Nikon those who received his forgiveness would also be pardoned by the great sovereign. This is why all the residents came to their arch-shepherd, their merciful father, and tearfully asked him for mercy and forgiveness, trusting his good will and asking for the great sovereign's mercy for the town. His eminence Nikon reasoned with, taught, and enlightened the Novgorodians using the Scripture for more than three hours, pleading with them not to act like this again.[i] Seeing that the residents were sincere in their penitence and crying, his eminence the metropolitan forgave their sins against him, removed his curse,[ii] and promised to ask the great sovereign to forgive their crimes. His eminence Nikon ordered to capture the instigators and masterminds of the rebellion and imprison them under strict guard. The Novgorodians immediately followed the order and imprisoned more than three hundred people.

After exhortations by his eminence the metropolitan, hopeful of the great sovereign's mercy, the Novgorodians calmed down entirely (and we, the members

---

[i] In the printed Iverskii version, there is the following passage inserted here. "His homily started in the following way: 'I beseech you, as the Prophet David who said: 'the fire consumed them and the sinners perished in flames.' While he started with these words, he ended with the following: 'pray and you shall not fall into danger, so that you will not feel God's wrath and will not go astray from the righteous path when His wrath enflames. Blessed are those who have hope in Him."

[ii] In the Iverskii printed version, there is an additional interjection at this point: "by saying: 'The grace of God our Lord and Savior Jesus Christ be with you all.'"

of his eminence the metropolitan's household, could freely walk around the town. Before, not only the adults, but even I, who write these words and who was then but a child, were in danger in the town because the residents called us co-conspirators and traitors and wanted to assail and beat us).

The insurgency in Pskov happened even before the one in Novgorod and the Pskovians rebelled even worse. The townsfolk imprisoned the archbishop and killed the governor and many members of the nobility. They called the great sovereign's letters to them treason. To suppress the rebellion, the great sovereign sent governor, prince Ioann Nikitich Khovanskii with an army to Pskov. Having first arrived in Novgorod the Great, prince Ioann Nikitich Khovanskii punished the instigators of the rebellion in accordance with the sentence by his eminence the metropolitan, because the great sovereign ordered to rely on the sensible judgment of metropolitan Nikon in the investigation of the Novgorodian rebellion. The main instigator, the "Wolf," was beheaded. Ioann Zheglov and his minions, about ten of them, were whipped and sent to eternal exile in Siberia. Others were released after receiving minor punishments, or being forgiven altogether. Then everything finally calmed down in Novgorod the Great.[33]

After completing his work in Novgorod, prince Ioann Nikitich Khovanskii went to Pskov where he was greeted with war, not with peace. The Pskovians shut the town gates and battled the governor's army as if it were the enemy. Because of this, much Christian blood was shed on both sides.[34]

Having learned about this, the great sovereign consulted with his holiness patriarch Iosif and with the entire holy synod and sent hierarchs, archimandrites, and abbots with his and the patriarch's degrees to the Pskovians. The Pskovians received them, read them and, although not immediately and after some persuasion, submitted to the sovereign. Since then the most pious *tsar* began to show his eminence metropolitan Nikon his special good will and often send him short personal letters. In them, the *tsar* praised his eminence Nikon for his pastoral care in managing Novgorodian affairs and preventing bloodshed even at the expense of his own well-being.

The souls of the great sovereign and his eminence the metropolitan were united in such great mutual love that the sovereign wished his eminence Nikon to be in Moscow so that they could enjoy conversing and seeing each other at all times. Although it was impossible because of the metropolitan of Novgorod's pastoral duties, his eminence Nikon came to Moscow every year and lived there for several months all the same.[35]

Once during a trip to Moscow, his eminence Nikon noticed the scarcely populated area next to Lake Valdai, about ten *poprishches* long and wide.[i] The lake contained several islands, was deep, rich in fish, and connected to several other lakes. The metropolitan so much liked the land and the lake that he immediately wanted to build a monastery on the largest island. This would be done in the future; but it will be told later.[36]

---

[i] About fifteen kilometers long and wide.

CR

When his eminence the metropolitan came to Moscow, the pious *tsar*, upon consultation with his holiness patriarch Iosif and the entire holy synod, [on March
11, 1652] sent his eminence together with a *boyar*, the chancellery secretary,
and several service nobles (*dvoriane*) to the Solovetskii Monastery to fetch the
remains of holy and blessed Filipp,[37] metropolitan of Moscow and all Russia.[38]
Others went with them to keep a prayer oath.[39] When [on May 14–16, 1652]
they reached the White Sea and sailed towards the island, the wind intensified
and a strong storm ensued. All the ships were wrecked; the boat, in which the
chancellery secretary and other people sailed, was lost, but all the other travelers
were saved by the mercy of God.[40]

After the frightening shipwreck, his eminence the metropolitan and his companions boarded other vessels without delay and again set sail. [On June 3,
1652] they successfully reached the Solovetskii Monastery, took the remains of
metropolitan Filipp and immediately set sail to return. On the way to the ruling
city of Moscow, pious people revered the honorable remains of metropolitan
Filipp. The remains were greeted by holy crosses and holy icons.[41] On these
occasions, by the Grace of God, many of those who came with faith to the holy
remains were cured of various ailments. When his eminence Nikon was traveling [from Novgorod the Great], his holiness patriarch Iosif left this world for
eternal life [on April 15, 1652].[42]

When the holy remains approached Moscow, the pious *tsar*, together with the
holy synod, bearing holy crosses and holy icons in proper decorum, came to
meet the remains. Together with him was his eminence Varlaam, metropolitan
of Rostov and Iaroslavl'. The pious *tsar* tried to persuade the elderly Varlaam
not to go greet the remains, but the metropolitan, wishing to see them, went all
the same. Walking, his eminence Varlaam was almost within a stone's thrown of
the holy remains, when he grew weak, sat down on a chair, and at once left the
earthly life.

After Varlaam's passing away, the remains of great metropolitan Filipp were
brought closer and the pious *tsar*, all his Council (*synclete*), the entire holy
synod, and a countless multitude of people cheerfully uttered their praise to God
and expressed their gratitude to Him for allowing them to see the holy relics of
His servant. [On July 9, 1652], having touched the holy remains with heartfelt
happiness and received a blessing from his eminence metropolitan Nikon, the
pious *tsar* returned to the ruling city of Moscow and ordered to put the holy remains of metropolitan Filipp in the middle of the Dormition [*Uspenskii*] Cathedral where they lay for three days. And during each of three days, the church
was full of people, wishing to touch or kiss the remains.

By the Grace of God, during both the translation of the holy relics and the period when they lay in the middle of the cathedral, the remains cured many afflicted people, especially the possessed. Prayers against evil spirits were read
over the relics. After his eminence metropolitan Nikon placed his hands over the
possessed, they were cured.[43]

After the translation of metropolitan Filipp's relics, the pious *tsar* started to
show his eminence Nikon even greater love and favor for the metropolitan's

labors. [On July 17, 1652], as a sign of his gratitude, the *tsar* benevolently bestowed upon the metropolitan many expensive clothes and vestments and assigned several villages to his St. Sophia residence in Novgorod; the *tsar* also recompensated all members of the metropolitan's choir.[44]

ભ

The pious *tsar*, seeing that there was no hierarch equal to his eminence Nikon either in intelligence or piety,[45] upon consultation with the holy synod, [on July 22], beseeched his eminence to assume the patriarchal throne, even though his eminence had no desire to do so and refused, giving many reasons.[46] But upon the sovereign's pleas, his eminence accepted the patriarchal throne and was installed on the twenty-fifth day of July, 7160 (1652).[47]

After assuming the patriarchal throne, his holiness Nikon, keeping the oath he gave earlier, asked the sovereign for the village and the lake at Valdai to construct a monastery honoring the Icon of the Iverskaia Mother of God.[48] The great sovereign fulfilled Nikon's wish without delay by granting him the rights to the village and the lake and ordered to confirm the finality of this gift in royal decree with a golden seal.[49]

His holiness the patriarch at once sent a respected abbot of the hermitage (*starets-stroitel'*) together with a junior *boyar* (*boyarskii syn*) and others from his patriarchal household to start the construction and gave them enough gold, silver, church utensils, and books for the new monastery. They reached the place without delay and started the construction with due diligence. Some cut wood, others built the cells, still others put up the fence around the monastery. The church was founded and built at the same time.[50]

Soon thereafter, having received the news about the construction of the holy monastery, the patriarch himself went there to finish the endeavor he started. He brought with him fragments of the relics of four Moscow metropolitans and miracle-workers Piotr, Aleksei, Iona, and Filipp in a gilded silver ark. Even before his arrival, his holiness Nikon ordered his eminence Makarii, metropolitan of Novgorod and Velikie Luki, to bring the honorable relics of holy Iakov Borovitskii to the newly built monastery.[51]

When his holiness the patriarch visited the monastery [on February 25/26, 1654], the inhabitants of the nearby villages came with stories that on the night of his arrival with the holy relics of the four Moscow metropolitans, they saw four fiery columns rising up above the monastery; some saw just one pillar over the church.[52]

After staying in the newly built monastery for a short time and attending to all its needs, his holiness the patriarch returned to the ruling city and at once sent a letter to holy Mount Athos asking for a copy of the miracle-working icon of the Iverskaia Mother of God for the newly created monastery. During the travel of this copy, first to the ruling city of Moscow, and then to the new monastery, Jesus Christ, the source of miracles and the Light of the world, graced it to perform new miracles[53] which are described in the book about the Iverskii Monastery called *Mental Paradise* [*Rai Myslennyi*].[i]

Ruling over the Russian Church, his holiness the patriarch protected it against deprived oppression and did not allow the clergy to be put on trial in any offices but his own (*patriarshii prikaz*). He treated the kind and obedient with humbleness and fatherly love and punished the evil and disobedient with reasonable severity. This is why he was respected by all, especially the sovereign, who treated his holiness the patriarch as his beloved father. The great sovereign did not do anything without the advice and blessing of his holiness Nikon. It was upon his pastoral advice and blessing that [in March 1654] the great sovereign launched the battle against the Polish and Lithuanian king to protect the Orthodox Christian faith and for other reasons. The *tsar* entrusted his family, his spouse, her majesty the pious and virtuous sovereign Mariia Il'inichna, his sisters and children, and the very ruling city of Moscow to his holiness the patriarch. The *tsar* asked his holiness to take care of them and rule in good faith in his stead.

By the will of God, the great sovereign conquered many Lithuanian towns during this campaign, and after his victory returned to the ruling city where he praised God.[54]

The same year [February 1654], a son, *tsarevich* Aleksei Alekseevich, was born to the pious *tsar*. Asked by the great sovereign, his holiness the patriarch became the boy's godfather. Later, because the great sovereign liked his holiness the patriarch, his holiness Nikon became the godfather of the *tsar's* other children.[55]

In the spring [on March 11, 1655], the great sovereign again entrusted his family and Moscow to his holiness the patriarch, when the *tsar* embarked on another campaign against the Polish king.[56]

That year [1654],[57] because of our sins, the ruling city of Moscow was besieged by a deadly plague.[58] To save the ruling house, [on June 24] his holiness the patriarch, together with her majesty, the virtuous and pious sovereign and grand princess Mariia Il'inichna, the noble *tsarevich* and virtuous *tsarevnas* went to the Monastery of the Trinity and St. Sergius [*Troitse-Sergiev*],[59] then to the monastery of the reverend Makarii of Koliazin, and then to the town of Viaz'ma.[60] On their way, his holiness took very good care of the *tsar's* family, protecting them from illnesses. He personally attended to them, ordering to blaze trails through inhabited areas, build sturdy protective fences, and burn big fires to purify infected air, doing everything in his power to protect them against the plague.[61]

The virtuous *tsarina*, seeing the fatherly care of his holiness the patriarch took a liking to him and started to respect him as her own father.[62] The sovereign's sisters and children also had a great love for him and, with God's help, and thanks to the careful protection of his holiness the patriarch, none of the travel-

---

[i] In the printed Iverskii redaction, there is an additional passage describing the construction of the Iverskii Monastery, an abridged description borrowed from *Rai Myslennyi*.

ers died from the deadly plague. All remained healthy and intact, but a countless multitude of people, almost everyone, died in the ruling city.[i]

[On October 21, 1654], when his holiness the patriarch lived in the town of Viaz'ma together with the *tsar's* family, the pious *tsar* arrived there victorious. Having seen his family healthy and intact, and having learnt about his holiness the patriarch's diligence and care, the pious *tsar* became elated. After giving great thanks to God for the victory over the Polish king and especially for the protection of his family, the great sovereign repaid his holiness Nikon with even greater affection for the love his holiness the patriarch had shown.[63] The *tsar* considered his holiness Nikon God's angel and the protector of his family and held him in such a great esteem that others were in wonder. When the plague was over, the *tsar*, his family, and his holiness the patriarch went from the town of Viaz'ma to Moscow where they arrived safely [in early Feburary 1655].[64]

℞

Upon return to Moscow, his holiness the patriarch heard from many people that Slavonic books were incorrect because they did not agree with the Greek ones.[ii] Wishing to correct this, his holiness the patriarch consulted with the great sovereign and the holy synod regarding the need to compare the church books against the ancient Russian and Greek parchments and to bring them in line with each other in words, order of service, and canon. He also wished to consult with the ecumenical and other patriarchs, as well as the monasteries at holy Mounts Sinai and Athos on the most difficult questions.[65]

The pious *tsar* praised the patriarch's zeal and ordered to assemble a council consisting of all Russian church hierarchs, archimandrites, abbots, and arch-priests in the ruling city of Moscow, which was to agree on the reform.[66]

After all the assembled had consulted each other, a declaration was made that a book reform was necessary to correct the mistakes in Russian church books by using ancient Greek and Russian parchments and comparing the order of service against these ancient church rules. It was decided that difficult and unresolved questions should be referred to their holinesses the ecumenical patriarchs and the monasteries at holy Mounts Athos and Sinai. The agreement to correct the books was signed personally by the pious *tsar*, his holiness the patriarch, other hierarchs, and the entire holy synod, thereby affirming the reform.[67]

Immediately after the conclusion of the council of the holy synod his holiness the patriarch ordered to collect all ancient Greek and Slavonic parchments from the old repositories so that skillful and pious people, able to distinguish truth from error and to translate from the Hellenistic Greek language to Slavonic, could read these books with great care, correct the mistakes of unskilled transla-tors and copiers, and write everything down for the sake of improved correc-tions. The pious *tsar* and his holiness the patriarch wrote about the corrections as

---

[i] In the printed Iverskii version, this passage reads "nearly everybody died and if four or five people were left on a street it was a source of great wonder."

[ii] In the printed Iverskii version, an important section about "the correction of the books" is absent, but it is included in the Rumiantsev version.

well as about all the difficult and unresolved questions to the ecumenical and other Orthodox patriarchs and sent their missives with Manuel the Greek.[68]

After receiving the missives, the ecumenical patriarch Paisius convoked a patriarchal council and, replying to the questions of the great sovereign and his holiness the patriarch, wrote to the pious *tsar* and Christ-loving patriarch about the decisions of the council. He also sent the decisions made by the previous council. This happened in the year 7163 (1655). The ecumenical patriarch decreed to follow the works of the great Orthodox teachers of the Eastern Church contained in ancient Greek and Slavonic books.[69]

In his epistle, his holiness patriarch Paisius wrote: "Your most blessed holiness Nikon, the patriarch of highest Moscow, *kyr* of all the Russian lands (which means lord), beloved brother in the Holy Spirit and concelebrant of our humbleness! In regards to the issue about which you wrote to us, my response, most blessed brother, is that you need to correct everything accordingly, because God will reveal Himself in due time in order to explain and correct everything which is incorrect. I am happy about this, for God is alive. I constantly have you in my soul and am amazed at your mind and deeds and truly praise you, your blessedness, for your constant search for salvation. You are a true shepherd caring for your spiritual flock, providing clean, firm, and true nourishment for them. I praise you for endeavoring to correct all elements of the holy canon in accordance with the statements of the great church so that we will not have any differences because we are children of one and the same mother, the great eastern catholic and apostolic church (*sobornaia i apostol'skaia tserkov'*) of Christ. Let us not give evil heretical mouths a single reason to talk about our differences. Let us stand in true concord as firm and undefeated pillars. And so on and so forth."[70]

And so, the pious *tsar* and the Christ-loving patriarch, having received the reply from the ecumenical patriarch Paisius and having read the council's records, became even more zealous in their good will. Considering it insufficient for the reform to collect ancient Greek and Slavonic books in Russia alone, the great sovereign and his holiness the patriarch both consented to send elder Arsenii Sukhanov[71] to Mount Athos and other ancient holy places so that he could exchange generous donations for old books and send them to Moscow. And so it was done; Arsenii Sukhanov brought about five hundred ancient books in Greek from holy Mount Athos.[72]

The patriarchs of Alexandria, Antioch, Jerusalem, Serbia, and Ohrid,[73] metropolitans, archbishops, and hierarchs from other Orthodox countries also sent no less than two hundred ancient holy books to the ruling city of Moscow.[74]

And so the pious and wise in God pair, Aleksei Mikhailovich, the great sovereign, *tsar* and grand prince of all Great, Little, and White Russias, and the great lord, his holiness Nikon, patriarch of Moscow and all Russia, by an act of God the Pantocrator, were moved to preserve the true dogmas of the holy faith by collecting all the holy books, studying their content together, and correcting the incorrect books.[75]

To confirm the book reform, another patriarchal council was summoned to the ruling city of Moscow. Nikon, by the Grace of God his holiness the patriarch of Moscow, Macarius, patriarch of Antioch, Gavriil, patriarch of Serbia, metropolitans, archbishops, bishops, archimandrites, abbots, and the entire synod were present.[76]

And so they studied the records of the council sent by his holiness the ecumenical patriarch Paisius with great care and reckoned that these decisions were indeed inspired by the Holy Spirit. Then, after comparing the ancient Greek and Slavonic books, the council discovered that the ancient Greek manuscripts were identical to the ancient Slavonic ones, but that the new Greek printed books and the new Moscow printed books were very different from the ancient Greek and Slavonic originals and contained many errors. The council of the holy synod decided to correct the new books so that they would agree with the ancient holy Greek and Slavonic manuscripts and so that all Orthodox Christians, wishing to have a correct understanding of the faith which would not contradict the ancient Greek manuscripts and canons, could avoid punishments for transgressions against piety even though these transgressions might be committed in ignorance. The Orthodox Christians could then live happily for many years here on earth and enjoy eternal happiness and bliss in the future life. Amen.[77]

The year before the council, the pious great sovereign with his army went on campaign against the Swedish sovereign; the *tsar* conquered many towns and defeated the Swedish king's army.[78]

CR

His holiness patriarch Nikon remembered the oath he swore during the storm at sea when he was thrown on the Isle of Kii and promised to build the Cross [*Krestnyi* or *Stavros*] Monastery there.[79] To this end, he sent a skillful monk together with a junior *boyar* to the island and ordered them to build a monastery dedicated to the Cross and to call it *Stavros* in Greek, or *Krestnyi* in Russian.

His holiness patriarch Nikon himself ordered a cypress cross to be made in Moscow for the Cross Monastery. The cross was to be equal to Christ's Cross in height and width and adorned with silver, gold, precious stones, and pearls; inside it three hundred relics were to be enclosed.[80]

Splendid holy icons were also skillfully painted and adorned and sent together with the holy cross to the Cross Monastery after his holiness saw them off with appropriate honors and piety. [81] His holiness Nikon, together with an assembly of clergy, accompanied the holy cross from the cathedral, beyond the Sretenskiie Gate, to the spot called Filipp's Cross; then he returned to the cathedral and served the liturgy there.

On this day [on July 31, 1656], God our Lord willed for the great sovereign to take the German town of Dünaburg, which was renamed in honor of *tsarevich* Dimitrii because the city was taken on *tsarevich* Dimitrii's day of commemoration.[82]

Soon thereafter [in late summer 1656], for our sins, by God's righteous will, the Russian land was again overcome by a deadly plague.[83]

His holiness patriarch Nikon, as a loving father and loyal protector of the sovereign's family, again left the ruling city of Moscow together with the *tsar's* entire family for the town of Tver' and from there for the town of Viaz'ma, where they remained until the great sovereign's return from Lithuania.[84]

When [on November 26, 1656] the great sovereign returned to the town of Viaz'ma victoriously and safely and found his whole family in good health, he uttered ardent thanks to God for their protection.[85] The *tsar* thanked his holiness the patriarch for his diligent care and zealous protection of his family by giving his holiness a great recompensate.[86] And so the *tsar's* love increased even more the fatherly love that the patriarch felt for the great sovereign.[87]

So great was their mutual love, that the Russian land has never seen such a love between a *tsar* and a patriarch. It was not only the subject of great rejoicing in the entire Russian tsardom, but the object of wonderment in the neighboring lands.

After the plague subsided, the great sovereign, together with his family, a large army, and his holiness the patriarch, returned from Viaz'ma to the ruling city of Moscow where they lived in peace and prosperity.[88] The patriarch and *tsar's* love towards each other increased daily and hourly to everyone's wonderment.

At this time [June 3, 1656] his holiness patriarch Nikon bought the village of Voskresenskoe for the Iverskii Monastery from one Roman Bobarykin.[89] The village was located forty-five *poprishches* from Moscow.[i] He started to go there frequently on account of the monastery's needs. It soon occurred to his holiness the patriarch to build a monastery in the village so that he could live there, not in the village during his visits.

And so, with the permission of the great sovereign, his holiness the patriarch started to cut wood to build the church and cells of the Resurrection [*Voskresenskii*] Monastery.

When it was time to consecrate the church, his holiness the patriarch invited the great sovereign to the occasion.[ii] After visiting the Resurrection Monastery, the pious *tsar* took a liking to the place and soon after his trip wrote to his holiness the patriarch in his own hand that "from the very beginning it was God's will to prepare this place for the founding a monastery; it is beautiful and looks like Jerusalem."

Happy to receive this letter, his holiness patriarch Nikon put the epistle into a silver-wrought ark which stood underneath the holy throne (*prestol*) and ordered to call the Resurrection Monastery "New Jerusalem," according to the *tsar's* words.[90]

After this, his holiness sent the cellerer (*kelar'*) of the Monastery of the Trinity and St. Sergius, elder Arsenii Sukhanov, to the holy city of Jerusalem in Palestine to bring a likeness of Jerusalem's great Church of the Holy Resurrection, which was originally built by pious and Christ-loving *tsarina* Elena, mother of St. Constantine the *tsar*. The cellerer went to Jerusalem at once and carried out the order.[91]

His holiness patriarch Nikon ordered to build at the Resurrection Monastery a large and spacious church in the likeness of the holy church of Jerusalem which would have no equal either in Russia or any other land because the Jerusalem church itself was destroyed by Turkish assaults and damaged by non-Orthodox

---

[i] About sixty-eight kilometers.
[ii] The printed Iverskii version dates this event to 7165 [1657].

Christians who followed their own customs.[92] And so blessed Nikon built this church.

CR

Some time later, the common enemy of humanity, the devil, started to envy the great love between the pious *tsar* and his holiness patriarch Nikon and ill-will and enmity between them ensued, ignited by the evil people who were emblazoned by the enemy. Before, the *tsar* would enter the cathedral during holy days and partake in the reading of the litany of supplication (*ektin'ia*) and singing of hymns. Now, instigated by the ill-will of his privy *boyars* (*blizhnii boyarin*), the pious *tsar* stopped these usual processions.

His holiness the patriarch often waited for him, continuing to ring the bell (*blagovest*), but the pious *tsar* would send a message ordering [the patriarch] not to wait for him. That was the cause of the ill-will and enmity between them. [93]

Once, his holiness the patriarch allowed his rage to overcome him; on July 10 [1658] he left the pastoral throne (*patriarshii prestol*) and staff (*posokh* or *zhezl*) in the Cathedral of the Holiest Mother of God during the celebration of the Deposition of the Venerable Robe [*Polozhenie rizy* or *khitona*] of Our Lord and Savior Jesus Christ.[94] And he also sent a note to the pious *tsar* asking to be granted a monastic cell in which he could reside.[95]

The pious *tsar*, learning about this, sent his privy *boyar*, prince Aleksei Nikitich Trubetskoi, to the patriarch at the cathedral and the people who witnessed this unusual event started to scream and lament and did not allow his holiness the patriarch out of the cathedral.

The privy *boyar*, after seeing his holiness the patriarch in a black monastic hood (*klobuk*)[i] and with a simple staff in his hands, relayed the *tsar's* words. "The great sovereign ordered me to ask you: 'Why are you requesting a cell since you already have cells that you built at the patriarchal palace?'"[ii] His holiness the patriarch replied: "They are not mine, let he who has the good will of the sovereign live in them, and I should be rewarded by the great sovereign and released to go to a monastery."[96]

The *boyar* returned to the *tsar* and, after a brief stay, again came to his holiness the patriarch repeating his earlier words and adding: "the great sovereign ordered me to ask your holiness whether or not you have something against the great sovereign or some reproachful words against him. Kindly respond!" His holiness the patriarch replied: "I have nothing against the great sovereign, nor any reproach against him or anybody else. I am leaving the throne knowing my numerous sins which were the cause of many diseases, wars, and other calami-

---

[i] It was customary for the Russian patriarchs to wear white monastic hoods (*klobuks*) with an elevated cross on the top, while lower ranks in the black clergy hierarchy wore black covers. Hence Trubetskoi and others witnessing this scene could only interpret Nikon's action as self-demotion.

[ii] In Shusherin's time, the patriarchal palace was located in the heart of the Moscow Kremlin, across the square from the Dormition Cathedral.

ties here in the ruling city. This is why I am leaving my throne and my patriarchal primacy."[97] After hearing these words, the *boyar* again returned to the *tsar*.

The pious people locked the church doors tightly, not allowing him out of the church. Every one lamented that they were loosing such a great shepherd and teacher. And so they held his holiness Nikon in the church, waiting for the *tsar's* arrival.[98]

His holiness the patriarch sat on the lower step of the patriarchal stall (*patriarshee mesto*) in the middle of the church across from the western door and rose up frequently wishing to leave. The people weeped and tried to stop him, and seeing their tears, he shed tears himself.

The same *boyar* came for the third time, this time with others and said: "the great sovereign ordered me to tell you to select whatever monastery and cells you wish." His holiness bowed to the *boyar* and said: "I humbly bow to the great sovereign for his favor" and left the cathedral.[99]

Seeing a coachman with a cart, his holiness the patriarch wanted to ride in it because Ivanovskaia Square was muddy at that time. But when the people noticed it, they destroyed the cart, cut up the hame-strap, and unharnessed the horse.

His holiness the patriarch, seeing that he was not to ride in the cart, walked across the muddy Ivanovskaia Square. There he was offered a carriage, but he refused to take it. Many people followed his holiness Nikon. And trying to stop him, they locked the Savior Gates of the Kremlin. His holiness the patriarch sat down in one of the niches of the Kremlin wall and many cried because he was leaving them as a shepherd leaving the sheep. Soon thereafter the *tsar's* dignitaries came to the gates and they were opened.

His holiness the patriarch stood up and walked across the Red Square along Il'inka Street to the town lodge of his Resurrection Monastery. He was followed by a large crowd which cried and tried to persuade him [to return]. When his holiness Nikon entered his cells at the town lodge of the Resurrection Monastery, he blessed all present, offered them peace, and released them. His holiness patriarch Nikon spent three days and three nights in the lodge, then asked for two wicker carts to be sent from the New Maiden [*Novodevichii*] Convent.[100] He put his belongings on one and sat in the other and went to his Resurrection Monastery.

The pious *tsar*, after learning that his holiness was traveling to the monastery in a simple cart, sent the same *boyar,* prince Aleksei Trubetskoi, after [the patriarch] to offer him a carriage in which his holiness the patriarch could travel. The *boyar* departed at once to follow the patriarch, but could not catch his holiness and so the *boyar* went to the Resurrection Monastery where he announced the *tsar's* edict (*ukaz*) to accept the carriage. His holiness the patriarch refused it; then the *boyar* took the carriage and brought it to the monastery's village called Chernevo and left it there. The carriage remained in the village of Chernevo for a long time.[101]

ଔଠ

His holiness patriarch Nikon started to wear metal chains, committed himself to prayer, fasting, and moderation, and personally looked after the building of the great church. He carried bricks with his own hands and on his own shoulders and labored together with the brethren of the Resurrection Monastery, carrying bricks every day of the week.

His holiness the patriarch also ordered to dig out ponds around the monastery and to raise fish in them; he also built mills and planted vegetable gardens. Together with the brethren, he cut down trees and extended the arable land. They dug out ditches near the swamps, making them into meadows on which to mow grass and rake hay. His holiness Nikon partook in every labor, setting a good example in everything. He came to work first and left work last. And so he lived increasing the fruits of his labors.

The pious *tsar*, hearing about the labors and patience of his holiness the patriarch, frequently sent generous donations of a thousand or two thousand rubles as well as food for the nourishment of the brethren. The great sovereign also showed his holiness Nikon royal favor by giving him the three great monasteries that he built: the Iverskii, Cross, and Resurrection Monasteries, so that [the patriarch] could rule all of them, live on the profits from peasants and lands belonging to these monasteries, and continue building God's great church. The *tsar* ordered these monasteries and their possessions to be exempt from all the royal levies and quitrents. Together, those monasteries then had more than six thousand peasants assigned to them.[102]

Every year the pious *tsar* also sent his holiness the patriarch two thousand rubles from the salt works in the Kama lands.[103] Using the silver donated by the grace of the *tsar* and the profits from the newly built monasteries, his holiness the patriarch continued to build God's church, always setting a good example with his labors.

Soon, about a year after his holiness the patriarch came to the Resurrection Monastery [in the summer of 1659], the pious *tsar* sent his privy *boyar* with the news about the invasion by barbarous Crimean Tartars, who already came very close to the Russian borders.[104] "And so you, our devout father and God-entreater," [said the note] "will not escape the invasion nor will survive the siege in such a new and scarcely populated place like the Resurrection Monastery." At this time, the monastery had low and poorly fortified walls. [The messenger] also asked his holiness the patriarch to take the advice of the pious lord the *tsar* and to kindly go to Makarii's monastery in Koliazin, which had strong stone walls, [to escape] the invasion of the barbarians.

His holiness the patriarch replied to the messenger: "Tell the pious *tsar* that I will not go to the monastery in Koliazin, I would rather go to the Monastery of the Conception of the Immaculate [*Zachat'evskii*] at the corner of Kitai Gorod, than to the monastery in Koliazin."[105] "I have," he added, "thanks to the help of great God and the *tsar's* favor, my own fortified monasteries, the Iverskii and the Cross, above and beyond the monastery in Koliazin, and I, after reporting to the great sovereign, will go to my own monastery. And now convey to the great sovereign that I will come to Moscow to tell the *tsar* about my needs." The messenger asked: "What Monastery of the Conception of the Immaculate, which is better than the one in Koliazin, does your holiness talk about?" His holiness the patriarch replied: "That monastery which stands on Varvarka Street at the foot of the hill next to the Church of the Conception of the Immaculate." (Then a big jail stood at the foot of the hill). The messenger noted that there was only a jail there, not a monastery, and his holiness Nikon replied: "This indeed is the Monastery of the Conception of the Immaculate." And he released the messenger with a blessing.

His holiness the patriarch set out for the ruling city of Moscow without delay. Moscow was then preparing for a siege by building wooden walls over the earthen ramparts.

Without delays in his trip, his holiness the patriarch reached the ruling city the same day; there, staying at the town lodge of his Iverskii Monastery, he sent word to the great sovereign that he had come for some necessities and wished to have an audience with the *tsar* to offer peace and blessing before fleeing the Tartar invasion to wherever God wishes and the *tsar* orders.

That evening, the pious *tsar* did not seek counsel from the *boyars* and did not deign his holiness the patriarch to visit. In the morning, together with the *boyars*, he decided to send the secretary of the Council (*dumnyi d'iak*) Almaz Ivanov to ask his holiness the patriarch about the reasons that brought him to Moscow; his holiness was to tell the secretary of the Council, who then would relate the reasons to the great sovereign and the Council [of the *boyars*] (*Duma*).

Hearing this, his holiness said: "I will not talk to you about my requests and will not send my blessing with you, that is, a complete blessing done with the making of the sign of the cross and the laying of hands." After these words, the secretary of the Council returned to the *tsar* and on that day the great sovereign again did not allow his holiness the patriarch to visit.

On the third day, the great sovereign again sent the same man to say that he would graciously allow his holiness the patriarch to visit the court that night. His holiness the patriarch had not eaten anything for three days, since his departure from the Resurrection Monastery, because he did not take any edible supplies with him.

The Muscovites exalted in seeing their shepherd. The same day, the news came that the Crimean Tartars retreated. And when the evening came, the secretary of the Council returned to announce that the time had come to go to the *tsar's* court.

His holiness the patriarch went and arrived, as before, in the upper chambers. The pious *tsar* greeted him at the front entrance. Upon entering the chambers, his holiness the patriarch read the prayer "Lord all merciful" and others according to the order and added supplications for the *tsar*, *tsarina*, the entire *tsar's* family, and the army. Immediately after the prayer, the pious *tsar* and his holiness the patriarch sat down and peacefully conversed, asking each other about their health and salvation. A short period of time passed. The *boyars* were also present at the conversation. Then the pious *tsar* and his holiness the patriarch went to the pious *tsarina* and *tsar's* children and stayed there until the fourth hour of night.[i] The pious *tsar* released his holiness the patriarch to go to the Resurrection Monastery, allowing the patriarch, upon his request, to go to the Iverskii and the Cross Monasteries. The *tsar* also invited his holiness Nikon to

---

[i] About ten o'clock in the evening.

attend dinner in the upper chambers the next day. His holiness the patriarch declined, explaining that he would leave early in the morning.

The pious *tsar* sent him two thousand rubles in silver in place of the dinner and for travel expenses and ordered his holiness to take twenty *strel'tsy* with captains (*sotnik*) from the St. Savva [*Savvin*] Monastery for protection against evil people when traveling to the Resurrection Monastery. Soon thereafter, his holiness the patriarch left the ruling city of Moscow and returned to his Resurrection Monastery.[106]

෨

At that time, the monastic deacon (*chernyi d'iakon*) Feodosii came from the ruling city of Moscow to the Resurrection Monastery. Feodosii was formerly in the service of Pitirim, metropolitan of Krutitsa,[107] and now told his holiness many wretched words about the metropolitan, calling him a tormentor, fornicator, and many other names. Feodosii begged his holiness the patriarch to allow him to stay at the Resurrection Monastery.[108]

His holiness the patriarch blessed him to be part of the brethren. When his holiness patriarch Nikon decided to go to his Iverskii and Cross Monasteries, monk Feodosii was constantly pleading with his holiness the patriarch to allow him to go to the aforesaid monasteries.

His holiness the patriarch, not suspecting Feodosii's treachery and duplicity, ordered him to come and serve at the patriarch's private church (*krestovaia sluzhba*), and eat and drink with the monastery elders (*keleinyi starets*). His holiness the patriarch lived in the Iverskii Monastery and at the Galilee Hermitage for some time [October 1659–Janurary 1660(?)]; then he went to the Cross Monastery and spent almost a year there [February–September 1660 (?)].[109] During his stay [at the Cross Monastery], the new stone church in honor of the Exaltation of the Venerable Cross of the Lord [*Vozdvizhenie chestnago kresta Gospodnia*] was built.[110] A well was dug in the rock and a stone church in honor of the Procession of the Precious Wood of the Venerable Cross of the Lord [*Proiskhozhdenie drev chestnago kresta Gospodnia*] was built near it. This new well was very useful; it contained plenty of water, enough for all the monastery's needs. The new well was built by the prayer and labor of his holiness patriarch Nikon himself, for there was no such well in the Cross Monastery before and it lacked water. The old well froze in the winter and dried up in the summer because it was very small and shallow.

His holiness the patriarch was very saddened by this and prayed to God to show him the place to dig a new well. Shortly thereafter, instructed by God, his holiness the patriarch selected the place where a deep well was dug. His holiness the patriarch took interest in founding other buildings, but he took particular care building churches.[111] His holiness Nikon himself worked alongside the local peasants, and the brethren, and the monastery workers who came with him.

But enough about that. Let us return to aforesaid deacon Feodosii. He lived in his holiness the patriarch's household, became close to him, and started to accuse other people unfairly. His holiness the patriarch, not suspecting his treachery, did not pay any attention to him.

On the island there was a bathhouse built for the laymen. In this bathhouse, the servants of his holiness once saw deacon [Feodosii] with a certain man, engaged in some activities. When asked [what they were doing], the deacon left for the monastery without responding. Then, the servants captured his myrmidon and interrogated him about the essence of their activities. He revealed that the deacon was concocting a poisonous drink. The servants relayed this to his holiness the patriarch.

His holiness the patriarch ordered his service noble, Vasilii Poskochin, to interrogate the deacon and his accomplice. The deacon wrote a detailed confession about concocting a potion in the bathhouse. He wrote: "I was sent from Moscow by Pitirim, metropolitan of Krutitsa, and Pavel, archimandrite of the Monastery of the Miracles of Archangel Michael [*Chudov*][112] to hex his holiness the patriarch. In return, they promised me the metropolinate of Novgorod the Great. I acted solely on their instigation. First, I slipped [poison] in his holiness the patriarch's drink and offered it in a crystal tankard. He saw that the drink was cloudy, poured it out saying that it is very cloudy, and ordered a fresh drink. This is how he got rid of the first poison. I put small doses of the poison in the drinks of his cell companions so that they would be kind to me, and they drank it without looking closely.

This time, acting on the instigation of the aforesaid people, I concocted a deadly poison for his holiness the patriarch. For this, I secretly took hair from his head, beard, bed, shoe insoles, and foot steps, and the soap with which his holiness lathered himself and from this I created a concoction. My accomplice did not know anything and simply helped me."[113]

Hearing this from his chancellery courtier (*prikaznyi dvorianin*), and reading the handwritten confession of the deacon, his holiness the patriarch was amazed at the strength of the Almighty God who protected him from the deadly poison and praised Christ for saving him from the treachery of these malefactors. His holiness the patriarch recalled how he poured out the cloudy drink from the crystal tankard given to him by the deacon.

His holiness at once ordered the handwritten confession and the records of the interrogation to be sent to the pious *tsar* in Moscow together with the shackled deacon and his accomplice. When the pious *tsar* read Feodosii's confession, he ordered his highest *boyars,* prince Aleksei Trubetskoi and others, to interrogate Feodosii again in order to learn the truth. At the interrogation [September 5, 1660], Feodosii recanted, saying that he knew no such thing and that he never even thought about it. When the *tsar* was informed, he ordered the deacon to stand a regular trial and to be interrogated under torture like other common criminals.

Then Feodosii repeated his previous confession recorded at the Cross Monastery, [explaining] that he was concocting poisons to kill his holiness the patriarch.[114]

Having spent some time at the Cross Monastery, where he attended to all necessary needs, his holiness the patriarch returned to the Resurrection Monastery.[115]

When the pious *tsar* learned that his holiness Nikon returned from the White Sea to the Resurrection Monastery, he sent his privy *boyar*, Irodion Matveevich

Streshnev, with the news about deacon Feodosii who was sent from the Cross Monastery to Moscow. Feodosii finally told the truth, admitted to everything, and asked for the great sovereign's forgiveness. Everything that his holiness the patriarch wrote to the great sovereign from the Cross Monastery was confirmed. "Now," [ordered the *tsar,*] "let your holiness decide the deacon's fate. You can either condemn him to death as a lesson to others or, if you want, exile him, or free him."

His holiness patriarch Nikon, hearing the words of the pious *tsar* from the messenger, humbly thanked the merciful sovereign who carefully investigated the charges and was able to get to the truth. The patriarch said: "Let the great sovereign decide this issue. I am free of the evil treachery of this deacon who wanted to poison me at the instigation of wicked people. Since the Almighty's arm saved me from their evil, I will not testify against this deacon. Besides, he revealed to the great sovereign the intrigues against me perpetrated by the metropolitan of Krutitsa and Pavel, archimandrite of the Monastery of the Miracles, as well as their minions. So let the great sovereign express his will about the deacon." And he released the messenger to go to Moscow.

ଔ

Once, acting on the devil's envy, the *tsar's* table attendant (*stol'nik*) Roman Bobarykin falsely accused his holiness the patriarch in the presence of the great sovereign, saying that [on July 15, 1663] his holiness the patriarch put a curse on the great sovereign during the prayer service (*moleben*) when he read the psalm (*psalom*) "Lord! Do not be silent at my praise" containing the line "let his court be empty, his wife be a widow, and his children be orphans" mixed with other psalms fit for the occasion.[116]

The great sovereign was wroth; [on July 15–16, 1663] he assembled all the Muscovite hierarchs and his officials and tearfully told the hierarchs how his holiness the patriarch cursed him.[117]

The Russian and Palestinian hierarchs and the *tsar's* Council advised the great sovereign to capture his holiness the patriarch and to send him to a remote and severe exile. One or two hierarchs told the pious *tsar* to first interrogate his holiness the patriarch himself. In the case that he was to deny the charges, the *tsar* should interrogate his servants and serfs and only then dispense punishment.[118]

The great sovereign decided to do just that and [on July 17, 1663] sent Paisius, metropolitan of Gaza, Iosif, archbishop of Astrakhan', archimandrites and abbots, representing the clergy and the *boyars,* prince Nikita Ivanovich Odoevskii, the lord-in-waiting (*okol'nichii*) Irodion Matveevich Streshnev, the secretary of the Council Almaz Ivanov, colonel Vasilii Filosofov, together with fifty *stel'tsy,* numerous service nobles and junior *boyars* (*boyarskie deti*) representing the court to the Resurrection Monastery.[119]

[On July 18, 1663], upon arriving at the Resurrection Monastery and entering the patriarch's cells, the delegation started to ask Nikon how he conducted the prayer service, how he cursed [the *tsar*], and what psalms he read.[120] He responded: "I solemnly declare, I did read the prayer service and the psalms, but they were not against the great sovereign. The prayer which I uttered and the psalms which I read I can repeat now in your presence. Those psalms I read while praying to God were against my enemy, Roman Bobarykin," for at that time, based on Roman's petition, his holiness the patriarch lost lands which were added to the village of Bobyrevo.[121] Later, [in 1681] the pious sovereign Fedor Alekseevich, *tsar* and grand prince of Great, Little, and White Russias, deigned to append the entire village to the Resurrection Monastery.[122]

The messengers responded: "We will not listen to your prayer service without the *tsar's* edict; we do however have an order to interrogate the archimandrite, the brethren, the junior *boyars*, and the servants that were present at the prayer service." His holiness the patriarch replied: "Do as you please." And the *tsar's* messengers interrogated everyone, bringing in one person after another, and asking how the prayer service was conducted and what was read. The iterrogated responded that during the litany of supplication, which was part of the prayer service, his holiness the patriarch prayed to God for the great sovereign, but did not mention who he meant during the reading of the psalms. And so, after the interrogations, the archimandrite and brethren were released, but forbidden to leave the monastery until the *tsar's* majesty decreed otherwise. All the laymen were detained by the Moscow *strel'tsy* after being interrogated.

The next day [on July 21, 1663], his holiness the patriarch was told that the bricks in one of the furnaces were ready and should be removed. As was customary, he ordered to ring the bell to summon everyone to work.[123]

Having learned from those living in the monastery that his holiness the patriarch intended to work with the brethren and take the bricks out of the furnace, the *tsar's* delegation ordered his holiness the patriarch not to leave the monastery until the great sovereign decreed otherwise. They put the Moscow *strel'tsy* around the monastery so that no one from the outside could enter, and the brethren and the patriarch could not leave. The Resurrection Monastery was under guard for more than a month.[124]

The hierarchs and *boyars* soon left for Moscow leaving only the colonel and *strel'tsy* at the monastery.[125]

At this time, his holiness patriarch Nikon increased his prayers to the Lord. After leaving Moscow and settling in the Resurrection Monastery, he established the following rule. Everyday after the liturgy, he prayed to the holiest Mother of God, reading and chanting in Greek. Being imprisoned in his monastery, his holiness the patriarch added to the prayers a Russian hymn (*stikhira*) "Blessed, you intercede for every one," which he sang as a Kievan chant; and his prayers were always filled with tears. And so, after a month, there came an order from the great sovereign for colonel Vasilii Filosofov to return to Moscow, free the monastery, and release the detained. So, by the grace of God, the enmity ended.

His holiness the patriarch devoted many efforts to the building of God's church. By the order of the great sovereign, his holiness the patriarch was protected by a captain and twenty *strel'tsy* from the St. Savva Monastery in Zvenigorod.

After the enmity ended, the great sovereign heard many other falsehoods and slanders about his holiness the patriarch. At this time, the Resurrection Monastery was frequented by foreigners, Greeks, Poles, Ukrainians, Byelorussians, newly converted Germans and Jews, and both black and white clergy, who came from different countries to see his holiness the patriarch and the construction of the great church. The patriarch happily received everyone.[126]

It was reported to the great sovereign that the patriarch told the foreigners inappropriate things about the great sovereign, complaining that the great sovereign ruled not only over the tsardom, but also over the church hierarchy.[127] Another delegation from the great sovereign came to reprimand the patriarch; other discords and enmities were also frequent.

The pious *tsar* was still quite magnanimous towards the patriarch even though [the sovereign] had heard many false accusations about him. When a son or daughter was born to the pious *tsar*, [the sovereign] always sent his holiness Nikon donations as well as vegetables, expensive confectionaries, and precious fabrics. His holiness the patriarch shared everything with the brethren. And so it was. When the *tsar's* family celebrated patron saint days, the pious *tsar* sent commemorative breads which his holiness the patriarch also shared with the brethren.[128]

ରଞ୍

Soon thereafter [in 1664], his holiness the patriarch and the great sovereign had another dispute. It happed like this. Nikita Andreevich Ziuzin, a *boyar* of the *tsar's* Council, and a pious and God-fearing man, saw the unrelenting hostility and enmity between the great sovereign and his holiness the patriarch, and recalling their previous great love, wanted to restore it, but could not because God did not will so. So desiring, the *boyar* wrote to his holiness the patriarch as if the pious *tsar* sent him, Nikita, his privy *boyars*, Artamon Matveev and Afanasii Nashchokin,[129] who ordered Nikita to write a letter to his holiness the patriarch on [the *tsar's*] behalf, asking his holiness to come to the ruling city of Moscow to attend the morning prayer on a particular Sunday and to introduce himself as the archimandrite of the St. Savva Monastery to the guard at the gate. Then, he was to go to the cathedral, stand at the patriarchal stall, and take his hierarchal staff which he left when he departed Moscow [in July 1658]. Then the pious *tsar* would send the *boyars*, first with accusations; then he would send the *boyars* and high functionaries again, and at this point his holiness the patriarch was to ask for the keys to his cells. During the third visit, "I would send him the keys," wrote Ni-kita as if in the *tsar's* words, so "let him go to his cells. Some time later, I myself will come to him and we will talk about everything. I have no one, but you, Nikita, to write to him because his holiness the patriarch does not like the *boyars* but he respects you."[130]

Nikita supposedly heard all this, wrote a letter and sent it with the Novgorodian priest Sysoi Andreev to his holiness the patriarch.

His holiness the patriarch, having received this letter, ordered it to be copied, and returned Nikita's original with the same priest because Nikita asked that his handwritten originals be returned to him.

His holiness the patriarch also sent a reply in which he wrote that it was impossible for him to come to Moscow in such a way.

In a week [on December 14, 1664], the same *boyar* summoned the patriarch's sub-deacon (*ipod'iakon*) Nikita Nikitin and told him: "The great sovereign ordered you to go to his holiness patriarch Nikon knowing his love for you and your love for him." The *boyar's* spiritual father monastic priest Aleksandr, formerly archpriest Andrian, was also present and the *boyar* listed him as a witnesses. The *boyar* sent a second letter of the same content with the sub-deacon, but in the second letter he added: "The great sovereign again sent the same privy *boyars* to me with the *tsar's* handwritten letter. The privy *boyars* were to repeat what the sovereign has already said and written. And so I am to believe their words and that you, your holiness, should also believe them and come."

His holiness the patriarch, having received this letter, again ordered his trusted servants to copy it and sent the sub-deacon back saying that this was impossible. [The patriarch] gave the sub-deacon the letter because the *boyar* asked for his letters to be returned.

Three days later, the same *boyar* sent the sub-deacon again with a letter similar to the first two in which he added: "The great sovereign said that if you, your holiness, do not return this time, do not heal God's church, and do not reconcile with him, God's church would be forever in discord. But if you return this time, everything will be according to your will, as you and God wish."

After receiving the third letter through the sub-deacon, his holiness the patriarch told him: "I do not want my throne, but I want peace and the *tsar's* favor for God's church. This is why I put this in God's hands and obey the *tsar's* order. I am concerned about one thing, whether or not this is a ploy." The sub-deacon replied that Nikita Ziuzin sent him in the presence of his spiritual father, giving him the *tsar's* orders.

His holiness the patriarch did not return the third letter, saying: "Tell the *boyar* that I will come and bring the letter myself," and started to prepare for the journey. He left for Moscow a week before Christmas, on Saturday night [December 18, 1664] after the evening prayer. Upon arriving in the ruling city of Moscow, he introduced himself to the guards at the Gates of Smolensk as the archimandrite of the St. Savva Monastery and the guards opened the gates and allowed him and all his companions into the city. They went to the Kremlin and entered the great cathedral of the holiest Mother of God during the morning service when the verses of the first proper psalm were being read. As was customary during the entrance of an arch-hierarch, his holiness ordered those accompanying him to sing the prayer "Meet, it is in truth to glorify Thee" ["*Dostoino Yest*"], bowed, and kissed the holy icons.[131]

After the prayer and the litany of supplication, the service continued with the psalms during which his holiness the patriarch ascended to his patriarchal stall and took the staff of miracle-worker Piotr which he left when he departed Moscow. His eminence Iona, metropolitan of Rostov and Yaroslavl', who at the time oversaw the holiest patriarchal throne,[i] the archpriest of the cathedral, priests, and others present at the cathedral came to ask for [the patriarch's] blessing.

---

[i] In other words, metropolitan Iona was patriarchal locum tenens, an overseer of the patriarchal throne when the patriarch was away or incapacitated.

After that, his holiness the patriarch summoned the metropolitan of Rostov and the archimandrite of the Resurrection Monastery and sent them to the *tsar's* court to announce that he brought peace and blessing to the great sovereign, the entire *tsar's* household, and the ruling city. Obeying him, they went and announced to the pious *tsar* as they were ordered.[132]

The pious *tsar* hurriedly sent for his dignitaries and the prominent *boyars* who happened to be nearby and sought their advice on the arrival of his holiness the patriarch; they decided to ask his holiness the patriarch why and on what account did he come.[133]

Then the pious *tsar* sent his *boyar,* prince Nikita Odoevskii, and others to question his holiness patriarch Nikon. After coming to the church, they asked him, and in response, his holiness the patriarch said that he brought peace and blessing to the great sovereign, the *tsar's* family, and the entire flock. Having heard that, the messengers returned to the great sovereign.[134]

The pious *tsar*, after learning about these words, again asked the hierarchs and his privy *boyars* about how to respond to his holiness the patriarch. The hierarchs and the *tsar's* Council advised sending his holiness the patriarch away to the Resurrection Monastery without seeing the *tsar*.

Then the pious *tsar* decided to act on their advice. The hierarchs and the *boyars* returned to his holiness the patriarch with the order from the *tsar* to return to the Resurrection Monastery. Patriarch Nikon responded: "I wish to see the *tsar* and to bless his home," but the messengers reproached him for the improper manner in which he came at night, saying that he could not see the *tsar* at night and that the great sovereign already ordered to send letters to their holinesses the ecumenical patriarchs inviting them to come to Moscow. Until their arrival, which should not be long, [the patriarch] cannot see the *tsar*.

Then his holiness the patriarch told them: "Tell the great sovereign that I have to see him on very a important matter," but they refused, referring him to the ecumenical patriarchs. This entire conversation took place during the morning prayer at the end of which the messengers went to the great sovereign for the third time to give him the words of his holiness the patriarch. The great sovereign again ordered [him] to go to the Resurrection Monastery. This happened after the morning prayer in the same cathedral.[135]

His holiness patriarch Nikon, having heard this order, went to kiss the holy icons, left the cathedral, taking the staff of metropolitan Piotr with him, and got in a sleigh. The great sovereign sent his *boyar,* prince Dimitrii Dolgorukii, together with a colonel and *strel'tsy*, after him.

When sitting down in the sleigh, Nikon shook the dust off his feet and quoted the Lord: "'If any place will not receive you or hear you, shake its dust from your feet in testimony against them as you leave.'[i] And so, I shake the dust from my feet." The colonel who was present there said: "We are going to sweep away that dust." Then his holiness the patriarch uttered: "But you yourselves will be swept away by the broom which now appears in the sky." At that point of time, a comet in the shape of a broom appeared in the sky.[136]

---

[i] See Mk. 6:11 and Lk. 9:5

Then, shortly before the sunrise, his holiness, together with his companions, went to the Kamennyi Bridge, then to Nikitskii Gate; they were accompanied by the aforesaid colonel and a *boyar*. When they exited the gates of Zemlianoi town,[i] the *boyar* ordered them to stop in the name of the great sovereign. Having stopped, his holiness the patriarch waited for the *boyar* to speak. The *boyar* announced the *tsar's* title and said: "The pious *tsar* ordered to ask you, your holiness the patriarch, for a blessing and forgiveness."

His holiness the patriarch replied: "God will forgive him, if he is not behind this discord." The *boyar* asked him: "What discord do you mean?" His holiness meant his visit, and replied: "If the great sovereign is not behind my visit and it all happened without him knowing, God will forgive him. Tell this to the great sovereign." The *boyar* returned to the city and his holiness continued his travel until his village of Chernevo. The *boyar* returned to the great sovereign and told him about this and about Nikon's taking the staff of metropolitan Piotr. When his holiness the patriarch was still inside the cathedral, the key keepers of the cathedral asked him to give back the staff, but he refused, saying: "I left it and I will now take it. What business is it of yours?"

The great sovereign again sought the advice of the hierarchs and the Council on how to retrieve the staff. They decided to send people after his holiness and, should the staff be carried by the sub-deacon, to take it by force, but should the staff be in the sleigh or in the hands of his holiness, to ask for it in a proper manner. They also decided to ask his holiness about his words to *boyar* Dolgorukii at the border of Zemlianoi town when he granted forgiveness to the great sovereign. What trouble did he have in mind? [They decided] not to leave him until he explained himself and returned the staff.[137]

Pavel, metropolitan of Sar and Don,[138] Ioakim, archimandrite of the Monastery of the Miracles, lord-in-waiting Irodion Streshnev, the secretary of the Council Almaz Ivanov, together with a colonel and *strel'tsy* were sent to carry out the *tsar's* order.[139]

Having caught up with his holiness the patriarch in the village of Chernevo, the messengers told him the *tsar's* order. He was to explain his words about trouble to the great sovereign and return the staff of metropolitan Piotr. Patriarch Nikon did not give up the staff and did not explain his words about the discord. The messengers stayed in the village relentlessly pursuing his holiness for two days; his house was surrounded and guarded by the colonel with numerous *strel'tsy*.[140]

His holiness patriarch Nikon, having had enough of these oppressions, sent the staff and the letters of *boyar* Nikita Ziuzin with Gerasim, archimandrite of the Resurrection Monastery.[141] Then the church hierarchs, the *tsar's* Council, and the colonel with *strel'tsy* left and his holiness the patriarch went to the Resurrection Monastery. Upon return to Moscow, the *tsar's* messengers told the great sovereign about the arrival of the archimandrite of the Resurrection Monastery who came with the staff and the letters because his holiness the patriarch

---

[i] In the seventeenth century, Moscow's perimeter was demarcated by earthen ramparts, hence the name, *Zemlianoi* or Earthen, town; it roughly corresponds to the present day Garden Ring [*Sadovoe Kol'tso*].

ordered the archimandrite to deliver the staff and the letters into the hands of the great sovereign himself.

The pious *tsar* himself took the staff and letters from the archimandrite; he sent the staff back to the cathedral's patriarchal stall with Pavel, metropolitan of Sar and Don, and he himself read the letters; two of them were copied, the third was Nikita Ziuzin's original which was barely legible because Nikita could hardly write. After reading that Artemon and Afanasii Nashchokin were mentionned in the letters as witnesses, the pious *tsar* interrogated them. They said that they knew nothing. Then the *tsar* sent for Nikita Ziuzin, sub-deacon Nikita, and priest Sysoi. Having heard that Nikita Ziuzin was taken to be interrogated under torture, his wife Mariia, screamed, sighed, and expired instantly. After the interrogation, the sub-deacon and priest Sysoi were imprisoned. They said that they only carried the letters and did not know what was written in them. The sub-deacon testified that the *boyar* sent him to carry out the *tsar's* order in the presence of his spiritual father.

When Nikita Ziuzin was interrogated under torture about this, he said: "I did all this on my own will, for I wanted God's church to live in peace and for the great sovereign and his holiness the patriarch to live in concord. I wrongly accused Afanasii and Artemon, only to make his holiness the patriarch believe me."

Seeing that the *boyar* told the truth, the pious *tsar* ordered to end the torture and imprison him in the house of one of his privy *boyars*. The aforesaid sub-deacon Nikita, after spending days under guard, commended his soul to God. The *tsar's* Council advised the *tsar* to execute Nikita Ziuzin, but the pious *tsar* saved him from death and exiled him to the town of Kazan', decreasing his rank to the service nobility. Priest Sysoi was exiled to the Solovetskii Monastery. Sub-deacon Nikita, according to his will, was brought to his holiness's Resurrection Monastery for a burial.[142]

His holiness the patriarch met him as a martyr outside the monastery and carried him to the monastery with crosses and after the burial service (*otpevanie*), [Nikon] interred Nikita with his own hands under the staircase [of the Church] of Holy Golgotha.[i] Such was the end of this discord.

૯૩

When living in the Resurrection Monastery, his holiness the patriarch continued to build the great holy church.[143] He was accustomed to conducting the divine liturgy during the great holy days of our Lord; he himself also found archimandrites for his Iverskii, Cross, and Resurrection Monasteries and the priests, deacons, sub-deacons, readers (*chtets*), and choir members (*pevchii*) for the monastery villages.

By that time, the ruling city of Moscow did not have a patriarch for eight years and five months. Based on the *tsar's* order, the patriarchate was overseen

---

[i] The tombstone with an inscription remains to this day indicating the site of his burial.

by Russian metropolitans, particularly by the preeminent metropolitan, Pitirim of Sar and Don,[144] who was once subject to his holiness the patriarch's curse.[145]

Another custom existed during his holiness patriarch Nikon's stay at the Resurrection Monastery. He ordered that all visitors to his monastery, and their horses and cattle, be given food and drink to their content; they were also allowed to stay for up to three days. [The patriarch] ordered to accept those who expressed a desire to take monastic vows at his monasteries and to give them monastic clothes without recording their donations. If someone wanted to make a donation to pray for the souls of their relatives and to remember them during the liturgy, or for the construction of God's church, his holiness the patriarch ordered to accept the donations without keeping record.[i] [In return,] during the litany of supplication and the office of preparation (*proskomidiia*), [the monastery inhabitants] were to pray that God grants health to the living and peace to the deceased, and were to write the names in the church books of the deceased and sick (*Sinodik*) to be mentioned in every service.

His holiness the patriarch had another custom. He always ate together with the brethren in the refectory during the holy days commemorating Lord, the Mother of God, and the great saints; on Saturdays and Sundays, and on the days commemorating the parton saints of the *tsar's* family, whatever was cooked for him was offered to the other monks; wanderers visiting the monastery ate at the same place. After dinner, [his holiness the patriarch] washed the feet of all the wanderers regardless of how many of them were there. At that time, wars with different lands were common, and the soldiers stopped to rest at his holiness the patriarch's monastery. He received, fed, and washed the feet of every visitor, no matter how many of them would come; sometimes there were one hundred, sometimes two hundred and sometimes even three hundred visitors a day.

His daily diet consisted of boiled cabbage with bread crumbs, cucumbers from the vegetable garden, and a fish soup which he ate only during the allowed days; on Wednesdays, Fridays, and Mondays he never ate fish, except on holy days commemorating the Lord and the Mother of God.

His dress consisted of sheepskin and a frock (*riasa*) made out of sheep's wool of ashen color. His mantle (*mantiia*), which he wore in church, was made of black cloth and adorned only with sources (*istochniki*);[ii] during construction and other work, he did not wear the mantle, but only a black monastic headdress (*kamilavka*), a black monastic hood, and a wide leather sash (*poias*)[146] the width of which exceeded a quarter of *arshin*.[iii]

During holy days commemorating the Lord and liturgies on other holy days, his holiness the patriarch put on soft clothes and took the hierarchical staff, but during the work days he walked with a stick made of simple wood. He fished

---

[i] In other words, Nikon forbade accepting monastic novices for a donation, a practice which was accompanied by issuing "donation receipts." These receipts described the conditions of acceptance which frequently caused discontent and conflicts.

[ii] *Istochniki* or sources are narrow ribbons of different colors, usually red or white, sewn onto the mantle of a hierarch; *istochniki* symbolize sources of grace, wisdom, and teaching emanating from a hierarch during his pastoral duties. See *Glossary*.

[iii] About eighteen centimeters.

frequently during both day and night, feeding the catch to the brethren. During all fasts, his holiness the patriarch retired to a secluded hermitage and lived a very austere life; he increased the number of prayers and bows, kept the strictest of fasts, and deprived himself of sleep; he only slept three hours a day.[i]

At that time, the number of schismatics who followed the heretical monk Kapiton increased.[147] They criticized his holiness Nikon for correcting the Divine Scripture, called him the Antichrist and other insulting names which cannot even be copied on paper.

The pious *tsar*, caring about the holy church, ordered to look for the schismatic Kapitonites everywhere, to destroy their secret asylums, and to execute or to imprison them for not submitting to God's holy church.[148]

Some time later [on November 2, 1666], at the great sovereign's request, the ecumenical patriarchs Paisius, patriarch of Alexandria, and Macarius, patriarch of Antioch, came to the ruling city of Moscow.[149] At that time, his holiness the patriarch had in his service two newly converted Jews, formerly of Judaic faith. One of them frequently went to Moscow to another recently converted Jew, named Daniil, a physician in the *tsar's* apothecary. One pious man told his holiness the patriarch that, when in Moscow, his servant engaged in Judaic rituals with Daniil, conducting ceremonies in Daniil's house, and that many other recent converts from all Muscovy convened there to observe Judaic rituals. Besides, the servant of his holiness the patriarch had been lying about his holiness and telling Daniil many falsehoods about his holiness which Daniil, in turn, told the great sovereign.

Having learned about this, his holiness the patriarch ordered to interrogate his servant and to subject him to torture, but he rejected all [the patriarch's] charges, did not confess, and for that he was jailed. His fellow servant, also a recently converted Jew, on the advice of the arrested, secretly fled to Moscow, went to the *tsar's* court and loudly yelled: "I came on the business of the sovereign!"[150] He was at once brought to the great sovereign where the new convert declared that his holiness the patriarch imprisoned a man in the Resurrection Monastery. "[The prisoner] asked me to tell you, oh great sovereign, so that you would order to release him from prison and bring him before you. Then the prisoner would tell you about the life and habits of his holiness the patriarch in great detail.

The great sovereign at once sent Ioakim, archimandrite of the Monastery of the Miracles, together with a colonel and *strel'tsy*, to the Resurrection Monastery to get the other convert out of prison. Upon his arrival at the Resurrection Monastery, archimandrite Ioakim ordered to surround the prison, and he himself went to the cell of his holiness the patriarch to give him the edict of the great sovereign which instructed the archimandrite to take the imprisoned away. His holiness the patriarch ordered to [obey the edict] and give the prisoner up.

---

[i] The printed Iverskii version includes an additional comment inserted here. "Here he created two churches one dedicated to the Epiphany (*Bogoiavlenie*), another to commemorate apostles Peter and Paul. The hermitage also contained sufficient cells; however the staircase to the upper cell was very narrow. It was there, in the small upper cell, that he usually stayed."

Having taken the convert, archimandrite Ioakim brought him to the great sovereign and the servant told many lies about his holiness, accusing the patriarch of taking their wives for fornication and beating them to death, and spreading other ridiculous lies.

To that, the great sovereign responded: "Do not tell anyone about this and do not discuss your master with anyone. If I hear from someone that you are talking, I will order to cut your tongue out." Then the pious *tsar* ordered to keep them under guard in the stables of the Monastery of the Miracles and brought their wives and children from the Resurrection Monastery so that they would live together.

Shortly thereafter, these vicious converts disappeared with their wives and children without a trace.[151]

ଓଃ

Around the same time, Arsenii, archbishop of Pskov, the archimandrite of Epiphany [*Bogoiavlenskii*] Monastery in Moscow, Sergii, archimandrite of the Savior [*Spasskii*] Monastery in Iaroslavl', and other abbots as well as a colonel of the *strel'tsy* were sent to his holiness patriarch Nikon.

Having come to his holiness the patriarch [on November 29, 1666], the messengers announced the sovereign's title, then the titles of their holinesses the ecumenical patriarchs and the resolution of the entire holy synod according to which his holiness the patriarch was to immediately go to Moscow to the council of the synod and explain to their holinesses the ecumenical patriarchs and the entire holy synod why he left his throne and settled in the Resurrection Monastery.[152]

His holiness patriarch Nikon responded: "From where did their holinesses the ecumenical patriarchs and the holy synod learn such abuse? They did not send for me according to the rules of the holy apostles and holy fathers. They sent archimandrites and abbots for me, your highest hierarch. The rules of the holy apostles and holy fathers say that if an archbishop or bishop, after leaving his seat, moves to another diocese, then after waiting for him for a long time, one needs to send two or three hierarchs for him and summon him to the council of the holy synod two or three times, and if he refuses and does not come, to judge him in his absense. And you, archimandrites and abbots, according to which rules did you now come?" Archimandrite Sergii of Yaroslavl', the most impertinent among them, stepped forward and said as if [being prompted] by a script: "Tell us, will you come or not? We are asking you not according to the rules, but on the sovereign's edict."

His holiness the patriarch replied: "I do not refuse to go, but I do not wish to listen to your words." Archimandrite Sergii said: "You are dishonoring us by this." Patriarch Nikon [replied]: "Is there a bishop among you? I will talk to him. I do not wish to talk to you monks because you came to me inappropriately." Then the archbishop said: "Explain what we should tell the great sovereign, will you be at the council of the holy synod or not?" His holiness patriarch Nikon [said] in response: "I will be at the council. But I will be a little late because I have to attend to my affairs." Upon their return to the travel lodge, the delegation at once sent a messenger to Moscow with a letter in which they wrote that his holiness the patriarch dishonored them and that, although considering going to Moscow, he still did not leave.[153]

At that time, his holiness the patriarch, having taken part in the evening prayers, ordered the archimandrite and the entire clergy to be ready to assist him in the liturgy. Having returned to his cell, he read his personal prayers and the prayers in preparation for the liturgy, as was his custom. Every evening he listened to the evening prayers and three canons in his cell; one to Jesus, one to the Mother of God and one to his patron saint.

After the prayers, his holiness ordered to collect and send to Moscow the rules of the holy apostles and holy fathers, the unabridged Book of Psalms, and the book of his replies, written in response to the thirty questions of *boyar* Simeon Luk'ianovich Streshnev answered by Paisius, metropolitan of Gaza.[154] [The patriarch] said not to take anything else, but the cross to be carried in front of him.

Some time later [on November 30, 1666], his holiness the patriarch ordered to ring the bell for the morning service, after which he summoned his spiritual father and confessed with sincere repentance. Then he and the entire monastery clergy (*pricht*) blessed the holy oil with which he anointed himself and the entire clergy and the brethren. He then returned to his cell where he read the Book of Hours (*chasy* or *chasoslov*) and prayers in preparation for holy communion.[155]

The archbishop and archimandrites sent word to his holiness the patriarch that they have to see him on the *tsar's* business. But he did not allow them to come, saying: "I am getting ready to go to the heavenly *Tsar*."

Soon his holiness Nikon ordered to ring the bells for the liturgy. When he entered the church, singing prayers together with candle bearers (*sveshchenosets*), he donned the hierarchical vestments and started the liturgy. At the same time, the archbishop with his companions also came to the Church of Holy Golgotha.

His holiness the patriarch called the sub-deacon, monk German, who subsequently became archimandrite of the Resurrection Monastery, and ordered [German] to tell Sergii, archimandrite of the Monastery of the Savior, to leave the church, for Sergii argued with many people about the recently corrected books and Greek chants. The sub-deacon relayed the patriarch's words, and the *tsar's* messengers, after talking to each other, all left the church and stood on the front porch of the Church of Holy Golgotha.

His holiness the patriarch ordered the choir to sing the liturgy in Greek with Kievan chants.[156] He himself partook of the sacrament of holy communion. After the liturgy, he delivered a lengthy homily from the Divine Scripture about patience and the joyful endurance of all calamities and woes for Christ's sake. He read from the apostle's epistles, and when the liturgy ended, his holiness the patriarch, granting peace and blessings, went to his cells again.

The *tsar's* messengers, who still stood on the porch, yelled disgracefully at him: "Why are you keeping us? You neither refuse nor agree." Archimandrite Sergii was especially rude to his holiness Nikon. His holiness the patriarch told him: "I do not listen to your words and do not hear them." After that, everyone entered the cell of his holiness. There his holiness the patriarch asked the archbishop: "Why did you send for me this morning? And what edict of the sovereign did you want to announce?" [The archbishop] replied: "[I meant] that edict of the *tsar*, which kindy asked you to come to the council of the holy synod in Moscow and answer why you left your throne. If you do not come, we will leave and tell the great sovereign."

His holiness patriarch Nikon uttered: "Glory be to God for everything. I am ready and am coming at once." He ordered to prepare his sleigh and promptly left the cell. The conversation occurred in the evening during the Christmas fast on the eve of the first of December. The entire brethren tearfully saw his holiness Nikon off as far as the cross on the hill called Mount of Olives, located across from the monastery. At the cross, his holiness the patriarch prayed, then ordered a deacon to read the litany of supplication and, after praying for the pious *tsar*, the entire brethren, and all Christians, offered peace, blessing, and forgiveness to the brethren and set out on his journey [around one o'clock in the afternoon on November 30, 1666].[157]

The brethren and all the other Orthodox inhabitants and workers of the monastery, after receiving the blessing and forgiveness, cried inconsolably, believing that they would never see their father again.

During the journey, the *strel'tsy* and a colonel named Ostaf'ev rode in front of his holiness the patriarch; the archbishop with the [*tsar's*] dignitaries traveled behind the patriarch. And so they reached the vicinity of the village of Chernevo, stopping one or two *poprishches* before it.[i]

There they were met by Filaret, archimandrite of the Nativity [*Rozhdestvenskii*] Monastery in Vladimir who ordered them to stop, and so they did. The archimandrite first announced the titles of the great sovereigns, their holinesses the ecumenical patriarchs, and the entire holy synod, and then said: "[The *tsar*] sent hierarchs, archimandrites, and abbots to you, but you dishonored them and refused to come to Moscow." [The patriarch] responded: "You are lying that I dishonored them and that I am not coming to Moscow. It is not me who dishonored [you], but you, who dishonored me by sending archimandrites to the highest hierarch."[158] Archimandrite Filaret told him: "We are under the orders of the *tsar*, their holinesses the ecumenical patriarchs, and the entire holy synod. Why do you refuse [to go]?"

His holiness the patriarch said: "I cannot complain about you to anyone but God and have heaven and earth as my witnesses." He added: "Heaven and earth, hear me!," and continued his journey. Soon they reached the village of Chernevo which his holiness the patriarch previously renamed "Nazareth."[159]

A short time later, Iosif, archimandrite of the New Savior Monastery, came to this village and gave the order to stop, which was followed. He asked for a light because, not remembering by heart the titles of their holinesses the ecumenical patriarchs, he had to read them from a handwritten paper. When given a light, he read from the paper the same words which the archimandrite of Vladimir said before and added: "After the first messengers were sent, Filaret, archimandrite of the Nativity Monastery in Vladimir, came to you, but you disgraced him and did not come to Moscow. You must come to Moscow on the third of December with a small number of people, three or four hours before sunrise or between three and four at night."[160]

---

[i] About three kilometers.

In response, his holiness the patriarch said: "Oh people full of lies and false-hoods! Was it long ago that the archimandrite of Vladimir left us? Perhaps he is still here? How was he disgraced? And who said that I am not coming [to Moscow]? Woe to your lies and falsehoods! Why do you order me to come at night with a small number of people? Do you want to strangle me like metropolitan Filipp whom they strangled when he was by himself?" [161]The archimandrite said: "I am but the [*tsar's*] dependent. I read whatever was written and given to me." Then they reached the village of Tushino where the colonel stopped and said: "We cannot go any further because the great sovereign ordered us to come on the third of December." Let us send a messenger to Moscow and give ourselves and our horses a rest."

His holiness the patriarch replied: "Do as you please," and ordered to prepare a house in which he could be alone. When the house was ready, he sang the evening prayers, read his prayers, and fell asleep for a short time.

Another edict of the great sovereign arrived; they were to come to Moscow without delay and be there three or four hours before sunrise. The company set off and arrived in Moscow at Vagan'kovo [on December 1] four hours before sunrise, passing the Gates of Smolensk and reaching the Kamennyi Bridge. At the gates of the Kamennyi Bridge many lights were lit to see who and how many people came with them.[162]

We then went to the lodge of the Archangel Michael [*Archangelskii*] Monastery located in the Kremlin near the St. Nicholas Gates. But suddenly, the gates were closed in front of us. I said: "I am a sub-deacon and the cross-bearer. Why did you close the gates?" The colonel told me: "A matter of state of importance." And two *strel'tsy* ran to the colonel and told him: "It is him." The colonel ordered me: "Dismount the horse and give me the cross, then go through, you are wanted on the business of the sovereign."

Even when we were still traveling, his holiness the patriarch already told me: "If someone captures you and starts to pressure you, give the cross to me." I dismounted the horse and gave the cross to his holiness the patriarch himself. The *strel'tsy* grabbed me by the armpits and carried me through the air, so that I barely touched the ground, and soon brought me to the sentinel post located at the Kamennyi Bridge and from there to the great sovereign himself. Then the great sovereign, who was alone, started to ask me about affairs which were unfamiliar to me, but I refused [to answer] and said that I knew nothing. The great sovereign ordered: "Tell me everything now, and if you do not reveal it to me, but to someone else, you will be imprisoned until God wills otherwise. But if you do tell me, you will be free at once." Without hesitation, strengthened by Holy God who gave me courage, I said that I knew nothing. I was immediately taken to the chancery of secret affairs (*prikaz tainykh del*)[i] where I spent eleven days. In the end, the colonel placed me under strict guard and I spent three years in prison and then was exiled to Novgorod the Great where I stayed for ten years.[163]

His holiness the patriarch, quartered in the lodge of the Archangel Michael Monastery, was very saddened as the last of his companions were kept sepa-

---

[i] Here the author means a torture chamber.

rately, under guard, and no one was allowed to visit them or talk to them. Even before the sub-deacon and cross-bearer was arrested, many among his holiness the patriarch's people were taken from the Resurrection Monastery and imprisoned. When, the same night, shortly before sunrise, his holiness the patriarch and his [small] entourage went to the house prepared for them (now this house is inside the Kremlin, on the corner near the St. Nicholas Gates and is called Lykov Court), the rooms were lit by many candles. After all his holiness the patriarch's companions assembled in the house, armed guards were placed at the doors and around the house so that no one could enter, exit, or even pass by.[164]

His holiness the patriarch, together with his companions, sang the morning prayers. When the day began, the St. Nicholas Gates were shut so that no one could pass the house where his holiness the patriarch was stationed, and even the big bridge near the gates was dismantled.

Having read from the Book of Hours and having sang his personal prayers, his holiness the patriarch ordered his housekeeper Feodosii to prepare food for him and his companions, but the housekeeper replied that all the food which was brought with them from the Resurrection Monastery was taken to the monastery lodge since the *tsar* ordered that no food was allowed here, neither at night, nor now [in the daytime], and on that account no one was allowed near the house. And the housekeeper showed the single loaf of bread which was left in his sleigh.

His holiness the patriarch ordered to break the bread for himself and others and said: "Let us not follow Judaic ritual and fast on Saturday which is against the canon." Together with the blessed patriarch Nikon there were more than thirty monks and laymen. And so they spent that day.

℀

On Sunday morning, December 2 [actually, on December 1], at the first hour of daylight,[i] Arsenii, archbishop of Pskov, Aleksandr, bishop of Viatka and Suzdal',[165] Pavel, archimandrite of Yaroslavl', archimandrite Sergii, and many other clergy came on behalf of the *tsar's* majesty, the ecumenical patriarchs, and the entire holy synod.[166] They entered, prayed, as was customary, sat down, and talked for a short time; then they stood up and told his holiness the patriarch that the *tsar's* majesty and their holinesses the ecumenical patriarchs were summoning him to the council of the holy synod.

His holiness patriarch Nikon, having heard that, said: "I am ready," stood up and, wishing to exit, ordered Mark, the lector [from his monastery], to carry the cross in front of him. Seeing that his holiness intended to go to the council with the cross, the messengers tried to stop him, saying that it was inappropriate to carry a cross to the council since it was Orthodox, not a non-Orthodox assembly.

His holiness Nikon quoted profusely from the Divine Scripture praising the holy and life-giving cross, its strength and victory over enemies, but they did not concede at all and tried to convince him to go without the cross.

---

[i] In other words, around seven o'clock in the morning.

His holiness the patriarch was likewise insistent and did not consent to go without the holy cross. The messengers sent a herald to the council, to the pious *tsar* and others, with the announcement that patriarch Nikon was coming to the council with the cross and that he would not concede to come without it. From there other messengers were sent again with the order to continue persuading him to come without the cross. And so arguing in this way, they slowly exited the inner cell into the front hall, where the messengers continued to pester the patriarch to leave the cross and go without it. The same continued at the door, then on the upper porch. On the lower porch, they stopped his holiness the patriarch for the last time and were especially insistent on his leaving the cross. But his holiness the patriarch did not budge and responded to everything with the words from the Holy Scripture as the Holy Spirit commanded him.

At that time, messengers carrying news about the developments were constantly running back and forth between the house where his holiness Nikon lived and the council. After a delay, seeing that the *tsar's* delegation will not persuade his holiness the patriarch, the council sent messengers with permission for patriarch Nikon to come with the cross.[167]

His holiness Nikon took the sleigh in which he came from his monastery and went to the council preceded by the cross.[168] A great number of people assembled between the house where his holiness Nikon lived and the Annunciation Church located at the *tsar's* court, as well as in the entire Kremlin, so that only his holiness the patriarch could pass, and even he with great difficulty.

When his holiness the patriarch approached the cathedral, in which at that time the holy liturgy was being conducted, he saw that the southern door was opened and wanted to enter, but the doors were closed in front of him. Seeing this, he bowed to the holy church, sat down in his sleigh and went to the Annunciation Church. Next to it stood the sleighs of the ecumenical patriarchs, excessively adorned and decorated with sable furs; a couple of the best horses was harnessed to each of their sleighs. And the sleigh of his holiness, which was the poorest and had the worst looking old mares, was put next to their sleighs and horses.

And so his holiness patriarch Nikon went up the porch of the Annunciation Church where the holy liturgy was being celebrated. When he reached the church door, it too was closed in front of him like the cathedral door before. And so he went upstairs to the refectory where the council of the holy synod took place.

As he was going towards the chamber, its doors were opened, but when he approached them, they too were closed and he stood outside for a short time while [inside] the council made the decision not to stand up, but to remain seated, when he entered the room. When the doors were opened, his holiness the patriarch came in preceded by the cross.

Seeing the cross in front of his holiness, the pious *tsar* and all those present unwittingly stood up. Although the pious *tsar* did rise up, he was still standing on the top step of his elevated throne. Next to him, to the left, were two highly decorated places near which stood the ecumenical patriarchs. In front of them was a table covered by a rug woven from golden thread on which a silver and gilded ark and several books were put.[169]

After entering and approaching the *tsar* and the ecumenical patriarchs, his holiness patriarch Nikon stood near the table in front of them and read the prayer "Lord the All-Merciful" and other prayers fit for the occasion. When finished, he handed his staff to his junior deacon (*prichetnik*), monk Serafim, and coming toward the *tsar's* throne, he bowed three times, as was the custom. But the *tsar*, who stood on top of his high throne, barely nodded. Then his holiness the patriarch bowed to their holinesses the ecumenical patriarchs, as was the custom, and turned to the hierarchs and bowed to them and then bowed to the other side, where the *tsar's* Council and his spiritual father stood.[170]

Having done this, his holiness the patriarch retook his staff and the monk who carried the life-giving cross in front of his holiness Nikon put the cross in the corner to the right of the *tsar's* throne. Then the pious *tsar*, standing on the upper step of his elevated throne, gestured to his right and, barely moving his lips, ordered his holiness the patriarch to sit on a bench. His holiness the patriarch replied: "Where do you order me to sit, oh *tsar*?" The pious *tsar* again pointed to the same place ordering [him] to sit down. The seat, unoccupied and located in the corner, was entirely unsuitable for a hierarch; it had neither a head nor a foot rest.

Seeing it, his holiness patriarch Nikon looked around and loudly told the *tsar*: "Pious *tsar*, I did not know about this your intention, otherwise I would have brought my own chair on which to sit. We already have a seat here, but it is occupied. But tell," added [the patriarch], "why did you summon us to come before the council you assembled here?" Seeing that his holiness the patriarch did not sit down, the monk who carried the holy cross in front of him, took the holy cross from the corner and stood it directly in front of the *tsar's* majesty and the ecumenical patriarchs' table.[171]

Having heard patriarch Nikon's words and seeing that he did not sit down, the *tsar* came down the steps of his throne and standing near the ecumenical patriarchs' table, said the following.

"Your holinesses the ecumenical patriarchs, judge who is right, me or this man who used to be our true shepherd guiding us and God's people to truth as Moses leading the Israelites?" And the pious *tsar* said many other equally praiseworthy words. "I do not know what happened to him after that. Suddenly, he left his flock and this city and went to his Resurrection Monastery where he now stays. Living there, he condemned many of our hierarchs and dignitaries of our Council for no reason. Your holinesses, pass your judgment on all these matters because it is for this occasion that I called upon your justice."[172]

The ecumenical patriarchs asked his holiness patriarch Nikon through their translator, archimandrite Dionysius: "What say you in response to the pious *tsar*?"

Nikon described in detail and with all possible boldness how and why he left the ruling city of Moscow and why he condemned those who were to blame.[173]

The pious *tsar* also said that patriarch Nikon sent a letter to Constantinople to his holiness ecumenical patriarch Dionysius, in which he disgraced and slandered the *tsar* distorting his words and deeds.[174]

His holiness the patriarch replied: "I wrote that because his holiness patriarch Dionysius is my older brother and he is Orthodox. If not from him, then from whom should I seek advice on these matters?"[175] And it was all that the *tsar's* majesty, the ecumenical patriarchs, and his holiness patriarch Nikon said to each other.

Then the sycophants and underlings or, better said, the slanderers of the patriarch, Pavel, metropolitan of Sar and Don, Illarion, metropolitan of Riazan', and Mefodii, bishop of Mstislavl', started impudently to utter libelous words, disgracefully opening their mouths and yelling all at the same time. One was saying one thing, others another, and all yelled different things altogether for it was known that they were told to do that. After the great commotion, the ecumenical patriarchs told his holiness patriarch Nikon to leave and return tomorrow, at which time he was to read his letter to ecumenical patriarch Dionysius in front of everyone.[176]

And so his holiness Nikon returned to the house prepared for him and as usual read from the Book of Hours. All his companions were very hungry as they had been without food for the third day. Seeing this, his holiness the patriarch took pity on them and said: "Let them not die from starvation," and sent one of his men to the captain of the *strel'tsy* (*sotnik*), who was in charge of the guard, requesting him to tell the pious *tsar* that his holiness the patriarch and his companions were dying from starvation and asking the *tsar's* majesty to allow free passage to the house necessary to bring the supplies. Being afraid, the captain did not dare relay the message to the *tsar*.

Seeing this, his holiness the patriarch became greatly upset and saddened, not so much about himself, as about the others; he went up to the top of the house and yelled to all the captains and *strel'tsy* around the court (all together there were more than a thousand guards) to tell the pious *tsar* that patriarch Nikon and his companions are dying from starvation.

One captain heard this and, acting either from pity, or from shame, he went to the *tsar's* court to tell the head guard, the colonel, about his holiness's request. The colonel told the *tsar's* privy *boyars* and so the request reached the pious *tsar* himself. He immediately ordered to take food and drink from his own supplies and load them onto carts.

Two clerks (*pod'iachii*), one from the food chancery and another from the *tsar's* cellars, came to his holiness the patriarch with the food and their arrival was announced to his holiness. He ordered to bring them before him. Upon entering, without saying a word, they bowed and handed his holiness patriarch Nikon two notes, or rather, two inventories, one for food and the other for drinks that were sent with them.

His holiness patriarch Nikon did not take the inventories but asked them: "From where and with what did you come?" They did not respond, but continued to extend the inventories to him, saying that their superiors, the *boyars* in charge of the food chancery and the *tsar's* cellars, sent the papers.

Hearing this, his holiness the patriarch told them: "Go back to your superiors with the food you brought and tell them that Nikon does not need it because it is written that it is better to eat grass with love than the fat calf with enmity. I never did, nor do I now ask the *tsar* for this. I am asking for one thing only, to grant us freedom so that we can enter and exit the house." His holiness Nikon quoted many more passages from the Holy Scripture and sent them away with the food. They returned to their superiors and told them everything. Having heard this, the superiors told the butler of the *tsar's* majesty and he told the pious *tsar* himself.

After hearing about this, the *tsar* was greatly saddened and even more wroth [with the patriarch]. He went to the ecumenical patriarchs at once and told them about what happened, as if complaining.[177] After that, already in the evening, the *tsar* issued a new edict, allowing the patriarch's people to freely enter and exit the house, but prohibiting anyone else to go in. [The detainees] immediately sent to the lodge of the Resurrection Monastery for the requisite food and drink and after the evening prayer thanked God for saving them from starving to death. In due time, they sang the evening and morning prayers, as was the custom.

CR

The next day, Monday, December 3, the same messengers, archbishop Arsenii and others, came again to invite his holiness the patriarch to the council of the holy synod. He went, as always, preceded by the holy cross of the Lord and so he entered the *tsar's* chambers. As last time, upon entering, he prayed and bowed.[178]

After a brief introduction, the council members started to read the letter that his holiness Nikon wrote to ecumenical patriarch Dionysius. Reading the letter not as it was written, but quoting only those passages that suited them and which they already underlined, they reached the passage where the letter said that the pious *tsar* exiled many because of patriarch Nikon, sending one whither, another hither, and that among them was Athanasius, metropolitan of Iconium and Cappadocia[i] sent by the ecumenical patriarch of Constantinople to the *tsar* in the ruling city of Moscow with a letter defending his holiness patriarch Nikon. For that Athanasius was imprisoned in the St. Simon [*Simonov*] Monastery.[179]

When the *tsar* heard that, he grabbed the letter and asked his holiness patriarch Nikon: "Do you yourself know this Athanasius?" His holiness the patriarch responded that he did not know him. Then the *tsar* called upon Athanasius, who stood among the hierarchs, and he approached the *tsar*. The *tsar*, pointing at Athanasius, told his holiness patriarch Nikon: "This is Athanasius himself."

Seeing him, his holiness uttered: "God and I bless this man." And Athanasius left and returned to his place. The reading of the letter resumed. During the reading [of the letter] the slanderers Pavel, Illarion, and Mefodii surrounded blessed Nikon and, like wild beasts, yelled at and insulted him by growling and screaming outrageously. The other hierarchs and clergy stood silently at their places according to their rank; the *boyars* and all the dignitaries of the *tsar's* Council stood on the other side also according to rank and were likewise silent.

Seeing that no one but these three men was willing to help him, the *tsar* yelled loudly, infuriated: "*Boyars, boyars,* why are you silent, why do you betray me, do you not need me?"

---

[i] Territories in Asia Minor. Historically, Iconium was a capital of Lycaonia, a territory incorporated into the Roman province of Galatia (cf. The Epistle of Paul the Apostle to the Galatians).

Hearing that, all of them were overcome with great fear and moved slightly forward from the places at which they stood as if preparing for battle or war. It appeared that they wanted to speak; yet not a word was uttered. Only one of the *boyars,* prince Yurii Dolgorukii, trying to oblige the *tsar,* briefly spoke in support of the *tsar,* humiliating his holiness patriarch Nikon in every possible way.

Seeing that he will not find any support, the *tsar* became greatly saddened. His holiness patriarch Nikon told him: "Oh *tsar*! For nine years you were making all these people now standing before you at this assembly to testify against us, preparing for this day. But what is happening? Not only do they say nothing, they cannot even open their mouths. Did not you teach them in vain? Oh *tsar,* I will give you advice: If you order them to stone us, they will do it at once, but even if you teach them for nine more years, they will hardly find the grounds to falsely accuse us."

Having heard that, the *tsar* became greatly wroth [with the patriarch] and buried his face in his throne, infuriated; and after a long time he rose up. One honorable man, Lazar' Baranovich, bishop of Chernigov, a kind and meek man skilled in philosophy, was present at the council. He stood in the place accorded by his rank, together with the other hierarchs. The *tsar* called upon him and said: "Oh Lazar', why are you silent and why do you not say anything? Why are you betraying me in this matter even though I held such high hopes for you?"

Bishop Lazar' stepped slightly forward from the other hierarchs. Piously holding his arms to his chest and obediently bowing his head, he replied: "Pious *tsar,* why would I ask for trouble? Why would I falsify and reject the truth?" Having said this, he returned to his place.

The *tsar,* not finding any support for himself, was utterly infuriated; the *tsar* had personally invited bishop Lazar' to the council before the arrival of his holiness the patriarch and told [Lazar']: "Oh bishop, although you have never seen or known patriarch Nikon, you probably heard that he is an intolerable man with a short temper. I beg you to help us in every way when he will be summoned to the council." Lazar' replied: "Oh *tsar,* if they find any falsehood in the words or deeds of patriarch Nikon, then I will not be silent." This is why the *tsar* called upon him at the council with the aforesaid words, but did not receive any help from him.

Some time later, the *tsar* came to his senses, and, standing near his throne, put his hands over his lips and was silent for a long time. Then he came very close to his holiness patriarch Nikon and, counting the prayer beads (*chiotki-lestvitsa*) in the patriarch's hand, said very quietly so that only the monks standing nearby heard it: "Oh your holiness the patriarch, how could you do such a thing that disgraces and dishonors me?" "What [have I done]?" asked Nikon. The *tsar* said: "When you left your monastery to come here, you first fasted, then confessed, then received extreme unction, and then conducted the holy liturgy, as if you were preparing to die. This is how you disgraced me."[180]

His holiness the patriarch replied: "It is all true, oh *tsar,* I did all that expecting not only suffering and torment from you, but death itself."

But the *tsar* swore: "Oh your holiness, not only did I not wish to do what you are talking about, but I did not even think about it, given the countless favors you showed my family and my children during the deadly plague.[i] When I fought at Smolensk and other enemy cities, you labored tirelessly, and like a hen with her chicks, you moved from city to city with them seeking air free of the deadly disease. For your prayers and labors all-merciful God protected my entire house as the apple of His eye. How can I repay you with viciousness for all your previous favors? No, I cannot even think about it." And the *tsar* swore by many other solemn oaths.

His holiness the patriarch, holding him by his hand, said quietly: "Oh pious *tsar*, do not swear such oaths. Trust me, you will bring me much evil and many calamities. Sorrows are being prepared on your behalf. He added many other quotes from the Holy Scripture, and after that, he told how the archimandrites inappropriately sent by the *tsar* falsely accused him at the monastery and during the trip to Moscow and how he exposed their lies. The *tsar* noted to the patriarch: "But you, too, disgraced me by writing to ecumenical patriarch Dionysius all the possible complaints against us."

His holiness patriarch Nikon said: "It was not me, oh *tsar*, who disgraced you, but you yourself. I wrote to my spiritual brother Dionysius in confidence, while you revealed your affairs not only to the subjects of your own tsardom, but to the people from all the corners of the world whom you assembled here. This is how you disgraced yourself more than I did. I discussed your affairs with one person who should know about them, while you revealed them to many."

Then the *tsar* talked to his holiness the patriarch about a peace and how to end the enmity between them. To that, his holiness the patriarch replied: "You have good and righteous intentions, oh *tsar*, but will you see them through? Be aware that it will not be up to you, because the fury of the wroth that you feel against us needs an appropriate conclusion." Having said this to each other, the pious *tsar* and his holiness the patriarch went to different corners.

Their conversation took place during the reading of Nikon's letter. During that conversation, his holiness the patriarch asked the pious *tsar*: "Where is your truth, oh *tsar*? When I traveled to the ruling city of Moscow, upon my orders, sub-deacon Ioann, called Shusherin, carried a holy and life-giving cross in front of me. I raised and brought up this Ioann. When we arrived at the house that you prepared for us, the soldiers, acting on your orders, unmercifully captured this Ioann, so that we could hardly protect the holy cross from the *strel'tsy*. We do not know whether this Ioann is alive or tortured to death upon your order."

The *tsar* said only that he did not know and added that the young man with the cross traveled not in the front, but in the back of the procession, but the *tsar* did not mention any other crime. Having heard the *tsar's* words, monk Mark who stood with the cross said under his breath: "You, oh pious *tsar,* were deceived in this matter."

Having heard these words, the *tsar* looked at the monk and exclaimed in fury: "Who asked you, monk? And who ordered you to speak?" The monk was greatly frightened by the *tsar's* dreadful exclamation because he was young and thought that he would be led away from the council. Afterwards, this monk

---

[i] The printed Iverskii version gives particular dates here. In particular, it mentions 7162 (1654) and 7163 (1655).

stood with the holy cross looking down both because he was afraid of the *tsar* and because he was thinking about what he had seen at the council.

Soon Anastasius, archdeacon (*arkhid'iakon*) of the ecumenical patriarchs, who stood by their chairs, came and stopped across from the *tsar* and the ecumenical patriarchs; he bowed to the holy icons three times, then bowed to the *tsar* and ecumenical patriarchs, and came to monk Mark who was holding the holy cross. [Mark] raised up his head and, seeing that the archdeacon was taking the holy cross away, yelled at his holiness the patriarch who, at that time was looking at and speaking to the *tsar's* Council: "Your holiness the patriarch! They are taking away our protection!" [The patriarch] turned his head and, seeing that they were taking the holy cross away, said: "God's will be in everything they do. If they decide to take away our last vestment and do something worse, we will not blame them, but will happily endure in the name of the Lord." And blessed Nikon added many more quotes from the Holy Scripture appropriate for this occasion and then ordered to hand over the cross.[181]

The archdeacon, having taken the cross, put it between the ecumenical patriarchs' staffs which stood to the left of their chairs. When the council finished reading his holiness patriarch Nikon's letter to ecumenical patriarch Dionysius, blessed Nikon was ordered to return to the house prepared for him. And so his holiness Nikon exited the chamber where the council took place and, on the order of the *tsar's* majesty, was accompanied to the house with candles because it was already the third hour of night.[i]

At the house he told his companions: "My children, did you hear the words of the *tsar* at today's council of the holy synod, when he swore that he would not hurt us in any way? Soon you will see what they are going to do to us. They have prepared for us great sorrows and intolerable torments!" His holiness patriarch Nikon lived in that house from that day until the twelfth of December.

His holiness Nikon's letter to ecumenical patriarch Dionysius, which was read at the council, was written in Greek by a Greek named Demetrius who lived in the Resurrection Monastery. [Demetrius] came together with blessed Nikon from the Resurrection Monastery to the ruling city of Moscow and lived together with his holiness the patriarch. Staying at the house, he walked around town whenever he wanted, without any fear.

Once, when he was absent, the pious *tsar* sent a chancellery secretary to his holiness the patriarch with an order to hand over Demetrius the Greek.

His holiness the patriarch replied that this man came with him from the monastery, but that he was not in the house. The messengers said: "On the order of the *tsar's* majesty, we will capture him wherever we find him." To this the patriarch responded: "If you were in our service, you would do what I told you, now do as you wish." They left. At this time, Demetrius the Greek, not suspecting a thing, was in the Kremlin where the soldiers soon found and captured him; he was taken to the chambers near the *tsar's* home, called the Embankment chambers [*Naberezhnye palaty*]. There, being greatly fearful of the *tsar*, he took a knife, stabbed himself, and so his spirit departed.[182]

---

[i] About nine o'clock at night.

CR

These very days the *tsar's* majesty, the ecumenical patriarchs, and all the hierarchs discussed the arrangements for the deposition and exile of his holiness patriarch Nikon.[183]

On the twelfth of December, early in the morning, the same messengers came to his holiness the patriarch to summon him once again to the council. This time the council of the holy synod was to take place not in the *tsar's* chambers, but in the monastery of St. Aleksei, metropolitan of Moscow, also called the Monastery of the Miracles, in the gateway Annunciation Church. The ecumenical patriarchs also resided at the entrance part of this church and so the council assembled in this church.

The ecumenical patriarchs, hierarchs, archimandrites, abbots and other clergy wore their liturgical vestments; the hierarchs wore bishop's scarves (*omofors*), all others were dressed according to their rank. The aforesaid Athanasius, metropolitan of Iconium, did not wear a bishop's scarf and simply stood watching the events.

Among the Russian hierarchs was one, Simon, archbishop of Vologda, who felt a strong love for blessed Nikon; he did not wish to go to the last meeting of the council and so he did not go. When summoned to come to the council as the others had done, he pretended to be ill and lay in bed so as not to be an accomplice in the unrighteous exile of blessed Nikon. Messengers came and told the council that Simon was ill and lay in bed, but the council declared: "Even though he cannot come on his own, he will be carried." At once, a delegation went to fetch him and brought him to the aforesaid church in a sleigh, carrying him on a rug, and put him in a corner of the church. Laying there, Simon watched the proceedings in great sorrow, drenched in tears, saddened by the loss of such a shepherd.

When the *tsar*, the ecumenical patriarchs, hierarchs, and all present at the council were setting their hands unto the scroll [confirming] the deposition and exile of blessed Nikon, Simon, knowing the innocence of his holiness patriarch Nikon, did not wish to do so. But he was forced to do so and, unable to refuse, he did the following. He took the scroll already signed by many hierarchs and wrote the following: "If this is true, let it be so and if this is not true, I do not confirm," and he put a four-ended cross in the middle of his statement. Seeing this, the heads of the assembly and all others became wroth with him, who did not want to act as they wished. And even though they did not hurt him there and then, [archbishop Simon] would be greatly harmed in the future.

Being summoned, as I already wrote, to the council and entering the church, his holiness patriarch Nikon bowed, as was the custom, to the holy icons and all present and then stood in the middle of the church. At that time, there also stood the *boyars* of the *tsar's* Council, prince Nikita Odoevskii, prince Grigorii Cherkasskii, prince Yurii Dolgorukii and many other functionaries. Then the resolution written in Greek [confirming] the deposition of blessed Nikon was read; as soon as the resolution in Greek was read, Illarion, archbishop of Riazan', started to read it in Slavonic. Hearing their unrighteous deposition verdict, which contained false and libelous accusations, his holiness the patriarch protested at one of the accusations, saying that it was not true. The said Illarion heard it and started to swear at his holiness the patriarch by indecently scolding him and calling him murderer, fornicator, predator, and other dishonorable words. Hearing the insults and reproaches from Illarion, his holiness Nikon uttered these words: "Child, blessed be your mouth," and many other quotes from the Holy Scripture, for Illarion had been ordained by his holiness the patriarch.

When the resolution about the [patriarch's] deposition was read, the ecumenical patriarchs, who wore bishop's scarves, moved from their places and stood in front of the royal doors (*tsarskie vrata*)[i] where they read several short prayers. Then, turning, they went to his holiness Nikon, gesturing and telling him through a translator to take off his monastic hood. His holiness patriarch Nikon wore a black monastic hood on which the venerable life-giving cross was depicted in precious pearls.

His holiness the patriarch asked why he was ordered to take off the monastic hood, to which the ecumenical patriarchs said: "Because the current council condemned you and your own deeds revealed [your essence], and so you are not to be called patriarch because, acting out of pride, you left your flock without permission and put a curse on them. To this Nikon said: "Even though this council unjustly condemned us and our actions, which never even transpired, and accused us of leaving the flock,[ii] I will not myself remove the monastic hood; when I took my oath accepting the monastic vows, I promised to keep it until my soul departs [my body]. And you, you do as you please. I know you, travelers from far away countries, from the ends of the earth; you came not to do good, not to make peace, but being enslaved by the Turks, you wander across the earth like beggars, not only to procure the things necessary for yourselves, but to pay a tribute to your masters." And his holiness patriarch Nikon added: "Let me ask you, where did you get these laws and canons according to which you now act so impudently? If I am guilty and deserve punishment, why do you act secretly like thieves? You brought me to this small monastery church; there are neither the *tsar's* majesty, nor his Council, nor the people of the Russian land. Was it in this small church that by the grace of the Holy Spirit I accepted my flock or my shepherd's staff? Trust me, this small church was built afterwards, by the labors of our humbleness.

We accepted the patriarchate in the holy cathedral in front of a magnitude of people, not because of our own wish or desire to receive a title, but [because] we were selected by the Holy Spirit and by the wishes, diligence, and constant tearful prayers of the most pious sovereign Aleksei Mikhailovich, *tsar* and grand prince of all Great, Little, and White Russias, for the sake of his great solemn oaths made before God Himself. If now you have the desire to unjustly condemn and depose us, let us go to God's holy church where we accepted the shepherd's staff. If it so happens that I deserve that which you desire, then do as you please in that church."

---

[i] In the Eastern Christian Church, a central entrance to the altar, part of iconostasis; the shutters flanking the royal doors usually depict four Evangelists and the Annunciation.

[ii] In the printed Iverskii version, a passage "I will not do this" follows after this phrase.

Having heard this, the ecumenical patriarchs said: "Here or there, it is all the same. This matter is being conducted according to the wishes of the pious *tsar* and all the hierarchs assembled here and that his majesty is absent now, it is his will."

The ecumenical patriarchs immediately removed the aforesaid monastic hood with the pearl cross and silver and gilded medallion (*panagiia*) with precious stones that blessed Nikon wore. Then blessed Nikon uttered: "You, travelers and slaves, divide all this amongst yourselves and receive, at least for some time, a consolation for your sorrows."

Hearing this, they took the monastic hood and medallion and handed them to monk Mark who stood near his holiness patriarch Nikon; blessed Nikon received another, simple monastic hood which was taken from a Greek monk standing nearby. At that time, they did not take the hierarchal mantle and staff from blessed Nikon fearing the people.

After that, they loudly announced to blessed Nikon that he could no longer be called patriarch and that he was not to live in the Resurrection Monastery that he built, but that he must go repent at a specific monastery, the Ferapontov[i] Monastery on the White Lake,[184] designated for this purpose. With that, he was released and left the church.[185]

When he was sitting down in his sleigh, he sighed and told himself: "Oh Nikon, all this happened to you as they say: 'Do not tell the truth and you will not loose the friendship.' Should you have prepared feasts and dined together with them, this would not have happened to you." Then he sat down in the sleigh and went straight home. The aforesaid archimandrites Pavel and Sergii were sent by the council to accompany him to the house and to stay there guarding him. Pavel was a humble and meek man, but Sergii was as proud and garrulous as an ancient Pharisee.[ii]

When blessed Nikon, talking to his men, rode back from the council, Pavel and Sergii followed behind them.

Barely did the patriarch say something when Sergii would yell from behind: "Quiet, Nikon, quiet!" He said that, swearing at the blessed not once, not twice, but many times, and at one point, his holiness said something to his companions, and Sergii, mocking him, yelled: "Quiet, Nikon!" Hearing this, blessed Nikon ordered his housekeeper, who traveled behind, to tell [Sergii]: "If you have the power, then come and close my mouth so that I would not talk." And so speaking to Sergii, the housekeeper Feodosii said: "His holiness the patriarch ordered to tell you that if you have the power, then come and close his mouth so that he would not talk." Having heard those words, Sergii yelled wildly at the housekeeper: "Why do you, monk, call another monk a patriarch? He is no patriarch, but one of the simple monks."

---

[i] For a number of monasteries, including Solovetskii, Ferapontov, and Kirillov, we use Russian names, which is the accepted practice. The names of all other monasteries are translated into English. See, for instance, our references to the Trinity and St. Sergius or the New Savior Monasteries.

[ii] In the printed Iverskii version, this phrase reads "as ancient Pharaoh."

When Sergii belched out these words, a man from the crowd, traveling behind the sleighs, yelled loudly: "How dare you scream unscrupulously? The name of patriarch was given to him from above, not by you, you arrogant man."

Hearing this, Sergii ordered the *strel'tsy* behind him to capture the man who said these words, but they replied that he was already captured and taken away. Blessed Nikon was followed by numerous guards for the fear that people may revolt. Seeing this, his housekeeper Feodosii said that everything happened as blessed Nikon prophesized.

His holiness the patriarch replied: "Blest are those persecuted for holiness' sake; the reign of God is theirs,"[i] and having arrived at the house, blessed Nikon sat down to read holy books to console himself after all that had happened, for he loved St. John Chrysostom's exposition of the Epistles of Paul the Apostle which he read most often.[186]

Sergii impertinently intruded into his holiness's inner cells and impudently sat across from his holiness the patriarch, taking off his monastic headdress and showing his shamelessness; he started to talk as if consoling blessed Nikon, all the while mocking and insulting him.

His holiness the patriarch said to him: "Oh Sergii, who ordered you to come here shamelessly and aggravate us?" and he replied: "The *tsar's* majesty and their holinesses the ecumenical patriarchs, and the entire holy synod." And [the patriarch] said: "Even though that might be true, all the same, stop insulting us like a hunting dog set out on our trail." Arrogantly, he continued to aggrieve the blessed with his cruel words.

Blessed patriarch Nikon became quiet, but first foretold prophetically: "Oh Sergii, Sergii, I see that you are pleasing the *tsar* and others, wishing and asking for my throne. Truth be told, soon you will be stripped of everything you now have and it will bring you shame." This, indeed, soon happened, as blessed Nikon prophesized. Soon archimandrite Sergii was deposed in disgrace and lived as a simple monk at the Tolga Monastery in the town of Yaroslavl'.

When the time came to conduct the evening prayers, they read all the prayers as they usually did in the monastery; during the litany of supplication they mentioned his holiness patriarch Nikon, as was the custom. Hearing that, an arrogant Sergii yelled again, forbidding them to do so: "What are you doing? You call a simple monk patriarch!" The priest and others paid no attention to his proscribing.

When night came, Sergii took burning candles and went to the inner cells where his holiness the patriarch was, then to the hall and the porch, and inspected everything, saying: "Lest Nikon escapes." At night, in Kitai-gorod, outside the Kremlin, at the town hall, separated from the house where his holiness the patriarch stayed by only a wall, on the order of the *tsar*, criminals were interrogated under harsh torture (this happened almost every night) as if to threaten his holiness the patriarch.

During these days and nights some [detainees] were subjected to unbearable tortures; the word came that Ioann Shusherin was also tortured, but it was not so. After this Ioann was captured and taken to the *tsar*, he was imprisoned.

---

[i] See Mt. 5:10.

Metropolitan Athanasius was later exiled to the monastery of the reverend Makarii on the Volga where his life ended.[187] Not only these people, but many others, who felt pity for blessed Nikon, suffered by being tortured, shackled, and imprisoned; but let us stop here, since they are too many to name.

After the morning prayer [on December 13, 1666], very early in the morning, the lord-in-waiting Irodion Streshnev came from the *tsar* and brought silver coins and many sable and fox furs, and said: "The *tsar's* majesty ordered to give these to you because you are embarking on a long journey." Hearing this and seeing the deliveries [the patriarch] said: "Return all this to him, who sent you. Nikon does not need anything." And he added many more appropriate quotes from the Holy Scripture. Irodion ardently pleaded with the patriarch to take the clothes, saying that the *tsar's* majesty would be wroth otherwise, for this Irodion Streshnev was an upright man skillful in conversation, but blessed Nikon did not listen to his words and did not accept the donation.

Then Irodion quietly and piously approached blessed Nikon and said: "The pious *tsar* Aleksei Mikhailovich, grand prince of all Great, and Little, and White Russias, ordered me to ask you to bless him, the *tsarina,* and his entire family." Hearing this, blessed Nikon said: "If the pious *tsar* wished to receive a blessing from us, he would not show us such disfavor; it could only mean that he did not want our blessing which will soon become more distant." And he added many more appropriate quotes from the Holy Scripture. Even though Irodion prayed and begged for his holiness Nikon's blessing for a long time, he did not succeed. Having bowed down, the *boyar* left, returned to the *tsar's* majesty, and told him what transpired, that blessed Nikon did not accept any donations and did not give his blessing. The *tsar* was greatly saddened by the discord and the absence of the blessing, but ordered to proceed with his intentions without delay.

Immediately after Irodion's departure, Aggei Shepelev, the commander of soldiers' regiments, came from the *tsar* to tell blessed Nikon that the *tsar's* majesty ordered him to set out to the designated place, that is, to the Ferapontov Monastery, without delay: "We, on his majesty's edict, are to accompany and protect you until you reach your destination." [The patriarch] responded: "I am ready; act on your orders and do as you please." Aggei then asked him whether he had horses for the trip. His holiness Nikon responded that he did not and so Aggei left.

Next, the messengers from the ecumenical patriarchs and the entire council of the synod came to blessed Nikon and said: "We are sent to you by their holinesses the ecumenical patriarchs and the entire holy synod to take your monastic hood and medallion, which were taken from you and given to the monk standing next to you, and to bring them to the ecumenical patriarchs." His holiness the patriarch ordered to return both without delay and said: "Lord's will be done," and so the messengers left.[188]

A short time later, the aforesaid colonel Aggei returned with the horses. He quickly bridled them and put blessed Nikon in the sleigh in which the patriarch came from the Resurrection Monastery. A great many people of Muscovy heard this and started to gather inside the Kremlin wishing to see the unjust banishment of the shepherd from the flock of his sheep.

The news about the crowd inside the Kremlin reached the *tsar's* ears and he decided to do the following. The soldiers were not to push or disperse the crowd with force, but to quietly say that patriarch Nikon will exit through the Gates of the Savior leading to Sretenka Street. And the people, hearing this, moved from the Kremlin to Kitai-gorod waiting for his holiness the patriarch there.

When the soldiers saw that the people left the Kremlin, they swiftly took blessed Nikon away from the Kremlin to the Kamennyi Bridge, then to the Arbat Gates, also called the Gates of Smolensk, leaving Zemlianoi town behind. On the order of the *tsar*, on his way out of the city, he was accompanied by four colonels with two hundred *strel'tsy*. Together with blessed Nikon were monastic priests and monks who decided to go in exile with him and many laymen who bade him farewell on his way out of town with tears and loud screams. All of them were surrounded by the soldiers who did not allow anyone inside [the original party]. And so the colonels and the *strel'tsy*, having accompanied his holiness the patriarch beyond Zemlianoi town in this way, bowed to him and returned to the city. The aforesaid warden (*pristav*) Aggei Shepelev and the fifty soldiers entrusted to him remained with blessed Nikon.

During his holiness the patriarch's journey along the wall of Zemlianoi town, to the Gates of Dmitrov and to the settlement called Sushchevo, up to a thousand *strel'tsy* with drawn weapons and lit torches stood inside the wall of Zemlianoi town. And when his holiness the patriarch crossed the border of Zemlianoi town, they marched parallel to his movement, on the inner side of the wall of Zemlianoi town. And when blessed Nikon reached the settlement of Sushchevo and turned away from the city on the Dmitrov Road, the marching *strel'tsy* left. Monks and laymen, screaming and wailing, saw his holiness the patriarch off beyond the settlement of Sushchevo. Consoling them, he quoted the Holy Scripture, blessing them and leaving them to God's mercy.

And so the guards rushed blessed Nikon off. Those who accompanied him [to this point] looked as he moved away with great sadness, feeling sorrow that they were loosing such a shepherd. Then, wailing loudly, they returned to the city. When the inhabitants of the city learned that blessed Nikon was already carried away, they became greatly saddened about their father and shepherd.

As blessed Nikon was traveling on the Dmitrov Road to his place of exile, the aforesaid warden Aggei Shepelev with soldiers rode horses in front of him,[189] but the blessed had the company of Iosif, archimandrite of the New Savior Monastery. The company was traveling very fast and under strict guard and the guards did not allow anyone approach or accidentally break the guard or even move towards the convoy.

And so his holiness Nikon traveled with great difficulties and deprivations. The blessed, who could tolerate hunger, found joy in the shortage of food, but he and his companions suffered from the winter cold, not having winter clothes.

Having reached the River Kliaz'ma, twenty-five *poprishches* from Moscow,[i] they stopped there and rested for two days.

Then, on the edict of the *tsar's* majesty, archimandrite Iosif of the New Savior Monastery was replaced by another Iosif, archimandrite of the Pechorskii Mon-

---

[i] About thirty-eight kilometers.

astery in Nizhnii Novgorod.[190] Seeing how long-enduring Nikon suffered from the cold, Iosif, the archimandrite of the New Savior Monastery, took pity on him and gave him his fur coat and a fur hat with earflaps, and plenty of food; and he himself, following the *tsar's* edict, returned to Moscow. I think that it was for this favor to his holiness Nikon that God our Lord repaid him in this world and willed that he become the metropolitan of Riazan' and Murom seven years later; and the same year when his holiness Nikon, his concelebrant, departed, he too went to see God. But enough about that; let us return to blessed Nikon.

Those who were with blessed Nikon suffered very much from the winter wind and cold.

One night, they rode very quickly, because his holiness had horses from the *tsar's* stables; the sleigh, moving at great speed, tossed the blessed against a tree and the head of the blessed got stuck in the tree trunk, so that it was almost severed. And after this blow his holiness the patriarch was ill for a very long time.

When they approached the town of Uglich, his holiness the patriarch, feeling pity for his companions, sent his people to buy warm clothes for them. Having learned about this, warden Aggei strictly forbade it. And when the travelers approached the city, its residents, knowing about the arrival of his holiness Nikon, came to greet him, carrying everything that he needed. Seeing this, warden Aggei ordered to push them away unmercifully and the soldiers beat up many people. The sleigh procession passed the city at great speed and no one was able to approach the travelers. Having gone fifteen *poprishches* from the town,[i] they arrived at a village which had a fair that day. The warden sent the guards ahead and told them to disperse the traders unmercifully. And so they reached Mologa and in all the villages where they stopped to spend the night and feed the horses, the warden first sent the guards to clear out the houses in which his holiness the patriarch and his followers were to be stationed, throwing the dwellers out.

In one of the villages where the travelers happened to spend the night, an old woman, the mistress of one of the houses that were cleared out, hid in a secret place, that is, in the cellar. When the *strel'tsy* left the house and blessed Nikon entered it, the woman was hiding in the secret place. When Nikon and several of his closest followers were there alone, and the widow recognized that the *strel'tsy* had gone, she came out of the hiding place at once and asked those in the house, who among them was blessed Nikon. They showed him to her and she fell to the feet of the blessed and sorrowfully, with tears and moaning, said: "Where are you going, shepherd of the sheep? Why are you leaving your sheep to be stolen?" She had many other sorrowful words. She also said that the day before when she was at home, she saw a handsome man in a dream; he said: "Woman, here is my servant Nikon who is exiled and is traveling to his imprisonment in great deprivation and poverty. Help him as much as you can." The woman said this, swearing an oath that this was the truth. She gave his holiness Nikon twenty silver rubles and warm clothes. When, early in the morning, the procession set out to travel, the woman cried bitterly and again disappeared into

---

[i] About twenty-three kilometers.

her hiding place, waiting until everyone left. And so they reached the settlement called Mologa where they spent the night.

Next to the settlement of Mologa stood the St. Athanasius [*Afanas'evskii*] Monastery, [which was previously] assigned to his holiness patriarch Nikon. The warden in his cruelty and ferocity did not allow his holiness to stay in his monastery.

In the morning, as they set out on their journey again, the procession passed by the holy gates of the monastery. Sergii Prokopiev, a steward (*stroitel'*) of the monastery and a follower of blessed Nikon, went to greet his holiness together with all the residents of the monastery. The unmerciful warden threatened and pushed them away and the sleigh procession quickly passed the monastery. When the travelers reached the area of the River Sheksna at night, the guards were pushing the horses to run quicker, and by intent or accident, God only knows, they ran over a very sharp log protruding from the road, and the sleighs, moving so quickly, ran over the log, puncturing the sleigh in which his holiness patriarch Nikon rode, tearing up the thick felt on the bottom, and hitting blessed Nikon so strongly that he barely survived. The log, which broke when the sleigh ran over it, injured the blessed very badly. When they stood next to the pothole, the guard, showing mercy to blessed Nikon, took a fragment of the log when no one was looking and hid it in the sleigh. And so they traveled to the designated place, which was the Ferapontov Monastery.

Before reaching it, the warden sent a messenger to Afanasii, abbot of the monastery with news that, by the edict of his majesty, they were bringing monk Nikon, for whom he, Afanasii, was to prepare the cells. Hearing this and seeing messengers with weapons in their hands abruptly entering the monastery, the abbot and the brethren were overcome with fear.

Shortly before blessed Nikon's arrival in this monastery, there was a fire and the entire monastery, except two hospital cells, was burned. When [on December 21, 1666] before sunrise blessed Nikon was brought into the monastery, following the order of the warden, he was greeted only by the abbot, and not the brethren. And so the blessed entered the hospital cells, blackened by smoke and stinking beyond description, designated for him.

In all these deprivations, his holiness Nikon thanked God for everything, consoling himself with the Holy Scripture. He suffered greatly from the wound inflicted during the trip.

In the morning came the aforesaid warden Aggei, Iosif, archimandrite of the Pecherskii Monastery, the abbot of Ferapontov Monastery, and a cell monk and they ordered to announce their arrival to blessed Nikon. They said that they came on the edict of his majesty to tell him about certain matters.

His holiness Nikon, exhausted with pain, ordered to tell them that they could not see him and wanted to know on what account did they come. They replied that his holiness the patriarch was to go to the church to obey the *tsar's* order. The blessed refused to go because of his illness, and asked for the letter which would explain why and with what order did they come. They said that, by the edict of his majesty and the blessing of their holinesses the ecumenical patriarchs and the entire holy synod, they were to take the hierarchal mantle and staff from monk Nikon.

Hearing this, blessed Nikon was in great doubt, but ordered to surrender all that was requested at once and quoted the Holy Scripture suitable for the occasion. Archimandrite Iosif, who was sent with them, took both, that is, the mantle and the staff, and carried them to Moscow.[191]

At the monastery, blessed Nikon ate the same food as the brethren, even though his warden Aggei was ordered by the *tsar's* majesty to cook for the blessed separately, [using fare] from the *tsar's* supplies. Blessed Nikon never requested this and warden Aggei, greatly saddened, pleaded with him to eat from the *tsar's* majesty generosity. But the blessed refused and said: "Even when I am dying, I will not do this." And so the warden stayed with his holiness for more than a month.[192]

Suffering from harsh imprisonment and deprivations, blessed Nikon sent a short message to Sergii, abbot of the hermitage at the Resurrection Monastery, asking him to beg the most pious *tsar* for permission to bury Nikon's body in his Resurrection Monastery in the Church of John the Baptist under holy Golgotha. This did happen in fifteen years, on his petition, but this will be told later.

Shortly thereafter [on January 19, 1667], by the edict of the *tsar's* majesty, the warden of his holiness the patriarch was replaced by a certain Moscow service noble, Stefan Naumov, son of Lavrentii;[193] Iosif, the former archimandrite of the New Savior Monastery, [was sent to represent] the clergy. Stefan was very cruel and unmerciful towards blessed Nikon; he ordered to put iron bars on the widows of the cells in which blessed Nikon lived and left unlocked only those doors that were heavily guarded. Soldiers vigilantly watched the doors and the cell and did not allow anyone to pass it, or even approach the monastery. A big road ran near the monastery wall and it was rerouted through another place.

Blessed Nikon, living in need and deprivation, collected his own firewood, went to the lake for his water, prepared food for all his companions, and labored incessantly. He never grumbled, but always thanked God for everything, going to the church, called the Gateway Church, in which the priest who came with him from the Resurrection Monastery conducted the services and always remembered his holiness patriarch Nikon in the litany of supplication. When he and his followers wished to go to the church, they had to go under guard. And so he spent his days in suffering, thanking God and praying for those harming him with these words: "God, do not consider this their sin."

Once [on September 7, 1667], warden Stefan came to blessed Nikon and pleaded with him, begging him to grant forgiveness and blessing for the *tsar's* majesty and his entire family.

Hearing this, blessed Nikon said: "You, Stefan, diligently beg us to give a blessing and forgiveness to the *tsar's* majesty and his entire family. But do tell me who taught you this and why are you doing it?" Stefan swore an oath, saying: "I received a letter from Moscow with an order to diligently beg you." And blessed Nikon said: "If this is true and there is no cunning in it, if the pious *tsar* stops being wroth with us and ceases torturing us for without a reason, then I will do what you ask." And his holiness the patriarch wrote a letter to the pious *tsar* which contained the following:

"A missive from his holiness patriarch Nikon to the pious *tsar*:

To the great sovereign Aleksei Mikhailovich, *tsar* and grand prince of all Great, and Little, and White Russias, his pious *tsarina* and grand princess Mariia Il'inichna, and noble children: noble *tsareviches* and grand princes Aleksei Alekseevich, Fedor Alekseevich, Simeon Alekseevich, Ioann Alekseevich, and noble *tsarevnas* and grand princesses Irina Mikhailovna, Anna Mikhailovna, Tatiana Mikhailovna, Evdokiia Alekseevna, Marfa Alekseevna, Sofiia Alekseevna, Ekaterina Alekseevna, Mariia Alekseevna, and Feodosiia Alekseevna, your devout God-entreater, humble Nikon, by the grace of God patriarch, petitions and prays to God.

On the seventh day of September, in the year 7176 from the creation of the world [1667], Stefan Naumov came to me, your devout God-entreater, and gave me your word, oh sovereign, that he was to ask and beg me for reconciliation on the sovereign's edict so that I, your devout God-entreater, would give a blessing and forgiveness to you, the great sovereign, *tsar* and grand prince of all Great, Little, and White Russias, and that you, the great sovereign, would grant me, your God-entreater, a favor as you see fit. And so I, the humble, am blessing and forgiving you, the great sovereign Aleksei Mikhailovich, the *tsar* and great prince, her majesty, the pious *tsarina* and grand princess Mariia Il'inichna, and noble *tsareviches* and *tsarevnas* and when I, your God-entreater, will come before your eye you, I will bless and forgive you with holy prayers as the Gospel and the Acts of the Apostles describe our Lord Jesus Christ doing. They always granted forgiveness and healing by the laying of hands. I, humble Nikon, by the grace of God patriarch, testify for the fear of God that I have written and signed this letter with my own hand. I, Stefan Naumov, on the edict of the great sovereign Aleksei Mikhailovich, the *tsar* and great prince, talked about the mercy of the great sovereign and dutifully begged and asked for reconciliation and blessing and I hereunto set my hand."[194]

Having taken the letter, warden Stefan Naumov promptly sent it to the ruling city; the *tsar* received it[i] and shortly thereafter sent his crown agent (*striapchii*) Ioann Obraztsov, carrying a thousand rubles from the *tsar's* coffers, to blessed Nikon; the *tsar* also ordered to unbar the windows and doors [of patriarch's cell]. The *tsar* appeared to be wroth with the warden, as if the warden did everything on his own volition without the *tsar's* order; the *tsar* also ordered to build new cells for blessed Nikon, easing his imprisonment greatly[ii] and allowing the blessed and his followers to walk freely and to receive visitors with the warden's consent.[195]

And so the blessed continued to live in great deprivation; he refused the food and drink sent for him from Moscow by the orders of the *tsar*,[196] using the fruits of his labor, fishing, and catching enough fish not only for himself, but for the abbot, brethren, and the monastery workers. Every day there was enough fish in the monastery.[197]

---

[i] In the printed Iverskii version another phrase is added here: "and after reading it, the *tsar* was elated."

[ii] In the printed Iverskii version, "a little" is written in place of "greatly."

CR

Some time later, during Shrovetide (*maslenitsa* or *syrnaia nedelia*),[i] [on February 2–8, 1668] the *tsar* sent blessed Nikon a bounty of fresh sturgeons and big barrels of red Rhine, Italian, and communion wine. After announcing this, the warden asked blessed Nikon to accept the *tsar's* delivery, but the blessed refused and only after long and persistent requests and multiple refusals, his holiness accepted the delivery.

On the Sunday before great Lent [February 8, 1668], his holiness the patriarch deigned to dine in the common monastery refectory together with the abbot, the brethren and the monastery workers, ordering to cook all that the *tsar* sent for this dinner, and leaving only a little wine for himself. The blessed himself did not touch the delivered food and drink and he required penance (*epitim'ia*) of those among his monks who unknowingly drank the delivered wine.

One day, during holy Lent, when his holiness the patriarch and his monks sang the morning prayers in his cells, he told his followers about a vision that he had the night before. "I was in a great stone building," said the blessed, "with me was Mikhail, archpriest of the big Moscow cathedral, who appeared to call us to consecrate a church. Together, we went from this chamber to another, then to another and no matter how long we walked, we came into a new chamber which was more beautiful that the last.

When we came into the inner chamber, perhaps the fifth or sixth one, which beauty defied description, we stopped to marvel at its splendor and greatness. Suddenly, a handsome youth appeared and told me: 'Your holiness, why are you amazed at this building?' I replied: 'How can one not wonder at the sight of such greatness and beauty?' He asked me: 'Do you know whose building this is?' I responded: 'No, my lord, I do not.' 'The building which you see is yours; you built it with your patience, but be diligent in completing your life's journey. I will tell you more; today you will eat your own bread.' And the youth became invisible at once and the vision ended." Blessed Nikon told all this to the brethren who were with him and they, having heard about the vision, kept it in their memory.

The same day, during the bell ringing signaling the holy liturgy, the warden, the archimandrite, the abbot and the cellarer of the monastery came to blessed Nikon to accompany his holiness the patriarch to church as was usual. They sat down and the blessed continued his homily about the spiritual good; a messenger came from a hostel to tell that a monastic priest named Misail and other monastery workers came from the New Jerusalem Resurrection Monastery, built by his holiness the patriarch. The blessed ordered them to come in. Upon entering, they bowed on behalf of archimandrite and the entire brethren, and, shedding tears of joy, asked for and received a blessing; they also delivered to the blessed two hundred rubles, ten loaves of bread, baked by the brethren, abundant fish and other supplies.

After joyfully and tearfully accepting the delivery, his holiness Nikon thanked God Almighty who gives food to every creature and said: "Today, the vision

---

[i] The week before great Lent, when the faithful indulge in pancakes and dairy treats.

from last night in which I was told that I would be eating my own bread, came true." Blessed Nikon spent great Lent fasting, praying, working tirelessly, and reading the writings of the saints as he used to do in his hermitage at the Resurrection Monastery.

On holy Easter day [March 22, 1668], after the holy liturgy, his holiness the patriarch deigned for archimandrite Iosif, the warden, the abbot and the cellarer of the monastery to dine in his cells. During the meal, his holiness ordered to bring the *tsar's* wine which was sent to him during Shrovetide. Having taken [the wine] in his hands, he said, so that all could hear: "After the *tsar's* order and to this day, we are imprisoned in this harsh place, and until this day, we not once partook of the food and drink that the pious *tsar* sent on several occasions.

Today, we, following the humility of the highest word, the Word of God, will recall Him who said: 'Love you enemies, pray for your persecutors.'[i]

Although the pious *tsar*, who is angry at us, imprisoned us here, we follow the words of our Savior which He said in his prayer during the Crucifixion: 'Father, forgive them; they do not know what they are doing,'[ii] and on another occasion: 'The sun must not go down on your wrath.'"[iii] He added many other quotations from the Holy Scripture and then, after thanking God, said: "Our conflict with the pious *tsar* must not last forever," and uttered a greeting, as was customary: "Here today, together with everyone, I partake of this wine and drink to the health of the most pious *tsar*. In the future, I will not refuse his deliveries."

Having heard these words, the archimandrite, the warden, and his holiness's followers, who were present, rejoiced, and having risen from their seats, they bowed to him to the ground. The same day a letter was sent to the ruling city to the pious *tsar* announcing what had happened, and from that time forward [the patriarch] accepted all the *tsar's* deliveries.[198]

Some time later, the pious *tsar* sent blessed Nikon a Gospel, silver church vessels, and many other essentials necessary for the church.

His holiness the patriarch selected one church in the monastery, a gateway Church of the Epiphany [*Bogoiavlenskaia*], and it was there that he went to glorify God. During his imprisonment, the monks of the Resurrection Monastery who were ordained and tonsured by his holiness himself conducted the divine liturgy with him. Others came later, on their own will, not the *tsar's* order, to endure together with the blessed. They were monastic priests Pamva, Varlaam (who later became the patriarch's spiritual father), and Palladii, monastic deacons (*ierod'iakon*) Markell and Mardarii, members of the choir, simple monks Vissarion and Flavian, and many other brothers who had to endure persecution and harsh imprisonment in Pomor'ie[iv].[199]

The aforesaid brothers were taken to Moscow and spent many years in prisons there, wearing heavy shackles and tormented by hunger; they were exiled to remote monasteries where they endured severe misery and some even lost their

---

[i] See Mt. 5:44.

[ii] See Lk. 23:34.

[iii] See *The Epistle of Paul the Apostle to the Ephesians*, 4:26.

[iv] Pomor'e, the region in which the Ferapontov Monastery was located, was a remote and inhospitable territory near the shore of the White Sea, a traditional place of exile.

tormented lives. For that reason and fearing such fates, pious people were afraid to come for [the patriarch's] blessing.[200]

ɒβ

His holiness the patriarch was accustomed to incessant work; he cut down trees and cleared land near Ferapontov Lake at the place called Leshchevo. And at this place, he planted a vegetable garden and sowed wheat.[201] Across from this place, in the middle of the lake, he put together stones to make an island; the lake was almost two *sazhens* deep in this place.[i] He and the monks who stayed with him carried the stones themselves, covering a distance of two *poprishches*[ii] on rafts. The island was twelve *sazhens* long and five *sazhens*[iii] wide.[202]

On this island, he erected a holy and life-giving cross of our Lord with the following inscription:

"Nikon, by the grace of God patriarch, erected this cross of the Lord being imprisoned in the Ferapontov Monastery on the White Lake for the word of God and the holy church." In the winter [when the water was frozen], a big road passed across the lake where he erected a cross on the island he put together, and many who passed by read the inscription.

[The patriarch] erected two other crosses with the same inscription on other islands in the lake. And later, during the rule of the pious *tsar* Fedor Alekseevich, by the order of his holiness patriarch Ioakim,[203] all these crosses were taken away and their inscriptions erased.

The same inscriptions were engraved on all the silver, copper, and tin vessels that blessed Nikon had in his cell; these inscriptions were erased and some of the copper and tin vessels were melted down.

The inscriptions on the crosses and vessels were engraved by Iona, a monk from the Resurrection Monastery, who was skilled in silver smithing. This Iona had a strong passion for intemperate drinking; he was quarrelsome and given to unrestrained talking, and he was also a slanderer. Without his holiness's knowledge, he secretly visited the warden to spread lies about the blessed. Once he got drunk at the warden's, as usual, and insulted his holiness the patriarch and the brothers. Some were insulted by his dog-like barking, others he hit impudently with his fists. For that, his holiness wanted to send him to work in the bakery for penance, but he escaped from the monastery, went to the warden and spread a ridiculous lie about his holiness, after which he went to the ruling city. And so on his journey to the ruling city, like a dog, he fiercely spread spiteful rumors about his holiness the patriarch to heads of monasteries[iv] and people of various ranks in different towns. The human mind can hardly imagine the foul language that he uttered, not to mention his assurances that all this indeed actually happened. He also carried with him the inscriptions which he, by his holiness's order, engraved on the crosses and vessels from the patriarch's cells. Iona showed

---

[i] One *sazhen'* equals two meters, so the lake was about four meters deep.
[ii] About three kilometers.
[iii] About twenty-four meters long and ten meters wide.
[iv] In the printed Iverskii version "governors and military commanders (*voevoda*)."

these inscriptions everywhere and disgraced his holiness, saying: "Patriarch Nikon lives in the Ferapontov Monastery and willfully writes these inscriptions on crosses and vessels, concocting stories about his suffering in the prison of Ferapontov Monastery for God's word and for the church." And he spread many other lies in different places. All this spiteful language was described by the warden in a letter to the pious *tsar* and finally reached the ear of his holiness patriarch [Ioakim].[204]

Hearing this, the pious *tsar* paid no attention to it; and the cursed monk Iona did not even reach the ruling city, but having stopped at a brewery in the town of Per'iaslaval', he got drunk and fell into a caldron with boiling water and was boiled alive. And so he died a horrifying death, meeting his end like Judas who betrayed the Lord.

Some time later [on March 3, 1669], the spouse of the pious *tsar*, the pious *tsarina* Mariia Il'inichna left this world for eternal rest. Then the pious *tsar* sent to his holiness the patriarch his privy *boyar*, the lord-in-waiting Irodion Streshnev, with five hundred rubles to remember the soul of the pious *tsarina* Mariia Il'inichna in prayers. The blessed did not accept the money, saying: "I must pray for the soul of the pious *tsarina* Mariia Il'inichna with as much strength as God gives me, without payment." Irodion pleaded with the blessed to take the donation, but did not succeed and so he returned to the ruling city.[205]

After Irodion's departure, his holiness the patriarch ceaselessly prayed for the soul of the pious *tsarina* as the church canon instructed him and as was the custom.

He also remembered the pious *tsarevich* Aleksei Alekseevich in his prayers.

Some time later [on January 22, 1671], the pious *tsar* entered holy matrimony for the second time and sent Fedor Lopukhin to his holiness the patriarch with seven hundred rubles, sable, fox, and squirrel furs, wool cloth, black taffeta, fifteen fine linens, and twenty towels.

Having accepted the delivery, his holiness the patriarch thanked God and conducted a prayer service to ask for the health of the *tsar* for many, many years; he generously received and fed the *tsar's* messenger and released him in peace.[206]

Shortly thereafter [on December 24/25, 1671] his holiness the patriarch sent his cell monk (*keleinik*), a deacon named Mardarii, to the ruling city to petition to the pious *tsar* for [his] most pressing needs.[207]

The pious *tsar* fulfilled all his requests and [in January 1672] sent Koz'ma Lopukhin with forty large sables, sable furs, five hundred rubles, not a small number of silver tableware, and plenty of food and drink.[208] The deacon was soon released and given ten rubles from *tsar's* charity.[209]

When Koz'ma Lopukhin was still visiting his holiness the patriarch, his brother, Fedor Lopukhin, came from the ruling city with the news that [on January 30, 1676] the pious *tsar* Aleksei Mikhailovich left this world for eternal bliss.[210]

When blessed Nikon learned about the death of the *tsar*, he sighed with his entire heart, shed tears, and said: "So be the will of God. Although he did not receive our forgiveness in this world, the Lord will judge us on the day of his final Coming." Fedor Lopukhin dutifully pleaded with his holiness the patriarch to issue a written absolution forgiving the most pious *tsar*. To this, the blessed said: "Following the words of Christ, our teacher, written in the Holy Gospel: 'Forgive and you will be forgiven,' I now say: God will forgive him, but I will not write it on paper, because he did not free us from imprisonment during his life."

This messenger brought a one hundred ruble donation and black fox furs to ask [the patriarch] to pray for the pious *tsar's* soul. The blessed took everything and prayed as the canon of the holy church instructed him and as was the custom.

જી

After the death of the pious *tsar* Aleksei Mikhailovich, the throne and scepter went to his son, the most noble *tsarevich* Fedor Alekseevich. Crowned in his youth, he became the *tsar* of all Great, Little, and White Russias.

Blessed Nikon endured another storm caused by the devil who acted through his weapon, the evil people, who did not forget the ridiculous rumors of the aforesaid monk Iona. And so his holiness patriarch Ioakim became angry at blessed Nikon. As before, the cruel wardens, prince Samuil Yusupov and Ioann Adadurov, a captain of the *strel'tsy*, together with thirty *strel'tsy* were again sent to [the patriarch]. These wardens inflicted much misery, oppression, and deprivation on the blessed, who endured everything thanking God and saying: "God, do not consider this their sin."[211]

After [patriarch Nikon] spent a long time in deprivation, [on May 16, 1676], Pavel, archimandrite of the Monastery of the Miracles, service nobleman Ioann Zheliabovskii, and the chancellery secretary Semen Rumiantsev were sent from Moscow to the Ferapontov Monastery on the orders of the sovereign and the patriarch. They were given papers with many false accusations against blessed Nikon made by disgraceful perjurers and sycophants mired in earthly troubles, especially flattery. The messengers were ordered to inquire about the details of the written accusations and then transfer the blessed to the Kirillov Monastery,[212] also on the White Lake, so that he could be imprisoned there.[213]

The messengers reached the Ferapontov Monastery [on June 4, 1676] and abruptly entered first the monastery and then the church, but the blessed did not know the reason for their arrival. They sent for his holiness Nikon to tell him to come to the church where they were. Without the slightest delay, the blessed came to the church and bowed as was the custom. The messengers announced to [Nikon] the order of the sovereign and the patriarch as well as the reason for their arrival. Blessed Nikon, after honoring the *tsar's* majesty and the patriarch replied: "Let the will of the Lord and the great sovereign be. 'I fear not the myriad of people arrayed against me on every side.'[i] I am ready to suffer and even die." Warden Ioann, growling like a lion and barking like a dog, fiercely yelled at the blessed, ferociously insulting him.[214]

Blessed Nikon quietly told the archimandrite: "Although you have been sent to us in defiance of church canons, it is better you talk. Order him to be quiet."

---

[i] See The Book of Psalms, 3:7.

Soon they started to read the order and then the accusations against the blessed, full of any imaginable falsehood. Those false accusations filled more than three hundred pages and [the patriarch] was interrogated in detail on every one them.[215]

The blessed responded as the Holy Spirit instructed him and he also cited appropriate quotes from the Holy Scripture.[216] When the interrogation was over, the blessed was forbidden to go to his cells and, shortly thereafter [on June 4, 1676] was sent, under strict guard, to be imprisoned in the Kirillov Monastery on the White Lake, where the *strel'tsy* were ordered to guard him very closely.[217] The cells in which he was imprisoned were utterly unfit, overheated, and full of smoke. From this the blessed became so ill that he almost died.

The brothers who lived in blessed Nikon's cell at the Ferapontov Monastery, monastic priest Varlaam and monastic deacon Mardarii were placed under strict guard and endured many sufferings.[218] Shortly thereafter, they were imprisoned in the Cross Monastery on the White Sea which his holiness patriarch Nikon built. There they stayed imprisoned for seven years.

[On June 7, 1676], the messengers recorded the contents of the coffers and all the items that the blessed kept in his cell and brought them to the Kirillov Monastery where they deposited them in a separate chamber which was ordered to be sealed and closely guarded. The blessed did not receive even the most necessary items from his personal belongings.[219] Having carried out all their orders, the messengers returned to the ruling city of Moscow reporting their actions and the answers of blessed Nikon to their questions to the sovereign and his holiness patriarch [Ioakim].[220]

Pitying blessed Nikon, who almost died from the smoke in his cell, archimandrite Pavel asked his holiness patriarch Ioakim to allow the building of a new cell for the blessed so that he would not die prematurely, for at that time the blessed was suffering from strong headaches. But his holiness Ioakim, burdened by a magnitude of daily clerical and lay matters to which he had to attend, forgot about that letter.

Some time later, his holiness the patriarch sent Ioakinf, his vestry deacon (*riznichii*), to blessed Ioann in the Kirillov Monastery with an order to take the medallion from blessed [Nikon] which he had since the time when he left the Resurrection Monastery. [He also ordered to remove] two silver seals; one large one depicting the Resurrection and another, smaller, folded one, belonging to his holiness Iosif who was the patriarch of Moscow before [patriarch Nikon]. After arriving at the Kirillov Monastery, deacon Ioakinf carried out all the orders.

Blessed Nikon gave up everything without a murmur; Ioakinf ordered the abbot of the monastery to build new cells for blessed Nikon by the decree of his holiness Ioakim.[221] When giving up the medallion and seals, blessed Nikon cited the appropriate passages from the Holy Scripture to Ioakinf and then sent him off with peace to the ruling city. Blessed Nikon spent a long time exiled in that monastery, suffering no less than in the Ferapontov Monastery. He did not leave the cells but to attend church services; he prayed to God for the *tsar's* health and the wellbeing of the entire world and increased the fruits of his labor as was his custom. During all the days of his life, his holiness Nikon cared incessantly about the Resurrection Monastery and the holy church that he founded, but did not get a chance to finish. And this was a source of great sorrow for him. He tirelessly prayed to God to allow him to live in the Resurrection Monastery again and to finish the great stone church, but his request was not granted in this life.

CR

When the pious *tsar* Fedor Alekseevich reached maturity, he started to inquire about the reasons for blessed Nikon's exile and imprisonment, asking many people about his fate.

The noble and pious *tsarevna* and grand princess Tatiana Mikhailovna, an aunt of pious *tsar* Fedor Alekseevich, was very fond of his holiness Patriarch Nikon since the time of her childhood and respected him as a father and a shepherd. Seeing that the blessed had been suffering in exile and enduring injustices from cruel wardens for a long time, and remembering the favors and labors that the blessed showed during the deadly plague when the entire *tsar's* household was entrusted in his care, she was moved with her whole heart and soul. The pious *tsarevna* remembered how the blessed carried them from town to town and from place to place seeking air free of infection to save and protect the *tsar's* family.

Seeing the zeal of her nephew, the pious *tsar* Fedor Alekseevich, for the well-being of blessed Nikon, the pious *tsarevna* began to frequently remind him how his father, the pious *tsar* Aleksei Mikhailovich loved the blessed when he was still the patriarch and how his holiness the patriarch saved the *tsar's* family from the plague and did other favors; she described in detail how the blessed was exiled and suffered in imprisonment.

She also told him about the construction of the Resurrection Monastery and about the founding of the great stone church which the blessed established in the likeness of the Church of the Resurrection of Christ our God in the holy city of Jerusalem, inside which were the Savior's sepulcher, holy Golgotha and other [signs of] the saving Passions of our Lord. The church that [the patriarch] started was not completed and stood in desolation and no one cared to complete this great church. [The *tsarevna*] asked the *tsar* to finish building the great church and to release blessed Nikon from his imprisonment.

Having heard from many about blessed Nikon, the construction of the Resurrection Monastery, and about the beautiful holy church which was incomplete and stood in desolation, the pious *tsar* Fedor Alekseevich started to think about it and divine inspiration from the Holy Spirit shone in his heart; his eyes opened up to mercy and generosity. First, the pious *tsar* showed his favor to the holy Resurrection Monastery by wishing to see it; although there were many obstacles to this, the pious *tsar* was firm in his good intention to see the monastery with his own eyes.

Shortly thereafter, on the first of December, the same year 7187 (1678 sic),[222] to fulfill his good intentions, the great sovereign Fedor Alekseevich, *tsar* and grand prince of all Russia, deigned to travel to the holy Resurrection Monastery or New Jerusalem, so called by the blessed, shining with piety, ever-memorable, and pious sovereign Aleksei Mikhailovich, *tsar* and grand prince of all Russia, when he visited the monastery during the consecration of the first wooden Church of Christ's Resurrection. And the pious *tsar* deigned to write to his holiness patriarch about this with his own hand.[223]

Staying at the Resurrection Monastery, the most pious *tsar* Fedor Alekseevich saw with his own eyes the buildings of the holy monastery, the incomplete great stone church, and the beauty of the monastery's location, and took a liking to it. The pious *tsar* was in wonder that such a beautiful building was left in great desolation. Sighing with his whole heart, he burned with fervor for God, following the examples of the ancient pious Greek *tsars* Constantine the Great, Justinian, and Theodosius. In his heart and mind, he decided to complete the great stone church which did happen later. And the pious *tsar* deigned to entrust the care of the holy monastery and construction of the great holy church to his man Mikhail, called Likharev.

So God, our Lord, graced the holy monastery with divine mercy as he did in ancient Jerusalem, and the construction of the deserted building began. The holy monastery was in disrepair and the great church was deserted for fourteen years and three months from the day when his holiness was taken from the Resurrection Monastery to the Ferapontov Monastery. And so by the will of the great Savior, our God, Who builds everything through His omnipotent word, and by the pious *tsar's* diligence, in both words and deeds, the construction of the great church neared completion.

The pious *tsar* spent many days in the monastery, conferring generous favors on the brethren, and returned to the ruling city of Moscow. And so the *tsar* began to go frequently[224] to the holy monastery.[i]

ଓ

Once [on December 2, 1680], at a time when the most pious *tsar* was in the holy Resurrection Monastery, Varsonofii, its archimandrite, left this world and the *tsar* ordered the brothers to select a new archimandrite. The *tsar* added, for the Sun of Truth, Christ our God, shone over him and put a good thought in his heart: "If you want patriarch Nikon who started this monastery and founded the great church to live here, write a petition to me and merciful God will help arrange this matter."

German, steward of the monastery, Sergii, the treasurer, and many other brothers who were with the *tsar* at this moment and heard these words rejoiced with their whole hearts and told the *tsar's* words to the rest of the brethren. The brethren sent praise and glory to the Holy Trinity and the holiest Mother of God for the blessings that God gives those who love Him. Immediately, all of them unanimously wrote a petition to the great sovereign, which read:

"To the great sovereign Fedor Alekseevich, *tsar* and grand prince of all Great, and Little, and White Russias, your devout God-entreaters, German, abbot of the hermitage in the Resurrection Monastery, elder Sergii, the treasurer, and the brethren petition you. Oh great sovereign, the grace of God, who in His

---

[i] This paragraph is absent from the printed Iverskii version and is found only in the New Jerusalem manuscripts.

great mercy exceeds not only human thought, but corporeal meaning, this infinite God of ours and yours, the Lord and *Tsar* of all Christians who always glorifies that which He loves, and which in turn loves Him, He who directs the *tsar's* heart towards good deeds which only He Himself knows in His wisdom, He looked down with His infinite favor and mercy on this holy monastery and this great church, a likeness of the original church built on the site of Christ's passions, and his life-giving joyful Resurrection, and on us, your humble and devout God-entreaters. We rejoice about this with unspoken joy and celebrate this with great festivities as the Israelites who, led by Moses, crossed the Red Sea of suffering and sorrow and found the Promised Land, we rejoice as those who rejoiced about Christ's Resurrection in Jerusalem.[i] We are missing just one thing, our kind master, to be truly like the ancient Israelites who carried the bones of Joseph, who saved them from starvation, out of Egypt,[ii] or the new residents of Constantinople who convinced the pious *tsar* Theodosius to bring St. John Chrysostom back from Comene.[iii] And until today, we did not petition about our father who delivered us from spiritual starvation and neglect of God's words and who fed us with the body of the Lamb which gives those who partake in Him eternal life. We now pray for your God-like mercy, oh our most pious sovereign, the *tsar*. Have mercy on us, your destitute God-entreaters, and grant the church to be complete. Bring back the captain to the ship, return the shepherd to the flock, unite the head with the body, and order to return to us our Christ-following teacher, his holiness Nikon, who, like Moses, carried us through the sea of life. Order that we inherit the Promised Land through your generous and abundant donations. Let [patriarch Nikon], who knows everything, divide this inheritance between us, after careful consideration, as the venerable Joshua, the son of Nun, and Eleazar did in the past. Release his soul from prison as blessed Ignatius, Patriarch of Constantinople, was once released from imprisonment, order [the patriarch's] release from the Kirillov Monastery and bring him to the Resurrection Monastery which is growing like a fertile tree being nourished and propagated by your generous gifts and is glorified by all. Allow him to enjoy your generosity together with us and allow him to rejoice in his old age. Sovereign *tsar*, have mercy!"[225]

Sixty brothers set their hands to the petition written by the steward and the treasurer which was handed to the most pious *tsar* with a tearful prayer to release blessed Nikon from imprisonment.[226]

Having accepted the petition with the brethren's pleas and having spent sufficient time at the monastery, the pious *tsar* returned to the ruling city of Moscow. Arriving at his court, the most pious *tsar* revealed his thoughts about patriarch Nikon to his holiness Ioakim, patriarch of Moscow and all Russia, intending to release patriarch Nikon from imprisonment and to bring him to the Resurrection

---

[i] An allusion to the Bible. See Exodus 14:30.

[ii] See Exodus 13:19.

[iii] Comene was a Byzantine city where the saint died in 407 en route to his exile, ordered by Eudoxia, empress of Byzantium. The translation of John Chrysostom's relics occurred in 438 by the orders of Eudoxia's son, emperor Theodosius II.

Monastery, to complete the construction of God's church that [the patriarch] already started.

Having heard this, patriarch [Ioakim] objected, saying: "It was not us who imprisoned him, but the great council of their holinesses the ecumenical patriarchs, and we cannot do anything without their consent, and this, oh *tsar*, should be your majesty's order."

Seeing that patriarch [Ioakim] did not agree with his intentions, the pious *tsar* was greatly saddened and frequently reminded his holiness about blessed Nikon and his release from imprisonment, but the patriarch was adamantly opposed to it and only increased his objection and resisted the *tsar's* wishes.

Shortly thereafter, the pious *tsar* assembled all the hierarchs and the entire holy synod in the Cross Chamber of the patriarchal palace, and the *tsar* and his Council were also present there. At once, the *tsar* announced his intention to release patriarch Nikon from imprisonment on the prayers and petition from the brethren.

But patriarch Ioakim insisted on keeping Nikon in the Kirillov Monastery. Many hierarchs, although fearing the patriarch, ardently supported the *tsar* saying both privately and openly: "Patriarch Nikon should be taken from imprisonment and brought to the Resurrection Monastery that he built and allowed to live there." But his holiness patriarch Ioakim did not consent and the council of the holy synod ended [without resolution].

Shortly thereafter, the pious *tsar*, seeing that it was not to be, invited patriarch [Ioakim] to his chambers and together with his aunt, the noble *tsarevna* and grand princess Tatiana Mikhailovna again diligently pleaded with the patriarch to release patriarch Nikon from imprisonment. But patriarch Ioakim was adamantly against the *tsar's* request to do a good deed and ease Nikon's fate. [Patriarch Ioakim] was now even more against it, saying: "It was not us who did it, but the great council of the holy synod and the ecumenical patriarchs, and we dare not release him without [the consent of] the ecumenical patriarchs."

The pious *tsar* was greatly saddened that the patriarch did not allow the release of patriarch Nikon for whom the sovereign felt pity on account of his suffering and exile. The *tsar* wrote a consoling letter to the blessed in which he told [patriarch Nikon] to pray to the Holy Trinity, the holiest Mother of God, and all saints for the *tsar's* health for years to come and for the well-being of the entire world; and to expect a favor from the *tsar's* majesty and a just investigation.[227]

The pious *tsar* sent this letter with monastic deacon Mardarii, who was freed [in 1680] together with monastic priest Varlaam from imprisonment in the Cross Monastery on the White Sea.[228] At the same time, the *tsar*, upon the request of her highness Tatiana Mikhailovna, pious *tsarevna* and grand princess, returned cleric Ioann Kornil'ev [Shusherin] from exile in Novgorod the Great.

Blessed Nikon received the *tsar's* letter in which he happily read that the *tsar's* majesty cared for him greatly and wished to release him from imprisonment and to transfer him to the Resurrection Monastery, where the blessed was to complete the task that he started and to build the great Church of Christ's Resurrection. And the most pious *tsar* also wished to see blessed Nikon because he heard from many people that the blessed was truly wise, knew the Holy Scripture, protected the holy and pure faith, and upheld divine dogmas.[229]

Having read the letter, the blessed rejoiced in God our Lord with all his heart and soul and gave praise to God our Savior, for He, in His holy divine grace, looked down on the humbleness of His servant and put thoughts about blessed Nikon, the Resurrection Monastery, and the completion of church in the heart of the pious *tsar*. And this gave blessed Nikon small consolation in his sadness and sorrow.

The blessed *tsar* shone with great love for the holy monastery and wished to complete the construction of the great church and to free blessed Nikon from imprisonment. And so the pious *tsar*, acting on his good intention, and with faith in God, began to build the roof of the great church, donating an abundant amount of money from his treasury.[230]

CR

Although blessed Nikon found the *tsar's* favor, he fell gravely ill and suffered very much and the *tsar* too was seriously ill and for this reason the *tsar's* intention to bring the blessed from the Kirillov Monastery to the Resurrection Monastery was delayed.

When the illness of the blessed worsened, archimandrite Nikita wrote to his holiness patriarch [Ioakim] in the ruling city of Moscow announcing that blessed Nikon was in great pain and near death (the blessed already accepted the *skhima*[i] and, seven days later, received extreme unction, but did not change his old name). The archimandrite asked what his holiness patriarch [Ioakim] wanted to do when God takes blessed Nikon from this life. Who should conduct the burial and how? How he should be remembered in prayers, where should his body be laid? And he asked about everything and what they should do. And patriarch [Ioakim] soon received the letter from the archimandrite of the Kirillov Monastery, and having seen what was written about blessed Nikon, replied at once ordering the archimandrite to give blessed Nikon the *skhima* and to arrange a Christian burial fit for a simple monk after his demise; his body was to be laid on the church porch. And the pious *tsar* knew nothing about this exchange.

When the pious *tsar* learned that the letter about the blessed was sent to the Kirillov Monastery, he ordered patriarch [Ioakim] to retrieve his missive, but [the patriarch replied] that the letter already arrived there.

Blessed Nikon, being gravely ill and feeling his imminent demise, wrote a short letter to his children, followers, and the entire brethren at his Resurrection Monastery, which read:

"Patriarch Nikon sends his blessing to his children: archimandrite German, monastic priest Varlaam, monk Sergii, monk Ippolit and the entire brethren. Please know that I am seriously ill and unable to get up and go outside; I am bedridden and lay in the festering pus excreting from me. And the great sovereign showed his favor towards me; on your petition, he wanted to take me from

---

[i] In Eastern Christianity, *skhima* refers to the two highest monastic orders (lesser and greater *skhimas*), characterized by extreme mortification and asceticism. Often called the final vows, *skhima* requires complete rejection of earthly possessions, including the change of one's name.

here, and he kindly wrote me a letter with his own hand, but time has passed and his merciful edict did not come and I might die suddenly. My children, please forgive my rudeness and petition to the great sovereign about me again. Do not allow me to die an unjust death, for the end of my life is near. And for my current condition, Ioann who lives in our monastery's village of Bogoslovskoe will describe it to you in detail."[231]

When the letter reached the Resurrection Monastery and the archimandrite and brethren saw what the blessed wrote about himself, they cried, lamented, and wailed, knowing that their father and shepherd was so gravely ill and near death.

The archimandrite of the Resurrection Monastery gave the letter to the pious *tsar*, tearfully begging him to return their father to the monastery which blessed Nikon founded.

And the pious *tsar* took the letter and, having read that the blessed was seriously ill and near death, was touched and felt deep sorrow for the blessed and he again began to ask his holiness the patriarch and the entire holy synod to release patriarch Nikon from imprisonment saying that he was near death. The patriarch and the entire holy synod told the *tsar*: "Oh pious *tsar*, let your will be done."

Having received the blessing of patriarch [Ioakim] and the entire council of the holy synod, the *tsar* hurriedly sent the chancellery secretary Ioann Chepelev, head of the *tsar's* stables, to the Kirillov Monastery, ordering him to take blessed Nikon, alive or dead, from the Kirillov Monastery and bring him to the Resurrection Monastery.

The messenger set out on the journey and soon arrived at the Kirillov Monastery. A day or two before the arrival of the secretary, blessed Nikon, although gravely ill, started to prepare for a journey. Seeing his preparations, the brothers staying with him thought he did so because of his illness and loss of senses; and he did so not once, but several times.

On the day when the messenger from the ruling city arrived [in August 1681], blessed Nikon also started to prepare for a journey; dressing himself in his own clothes, he sat down in the chair which stood right there on the porch, and told those staying with him: "I am ready, why are you not getting dressed? Soon you will see that they will come for us." Hearing this, they thought that the blessed was delirious.

But suddenly the messenger with the *tsar's* order entered the cells, announcing to blessed Nikon the *tsar's* favor: "The pious *tsar* allows you to go to your Resurrection Monastery that you founded."

Gravely ill, the blessed could barely stand up to give the *tsar* the appropriate honor.

And they started to prepare a boat for the journey since the voyage was to take them down the Sheksna River. When everything was prepared for the river voyage, the blessed was put in a sleigh and carried to the river where the boats stood ready. They put him in the boat with a great difficulty for the blessed was greatly weakened from illness. Then they set out down the river.

The archimandrite of the Resurrection Monastery and the brethren sent monastic priest Varlaam, who previously lived with blessed Nikon for many years in the Ferapontov Monastery and who was described above, monastic deacon

Serafim, steward of the St. Athanasius Monastery, a possession of the Resurrection Monastery, in Mologa, and monastic priest Tikhon to meet and greet blessed Nikon.

The delegation met the blessed twenty *poprishches* from the Volga River[i] and received his blessing for themselves and asked for a blessing for the archimandrite, and the brethren of the Resurrection Monastery.

The blessed gave all of them peace and blessing and the journey down the river continued. When they reached the Volga River, the *tsar's* messenger wanted to sail up the river.

But blessed Nikon did not consent and deigned to go down the river towards the town of Iaroslavl'. When they sailed down Sheksna and Volga and passed towns and villages [on the banks these rivers], their residents went out to greet the boats, bringing everything necessary and bidding tearful farewells to the travelers.

In the early morning of August 16 [1681], the travelers reached the Monastery of the holiest Mother of God on the Tolga River, six *poprishches* from Yaroslavl'.[ii] About half a *poprishche* from the monastery,[iii] the blessed ordered to land the boat because he was exhausted from illness; he received holy communion of the most pure body and blood of Christ from his spiritual father Nikita, archimandrite of the Kirillov Monastery, which was preserved since holy Thursday.

And then the boats landed near the monastery whose abbot and brethren came to greet [the boats]. Among them was the aforesaid Sergii, the former archimandrite of the Monastery of the Savior in Yaroslavl'. During the banishment of blessed Nikon, this Sergii insulted the blessed the most, both at the council of the holy synod, in the presence of the ecumenical patriarchs, and in the house where the blessed lived under guard. About this Sergii we already told earlier.

This Sergii, seeing that blessed Nikon was dying, fell to Nikon's feet and tearfully and touchingly said: "Forgive me, your holiness, I am guilty of all the abuse that you had to endure. I insulted and abused your holiness during your banishment to please the council."

And to this he also added: "Today, after the holy and divine liturgy, and after partaking in common meals with the brethren, I lay down to rest and soon dreamed that his holiness patriarch Nikon came to me and said: 'Brother Sergii, raise up, I will give you my forgiveness.' And immediately the monastery guard knocked on my door saying that his holiness patriarch Nikon sails along the Volga and is approaching the monastery. The abbot and the brothers went to greet him and I, after this vision and the words of the guard, trembled in fear, rose up and, barely coming to my senses, quickly ran following the brothers. Here I am, my master, asking your holiness for forgiveness." Then Sergii received forgiveness from the blessed and told everyone about his vision.

But blessed Nikon already began to feel the agony which precedes death. The boats landed at Yaroslavl' and the town's residents, having heard about the arri-

---

[i] About thirty kilometers.
[ii] About nine kilometers.
[iii] Less than a kilometer.

val of the blessed, happily ran to him to receive the blessing from the shepherd returning to his flock. But seeing him laying on his deathbed and learning that his death was imminent, the people fell to his feet, wailing and crying, asking for forgiveness and blessing and kissing his hands and feet.

And so, because of the crowds, the boats could barely enter the Kotorosl' River; people were pulling the boat with the blessed, some from the shore, others walking in the thigh-high water. Near the Monastery of the Savior they landed again. Here the town's military commander and governor came with a magnitude of people and the archimandrite of the Monastery of the Savior and a delegation of clergy from the monastery and the town. They brought everything necessary and asked for [patriarch Nikon's] blessing.

However blessed Nikon was so exhausted that he could not speak and only gave his right hand to be kissed. The crowd around him was burdensome, and so, seeing that the crowd was still increasing, Nikita, archimandrite of the Kirillov Monastery and blessed Nikon's spiritual father, and the chancellery secretary sent by the *tsar*, ordered to bring the boat with the blessed to the other shore.

When evening came and the bells in the town called for evening prayers, blessed Nikon, who was losing his last strength, started to look around, as if seeing people coming for him; he carefully straightened his hair, beard, and dress as if preparing for a journey. Archimandrite Nikita, the brethren, and the chancellery secretary, seeing that the blessed was drawing his last breath, started to read the prayers for the soul leaving the body.

The blessed lay down on the prepared bed, gave a blessing to his followers, folded his hands on his chest, and reverently and in good conscience thanked God for everything, even for the painful end of his life's journey, and died in peace, putting his soul in the hands of God, Whom he loved. He left this life for eternal bliss in the year 7189 from the creation of the world (1681) on the seventeenth day of August.

The archimandrite of the Yaroslavl' monastery and all the assembled clergy were able to conduct only earnest entreaties (*litiia*) for the dead. Then came the town's military commander and governor with a large crowd of people crying and lamenting the loss of their shepherd and teacher. The chancellery secretary promptly went to the pious *tsar* in the ruling city of Moscow with the news that blessed Nikon left for eternal rest.

ଓ

The pious *tsar*, not yet knowing about the demise of blessed Nikon, sent his carriage and his best horses for him. On the second day after the demise of the blessed, the messengers and the carriage reached the place and saw that the blessed had died. They then put together a sturdy carriage, placed the coffin with the body of the blessed on it and set out for the ruling city of Moscow. In the cities and towns, the body of the blessed was greeted with psalms and earnest entreaties for the dead and was seen off with tears.

When the mourning procession reached Alexandrov Sloboda, the mother superior with all the nuns, numbering no less than two hundred, went out from the nunnery to meet the body of the blessed. The bells knelled, the nuns prayed, and sang earnest entreaties for the dead. The nuns shed tears and cried out loudly, lamenting the loss of their shepherd and teacher. After accompanying the body of the blessed for one *poprishche*,[i] they kissed the body of the blessed and returned to the nunnery sobbing loudly.

When the mourning procession approached the Trinity and St. Sergius Monastery, Vikentii, its archimandrite, together with clergy and brethren, came to greet the body of the blessed. They stopped in front of the holy gates and together they sang earnest entreaties for the dead. Then they bid the body of the blessed farewell and returned to the monastery crying.

The mourning procession barely left the monastery when the aforesaid chancellery secretary came from Moscow announcing the *tsar's* order for Nikita, archimandrite of the Kirillov Monastery, to promptly go to the ruling city. In his stead, Vikentii, archimandrite of the Trinity and St. Sergius Monastery, was to accompany the body of the blessed. And so they continued the journey.

When the aforesaid chancellery secretary was presented to the sovereign, the *tsar* asked him about blessed Nikon: "How did you find him when he was still alive? How did he die and [did he leave] a will?" The chancellery secretary described everything in detail and added about the will: "Oh pious *tsar*, I reminded blessed Nikon to write a will, but he replied: 'I do not wish to write a will. Instead, I will say just one thing. Let there be peace and blessing for the most pious sovereign Fedor Alekseevich, *tsar* and grand prince of all Russia, and for the *tsar's* family. Let him, the most pious *tsar*, take care of my soul, sinful body, funeral, and remembering me in prayers. Let him be the executioner of my will, and as he decides, so be it.'"

Hearing this, the pious *tsar* was touched and, pitying the blessed, said: "If his holiness patriarch Nikon put his hope in my hands, then so be the will of God. For as long as God helps me, I will not forget him." And he ordered to carry the body of the blessed to the Resurrection Monastery.

The pious *tsar* sent an order to his holiness patriarch Ioakim summoning him and the entire holy synod to the Resurrection Monastery for the burial of blessed Nikon. The patriarch replied to the messenger: "Let the sovereign's will be done. I am ready to go, but during the burial, in the course of the litany of supplication and other prayers, I will not call Nikon patriarch, but a simple monk, as the council of the holy synod decreed. If the pious *tsar* wishes to remember Nikon as patriarch in prayers, I will not do this."

The *tsar* pleaded with patriarch [Ioakim] at length to go to the burial of blessed Nikon and remember him as patriarch in prayers, but the patriarch refused many times, saying: "I will go, but will not call him patriarch because it was not me, but the ecumenical patriarchs who called Nikon a simple monk and the council confirmed this."

But the pious *tsar* said: "If the ecumenical patriarchs will reprimand you, let this sin be on me. I will beg their holinesses the patriarchs and they will send us

---

[i] About one and a half kilometers.

their blessing and forgiveness for patriarch Nikon, allowing the prayers for him."[232]

The patriarch did not deign to go to the funeral, but he blessed Kornilii, metropolitan of Novgorod the Great, to go. [The patriarch] ordered the metropolitan to mention Nikon in the course of the litany of supplication as the pious *tsar* wished.

※

The pious *tsar* arrived at the Resurrection Monastery [on August 25, 1681] with his household and Council, and metropolitan [Kornilii] and the holy synod arrived at the monastery before the body of the blessed was brought there to prepare everything that was necessary for the funeral as the church canon instructs. They conducted evening prayers and an all night vigil to remember [patriarch Nikon's] soul as the book of devotions (*Trebnik*) by Piotr Mohila published in Kiev prescribes.

The following day, early in the morning, Vikentii, archimandrite of the Trinity and St. Sergius Monastery, arrived with the body of the blessed. The coffin was laid across from the monastery near the holy cross erected by the will of pious *tsar* Aleksei Mikhailovich and with the blessing of his holiness patriarch Nikon, as a symbol of their mutual love and concord during the founding of the new monastery and its being named New Jerusalem. A Slavonic inscription engraved on the stone cross testifies to this.[233] It was announced to the *tsar* that the body of blessed Nikon had arrived. It was August 26, 7189 from the creation of the world (1681); on the day that the body of the blessed arrived at the first hour of daylight,[i] the bells rang one after another, as if during a procession of the cross (*krestnyi khod*).

When the time had come to go to the coffin of the blessed, everyone assembled in the great stone Church of Holy Golgotha where the cross stood; the great church was still not competed and not consecrated. Among the assembled were the *tsar* and his Council and metropolitan with the holy synod. All members of the clergy assembled in the Resurrection Monastery for the burial of blessed Nikon, donned liturgical vestments. Present at the burial were: Kornilii, metropolitan of Novgorod the Great, Vikentii, archimandrite of the Trinity and St. Sergius Monastery, Silvestr, archimandrite of the St. Savva Monastery, German, follower of blessed Nikon and archimandrite of the Resurrection Monastery, Nikita, former spiritual father of blessed Nikon and archimandrite of the Kirillov Monastery on the White Lake, other monastic priests, monastic deacons, brethren of the Resurrection Monastery and many other archimandrites, parish priests, deacons, and ordinary people. The clergy took holy banners, the holy cross, and holy icons and exited the monastery as instructed by the church canon and went to the holy cross where the coffin with the body of the blessed lay.

The pious *tsar* walked and together with the church choir sang a hymn praising the Lord, in Kievan chant: "Today we are assembled by the grace of the Holy Spirit" and so did all standing there. And soon they reached the holy cross

---

[i] Approximately six o'clock in the morning.

were the coffin of the blessed lay and lit big candles—some a *sazhen* long, others—six *chetvert's,* and still others—half an *arshin* long.[i] These different candles, paid for from the *tsar's* coffers, were made for the burial and painted black.

The metropolitan gave everyone a candle according to rank, first to the *tsar,* then to the archimandrites, the *boyars* and the *tsar's* Council. Vikentii, archimandrite of the Trinity and St. Sergius Monastery, gave candles to the monks and the priests and the multitude of laymen. After that, the priests lifted the coffin with the body of the blessed and carried it to the monastery above their heads. Next to the coffin walked twelve youths, members of the *tsar's* choir, carrying large candles and dressed in vestments, similar to tunics (*stikhar'*), made for this occasion from expensive Chinese silk of mourning colors. At the head of the procession were the holy banners, the holy cross, and holy icons, followed by the metropolitan with the holy synod, and the *tsar* and his Council. Behind them, the priests carried the coffin with the body of blessed Nikon, followed by a multitude of people mourning their father and shepherd with tears, loud screams, and sobs.

Again, the pious *tsar* together with his choir sang the aforesaid hymn, "Today we are assembled by the grace of the Holy Spirit." [He sang] with such a sorrowful and touching voice that it moved all to tears. And so the coffin with the body of the blessed was carried into the monastery and all the bells knelled. And it was brought to the great stone church, and once inside, to the Church of the holiest Mother of God, also called the Dungeon [*Temnitsa*], and there the coffin was laid down. The divine liturgy started, followed by a burial service fit for a hierarch.

The pious *tsar* ordered metropolitan Kornilii and the clergy celebrating with him to remember blessed Nikon as patriarch in all supplications as was customary for all the other Moscow patriarchs, as so it was done as he ordered.

The pious *tsar* deigned to work during the burial service until the dismissal prayer (*otpust*); he read proper psalms, epistles of the apostles, and sang together with his choir throughout the burial. When it was time to take a leave from the deceased by kissing him in the coffin, the pious *tsar* took the right hand of the patriarch from underneath the *skhima* pall[ii] and lovingly and tearfully kissed it, and so did his family, his Council, clergy, brethren, and the entire crowd of people, and every man and woman did so.

After the burial service, the priests again took the coffin with the body of blessed Nikon and carried it to the southern side of the great stone church to the Church of John the Baptist beneath Golgotha itself. In Jerusalem, this church is carved in the rock which split in half during the Crucifixion of our Lord Jesus Christ and the Lord's saving blood flowed from His rib into this ravine onto Adam's head, and the crypt of Melchisedek, the first hierarch of Jerusalem, is located there and can be seen there even now. Our shepherd and father, his holiness patriarch Nikon, when still alive, asked to be buried in the Church of John

---

[i] About two meters, a meter, and thirty-five centimeters respectively.

[ii] The dark cover symbolizing a great habit of a monk having taken the monastic *skhima,* or the strictest monastic vows.

the Baptist and God did as his heart desired. There, the proper prayers were sang over the body of the blessed.

Although the pious *tsar* had never seen blessed Nikon when he was alive, he loved him with all his heart, because when blessed Nikon placed his soul in God's hands, he entrusted the *tsar* with his burial and the commemoration of his soul, as is written above. And so, after the singing had ended, the pious *tsar* together with the metropolitan, lowered the coffin of the blessed into the grave with his own hands. He sobbed and sang: "Holy God."

The metropolitan and the entire holy synod, the *boyars*, the *tsar's* Council, and all assembled laymen looked in wonder and were moved to tears seeing the pious *tsar* doing so and showing such heartfelt love for his holiness patriarch Nikon. Today there are no *tsars* capable of actions, which will create such a sense of wonder in the generations to come.[234]

After the death of his holiness patriarch Nikon, Fedor Alekseevich, the most pious *tsar* and grand prince of all Great, Little, and White Russias, showed such love and purity of heart and arranged such an honorable burial that everyone who saw and heard about it were in wonder.

That day these sacraments were conducted over the body of his holiness patriarch Nikon: the procession to the cross to collect his body, the divine liturgy, and a burial service. They lasted for ten and a half hours and the pious *tsar* labored during this period with both spiritual love and corporeal strength.

At the end of burial ceremonies, the pious *tsar* went to the [monastery] vestry to see the hierarchical liturgical vestments [of the deceased]. From among them he choose and gave Kornilii, metropolitan of Novgorod the Great, the best bishop's chasuble (*sakkos*) made of white silver-threaded material and a bishop's scarf made of gold-threaded material, priceless hierarchal vestments, and one hundred rubles. The great sovereign also generously gave money from his own treasury to other archimandrites, the holy synod, and the clerics present at the burial; and he also rewarded the brethren and gave generous donations to the beggars.

The *tsar* rewarded all the brothers, tonsured by his holiness the patriarch, who lived with him in the Resurrection Monastery and then shared exile with him in the Ferapontov and Kirillov Monasteries, by giving them frocks, warm coats (*kaftans*), various light clothes, and other personal belongings of the deceased Nikon. [The gifts] were divided according to rank and labor. Everything given to the brethren was brought from the Kirillov Monastery after his holiness the patriarch left it. Many silver, copper, and tin utensils and personal belongings kept in his cells were given to the monastery treasury,[235] and one thousand rubles were given to the treasury to build the church.

And after honoring the metropolitan and the holy synod, the pious *tsar* released them with peace.

Having spent sufficient time in the monastery and having generously rewarded the brethren, the pious *tsar* returned to the ruling city of Moscow. Taking great care of blessed Nikon and saddened that his holiness patriarch Ioakim did not allow blessed Nikon to be called patriarch, the most pious *tsar* decided in his heart to write about this to the ecumenical patriarchs, which he did.

The great sovereign took the rest of blessed Nikon's hierarchical vestments, miters (*mitra*), bishop's chasubles, richly adorned mantles with sources, monastic hoods, and other items of clothing, to Moscow. He left one complete set of hierarchal vestments consisting of bishop's chasuble and scarf, mantle, and other garments, and a hierarchical staff in the monastery for the future brethren and other residents of the monastery to remember.[i] And the great sovereign ordered to carefully keep all in the vestry.[236]

The *tsar* sent the miter, and bishop's chasubles which were brought to Moscow to his holiness Ioakim to commemorate blessed Nikon, but the patriarch did not accept them. And so the miter was given to Simeon, metropolitan of Smolensk.

The rest of the bishop's chasubles, monastic hoods, mantles and other hierarchal vestments were given, at the *tsar's* discretion, to hierarchs to commemorate his holiness patriarch Nikon.

෪

Let it be known how his holiness patriarch Nikon was buried. After his demise, his body was brought to the monastery mill called Voskresenskii, which stood on the Pesochnia River one *poprishche* from the monastery.[ii] There, by the order of the *tsar*, the [mourning procession] stopped and the coffin of the blessed was carried into a cell and archimandrite German and the priests who came from the monastery brought fresh clothes: a Greek shirt made of white camel wool, which the blessed prepared many years ago when he was still living in the Resurrection Monastery before his exile (this shirt was kept in the treasury of the Resurrection Monastery until the death of the blessed), a frock of dark red velvet, a hierarchical mantle with sources and pomata (*skrizhal'*), medallion, and *skhima* pall.[237]

The archimandrite, together with the priests, dressed blessed Nikon in these clothes. His body was completely unscathed and he did not show any sign of decay even though ten days have already passed since his death. Even though the weather was very warm, his body was intact, as if he just died; his face and entire body did not change and remained intact and had no sign of putrefaction.

Next, the body of the blessed was again put in the coffin and brought to the monastery. After the funeral service, the oak coffin with the body of the blessed was put into a new crypt carved in stone. The stone, from which the crypt was made, was brought by the order of his holiness patriarch Nikon from the White Sea to the church and paid for back in those days when his holiness the patriarch lived in the Resurrection Monastery before his exile.

When God deigned to take blessed Nikon from this life, the pious *tsar* ordered to carve a crypt out of this stone and so it was done. When the masons were carving the stone first they cut off a slab two *vershoks* wide[iii] from the stone, and

---

[i] The printed Iverskii version this sentence also contains a phrase "to the future people."

[ii] About one and a half kilometer.

[iii] About nine centimeters.

then started to carve inside it, so that the wooden coffin could fit into it. Carving the stone was very difficult because it was very hard. This valuable stone is called alabaster and there is no other like it. In the Church of John the Baptist under holy Golgotha, to the right of the door in the corner, a hole was dug in which the stone crypt was placed. And at the end of the funeral service, the coffin with the body of the blessed was carried to the Church of John the Baptist.

The pious *tsar* together with his eminence the metropolitan, deigned to lower the wooden coffin with the body of blessed patriarch Nikon into the newly carved alabaster crypt with his own royal hands. During the lowering, the pious *tsar*, the metropolitan, and others sang the appropriate hymns. And the crypt was covered with the slab cut from the stone, and on top of it the lid of the wooden coffin was placed. A layer of bricks was laid over the crypt and the tomb was leveled with the floor of the church.

03

The pious *tsar* lamented incessantly that blessed Nikon was not remembered in prayers as patriarch. [On June 26, 1681] the *tsar* deigned to write about this to all four ecumenical patriarchs in Palestine and sent letters with a messenger, chancellery secretary Prokopii Voznitsyn, asking for permission to call Nikon a patriarch in prayers which the holy synod still forbade.[238]

The pious *tsar* pleaded with their holinesses the ecumenical patriarchs to allow Nikon to be called patriarch, to forgive the sins of blessed Nikon, who died in exile, and to remember him as patriarch [during remembrance services] in the great cathedral and throughout all of Russia during every liturgical service, like all other patriarchs of Moscow. And the *tsar's* letter soon reached the ecumenical patriarchs.

And as the heartfelt faith of the pious *tsar* in the monastery and his love for blessed Nikon grew, the sovereign wished to complete the construction of the great church as soon as possible and ordered the builders to work on its roof without delay.[239]

He generously ordered to give treasures from his coffers for the church needs: gold, silver, money, church utensils, liturgical vestments, albs (*stikhar'*), liturgical cuffs (*poruchi*), stoles (*epitrakhil'*), priceless gold and silver vessels, and many other utensils for the holy church and the altar.[240] The great *tsar* assigned as eternal possessions of the [Resurrection] Monastery many smaller monasteries which came with peasants and estates.[241] The *tsar* also gave the village of Troitskoe, together with smaller villages, located near the monastery and which previously belonged to Roman Bobarykin, to the monastery as an eternal possession.[242] But the strongest desire of his heart was to complete the construction of the great church about which he cared incessantly during all the days of his life.

But great God, our Savior, deigned differently. Because death is the common fate of all humanity, the life of the pious Fedor Alekseevich, *tsar* of all Russia, ended and his noble soul went to the Lord for eternal bliss. His body was buried in 7190 (1682) on the twenty-seventh of April. The pious *tsar* did not receive that which his heart and soul desired so strongly, to see the great church completed and consecrated.

The ecumenical patriarchs accepted the *tsar's* letters that the messenger brought them, and reading his pleas and prayers, saw the strength of the *tsar's* desire and his spiritual and heartfelt love for blessed Nikon, his ardor to receive their forgiveness for the sins of the blessed and [to secure] their permission to commemorate him during every liturgy together with the other Moscow patriarchs. The *tsar* wrote that blessed Nikon was a worthy man who lived his life virtuously, courageously enduring all torments during exile, and who went to the Lord being repentant. Having read about all of this in the *tsar's* letter, the ecumenical patriarchs were in great wonderment and thanked God the Almighty Savior who gave the pious *tsar* such diligence and great desire to take care of the soul of the blessed as only a son could care about his spiritual father and his fellow in the Holy Spirit.

Guided by the Holy Spirit, their holinesses the ecumenical patriarchs granted the *tsar's* desire and request.

They wrote the decrees forgiving and absolving blessed Nikon and allowing his inclusion together with all other Moscow patriarchs and his remembrance during liturgies in the holy and great cathedral and in all of Russia as his holiness the patriarch, as befits a Moscow patriarch. They signed the decrees with their own hands, sealed them with their own seals, and sent them back to the ruling city of Moscow with the same messenger. This happened in September of 7191 (1682).[243]

At that time [on April 27, 1682], Fedor Alekseevich, the most pious *tsar* of all Russia, left this life for heavenly bliss and eternal rest.

[On September 9, 1682], already after the *tsar's* death and during the reign of his brothers Ioann Alekseevich and Piotr Alekseevich, the pious *tsars* and grand princes of all Russia, the messenger brought the decrees of the ecumenical patriarchs.[244]

The pious sovereigns and *tsars* [Ioann Alekseevich and Piotr Alekseevich] received the decrees of the ecumenical patriarchs and ordered to translate them into Russian because the decrees were written in Greek. And having translated the decrees, they sent the translation to his holiness patriarch Ioakim, saying: "These decrees were sent to our brother, Fedor Alekseevich, the *tsar* of all Russia, let his memory be blessed, from the ecumenical patriarchs, announcing the forgiveness, dispensation, and inclusion of patriarch Nikon together with all the other Moscow patriarchs, and permission to remember him in prayers during the liturgies as all other Moscow patriarchs."

Having taken the letters and having listened to these words, patriarch Ioakim said: "If you do not bring me the original decrees sent by their holinesses the ecumenical patriarchs with their own signatures and seals, I will not believe you." When he returned, the messenger told the *tsars* the patriarch's words and the *tsars* at once sent the original decrees that the patriarchs wrote to patriarch Ioakim.

Seeing the original decrees with the signatures and seals of the ecumenical patriarchs, the patriarch ordered the translators to read them. And having learned what they have written about patriarch Nikon, he said: "Those are indeed the authentic decrees of the ecumenical Orthodox patriarchs signed with their own hands and bearing their own seals." And having seen the decrees, he said: "Then so be it."[245]

From that time forward, blessed Nikon, like all other Moscow patriarchs, was remembered in prayers in all the liturgies in the great cathedral and in all Russian churches as his holiness the patriarch. Patriarch Ioakim ordered to write the name of the blessed in the church book of the deceased and sick, and the decrees, as authentic testimonies, were placed in the vestry of the patriarchal palace. His holiness patriarch Ioakim himself remembers blessed Nikon in prayers as his holiness the patriarch during memorial services (*panikhida*) when he visits the Resurrection Monastery.[246]

After the death of Fedor Alekseevich, pious *tsar* of all Russia, the great church remained incomplete.

But our merciful God, Creator of the World, on the prayers of our father the great hierarch, his holiness patriarch Nikon, did not forget the monastery and put good thoughts about the completion of the great church [at the Resurrection Monastery] into the hearts of the great sovereigns Ioann Alekseevich and Piotr Alekseevich, *tsars* and grand princes of all Great, and White, and Little Russias, and their highnesses Tatiana Mikhailovna, Sofiia Alekseevna, noble *tsarevnas* and grand princesses, and others, as he did previously for the great sovereign Fedor Alekseevich, *tsar* and grand prince of all Russia.[247] [In 1685], with faith in our Lord and Savior and with love for the holy monastery, by the diligence of their majesties, they soon completed the building of the great stone church which patriarch Nikon founded in honor and glory of Christ our God and in praise of the Russian state. There is no other church like it in size, appearance, beauty, and likeness to the church in Jerusalem.[248]

So, by the will of our God and great Savior, and by the prayers of the builder and founder of the holy monastery, his holiness patriarch Nikon, with the help and good will of the great sovereigns, *tsars* and grand princes, and noble *tsarevnas* Tatiana Mikhailovna and Sofiia Alekseevna, this holy great church was completed.

Her highness, noble *tsarevna* Tatiana Mikhailovna prepared everything that was necessary for the consecration [of the church] from her possessions. She donated gold and silver vessels, decorated a precious Holy Gospel, embroidered priceless paten and chalice veils (*vozdukh*)[i] for the Eucharistic offerings with her own hands, and arranged for the large carved iconostasis of exquisite workmanship, all gilded and covered with lacquer to [enhance its luster]. On her orders, icons of local saints and altar stand (*analoi*) icons adorned with gold, pearls, and precious stones were made for the iconostasis.

The [pious *tsarevna*] generously donated liturgical vestments, albs, liturgical cuffs, stoles, and sashes (*poias*) made of valuable fabrics, and books and utensils for the church and the altar. And she also donated money from her coffers to complete God's church.[249]

---

[i] The printed Iverskii version adds "gold, and precious gold and silver crosses" to this phrase.

Almighty God, Creator and Source of everything, arranged everything according to the wish and good intentions of pious *tsarevna* and grand princess Tatiana Mikhailovna, whose holy soul aspired incessantly to see the holy church completed. And so God, our Lord, completed and consecrated the church by the power the most holy and life-creating spirit acting through the shepherd of all Russia, great hierarch, his holiness Ioakim, patriarch of Moscow and all Russia.

During the consecration [on January 18, 1685], the clergy was represented by Varsonofii, metropolitan of Sar and Don,[250] Gavriil, archbishop of Vologda, Afanasii, archbishop of Kholmogory,[251] archimandrites, priests, deacons and many other clergy of different ranks. [252]

His majesty, the most pious great sovereign Ioann Alekseevich, the *tsar* and grand prince of Great, and White, and Little Russias, and grand princesses Tatiana Mikhailovna and Sofiia Alekseevna, and the other pious *tsarinas* and noble *tsarevnas* deigned to be at the consecration of the church together with the dignitaries from the Council and laymen of various ranks.[253]

The consecration of the holy and great church, which was built in the likeness of the Jerusalem church in the Resurrection Monastery called New Jerusalem founded by his holiness Nikon, patriarch of Moscow and all Russia, was on the eighteenth day of January 7193 from the creation of the world (1687 sic!),[254] on the day commemorating our holy fathers, miracle-workers Athanasius and Cyril, archbishops of Alexandria.

During the reign of the most pious great sovereigns Ioann Alekseevich and Piotr Alekseevich, *tsars* and grand princes of all Great, White, and Little Russia, Nikifor served as the archimandrite of the Resurrection Monastery and Sergii Turchaninov as the abbot of its hermitage; and they guided the monastery, attending to all its needs.[255] They diligently labored to complete the great holy church. It was elder Sergii who knew the skill of bell casting as no one else and who cast all the bells, except one big one, but he did help with its casting, working together with a master assigned to the treasurer, monastic priest Varlaam, who, as I mentioned earlier, shared exile with his holiness patriarch Nikon in the Ferapontov Monastery.[256] The monastery then had no less than two hundred brothers, and if one counts all the smaller monasteries assigned to it, no less then four hundred.

And so in 7186 (1678), the great sovereigns, pious *tsars* and grand princes of all Russia, kindly assigned 2,097 households possessed by smaller monasteries and their surroundings to the [Resurrection] Monastery. They also assigned salt mines in Perm' on the Kama River, the rights to fish in the White Sea and on the River Panoi and the rights to hunt deer, wolf, fox, and other fur animals in the tundra. [257]

And so since the time when God, our Lord, looked down on the holy monastery in His mercy and opened the heart and mind of Fedor Alekseevich, the pious *tsar* of Russia shining in piety, and Who, after his departure from earthly life, opened the eyes of his brothers, the pious sovereigns Ioann Alekseevich and Piotr Alekseevich, *tsars* and grand princes of all Great, White, and Little Russias, and pious *tsarinas* and noble *tsarevnas* and grand princesses Tatiana Mikhailovna and Sofiia Alekseevna, the monastery continues to grow. Upon their good intent and faith in God, our Lord, and thanks to their majesties' generosity, the monastery is not lacking in anything and the sovereigns frequently grace it with their visits.[258]

CR

A pious man and ardent follower of God and his spiritual shepherd and father, his holiness Nikon, patriarch of Moscow and all Russia, diligently labored over this tale. He who knows will understand the name of the author of this story. His name has five letters, amongst them three vowels, one consonant and one hard sign; the name has four syllables and contains the number 131. His patronymic consists of eleven letters: five consonants, four vowels, one soft sign, and one hard sign making four syllables and containing the number 297.

In another book,[259] his patronymic is given as thirteen letters, six consonants, four vowels, two soft signs, and one hard sign, making four syllables and the number 393.

His last name consists of eight letters, four consonants, three vowels, and one hard sign, making up three syllables and the number 563. Together, the name, patronymic, and the last name add up to 991.

[The author] is a clergyman well known to his holiness patriarch Nikon because he was raised by his holiness the patriarch from childhood and grew up near him. During the exile of the blessed and at the time when the holy synod convened, this clergyman endured much harm; he was imprisoned in Moscow for three years and then exiled to Novgorod the Great[i] where he spent ten years. Upon the request of her highness, the great sovereign Tatiana Mikhailovna, *tsarevna* and grand princess, he was released from Novgorod and brought to Moscow during the reign of the pious *tsar* of all Russia, Fedor Alekseevich. This pious man had great faith in God, our Lord, and in the Resurrection Monastery. He took great care to complete the roof of the great church and petitioned to the noble *tsarevna* and grand princess Tatiana Mikhailovna to grant all that was necessary to complete and consecrate the church. This was possible because this man enjoyed the grace of her highness more than others of the same rank and served her noble highness, the sovereign and grand princess Tatiana Mikhailovna. He cared tirelessly about all the monastery's needs because he had the intention of being buried near his mentor, in the holy Resurrection Monastery after his life would end.

This pious man wrote this tale about the birth, upbringing, and entire life of his holiness patriarch Nikon, about the founding of the Resurrection Monastery and its great church, how they were founded and completed, and about the demise and burial of his holiness the patriarch. He described all the events from the very beginning and in great detail, witnessing some of what he has written and hearing some from his holiness and the rest from the brothers living with his holiness the patriarch who told [the author] about the life of his holiness in exile, where he endured calamities and deprivation until his death.

---

[i] In the printed Iverskii version the author adds another phrase here: "his hometown because he was born there."

All this he has written to glorify and honor the holy name of God and for the pleasure of readers and listeners so that the future brothers of the Resurrection Monastery, also called New Jerusalem, and the entire Christian fold would learn about these events and so that the name of his holiness Nikon, patriarch of Moscow and all Russia, and the founder of the monastery, would be remembered to the end of the world. Amen.

Ioann Kornil'ev Ripatov.
131   297   563[260]

Annotations to the Account

1. See also S. V. Lobachev, "K voprosu o rannei biografii patriarkha Nikona," in *Srednevekovaia Rus'* (St. Petersburg, 1995), 52–69.

2. Makarii Zheltovodskii Monastery of the Trinity, also commonly referred to in the *Account* as Makarii's monastery in Koliazin and monastery of the reverend Makarii Zheltovodskii in Koliazin, was founded in 1435 by the reverend Makarii Zheltovodskii on the left bank of the Volga River near Nizhnii Novgorod. Lake Zheltoe, located near the monastery, was a site of Makarii's reputed baptisms of pagans and Muslim Tartars. Situated on the main route of Tartar invasions, the monastery was frequently destroyed, but subsequently restored and, in 1663–1667, fortified with a thick stone wall. The monastery enclosed six stone churches and was a site of an important trading fair. Nikon was among its inhabitants circa the 1620s. See A. Ratshin, *Polnoe sobranie istoricheskikh svedenii o vsekh byvshikh v drevnosti i nyne sushchestvuiushchikh monastyriakh i primechatel'nykh tserkvakh v Rossii* [Moscow, 1852] (reprint Moscow, 2000), 327–328; and Lobachev, *Patriarkh Nikon*, 56.

3. The friendliness between the boys and the Tartar is not perhaps surprising, given the history of the monastery and the frequent interaction between its founder and the Muslims he baptized.

4. Moscow's Alekseevskii Convent was founded circa 1360, near the modern day Ostozhenka Street; it was subsequently transferred to the area where the Cathedral of Christ the Savior stands today. In 1837, to clear the land for the new cathedral, the convent was transferred again to Krasnoe Selo (present day central Moscow). The convent housed several aristocratic nuns and was a burial place for many noble families. Nikon's wife was buried there as well. See Ratshin, 238–240.

5. On Eleazar, see S. K. Sevast'ianova, *Prepodobnyi Eleazar, osnovatel' Sviato-Troitskogo Anzerskogo skita* (St. Petersburg, 2001). For a useful discussion on Nikon's relationship with Eleazar, see G. P. Gunn, "Patriarkh Nikon i Eleazar Anzerskii," in A. M. Panchenko, ed., *Drevnerusskaia knizhnost' po mater'ialam Pushkinskogo Doma* (Leningrad, 1985), 230–242.

6. The Solovetskii Monastery, located on islands in the White Sea, was established in the fifteenth century. In 1667, the brethren of the Solovetskii Monastery, then Russia's second largest, refused to accept the new Nikonian books precipitating a bloody and protracted conflict. In 1676, after almost ten years of intermittent siege, the monastery was captured by the royal forces led by prince Meshcheriakov. The revolt was immortalized in Simeon Denisov's *Istoriia o ottsakh i stradal'tsakh solovetskikh* (1710s). See N. V. Ponyrko and E. M. Iukhimenko, eds., *Simeon Denisov's Istoriia o ottsakh i stradal'tsakh*

solovetskikh (Moscow, 2002), 39–40. Historically, the monastery also served as a place of exile for both aristocrats and clergymen. On the history of the Solovetskii Monastery, see R. R. Robson, *Solovki: The Story of Russia Told Through Its Most Remarkable Islands* (New Haven, 2004); G. Michels, "The Solovki Uprising: Religion and Revolt in Modern Russia," *The Russian Review* 51, No. 2 (1992): 1–15; and Ratshin, 3–8.

Within the monastery was the Trinity Hermitage referenced in the *Account*. Located on the Isle of Anzer, the hermitage was founded in 1628 by the reverend Eleazar whose relics are deposited there. See Ratshin, 7. The founding and early history of the hermitage are detailed in Eleazar's *Zhitie*. See *Zhitie i chudesa prepodobnago ottsa nashego Eleazara chudotvortsa, nachal'nika Anzerskago skita. Sobrano ot mnogikh i vernykh skazatelei i spisano vkratse.* This work was published in *Pravoslavnyi sobesednik* (January 1860): 108–120.

7. Old Believer accounts attributed to Eleazar and dating to the early eighteenth century offer a different explanation for the elder's dislike of Nikon. Simeon Denisov's *Istoriia o ottsakh i stradal'tsakh solovetskikh* notes that "when Nikon, patriarch and instigator of innovations, was a novice of his, [Eleazar] prophesized that Russia will suffer a great evil from him. The residents of Anzer, truthful witnesses, told us that the saint [Eleazar] once saw a very big black snake twined around Nikon's neck while he was serving the liturgy (*liturgiia*). And he was very frightened and from that time started to be wroth with him and made him flee." Denisov, 39–40. The Old Believer *Povest' o zhitii i rozhdenii i vospitanii i o konchine Nikona, byvshago patriarkha moskovskago i vseia Rusi, sobrannaia ot mnogikh dostovernykh povestvovatelei, byvshikh vo dni otets nashikh* (early 1730s) [hereafter Old Believer *Account about . . . Nikon*] presented an even more complex version of the same event. After noting that Nikon became Eleazar's pupil, this tale added that the elder, who "had the ability to predict the future and this gift was given to him for true living," foretold that "Nikon will be the man who causes confusion and rebellion in Russia . . . he will confuse the whole country and fill it with misfortunes." Thereafter, Eleazar saw "a very large snake of awful appearance wrapped around his [Nikon's] neck during a church service." This occurrence "was truly witnessed by the people at the Anzer hermitage." A. K. Borozdin, *Protopop Avvakum: ocherk iz istorii umstvennoi zhizni russkago obshchestva v XVII veke* (St. Petersburg, 1900), No. 33, 146.

8. Nikon himself explained his departure from Anzer, shipwreck on the Isle of Kii, and erection of a cross in his *Gramota o Krestnom monastyre* (June 24, 1656). This source is published in archimandrite Lavrentii, *Kratkoe izvestie o Krestnom onezhskom arkhangel'skoi eparkhii monastyre* (Moscow, 1805), 1–22. The relevant passage reads: "In the year 1639, we, being a monastic priest (*ieromonakh*), sailed at sea from the Anzer hermitage and during a great maritime storm almost drowned. But believing in the power of God's divine life-giving cross, we received salvation near the mouth of the Onega River. Having landed on the Isle of Kii, we gave glory to Jesus Christ our Lord crucified on the cross for saving us. Being then on the same island, I erected a holy and life-giving cross at the same place in memory of my rescue." Nikon, *Gramota o Krestnom monastyre*, 2. Nikon's account was likewise presented in *Gramota tsaria Alekseia Mikhailovicha o postroenii Krestnogo monastyria* (Moscow, June 13, 1656). This source is also published in Lavrentii, *Kratkoe izvestie*, 23; *Akty Istoricheskie, sobrannye i izdannye Arheograficheskoiu komissieiu* (*AI*), Vol. 4 (St. Petersburg, 1848), No. 102, 244–245; and *Krestnyi monastyr' osnovannyi patriarkhom Nikonom. Istoricheskii ocherk* (St. Petersburg, 1884), 13–14.

9. Aleksei Mikhailovich's original grant is outlined in *Gramota tsaria Alekseia Mikhailovicha*, 24–25.

10. The first record of Nikon being referred to as the abbot of the Kozheezerskii Monastery is found in a decree dated August 13, 1643. See Lobachev, "K voprosu o rannei

biografii," 64; and S. K. Sevast'ianova, *Mater'ialy k 'Letopisi zhizni i literaturnoi deiatel'nosti patriarkha Nikona'* (St. Petersburg, 2003), 12.

11. For a brief historiographical treatment of Nikon's motives for visiting Moscow, see S. V. Lobachev, *Patriarkh Nikon*, 66.

12. On Iosif I, the fifth patriarch of Moscow (1642–1652), see Lebedev, 27–31.

13. The New Savior Monastery, one of the most important Russian monasteries in Nikon's day, was originally founded in the thirteenth century as the Savior Monastery. After being relocated from its initial site to the present-day location on the bank of the Moscow River (hence the new name) in the fifteenth century, it became a "royal" monastery, serving as a burial place for the Romanov dynasty. As late as the reign of empress Elizabeth (1741–1772), the monastery was referred to in royal decrees as a "court," "royal," and "private" monastery. Until the early eighteenth century, the monastery also contained royal chambers. The New Savior Monastery was nearly destroyed during the Time of Troubles and Nikon, serving as its archimandrite almost fifty years later, was responsible for the rebuilding and adornment of the monastery's main sanctuary, the Cathedral of Transfiguration (re-consecrated on September 19, 1647). See Ratshin, 188–194.

14. Note that Shusherin refers to patriarch Iosif as "great sovereign." This form of address as practiced by Nikon when he was the patriarch became a highly contentious issue and was brought up as one of the charges against him at the council of the holy synod of 1666–1667 that deposed Nikon. See Ligarides, 162–163.

15. Iosif, patriarch of Moscow, and Paisius, patriarch of Jerusalem, consecrated Nikon on March 9, 1649. See *Polnoe sobranie rossiiskikh letopisei* (*PSRL*), Vol. 3 (St. Petersburg, 1841), 190. Paisius wrote about Nikon's consecration in a letter to the *tsar* dated March 14, 1649. See *Sobranie gosudarstvennykh gramot i dogovorov* (*SGGD*), Vol. 3 (Moscow, 1822), No. 135, 447–449. Sevast'ianova dates Nikon's consecration to March 11, 1649. See Sevast'ianova, *Mater'ialy*, 19.

16. This monastery, located approximately eleven kilometers from Novgorod the Great, on the right bank of the River Volkhov, was founded at the end of the twelfth century. It was patronized by Novgorodian and Muscovite royalty and counted several Russian saints, including its founder Varlaam, among its inhabitants. In 1651, Nikon founded a printing house there. The famous court poet G. R. Derzhavin (1744–1816) is buried in the monastery. See Ratshin, 337–339.

17. The Old Believer *Povest' o zhitii i rozhdenii* co–opted and contested Shusherin's account of Nikon's encounter with Affonii. According to the tale, patriarch Iosif made Nikon the metropolitan of Novgorod, "because of the many sins of the people. And he, false monk, led to the death of Christian people because before his elevation he was anointed with Tatar vomit." After becoming metropolitan, "this sly fox" visited Affonii, "the very epitome of virtue and humbleness," and asked to be blessed. Affonii, who was partially blind, asked "who are you and where are you from?" Nikon responded: "I am metropolitan Nikon." Affonii, who also "had the gift of prediction," perceived that Nikon would "cause very great damage to the Orthodox people," and said: "it is so strange that the time has come when Nikon is becoming metropolitan. This is because the Lord's will has left us." Borozdin, No. 33, 148.

18. According to a decree of *tsar* Aleksei Mikhailovich dated February 6, 1651, Nikon was granted the right to judge all clerics, monastery workers and peasants living within his tithe in all criminal and administrative matters except thievery, robbery, and murder. It reads: "From the *tsar* and grand prince of all Russia Aleksei Mikhailovich to our patrimony Novgorod the Great and to our God-entreater Nikon, metropolitan of Novgorod and Velikie Luki. We deigned that in Novgorod the Great and in Velikie Luki, in the monasteries and districts of your tithe, all archimandrites, abbots, and brethren of the

monasteries, archpriests, and priests, and deacons of the cathedrals, and priests, and deacons, and members of the clergy of all parish and diocese churches, the monastery laborers, and peasants should be judged in all criminal and administrative matters by you, our
God-entreater, except in the matters of robbery, and thievery, and murder; and our *boyar,*
governor and military commander (*voevoda*), prince Yurii Petrovich Buinosov Rostovskii
and the chancellery secretary (*d'iak*) Isak Kudrin and all our future *boyars,* governors,
military commanders, and deacons who would be sent on our edict to Novgorod the
Great and the governors and military commanders of Velikie Luki should not judge archimandrites, and abbots, and brethren of the monasteries, and archpriests, and priests,
and deacons, and members of the clergy, and the monastery laborers, and peasants in
criminal and administrative matters and should not interfere with yours, our God-
entreater's, judgments in all administrative and criminal matters, except thievery, and
robbery, and murder, and about this we sent a decree to our *boyar,* governor and military
commander, prince Yurii Petrovich Buinosov Rostovskii and to the chancellery secretary
Isak Kudrin . . . You, our God-entreater, should judge all of them [white and black clergy
as well as laborers and peasants assigned to the monasteries] in all administrative and
criminal matters, and order your chancellery secretaries to judge them based on your, our
God-entreater's, judgment." *Dopolnenie k aktam istoricheskim, sobrannym i izdannym
Arkheograficheskoi komissiei* (*DAI*), Vol. 4 (St. Petersburg, 1848), No. 50, 70.

19. By this innocent reference, Shusherin introduces another, albeit less ideologically-
driven innovation that Nikon undertook in the course of his reforms. After adopting the
Byzantine form of Christianity, Russia also inherited its hymnology. The octophonic
znamennyi chant (*raspev*), which used special Russian notations denoting one, two, or
half notes, was the original type of music for the Russian Orthodox Church. Connected to
the Byzantine calendar, which subdivided the year into several eight-week periods, *znamennyi* chant also used eight tones, one for each week in a cycle. Often *znamennyi* chant
was sung in a polyphonic manner. As time passed however, the special *znamennyi* notations as well as polyphonic singing fell out of fashion. The square notations and Kievan
chants, often seen as simplified *znamennyi* chants, were introduced and by the mid-
seventeenth century supplanted *znamennyi* chants, especially given "unification" of Russia and Ukraine around this time. Kievan chants had clearly articulated major or minor
keys and were characterized by greater simplicity, shorter length, and increased repetition
of certain phrases of the text. Greek chants gained popularity during the reign of Aleksei
Mikhailovich when Greek deacon Meletius was invited to teach the *tsar's* and the patriarch's choirs the intricacies of new chanting. Patriarch Nikon supported the use of both
Kievan and Greek chants in liturgical services as part of his greater Greecophilia. Old
Believers eventually chose *znamennyi* chant over its later competitors and preserved its
unique notations, also known as *kruki*. On the history of Russian chants, see V. M. Metallov, *Ocherk istorii pravoslavnago tserkovnago peniia v Rossii* (Moscow, 1896).

20. On Nikon's restoration of Novgorodian churches, see Lobachev, *Patriarch Nikon,*
88–89.

21. Lobachev gives examples of Nikon's building projects funded by the tsar, including the construction and repair of churches, monastery lodges, town walls and towers in
Novgorod. See Lobachev, *Patriarkh Nikon,* 88–89.

22. Nikon refused to accept polyphonic *khomovoe* singing and later abolished the practice. See Paul Meyendorff, *Russia, Ritual, and Reform* (Crestwood, 1991), 85–86. Indeed
Nikon represented a broader consensus on the issue. On February 11, 1649, the holy
synod, on the instigation of patriarch Iosif, upheld the old polyphonic singing, but a number of key reformers, including Nikon, Stefan Vonifat'ev, the *tsar's* spiritual father, and
Ioann Neronov, openly defied it by refusing to sign the council's resolution. See Lobachev, *Patriarkh Nikon,* 85–86.

23. The uprising in Novgorod took place on March 15–April 16, 1650. For classic historical treatment of the revolt, see S. M. Solov'ev, Vol. 10, 650–679; and metropolitan Makarii (Bulgakov), *Istoriia Russkoi tserkvi* (St. Petersburg, 1882), Vol. 11, 164–173. For a Soviet analysis of these events, see M. N. Tikhomirov, "Novgorodskoe vosstanie 1650 goda," *Istoricheskie zapiski* No. 7 (1940): 91–114; and idem., "Dokumenty o Novgorodskom vosstanii 1650 g.," in M. N. Tikhomirov, ed., *Novgorod. K stoletiiu goroda* (Moscow, 1964), 286–296. For more current scholarship, see Lobachev, *Patriarkh Nikon*, 90–95.

24. His real name was Trofim Volk. See Solov'ev, Vol. 10, 650. The Russian word "volk" means "wolf" in English. Shusherin may be playing on the interesting contrast between Nikon as a good shepherd and the miscreant wolf.

25. Boris Ivanovich Morozov (1590–1661), Aleksei Mikhailovich's tutor and later brother-in-law, was an important statesman and diplomat who supported Western culture and lifestyle, especially German ones. See V.O. Kliuchevsky, *A Course in Russian History: Seventeenth Century*, trans. Natalie Duddington (Chicago, 1967), 281, 284, 312.

26. These events are also recorded in the letter sent by Nikon and F. A. Khilkov to Aleksei Mikhailovich dated March 16, 1650. This document is published as "Otpiska mitropolita Nikona, voevody F. A. Khilkova, i d'iaka V. Safonova o vosstanii v Novgorode," in Tikhomirov, *Dokumenty*, 286–287.

27. Nikon recounted the events that transpired on March 17 and 19, 1650 in a letter written to *tsar* Aleksei Mikhailovich and the royal family dated March 19, 1650. The missive reached the *tsar* on April 13, 1650. It reads:

"To the sovereign, *tsar* and grand prince of all Russia, Aleksei Mikhailovich and her majesty the pious *tsarina* and grand princess Mariia Il'inichna, and . . . princess Irina Mikhailovna, and . . . princess Anna Mikhailovna, and . . . princess Tatiana Mikhailovna, and . . . princess Evdokiia Alekseevna, your majesties' devout God-entreater, sinful Nikon, metropolitan of Novgorod, praises God and humbly petitions.

Your majesty, in the year 7158 [1650], because of our sins, in your lands in Novgorod the Great, on March 15, there occurred a great upheaval among various ranks of people. And I, your God-entreater, talked to them several times and they did not listen, and why the upheaval started both I, your God-entreater, and the lord-in-waiting (*okol'nichii*) and governor, prince Fedor Andreevich wrote to your majesty many times before.

And they took from my, your God-entreater's, guard a known thief, the former official of the [metropolitan's residence at] St. Sophia, Ivashka Zheglov and made him their leader and he, by his evil advice, teaches them various wrong things and, with unlawful intent, he wanted to make all Orthodox Christians take a cross-kissing oath for an unknown purpose.

And I, your God-entreater, on the seventeenth of March, called upon all ecclesiastical dignitaries and, praying to God to grant your majesties health for many years, put a curse on him, Ivashka, the traitor to your majesties . . . And now they wrote among themselves an unlawful statement that they will protect each other and that in their thievery they will not surrender anyone to your majesty and they ordered the officials and the clergy, and all other ranks to sign that unlawful statement under a threat of beating. And those who did not sign, those they wanted to beat and whip. . . .

On the nineteenth of March, around two in the afternoon, Ivashka Zheglov's accomplice, Gavrila Nesterov, a retired warden (*pristav*) who was cursed, came to the St. Sophia stead, as if wishing to repent, and I ordered to hold him while I attended the liturgy and, according to the tradition of the apostles and the holy fathers, I wanted to absolve him from the curse and to recite the absolution prayers. And at the same hour the traitor to your *tsar's* majesty, Ivashka Zheglov ordered to sound the alarm bell on the trading side [of the city]. And having assembled many people, he sent them to me, your

God-entreater, at the St. Sophia stead to take that warden. And they started to force them-selves upon the porch and started to destroy the doors of the church dedicated to the Birth of Christ and they destroyed the gates of the fiscal office.

And I, your God-entreater, came to them and started talking to them. And they grabbed me . . . and at that time started to insult me with various offensive words and hit me on the chest with a log and hurt my chest and, holding stones in their hands, they beat me with stones and fists on my sides.

And they beat the treasurer of St. Sophia, elder Nikandr, and my junior *boyars* who stood behind me. And they took me to the traitor to your *tsar's* majesty Ivashka Zheglov.

And as we reached the church, I wanted to enter through the doors, but they did not al-low me to go to the church at that time and Iakov, the cathedral deacon, opened the doors, but they beat him as well. And they carried me past the front doors to the town hall, but as we reached the golden gates, exhausted from their beating, I asked to sit down on the bench in front of the church. And I started asking them to release me with crosses to the Church of the Holy Sign [*Znamenskaia*], saying that I, the sinful, was preparing to serve the holy liturgy, and they almost agreed.

And I, your God-entreater, ordered to ring one of the church bells and together with the cathedral clergy and a few other priests, in great pain, barely reached the Church of the Holy Sign and there, standing and sitting, I conducted the holy liturgy in great haste and pain and dragged myself back into a sleigh in great pain.

And now I lie near the end of my life and cough up blood, and my abdomen is swollen, and, anticipating imminent death, I received the rites of extreme unction with holy oils. But I do not know for how long my life will continue, or will I be alive.

Whether or not it will be better, grant me, your devout God-entreater, your forgiveness and order me to receive a schema (*skhima*), but, if I will not soon receive your majesty's decree and I am not better, I wish to receive a schema without your majesty's order."

This document is published as "Otpiska novgorodskogo mitropolita Nikona tsariu i tsarskoi sem'e" (posle 18 marta 1650 g.)," in Tikhomirov, *Dokumenty*, No. 5, 290–291. See also Solov'ev, Vol. 10, 653–654.

Nikon later recounted the beating in a letter to the *tsar* written nearly twenty years later. See "Pis'mo patriarkha Nikona tsariu Alekseiu Mikhailovichu (9 maia–20 iulia 1667 g.)," published in S. K. Sevast'ianova, "Pis'ma patriarkha Nikona tsariu Alekseiu Mikhailovichu iz Ferapontova monastyria v 1667 g.," in E. M. Iukhimenko, ed., *Patriarkh Nikon i ego vremia* (Moscow, 2004), 247–276.

28. The petition sent to Aleksei Mikhailovich by the Novgorodians on March 22–25, 1650 painted a different picture of the rebels' treatment of Nikon. According to this ac-count, "Nikon the metropolitan went with crosses to the miracle-working icon in the Church of the Holy Sign on Il'in Street and at the Church of the Holy Sign, for his great wrath and the curse that he put on all of us Orthodox Christians of Novgorod the Great, on the day of your majesty's guardian angel [Aleksei Man of God] . . . by the grace of God and the prayer of the holiest Mother of God, in the presence of all the people, Nikon the metropolitan was revealed by the power of God, struck, and smashed to pieces . . . And after that, your majesty, Nikon the metropolitan, together with the lord-in-waiting, decided to write to you, oh sovereign, as if it was us who killed Nikon the metropolitan." This document is published as "Novgorodskaia chelobitnaia" (22–25 marta 1650 g.), in Tikhomirov, *Dokumenty*, 293–296.

29. Shusherin's account is corroborated by "Otpiska mitropolita Nikona," in Tikhomi-rov, *Dokumenty*, 287; and "Pis'mo novgorodskogo voevody kniazia F. A. Khilkova boyarinu Borisu Ivanovichu Morozovu (17 marta 1650)," in Tikhomirov, *Dokumenty*, 288.

The rebels' petition gives a different account of Zheglov's imprisonment and release. "Nikon the metropolitan fettered the warden, his former chancellery courtier, Ioann Zheglov in chains and irons, and . . . carrying him on a sleigh, beat and tortured him inflicting deathly tortures and so he extracted from the prostrated man three rubles. And after that, he imprisoned the said Ioann and kept him under guard and tortured him, the innocent, for a long time." "Novgorodskaia chelobitnaia," in Tikhomirov, *Dokumenty*, 294.

30. Records concerning the interrogation of Mark Zhinevlev, a Novgorodian messenger, conducted on March 22, 1650, corroborate Shusherin's explanation of the situation in Novgorod. See Tikhomirov, *Dokumenty*, 289–290.

31. In mid-May 1650, Nikon wrote to Aleksei Mikhailovich responding to the accusations raised in the rebels' petition to the *tsar*. The missive reads: "The good tax-paying townsmen stayed at my residence and I fed them and gave them drink and, on account of my good care, Ivashka and Ignashka suffered ruin and setbacks in all their bad deeds, and if I did not take care of this, it would become much worse than in Pskov; I constantly prayed to God for you, oh sovereign, and I wrote to you and, hiring people by all possible means, I sent to you a secret letter. And for that, by the slander of Ivashka Zheglov, I was disgraced and maimed; the same Ivashka with accomplices falsely petitioned to you as if I cursed all Novgorodians; but I cursed the thieves and not the good people and because of that revolt ensued; but I cursed on the third day after the revolt. . . . And now all is quiet in Novgorod the Great, and they weep loudly because of their short-lived sin against you. Merciful sovereign, *tsar* and grand prince Aleksei Mikhailovich! Be merciful and loving like God! When they will petition to you about their guilt, forgive; and I, when persuading them, avouched for your mercy and if I did not persuade them, then all of them would be driven to despair for their knavery and would commit even worse crimes; the entire town came to me and not for one day and asked for forgiveness for beating and disgracing me and for falsely petitioning against me." This letter is quoted in Solov'ev, Vol. 10, 662–663.

32. This letter is dated May 19, 1650. It reads: "You, our God-entreater, followed and fulfilled the Lord's commandments, by zealously adhering to the true faith of Christ, the teachings of the holy apostles and holy fathers, the former hierarchs, and the praiseworthy new confessor patriarch Hermogen. And we, the great sovereign, graciously praise you for your zeal and devotion, and suffering; and in the future you should fulfill your oaths to almighty God and be a zealous adherent to good deeds, so that you will continue what you have begun." The source is quoted in Solov'ev, Vol. 10, 663.

33. On May 22, 1650, patriarch Nikon and prince Ioann Khovanskii wrote to the *tsar* describing the aftermath of the Novgorodian uprising. "To the sovereign, *tsar* and grand prince of all Russia, Aleksei Mikhailovich, your devout God-entreater, his eminence Nikon metropolitan of Novgorod and Velikie Luki, prays to God and, with your servant Ivashka Khovanskii, humbly petitions. I, Ivashka, your servant, oh sovereign, wrote to you, oh sovereign, that your majesty's decree was sent to me, your servant: I, your servant, found the thieves and instigators whose names I ordered to write down; people of other various ranks surrendered these thieves and instigators to me, your servant, to be put in prison until your majesty's edict. And from the twenty-fourth of April to the seventh of May, oh sovereign, we located all these thieves and instigators, including Ivashka Zheglov with seven accomplices. [W]e found thirty people guilty of various crimes; the said crimes were reported by people of various ranks, and there was a total of one hundred and ninety-five people, and they were released on bail because there was no space in the prison and many other people pleaded guilty in minor crimes. . . . And on the fourteenth of May, oh sovereign, the *strel'tsy* and their commanders from both chancelleries came with their wives and children to the cathedral of St. Sophia to me, your majesty's God-entreater, and petitioned so that you, oh sovereign, would take pity on them and would not order to imprison those *strel'tsy* who were on bail, but to punish them accord-

ing to their crimes, but if all these people were imprisoned, then they and the guilty ones would expect death and execution. But they are ordered to serve your majesty in Pskov and the Pskovians might hear that many people in Novgorod are put in prison and the Pskovians would expect the same. . . . And on the fourteenth of May, oh sovereign, after a conversation I, your God-entreater metropolitan Nikon, and I, your servant Ivashka, hearing from people of various ranks that many people are imprisoned and are expecting execution and in order not to upset Pskovian affairs, we, your God-entreater and your servant, will sentence the thieves guilty of minor crimes, so they will be released on bail, and others will be imprisoned until the Pskovian affairs are settled and those who pleaded guilty in minor crimes will be assembled . . . and will be released on bail and we will order the service nobility and the junior *boyars* to guard them strongly at the aforesaid court. And those, oh sovereign, who pleaded guilty in more serious crimes and . . . Ivashka Zheglov with accomplices, those thieves and instigators, we ordered to put in secure prisons." "Otpiska mitropolita Nikona i kniazia Ioanna Khovanskogo tsariu Alekseiu Mikhailovichu o rezul'tatakh rozyska po Novgorodskomu delu (22 maia 1650 g.)," in Lobachev, *Patriarkh Nikon*, 348–349.

34. On the rebellion in Pskov, see Solov'ev, Vol. 10, 665–679.

35. For example, Aleksei Mikhailovich decreed Nikon to serve in Moscow from November 28 to December 6, 1650. See M. N. Tikhomirov, *Novgorodskii khronograf XVII v.* (Moscow, 1979), 389–390.

36. Nikon described this event in his *Rai Myslennyi* (1658). "[A] thought suddenly occurred to me about one place which I happened to see on the way from Novgorod, where I was then a metropolitan, to Moscow; passing Valdai, I saw a great lake and on it, many islands. Looking at the islands of the great lake, I asked the locals about its size, islands, and fisheries. And so it appeared to me that a monastery would be great at such a place suitable for monastic life. But, I did not know whether such a thought was pleasing to God." Nikon, *Rai Myslennyi*, 65.

37. Filipp (Kolychev), metropolitan of Moscow (1507–1568), rose to prominence during the later part of Ivan IV's (the Terrible) reign in the 1560s. Ivan turned to Filipp, his childhood friend and a former warrior, who was at that time the archimandrite of the Solovetskii Monastery, after his relationship with ecclesiastical powers soured over the newly established *oprichnina*. Filipp's two predecessors died under suspicious circumstances. In 1567, Filipp agreed to be metropolitan of Moscow on the condition that he could intercede on behalf of the oppressed. Two years later, during a service at the Moscow Kremlin's Dormition Cathedral, the new metropolitan forbade the *tsar*, who had just completed his latest spree of terror, to venerate the cross and reproached his murderous actions before the entire congregation. Thereafter, the metropolitan was deposed, imprisoned and finally strangled by the chief of the *oprichnina* on November 8, 1568. In 1590, Filipp's remains were translated to the Solovetskii Monastery. Filipp became recognized as a martyr and miracle-worker and was finally canonized in 1636; he is commemorated on December 23.

An important aspect of Filipp's veneration, clearly articulated in the metropolitan's *Zhitie* (1590s), was the acceptance of the church and its hierarchy as the moral guardians of the state. Nikon became acquainted with Filipp's cult and chose the saint as his spiritual paragon in the late 1630s and early 1640s, when he lived as a monk at the Solovetskii Monastery. As patriarch, Nikon promoted Filipp's veneration. In addition to translating his relics from the Solovetskii Monastery to Moscow in 1652, Nikon added St. Filipp to the list of commemorations recited during the Eucharist in the revised *Sluzhebnik* (1655), while eliminating more than a dozen formerly mentioned Russian saints. Nikon's promotion of Filipp was conducted not only ritualistically but concretely with the saint figuring prominently in the patriarch's justification for much of his expansive building

Annotations 117

program. The patriarch repeatedly cited Filipp in successful bids to gain the *tsar's* permission to found new monasteries. All three monasteries which Nikon eventually founded, the Iverskii, the Kii, and the New Jerusalem Resurrection Monasteries, had churches dedicated to Filipp. Nikon even commissioned an icon of Christ the Pankrator with images of himself and Filipp humbled at the Savior's feet. In 1656, this icon was included in the iconostasis of the Golgotha Church in the New Jerusalem Monastery. See G. P. Fedotov, *Sviatoi Filipp mitropolit Moskovskii* [Paris, 1928] (reprint Moscow, 1991); Meyendorff, 142, 148; P. Bushkovitch, *Religion and Society in Russia. The Sixteenth and Seventeenth Centuries* (New York, 1992), 90, 123, and 178; and Robson, *Solovki*, 28–75, passim. On the icon, see G. M. Zelenskaia, "Prizhiznennye izobrazhenia sviateishego patriarkha Nikona," in *Nikonovskie chteniia* (2002), 7–8.

38. Prior to Nikon's departure for the Solovetskii Monastery, Aleksei Mikhailovich composed a letter addressed to the deceased Filipp, begging forgiveness for his predecessor's transgressions against the saint. See "Molebnoe poslanie gosudaria tsaria Alekseia Mikhailovicha k moshcham sviatago mitropolita Filippa, otpravlennoe s Novgorodskim mitropolitom Nikonom i boyarinom kniazem Ioannom Khovanskim, ezdivshimi v Solovetskii monastyr' dlia privezeniia ikh ottuda v Moskvu," in *SGGD*, Vol. 3, No. 147, 471–472.

Other primary sources of Nikon's translation of metropolitan Filipp's relics from the Solovetskii Monastery to Moscow include "Raskhodnaia kniga denezhnoi kazny mitropolita Nikona," in *Vremennik Moskovskago obshchestva istorii i drevnostei Rossiiskikh* (St. Petersburg, 1852) and Nikon's correspondence with *tsar* Aleksei Mikhailovich. Selections from Nikon's communications with the *tsar* are published as "Shest' otpisok k gosudariu tsariu Alekseiu Mikhailovichu ot Novgorodskago mitropolita Nikona i boyarina kniazia Ioanna Khovanskago, posylannykh v Solovetskii monastyr', dlia privezeniia ottuda moshchei sviatago mitropolita Filippa v Moskvu, pisannyia imi na puti iz raznykh mest v iiune i iiule 1652 g.," in *SGGD*, Vol. 3, No 149–154, 474–479; Solov'ev, Vol. 10, 686–688; and "Otpiski novgorodskogo mitropolita Nikona i kniazia I. N. Khovanskogo tsariu Alekseiu Mikhailovichu vo vremia pokhoda v Solovetskii monastyr' za moshchami sviatogo mitropolita Filippa," in Lobachev, *Patriarkh Nikon*, 350–361. Nikon also commented on his trip to the Solovetskii Monastery in his *Letter to Dionysius, Patriarch of Constantinople* (December 1665). According to the missive, Nikon "was before metropolitan of Great Novgorod, the first metropolitan see of Great Russia, when it pleased God to take to himself the most holy Iosif, patriarch of Moscow and all Russia. After his decease on my arrival at Moscow—for I had been sent by the *tsar's* Council, with the blessing of our father of blessed memory the most holy patriarch Iosif, to the Solovetskii Monastery for the relics of the holy martyr, Filipp, sometime metropolitan of Moscow and all Russia, whom the *tsar* Ivan IV Vasil'evich persecuted unrighteously for his righteousness, the particulars of which for brevity I omit to relate." Nikon, "Letter to Dionysius," 381.

Paul of Aleppo explained that "Nikon was sent by the *tsar* to bring the body of St. Filipp, the celebrated metropolitan of Moscow; the reason of which was that this saint, from the time of his martyrdom [1568] and of his burial in the Solovetskii Monastery, had not worked miracles till now, when he wrought many. They sent therefore to fetch his body to Moscow, as he had appeared several times to the *tsar* in his sleep, saying, 'I have been long enough at a distance from the tombs of my brethren the metropolitans; send and fetch my body, and place me with them.' Thus urged, the *tsar* sent, in company with the metropolitan Nikon, a great number of archons, who brought his body, having been two whole years on the journey." Paul of Aleppo, 110. Another primary source gives the following description: "On the eleventh day of March, the sovereign, *tsar* and grand prince of all Russia, Aleksei Mikhailovich made an entrance to the Cathedral of the

Dormition of the Holiest Mother of God to partake in the prayer service (*moleben*) and to send Nikon, metropolitan of Novgorod, to fetch the relics of metropolitan Filipp, the miracle-worker from the Solovetskii Monastery." *Vykhody gosudarei tsarei i velikikh kniazei, Mikhaila Feodorovicha, Alekseia Mikhailovicha, Feodora Alekseevicha, vseia Rossii samoderzhtsev*, Bk. 18, P. M. Stroev, ed. (Moscow, 1844), 255. See also *PSRL*, Vol. 3, 190. For a specialized study of Nikon's retrieval of Filipp's relics, see P. F. Ni-kolaevskii, *Puteshestvie Novgorodskago mitropolita Nikona v Solovetskii monastyr' za moshchami sviatitelia Filippa* (St. Petersburg, 1885). See also Fedotov, 97–102.

39. For the full list of those commissioned, and later rewarded by the *tsar* for the trans-lation of Filipp's relics from the Solovetskii Monastery to Moscow, see *Akty Mosk-ovskago gosudarstva, izdannye Imperatorskoiu Akademiei Nauk*, Vol. 2, N. A. Popov, ed. (St. Petersburg, 1894), No. 471, 292.

40. Nikon and prince Khovanskii described the shipwreck in two letters written to Aleksei Mikhailovich in mid-May 1651. In the first message, the metropolitan and the prince recounted: "In the third hour of night, we left the Karelian monastery and being eighty *versts* from the Solovetskii Monastery, sailed quietly and comfortably; and on the fifteenth day of May, in the fourth hour of night, a sea wind, called the deep wind, started and so great was its force that it not only created a storm at sea, but also destroyed the foundation of the churches on the hills and uprooted trees; we stood anchored at sea until the sixteenth and at the end of the third hour of daylight, the anchors could no longer hold us because of the strong storm and great waves, the sails were torn and anchors de-stroyed; and having been carried on the waves in great discomfort as if on big mountains we all were driven to despair and became violently sick from being tossed by waves, worse than anyone could remember. And I, your devout God-entreater, was hit and flooded by waves in the stern storeroom and was barely alive. And the boat was tossed into the mouth of the Pudoga River. And the boat of your servant Ivashka was tossed onto the shore of the Karelian monastery of St. Nicholas the miracle-worker; and the other boat of your God-entreater with the chancellery secretaries and supplies and the boat of your servant with supplies and people and [another] boat . . . were tossed ashore near the mouth of the Pudoga River . . . and these boats were destroyed on the shore . . . And the chancellery secretary Gavrila Leont'ev and service nobleman (*dvorianin*) Ioann Pustynnikov are unheard from for twenty-two days . . . We expect that they have indeed drowned. And together with the chancellery secretary was your majesty's treasury, a thousand rubles, [intended] as charity for the brethren [of the Solovetskii Monastery]." Quoted in Nikolaevskii, *Puteshestvie*, 37–38.

In the second letter, received in Moscow on June 14, 1651, Nikon clarified that: "[We] found out that indeed the boat of the chancellery secretary Leont'ev was destroyed, it drifts at sea split in half and all the people drowned and your majesty's treasury was lost. And on the boat of the chancellery secretary was his son Piotr and Ioann Pustynnikov and many pilgrims of various ranks and his servants, all together sixty-nine people; and the supplies from that boat have been tossed on the summer shore; but the people have not been tossed ashore to this day." Quoted in Nikolaevskii, *Puteshestvie*, 39.

41. Nikon and prince Khovanskii described the honors shown to Filipp's relics by those who came in contact with the saint, in a letter to Aleksei Mikhailovich dated late June 1651. "On June, I, your God-entreater [Nikon], sailed down from the sea by the Onega River with the relics of St. Filipp the metropolitan and came to Kargapol' on the twentieth of June, at the first hour of the night. And the abbots, brethren, and priests, and deacons, and all the church clergy of Kargapol', and all the Orthodox peasants, men, and women with infants met the relics of St. Filipp the metropolitan with great honor, with crosses and icons, and candles, and incensories (*kadilo*), one *verst* from the town, and carried the relics of St. Filipp the metropolitan from the vessel and put them in the Cathe-

dral of the Nativity of our Lord, God and Savior Jesus Christ, and at that time I, your devout God-entreater, conducted a prayer service (*moleben*)." *SGDD,* Pt. 3, No. 150, 476.

42. Published primary sources offer extremely detailed and highly graphic accounts of the last days of patriarch Iosif's life and the preparations for his burial. Among the unpleasant and sad events, the *tsar* nonetheless found words of admiration, love, and respect for Nikon. "Chosen and strong standing shepherd and preceptor of our souls and bodies, the merciful, meek, pious, kind, but above all zealot and confidant of Christ, and overseer of the sheep of the Word . . . Oh mighty warrior and martyr for the heavenly King. Oh my beloved favorite and friend, holy father! Pray for me, the sinful, so that I may not be covered by the dark depths of my sins, for the power of your holy prayers; and trusting your most immaculate and kind and holy life, I write to you who brightly shines among the hierarchs, as the sun shining for the entire universe, so you are beaming to our entire tsardom by your good temper and your good deeds, to the great sovereign and our devout God-entreater, his most radiant eminence Nikon, metropolitan of Novgorod and Velikie Luki, our personal friend in soul and body. We are asking about your salvation, how does God our spiritual Light, protect you; and about us you already know, and we, by the grace of God and by the blessing of your eminence, who is called the true Christian *tsar* but who, because of my bad and abominable deeds, is not worthy of being a dog, not to say the *tsar* . . . And let it be known to you, great metropolitan, that for the sins of the entire Orthodox Christendom, but above all, for my accursed sins, God our Creator, deigned to take from this world our father and shepherd the great sovereign Iosif, patriarch of Moscow and all Russia, and deigned to deliver him in the places where Abraham, and Isaac, and Jacob live, and you, our father, should know about this; and our mother, the holy catholic and apostolic church (*sviataia, sobornaia i apostol'skaia tserkov'*) is a widow, and begs for her groom; and if one enters it and looks around, she, our mother, is like a dove in the desert without friends: so she is without her groom and she is in sorrow: and everything changed, not only in the churches, but in the entire tsardom, the spiritual affairs cannot be judged and children live badly without a shepherd. . . . And so, for God's sake, return to us soon to select a *theognostus* [patriarch], without you we will not start anything. And next, I ask for your blessing and forgiveness together with the entire tsardom; and about this, I diligently petition. Written in Moscow in May 7160 [1652], signed by the servant of God, *tsar* Aleksei of all Russia in his own hand." *DAI,* Vol. 4, No. 57, 76–77.

43. Paul of Aleppo offered a contemporary account of this encounter: "On the arrival of the body of St. Filipp, the *tsar*, the patriarch [Macarius of Antioch], the great officers of the state, together with the bishops, all the heads of convents, the clergy, and the whole population of the city went out to meet it, with candles, banners, and icons, and in their most splendid robes; and, as we were told by everyone, the saint performed a number of miracles—opening the eyes of the blind, raising the sick from their chairs and couches, and curing demoniacs—before they carried him into the cathedral and placed him in a silver gilt shrine, near the fifth door, on the south side of the sanctuary, where he still works many miracles." Aleppo, 111. See also *Vykhody gosudarei tsarei,* 260–261.

44. For a description of the *tsar's* donations to Nikon, see Nikolaevskii, *Puteshestvie,* 48.

45. Aleksei Mikhailovich clearly expressed these sentiments in a letter to Nikon dated May 25, 1652 in which he described the demise of Affonii, former metropolitan of Novgorod the Great whom Nikon had succeeded in 1649. In this letter, the *tsar* also lavished him with praise. "From the *tsar* and grand prince of all Russia Aleksei Mikhailovich to the great shinning sun, our most radiant God-entreater, his eminence Nikon, metropolitan of Novgorod and Velikie Luki, a bow from us the earthly *tsar*. Rejoice, oh great hierarch, working with all possible virtues! How does God show mercy to you, great metropolitan?

And I, sinful, am in good health by your prayers to God. Let it be known to you that the former metropolitan of Novgorod Affonii left us during the sixth week of great Lent, on Tuesday . . . would you please, great metropolitan, pray so that the Lord God will increase the years of my daughter's life, she is very fond of you . . . also do pray for my wife, so that she, for the power of your prayers, be blessed by God with child; for the sake of God, pray for her. . . . You, the great sovereign, asked us whether we should sing like that or differently, and how they sing for you, the metropolitan? So write about this to us. And also respond, oh great metropolitan, for the Lord's sake, to all my letters; as you deign and how God instructs you, so please write; and do not release the military commander without a letter for us. And after this, rejoice, oh great hierarch, and be joyful in good deeds; and bless and forgive us, oh holy father, in words, and deeds, and intentions, and pray for us sinful, and do not forget us in your prayers at any day and hour and about this I, very sinful *tsar*, dutifully petition. Written in Moscow on the twenty-fifth day of May, 7160 [1652]." *DAI*, Vol. 4, No 57, 75–76. The missive is also published in *Akty sobrannye v bibliotekakh i arkhivakh rossiiskoi imperii arkheograficheskoi ekspeditsiei Imperatorskoi Akademii Nauk* (*AAE*), Vol. 4 (St. Petersburg, 1842), No. 57, 364–367; and archimandrite Apollos, *Nachertanie zhitiia i deianii Nikona, patriarkha moskovskago i vseia Rossii* (Moscow, 1846), 27–28.

46. The controversial circumstances surrounding Nikon's acceptance of the patriarchal throne are well documented. Nikon himself left two accounts. The first appears in his *Replies,* see especially 582–583. The second is told in his *Letter to Dionysius*, 382–384.

In the twenty-sixth of his *Replies* Nikon recalled that, "the *tsar*, together with the sacred synod, besought Nikon then metropolitan of Novgorod, to undertake the patriarchate. And Nikon long refused so great a burden. And at length, after many entreaties from the *tsar* and from all the sacred synod, Nikon the metropolitan spoke to the *tsar* and grand prince Aleksei Mikhailovich in the holy great catholic and apostolic church: witness to the Lord God and our Savior Jesus Christ, and the most pure Mother of God and ever-virgin Mary, and the holy angels and archangels, and the holy and glorious prophet the forerunner of the Lord John the Baptist, . . . all laudable apostles, and the holy fathers, . . . and all the saints, before the sacred synod, and before *tsar's* Council (*synclete*), and before all the people, that if it pleased God that the metropolitan Nikon should be patriarch and that the metropolitan Nikon observed in the *tsar* and grand prince any fault contrary to the holy apostles and fathers, then he Nikon, as it is written in the Psalms, should, without being shamed, speak before the *tsar* of the commandments of the Lord and of the holy apostles and the holy fathers; and that he hossoudar [sic! we use "great sovereign" instead] the *tsar*, and the *tsar's boyars*, should hearken to him in all things." Nikon, "Replies," 582–583.

In his *Letter to Dionysius*, Nikon explained that after his return from the Solovetskii Monastery with metropolitan Filipp's relics, "there were words spoken on the part of the most pious *tsar* and grand prince Aleksei Mikhailovich, autocrat of all Russia, and on the part of all the Council, and on the part of the metropolitans and archbishops and all the people, for electing to the patriarchate of Moscow a patriarch, whom it should please God. And there was mention made, as from one mouth, from the *tsar* and his honorable Council and all the [holy] synod and all the people of our humility, that our unworthiness should be patriarch of Moscow and all Russia. And that was known to us: and on this account we were unwilling to go to the council [of the holy synod]. And when we were called for by the *tsar's* majesty, and by his Council, by the *boyars*, and the holy order of the clergy, not once, not twice, but many times, and we were unwilling to go, then at length the pious *tsar* sent some of his honorable *boyars*, and some of the metropolitans and archbishops and holy archimandrites and abbots and archpriests and other honorable people to bring me from my house, against my will, to the synod by constraint. And when they had come to the holy catholic church (*sobornaia tserkov'*), because it was there that the synod was being held by the most pious *tsar*, and the *boyars*, and the [priestly] order, and all the people, they set me in the midst before the *tsar* and all the people. And the most pious *tsar*, with all the assembly and synod, besought me much to be patriarch of Moscow and all Russia. And when I had for a long time refused, as not being of such capacity as to be fit to be alone the chief pastor, saying that I am a humble person, and of no great parts, and cannot teach the flock of Christ's rational sheep, and much time had now passed—the Lord God is my witness that this is the truth—the *tsar* prostrated himself on the ground, and so lay with all the people, and with many tears besought me that I would become their chief pastor. And I was unable to disregard the *tsar's* entreaty. I remembered how it is written that the heart of the king is in the hand of the Lord: and I wept myself not a little; and I caused the *tsar* to rise up, and began to speak to the most pious *tsar*, and to all the synod and to the people, in words such was these: . . . 'And therefore, Oh most pious *tsar*, and ye *boyars*, and all ye sacred synod, and all ye Christian people, if it be agreeable to you that our humility should be your patriarch, then do ye give your word, and make a covenant with me in this holy catholic and apostolic church, before the Lord God and our Savior Jesus Christ, and before his holy gospels, and before the holy Mother of God, and the holy angels, and all the saints, and promise to keep the commandments of Christ's holy gospels, and the canons of the holy apostles and the holy fathers, and the laws of the pious Greek emperors, unchangeably, and to obey us as your chief pastor and supreme father in all things which I shall announce to you out of the divine commandments and laws: and if you do this, then, seeing your zeal and your demand, I can no longer refuse this great chair.' Thereupon the most pious *tsar*, with all the honorable *boyars* and with all the sacred synod, earnestly and affectionately catching up our answer, did then in the holy catholic and apostolic church, before the holy gospel and before the venerable icons of Christ and the Mother of God, and of the other saints, promise to keep unchangeably all that we had mentioned, and they called to witness our Lord and God Jesus Christ, and our most holy, immaculate, and most blessed and glorious Lady the Mother of God and ever-virgin Mary, and the holy angels, and all the saints, and the sacred and holy gospel, and all the holy and venerable icons. And after that, thereupon, all was performed that concerned our becoming patriarch according to the accustomed order." Nikon, "Letter to Dionysius," 382–383.

Records of the *tsar's* activities note that "[o]n the twenty-second day of July, the sovereign was at the Cathedral of the Dormition of the most pure Mother of God, he listened to the liturgy; and after the liturgy, the sovereign spoke to Nikon, metropolitan of Novgorod about him becoming the patriarch." *Vykhody gosudarei tsarei*, 261.

Paul of Aleppo used Nikon's acceptance of the patriarchal throne to suggest that the patriarch was power-hungry. He explained that just before the arrival of Filipp's relics, patriarch Iosif died and there "was the unanimous vote of the assembly of the clergy to make Nikon patriarch. But he strongly refused to accept the dignity, until an order should be established that the *tsar* should confer no ecclesiastical sacerdotal offices whatsoever, as the previous sovereigns had conferred them. Having obtained his will in this respect, he further procured a royal decree, that his sentence should be absolute, without opposition or appeal. This prelate, immediately on his elevation, entered upon the exercise of uncontrolled authority." Aleppo, 110.

Archpriest Avvakum, an early Old Believer father, likewise treated Nikon's elevation to the patriarchal throne with disdain. "Nikon, our friend, brought down the relics of the metropolitan Phillip [Filipp] from the Solovetskii Monastery, and before his arrival, Stephen [Vonifat'ev], the chaplain, with the brotherhood and I with them, passed a week in prayer and fasting, concerning the patriarchate, even that God might give us a shepherd fitted to the saving of our souls. And the metropolitan of Kazan' and I, we signed our names to a petition and gave it to the *tsar* and the *tsarina*, concerning the chaplain

Stephen, that he might be made patriarch. But he did not wish it for himself and named the Metropolitan Nikon. And the *tsar* hearkened to him and wrote to Nikon to greet him on his arrival. 'To Nikon, the right reverend metropolitan of Novgorod and Velikie Luki and of all Russia, greetings,' and so forth. And when he arrived, he played the fox with us, and it was bowings and scrapings and 'Good morrow to you!' For he knew that he was to be patriarch and wished to remove all obstacles thereto. But I'll not waste my time telling all these cunning machinations." *The Life of Archpriest Avvakum by Himself* in S. A. Zenkovsky, ed., *Medieval Russia's Epics, Chronicles and Tales* (New York, 1974), 406–407.

47. "On the twenty-fifth day of July, the sovereign was at the Cathedral of the Dormition of the Holiest Mother of God when Nikon, metropolitan of Novgorod, was installed as patriarch." *Vykhody gosudarei tsarei*, 261. See also N. Gibbenet, *Istoricheskoe issledovanie dela patriarkha Nikona* (St. Petersburg, 1882–1884), Pt. 1, 9; and Sevast'ianova, *Mater'ialy*, 46.

48. The primary sources on the founding of the Iverskii Monastery include Nikon, *Rai Myslennyi*; and the documents published in archimandrite Leonid (Kavelin), *Akty Iverskago sviatoozerskago monastyria* (St. Petersburg, 1878).

Nikon described the founding of the monastery in the following manner: "I decided to check my intentions and relied on God's will and asked the great sovereign . . . Aleksei Mikhailovich for a place to build a monastery without delay . . . And the great sovereign, as if hearing from God, happily promised to give me the place together with the surrounding fields and villages. Having heard about the permission by the great sovereign, the *tsar* and the grand prince of all Russia, Aleksei Mikhailovich I, the humble, became very happy and, after hearing the news from God, tearfully thanked the Lord; some time later I started the endeavor. Soon I sent people skilled in building to find a place on one of the islands to build a monastery. They went and, having walked across and having seen everything, found one isle among others not particularly big, but very beautiful, surrounded by fisheries. Upon their return, they told me about this holy place and I ordered to cut down the trees on it." Nikon, *Rai Myslennyi*, 45–46.

Secondary sources on the founding of the Iverskii Monastery include archimandrite Piotr, *Opisanie pervoklassnago Iverskago Bogoroditskago monastyria, Novgorodskoi eparkhii (izvlecheno iz Istorii Rossiiskoi Ierarkhii, iz knigi Rai Myslennyi i Zhizneopisaniia patriarkha Nikona*. 2nd ed. (St. Petersburg, 1850); P. M. Silin, *Istoricheskoe opisanie valdaiskago iverskago sviatoezerskago bogoroditskago pervoklassnago monastyria* (Voronezh, 1912); and Il'in, 107–148.

49. In the twenty-fifth of his *Replies,* Nikon quoted Aleksei Mikhailovich's decree of March 6, 1654 in which the *tsar* "made grants to our father and beadsman the great hossoudar [sic!, we use "great sovereign" instead] Nikon . . . and according to our request and vow have bidden him to build the monastery of the most holy Mother of God, of her icon called the Hodigitria of the Iverskoi and of our the holy father the new confessor and martyr Phillip, metropolitan of Moscow . . . in the ridding of Novgorod . . . on an island in the Valdai Lake, now named anew by our imperial bidding and consent the Holy Lake." The decree continued to grant other territories in the area and elsewhere, including properties in Moscow. "On the request of our father and beadsman, the great hossoudar Nikon, patriarch we . . . have been graciously pleased to bid him to give to the same monastery of the holiest Mother of God, the Iverskaia . . . certain purchased properties of his own." The *tsar's* donation to the monastery also included numerous salt mines. Nikon, "Replies," 261–270.

50. Nikon recalled that "after summer past and fall was approaching winter, the trees [on the island] were cut down with the help of nearby residents. Then I ordered to found a

wooden church in honor of the holiest Mother of God and her Iverskii icon." Nikon, *Rai Myslennyi*, 47.

51. Nikon himself explained, "[t]he winter came. I had another desire, to make a silver ark and having put the fragments of the relics of the new martyr and confessor metropolitan Filipp in it, brought it [the ark] to the consecration of the monastery. I also heard about the relics of the righteous saint Iakov Borovitskii who was a great miracle-worker . . . I wanted to translate the relics of righteous saint Iakov Borovitskii, the miracle-worker, to the new Iverskii Monastery and so the creation of the silver reliquary began and soon it was completed . . . I had a vision that before my departure I prayed in the great holy cathedral. And so three metropolitans came to me as if they wanted to come with me to see the monastery. I asked them their names because none was familiar to me and one [of them] said: 'We are Piotr, Iona, and Filipp.' Being frightened by these words, I awoke and was at a loss about what it could portend and I decided that such a vision was not without a reason and made a resolution to take fragments of miracle-workers Piotr and Iona and, trusting God, did so." Nikon, *Rai Myslennyi*, 48.

52. The patriarch reported the sighting of a fiery pillar in a letter to Aleksei Mikhailovich dated February 27, 1654. According to Nikon, "Before our arrival at the new monastery of the holiest Mother of God and saint and holy martyr Filipp the metropolitan on your majesty's pilgrimage, early Friday, about three in the morning, there was a frightening vision over the monastery. A fiery column rose from earth to heaven and a great light shone from that fiery column for about three, five, ten, and twenty *versts* as if it was daylight. Seeing this unusual light, many in the villages were overcome with fear. And some villages located three or four *versts* could see the monastery as if in the daytime." "Pis'mo k tsariu Alekseiu Mikhailovichu ot Nikona patriarkha o byvshem v novom Iverskom monastyre iavlenii i o prochem," in Apollos, 143.

Nikon gave a more detailed account of the same events in *Rai Myslennyi*: "When we came to the holy monastery, that is the Iverskii Monastery, many told me that before our arrival, around four o'clock at night, on Friday, a frightening vision appeared over this place. A fiery column was seen rising from the earth to the sky. It spread above the monastery so that people thought it had caught on fire. . . . When we were at the holy monastery and were leaving it for the ruling city of Moscow, three honorable men hoary with age came to us. On the night the relics of the holy fathers Piotr, Iona and Filipp and blessed Iakov Borovitskii were brought to the monastery in the ark, these people decided to come to the monastery for the morning prayer celebrated at midnight. And when they set out on their trip, a bright light suddenly appeared. Frightened, they looked around and saw four fiery columns above the holy monastery. One of the columns was especially bright and shiny, the other three were smaller. The men observed this strange and frightful vision for a long time . . . and when they approached the monastery, the pillars became invisible again." Nikon, *Rai Myslennyi*, 55–58.

53. Nikon described the transfer of the icon to Russia in his *Rai Myslennyi*. "She [the icon of the Mother of God] hurries to leave the impious, who keep the laws of Mohammad, and is headed to Russia where She, Herself and Her only-begotten Son are being glorified throughout the entire land. She lightens a place for Herself similar to the old one, and chooses as a dwelling the second Zion, her divine church on the Holy Lake, the newly created monastery in honor of Her most pure name, called the Iverskii Monastery after the miracle-working icon of Portaitissa. But, slowing down a little, remember the transfer of this miracle-working icon to the Russian lands. It was brought by the Greeks from the Holy Mounts to his holiness patriarch Nikon in the ruling city of Moscow protected by God. But before it was transferred, on the road, the most pure Virgin and Mother of God sent a miracle. We will tell about it.

When the time had come to transfer the likeness of Her holiest image to Russia, the fathers living there started to search for those who could be entrusted with this most precious pearl. And they found father Kornilii, honored by the office of priest, who lived a hermit's life decorated by various virtues . . . They succeeded in entreating him to go to Russia with a certain virtuous monk Nikifor. They entrusted them, the poor monks, with the likeness of the holiest icon of Her divine face. Sailing across the great Danube River on the trip from their country to Russia, they encountered royal tax collectors. And because they could not pay, they considered going back. Then, at night, the most pure appeared before them, saying: 'My children, do not grieve. In the morning I, Myself, will arrange everything, simply do not abandon your intentions.' The same night, the most blessed Queen appeared before one of the Greeks, a rich man and Her loyal servant, Manuel Konstantinov, and ordered him to pay the road tax for the poor monks. Having obeyed the Queen and Mother of God, he did so. And so, when the icon reached the ruling city, he was compensated for everything he spent by his holiness patriarch Nikon, but he refused to take it. And then again, at the patriarch's insistence, he accepted double payment. So he learned the mercy of the most blessed Queen of the heavenly King, the Mother of Christ. But let this holy place, created now in Her name, chosen even before construction by the light and fiery columns, be glorified in signs and miracles." Nikon, *Rai Myslennyi*, 62–64. The patriarch also described the history of the original icon earlier in the same text. See Nikon, *Rai Myslennyi*, 56–62.

Importantly, Manuel Konstantinov also known as Manuel the Greek, was already en route to Moscow; he sent by Ioannikii, then patriarch of Jerusalem, to bring an ornate miter (*mitra*) that Aleksei Mikhailovich commissioned in Jerusalem and intended to present to Nikon on behalf of his son, *tsarevich* Aleksei Alekseevich. Manuel not only carried out this request, but played a central role in what Nikon describes as the icon's miraculous journey. In so doing, Manuel acquired a reputation of a righteous man and gained the confidence of both the *tsar* and the patriarch, roles that would prove fateful in the future (see note 68 below). See Makarii, *Istoriia*, Vol. 12, 85, 94, 132, and 147.

Paul of Aleppo offered an extremely detailed description of the icon's creation. "[P]atriarch Nikon, when he was archimandrite of the New [Monastery] of the Savior, asked the delegates of this convent of Iveron, who came regularly with others to beg the alms of the *tsar* . . . to get painted for him a copy of this their icon, and bring it to him; and so they did. . . . When the *tsarina* heard of this copy, she took it away from Nikon; and he ordered another, which they brought to him lately. Its cheek is wounded, and blood is flowing from it. For it is supposed that the Westerners, when they overran the holy mountain, struck this icon with a knife, and the blood has flowed from the wound ever since. The patriarch Nikon has been very munificent to the monks of his newly-founded convent [Iverskii Monastery], and has given them another lesser convent, opposite the *tsar's* palace . . . Next he gave them this icon; into the gold sheathing covering, of which, as I was told by persons of credibility, his goldsmiths put about forty pounds, i.e. a pood and a half, or twenty okas of gold. He adorned it . . . with a pood of pearls, and with thirty diamonds, worth above twelve thousand dinars, besides emeralds, jacinths, and rubies. On the head of our Lady, and on her shoulders and breast he set four stars of diamonds, which had belonged to the crests or pannaches of the sultan Ibrahim; for all these treasures have recently been brought hither by Greek merchants. The value of each star is above a thousand dinars. All this was displayed before us. On the neck of our Lady he had hung a necklace of emeralds of surprising beauty, reaching half round, in the form of a crescent; which had cost him, as we verified with our own eyes, above sixty thousand dinars. The icon itself is very large and imposing, and blood is flowing from its cheek. The back is entirely covered with satin and velvet. It is thus an object above all admiration; and has no equal, not even in the treasures of the *tsar*, or in his churches: for we have seen them all." Aleppo, 233–234. See also *Kratkoe skazanie o iavlenii chudotvornoi ikony Bozhei Materi Iverskoi, ob ustroenii Valdaiskoi Iverskoi obiteli i prazdnestva* (St. Petersburg, 1861). For a useful work on the original icon in English, see J. B. Bury, "Iveron and Our Lady of the Gate," *Hermathena* 10 (1899): 71–99.

54. In the course of the first military campaign against Poland-Lithuania, Aleksei Mikhailovich conquered Smolensk (September 23, 1654). See P. Longworth, *Alexis Tsar of All the Russias* (New York, 1984), 92–102.

55. Aleksei Alekseevich was born on February 5, 1654 and baptized shortly thereafter, on February 19, 1654. Nikon announced the birth in a decree to Makarii, metropolitan of Novgorod. See *DAI*, Vol. 4, No. 69, 106–107.

56. During the second campaign against Poland-Lithuania (March–September 1655), Aleksei Mikhailovich took Minsk, Homel, Kovno, Vilno, and many other Byelorussian and Lithuanian towns, adding the title "*tsar* and autocrat of White Russia" to his royal designation. See Longworth, 106–109.

57. The following three paragraphs should chronologically precede the one describing the second military campaign of Aleksei Mikhailovich. All the plague-related events happened in the second part of 1654–early 1655. See Longworth, 92–102.

58. Paul of Aleppo explained that some in Moscow believed that the plague was divine punishment for Nikon's actions, namely the patriarch's attack on "Frankish" icons. Aleppo reported that in the summer of 1654, Nikon collected "Frankish" and "Polish" icons "from every house where they were found . . . even from the palaces." Then the patriarch gouged the eyes out of the images, paraded them around Moscow, and published "an imperial proclamation" prescribing punishments for those who continued to keep such icons. "When they saw therefore . . . what the patriarch did to the pictures, they judged that he had sinned greatly. Uttering imprecations against him, and making a tumult, they denounced him as an open enemy of the holy icons. While they were thus minded the plague broke out, and there was an eclipse of the sun on the afternoon of the twelfth of August. They immediately said: 'All this is through the wrath of God, for our patriarch's contempt of our holy icons.'" Aleppo, 149–150.

59. The Monastery of Trinity and St. Sergius, located about sixty-six kilometers northeast of Moscow, was founded in the 1330s by St. Sergius of Radonezh (1314–1392), one of the most revered Russian saints. The monastery is connected to various important events in Russian history, including the Battle of Kulikovo, capture of Kazan', and the Time of Troubles. Since its founding, the monastery was considered one of the most important Russian religious centers. In Nikon's day, pilgrimage to the monastery was considered equivalent to the journey to Jerusalem in the Holy Land. On July 8, 1744, empress Elizabeth decreed that the monastery be elevated to the status of *lavra*, the highest classification for a Russian monastery. There are only three *lavras* in present day Russia and one in Ukraine. On the founding of the monastery, see Epiphanius the Wise, *The Life, Acts, and Miracles of Our Blessed and Holy Father Sergius of Radonezh*, in S. A. Zenkovsky, ed. *Medieval Russia's Epics, Chronicles and Tales* (New York, 1974), 262–290. See also Ratshin, 171–182.

60. This journey was made on June 24, 1654. See Sevast'ianova, *Mater'ianova*, 97. For recent research on the effects of the plague and Nikon's actions during the pestilence, see Lobachev, *Patriarkh Nikon*, 147–156.

61. In a patriarchal decree sent to the Koliazin monastery on August 20, 1654, requesting the preparation of cells, services, and supplies in anticipation of the arrival of *tsarina* Mariia Il'inichna and *tsarevich* Aleksei Alekseevich, Nikon wrote: "from the great sovereign, his holiness Nikon patriarch of Moscow and all Great and Little Russias, to the abbot, and cellarer, and brethren of the Trinity Monastery in Koliazin. On our edict, Osip Surmin is sent to you in the monastery and is ordered to clean cells at your monastery together with you, the abbot and the cellarer, for the arrival of her majesty pious *tsarina* and grand princess Mariia Il'inichna and his highness *tsarevich* and grand prince Aleksei

Alekseevich and their highnesses the *tsarevnas*, so everything would be clean and in order for their majesties' arrival; he is also ordered to clean and prepare all services both in the monastery and outside the monastery for the needs of their majesties . . . Written at our encampment at the Trinity and St. Sergius Monastery on the twentieth day of August, year 7162 [1654]." *DAI,* Vol. 4, No. 73, 111.

62. Paul of Aleppo offers a less flattering account of Nikon's relationship with the *tsarina*. According to his narration, after the patriarch delivered Mariia Il'inichna to the Monastery of Trinity and St. Sergius, he "left her there; and passed this season in the mountains and forests, dwelling in a tent, under the rain and snow, with no other companion but his fire." Aleppo, 150. In another instance, Aleppo claimed that Nikon "had passed [time] in the fields and forests through fear of the plague." Aleppo, 92.

63. Aleksei Mikhailovich proclaimed his thanks to Nikon and granted him numerous properties in a decree issued on December 5, 1654. It reads: "By the grace of God, we the great sovereign, the *tsar* and grand prince, Aleksei Mikhailovich . . . entrusted our father and devoted servant, the great sovereign, his holiness Nikon, patriarch of Moscow and all Russia, . . . [with our family]. . . . He, our father, the great sovereign, his holiness Nikon, patriarch of Moscow and all Great and Little Russias, asking God Almighty for mercy, protected [them] from the deadly plague and by the mercy of God and the holiest Mother of God . . . and by the prayers of our father and God-entreater, the great sovereign, his holiness Nikon . . . and his incessant diligence, our *tsarina* Mariia . . . Il'inichna, and our son . . . Aleksei Alekseevich, our sisters . . . and our daughters . . . were saved from the deadly plague and left intact and came to us, the great sovereign, in good health. And we, the great sovereign, the *tsar* . . . with our *tsarina* . . . for the mercy of God and the holiest Mother of God, giving thanks to Our Lord God and the holiest Mother of God, grant . . . [a list of territories] to the Iverskii Monastery . . . created by our father and God-entreater, the great sovereign, his holiness Nikon." *DAI,* Vol. 4, No. 78, 115–117; and Apollos, 139–140.

64. Nikon returned to Moscow on February 2–3, 1655. See Sevast'ianova, *Mater'ialy, 92.* Mariia Il'inichna arrived on February 9, 1655. Aleksei Mikhailovich returned the following day. For an eyewitness account of the *tsar's* triumphant entrance into the capital city on February 10, 1655, see Aleppo, 93–94.

65. Shusherin's account of the reform of the Russian church service books follows closely the official version of events published by Nikon in the introduction to the *Sluzhebnik* (1655). See *Sluzhebnik napechatannyi v Moskve, 1655 goda* published in *Opisanie staropechatnykh knig slavianskikh, sluzhashchie dopolneniem k opisaniiam bibliotek grafa F. A. Tolstova i kuptsa I. N. Tsarskago,* P. M. Stroev, ed. (Moscow, 1841), No. 89, 147–169 (hereafter cited as *Sluzhebnik*). Documents pertaining to the reform process are published in N. I. Subbotin, *Deianie moskovskago sobora byvshago v tsarskikh palatakh v leto ot sozdaniia mira 7162, ot voploshcheniia zhe Bozhiia Slova 1654* (Moscow, 1873).

The reform of church books and practices in the 1650s was one of the most controversial aspects of Nikon's patriarchate. A rich historiography developed on the subject in the nineteenth century. Among the most important works are Makarii, *Istoriia,* Vol. 12, 68–119; idem., *Patriarkh Nikon v dele ispravleniia knig i obriadov* (Moscow, 1881); N. F. Kapterev, *Patriarkh Nikon i tsar Aleksei Mikhailovich* 2 Vols. (Sergiev Posad, 1909–1912); idem., *Patriarch Nikon i ego protivniki* (Sergiev Posad, 1913); and idem., "Ispravlenie tserkovno-bogosluzhebnykh knig pri patriarkhe Nikone," *Bogoslovskii Vestnik* 3 (1908): 538–559; 1 (1909): 24–44; S. A. Belokurov, "Sobiranie patriarkhom Nikonom knig s vostoka," *Khristianskoe Chtenie* 2 (1882): 444–494. For a useful nineteenth-century historiography of the Nikonian reforms, see V. S. Ikonnikov, *Novye materialy i trudy o patriarkhe Nikone* (Kiev, 1888), 26–35. Important new works on the reforms include Meyendorff, 37–63; B. L. Fonkich, *Grechesko-russkie kulturnye sviazi v XV-XVII vv.* (Moscow, 1977); S. V. Lobachev, "Khronologiia tserkovnoi reformy Patriarkha Nikona," in *Nikonovskie chteniia* (2002), 105–111; and idem., *Patriarkh Nikon,* 113–129.

66. This section of Shusherin's narrative is out of chronological order. The early stage of the book reform described by the author happened before the deadly plague of 1654 and the journey to Viaz'ma. The council took place in March or April of 1654 in the *tsar's* chamber. See *Sluzhebnik,* 151–152; and Meyendorff, 42. The 1655 *Sluzhebnik* also records all those who took part in the council. See *Sluzhebnik,* 152–153.

67. For the official account of the reforms, see *Sluzhebnik,* 155–157.

68. In this section Shusherin follows the official description of the preparations for the reform. See *Sluzhebnik,* 157. Nikon sent the letter to Paisius, patriarch of Constantinople, on June 12, 1654 with Manuel the Greek (also known as Manuel Konstantinov). See Meyendorff 47; and Sevast'ianova, *Mater'ialy,* 86. Manuel Konstantinov first arrived in Moscow on February 28, 1654, bringing the precious miter (*mitra*) that the *tsar* ordered for Nikon. Already famous for his role in the miraculous delivery of the icon of the Iverskaia Mother of God, he was introduced to the *tsar* on March 4, 1654 (see note 53 above). Manuel returned to Moscow on May 15, 1655 with the replies of Paisius. See Makarii, *Istoriia,* Vol. 12, 85, 94, 132, and 147.

69. For an official version of these events which corroborates Shusherin's narrative, see *Sluzhebnik,* 158.

70. Patriarch Paisius's reply to Nikon arrived in Moscow on May 15, 1665 with Manuel Konstantinov. The text of the letter was published in *Sluzhebnik,* 157–158.

71. Arsenii (Anton) Sukhanov (circa 1600–1668), monastic priest (*ieromonakh*), elder of the Trinity and St. Sergius Monastery, and Nikon's primary assistant in the book corrections, was born near the town of Tula to aristocratic parents. The educated monk was frequently entrusted with important diplomatic missions, including trips to the ecumenical Orthodox patriarchates to compare Russian liturgical books and practices (1649–1653) and to acquire the Greek originals that Aleksei Mikhailovich and patriarch Nikon needed to launch reforms (1654). Sukhanov is the author of *Proskinitarii* (1653), an eyewitness description of the Holy Land, and *Spor s grekami o vere,* a dogmatic tract. See S. A. Belokurov, *Arsenii Sukhanov,* 2 Vols. (Moscow, 1891–1893).

72. For the official explanation of Arsenii's acquisition of books, see *Sluzhebnik,* 158. In his *Letter to Dionysius,* Nikon explained: "I wrote to thy predecessor . . . patriarch Paisius, concerning the holy creed, and concerning the other rules of the church; and we received from him a tome of answers to all; and by that we go in all things, according to the order which the holy eastern church is used to follow. On this account we sent with much money to the holy city of Jerusalem and the imperial city of Constantinople and to the holy mountain Athos, for ancient copies of holy books; and not fewer than five hundred were obtained and brought to us, some of them written a thousand, some seven hundred, some five hundred years ago; and what we from these divine books, by God's grace, have corrected and translated, that they call a new rule, and a tradition of Nikon's, that is, mine." Nikon, "Letter to Dionysius," 390.

Paul of Aleppo explained Arsenii's trip to the holy places and his collection of five hundred books. "[T]he patriarch and the *tsar* convoked a synod and sent him [Arsenii] to Mount Athos, with a large contribution of alms for the convents, and with letters to the superiors of them, requesting them to give him whatever they could command in the way of old Greek books. This was because the present patriarch and the *tsar* are lovers, to an extreme, of the Greek ceremonies and ritual; and they had observed that, through length of time, some alterations had crept into their own books. They had heard that on the holy mountain all the writings of the Greek tsardom had been collected. They therefore, sent this man to collect all he could find of what was curious among them. He went therefore and obtain of them about five hundred large books of various kinds. . . . On his arrival at Moscow, he brought all these things with him; and the books were deposited in the treasury. For there they have translators, natives of Greece; who translate them one after another, and print and publish them. In reward for these services which the archdeacon Arsenii had performed, namely for going at the command of the *tsar* and the patriarch to Mount Sinai, Egypt, Jerusalem, to our country (Syria), and to Georgia, to ascertain the condition of all those countries, and now for the second service the patriarch rewarded him by placing him in the highest situation." See Aleppo, 170.

Arsenii actually left Moscow on October 1653 and returned on February 22, 1655. See Makarii, *Istoriia,* Vol. 12, 86–88; and Meyendorff, 52.

73. Ohrid is a region in Macedonia. Here Shusherin refers to the heads of Slavic autocephalic churches in Serbia and Macedonia which were eliminated in the 1760s. Serbia did have a patriarchate at the time of Shusherin's writing, which was established in 1346 under an autocephaly of the patriarch of Constantinople. But Ohrid was patriarchate only in 990–1018 and was later demoted to the status of archbishopric under the patriarch of Constantinople.

74. This donation is confirmed by records in *Sluzhebnik,* 161–162.

75. Ibid., 162–163.

76. This council of the holy synod took place in Moscow on March 25–31, 1655. See *Sluzhebnik*, 163; and Meyendorff, 52–55.

77. The same version of the council's resolutions is found in official documents. See *Sluzhebnik,* 164–165. Metropolitan Makarii (Bulgakov) was the first to contest the chronology of events presented in the *Sluzhebnik* and accepted by Shusherin, explaining that Arsenii Sukhanov left Moscow before the council met in 1654 and that patriarch Paisius's reply arrived after the council of the synod met in 1655. See Makarii, *Istoriia,* Vol. 12, 86–88. More recently, Meyendorff challenged the chronology of the reform process adding that the council of 1655 lasted only one week and, thus, did not have sufficient time to study the collected books. Therefore, he concludes that the comparison of Greek and Slavic texts was done not at the council, but, most likely, earlier by Arsenii the Greek and Epifanii Slavianetskii, Nikon's chief correctors. See Meyendorff, 39, 52–54; and Lobachev, "Khronologiia," 105–111.

The Old Believer author Simeon Denisov offered a different version of the reform process. "After convincing the *tsar* and his Council and after convening all the hierarchs at the council of the holy synod, some by kindness and others by fear of the *tsar*, he [Nikon] involved them in his intention. On those not submitting he inflicted fetters, . . . wounds, and incarceration and deprived them of life by the most heinous deaths. And he ordered to print books with the aforementioned innovations and to send those everywhere in all corners of the Russian state and to conduct all prayer services according to those. Those were sent everywhere . . . but no one protested against those innovations . . . except Pavel, the good bishop of Kolomna, and the most zealous archpriest Avvakum and others who protested at the time of the first council of the holy synod." Denisov, 144–145.

78. Shusherin is incorrect in linking the Swedish campaign to the year preceding the council of the synod. Aleksei Mikhailovich declared war against Sweden on May 17, 1656, not in 1654 as it would appear from Shusherin's dating. See Longworth, 112–115.

79. Nikon listed his reasons for founding the monastery and recounted his misadventures at sea in his *Gramota o Krestnom monastyre*. In this decree, Nikon explained: "Having hope in Jesus Christ our Lord we will found a monastery honoring the holy and life-giving cross on the Isle of Kii which is in the sea near the mouth of the Onega [River], build a church, bring brethren there, and call this holy monastery *Stavros* in Greek or *Krestnyi* in Slavonic." Nikon, *Gramota o Krestnom monastyre,* 1–2.

Tsar Aleksei Mikhailovich granted Nikon's request to build the Cross Monastery on the Isle of Kii Island in his decree of June 13, 1656. The decree also described Nikon's ordeals and his pledge to build a monastery at the site of his rescue. "Our father and God-entreater, the great sovereign Nikon . . . humbly petitioned to us concerning how he . . . traveled from the Anzer hermitage and at that time almost drowned during a great storm at sea, but trusting the power of the life-giving cross, was saved near the mouth of the Onega River by landing on the Isle of Kii and, while on that island, remembering his rescue, he erected on that place a holy and life-giving cross; and how, according to our order, in the year 7160 [1652] he, the great sovereign Nikon, . . . was sent to retrieve the relics of metropolitan Filipp the miracle-worker from the Solovetskii Monastery. Traveling by sea from the Solovetskii Monastery with his miracle-working relics, God willed that he, the great sovereign, landed at the same place and saw the holy cross that he previously erected on that place which, by the power of the Crucified, was still standing there intact. That island was uninhabited and did not have any landholdings and no one settled there because the place consisted of bare stone. But by the power of the life-creating cross that was erected on that place, many who put their faith in Him were saved from drowning at sea. So he stood with the relics of the miracle-worker Filipp and promised to found a church and enclose a monastery at that place called *Stavros* in Greek and *Krestnyi* in Russian in honor of the holy and life-giving cross and the holy martyr and miracle-worker Filipp the metropolitan." *Gramota tsaria Alekseia Mikhailovicha*, 23–24.

80. This cross is known as the Kii cross [*Kiiskii krest*]. Nikon described the cross and its significance in his decree dated June 24, 1656. "This is the honorable life-giving cross which we sent to the Isle of Kii today. It was brought from Palestine and created from the noble wood of the cypress tree. Its width and height are identical to the life-giving cross on which Christ our Lord allowed Himself to be crucified for our salvation. It contains parts of the very life-giving cross, as well as the remains of numerous apostles, martyrs and others. Let this honorable life-giving cross protect and save everyone who appeals to it, having a certain need or by wise intent. He who will come to this life-giving cross with faith and will adore it, will not be denied the grace given by the power of the holy, honorable and life-giving cross, the grace equal to that given to the travelers to Holy Palestine." *Gramota o Krestnom monastyre*, 3–4. The cross exists today and is held at the Church of St. Sergius of Radonezh at Krapivniki in Moscow.

According to one Old Believer account, "Nikon ordered to make a cross of cypress wood with height and width like the cross of Christ, on which Christ was crucified for saving the world. This cross was decorated with silver, gold, precious stones, and pearls. Many relics of Greek and Russian saints were collected." Borozdin, No. 33, 151.

The Kii cross is described in greater detail in *Krestnyi monastyr' osnovannyi patriarkhom Nikonom*, 16–18. More recent works analyzing it include M. V. Osipenko, *Kiiskii krest patriarkha Nikona* (Moscow, 2000); K. A. Shchedrina, *Tsarei derzhava* (Moscow, 2000), 10–21; G. M. Zelenskaia, "Prizhiznennye izobrazheniia sviateishego patriarkha Nikona," 9; S. V. Gnutova, "Kiiskii krest," in Iukhimenko, ed., *Patriarch Nikon: Oblacheniia, lichnye veshchi, avtografy, vklady, portrety* (Moscow, 2002), 72–75; and K. M. Kain, "Patriarch Nikon's Image in Russian History and Culture," (Ph.D. Diss., Western Michigan University, 2004), 40–48.

81. Two icons accompanied the Kii cross. The first depicted Byzantine emperor Constantine, *tsar* Aleksei Mikhailovich, and Nikon himself. The second featured St. Helen, Constantine's mother, and Mariia Il'inichna, *tsar* Aleksei Mikhailovich's wife. The original icons, which are no longer extant, were described in *Krestnyi monastyr' osnovannyi patriarkhom Nikonom*, 17. There are however numerous seventeenth-, eighteenth-, and nineteenth-century copies of the entire "Kii cross system of imagery," which depict the cross flanked by the two icons (the first to the left of the cross, the second to the right)

in a single painted image. On these images and their significance, see G. M. Zelenskaia, "Prizhiznennye izobrazheniia sviateishego patriarkha Nikona," 9; O. P. Pasternak, "Ikonografiia Kiiskogo kresta i ego povtoreniia v XVIII veke," in *Original i povtorenie v zhivopisi* (Moscow, 1988), 47–60; L. A. Kol'tsova and E. M. Iukhimenko, "Kiiskii krest s predstoiashchimi (Poklonenie krestu)," in Iukhimenko, *Patriarkh Nikon*, 76–77; I. Thyret, *Between God and Tsar. Religious Symbolism and the Royal Women of Muscovite Russia* (DeKalb, 2001), 64–70; and Kain, 26–80.

82. Dünaburg (modern Daugavpils in Latvia) was taken by the Russian army on July 31, 1656. See Lobachev, *Patriarkh Nikon*, 371; and Longworth, 115.

83. See Gibbenet, *Istoricheskoe issledovanie*, Pt. 1, 20.

84. Nikon left Moscow together with the royal family in the first week of September 1656. The party spent six weeks in Tver' (September 6–October 18, 1656) on account of Nikon's being sick. The company finally arrived in Viaz'ma on October 28, 1656. For a detailed account of this journey and related events, see A. K. Zhiznevskii, *Pokhod velikago gosudaria sviateishago Nikona patriarkha moskovskago i vseia Velikiia, Malyia i Belyia Rossii, v 1656 g. v Tver', Viaz'mu i Iverskii monastyr'* (Tver', 1889), especially 16, 20. See also Gibbenet, *Istoricheskoe issledovanie*, Pt. 1, 21; and Sevast'ianova, *Mater'ialy*, 139, 140.

85. Aleksei Mikhailovich met his family and Nikon in Viaz'ma on November 26, 1656 and lived there for more than a month. See Zhiznevskii, 23; and Sevast'ianova, *Mater'ialy*, 142.

86. According to Nikon, "the great recompensate" Aleksei Mikhailovich granted him was the title "great sovereign." In the thirteenth of his *Replies*, the patriarch explained that "when the great hossoudar the *tsar* returned from Smolensk to Viaz'ma, and we met him there with the *tsarina* and the princesses, he, the *tsar*, then spoke to us of this, praying us much that we would write ourselves 'great hossoudar': but our consent was not given." Nikon, "Replies," 66.

87. See Kavelin, *Akty Iverskago monastyria*, 18–19; and Sevast'ianova, *Mater'ialy*, 142.

88. Nikon departed Viaz'ma after December 6, 1656 and went to the Iverskii Monastery where he stayed until late December. He returned to Moscow in early January 1657. Aleksei Mikhailovich and his family sojourned in Viaz'ma for almost a month. The *tsar* arrived in the capital city on January 14, 1657. See Zhiznevskii, 23–24.

89. The document of sale recorded by Roman Fedorovich Bobarykin states: "I, Roman Fedorovich Bobarykin, sold my patrimonial lands to the monastery of the most pure Mother of God of Iverskii and our holy father metropolitan Filipp and St. Iakov the miracle-worker in the Novgorod region which belongs to the great sovereign, his holiness Nikon, patriarch of Moscow and all Russia, . . . in the Moscow region . . . the village of Voskresenskii, formerly the village of Savatovo, on the Pesochnia River, and in that village the Church of the Resurrection of Christ with all the church buildings and offices and four households of people and the granary . . . And I, Roman, took from the patriarch's private treasury, from archimandrite Dionisii and brethren two thousand rubles for this patrimony. In the future my, Roman's, descendants will not lay claims to this patrimony because it was bought by my father Fedor Vasil'evich and me and not inherited; I, Roman, pledge to write this in the estate books, kept in the state chancellery, as belonging to the Iverskii Monastery, to which we testify. [Signed] Ioann Sokolov, . . . Year 1656, the third day of June." See Leonid (Kavelin), Archimandrite of the New Jerusalem Monastery, *Istoricheskoe opisanie stavropigial'nago Voskresenskago, Novyi Ierusalim imenuemago, monastyria* (Moscow, 1876), 2–3. On Bobarykin and the sale, see L. G. Nevzorova, "Roman Fedorovich Bobarykin (ok. 1605–posle 1682). Biograficheskii ocherk," in *Nikonovskie chteniia* (2002), 112–116; and Sevast'ianova, *Mater'ialy*, 132.

90. The monastery inventory (*opis'*) of 1679, "Opis' tserkovnago i monastyrskago imushchestva i knigokhranilishcha Voskresenskago, Novyi Ierusalim imenuemago, monastyria, 1679 goda, uchinennaia po ukazu tsaria i velikago kniazia Fedora Alekseevi-cha Moskovskago i vseia Rossii," shows that *tsar's* decree was still at the New Jerusalem Resurrection Monastery at that time. See Kavelin, *Istoricheskoe opisanie*, 205. This document however is no longer extant. Kavelin believed that the *tsar's* decree was lost during the church property reforms of Catherine the Great in 1764, not after Nikon's downfall. After all, Kavelin argued, the decree was still intact even after Nikon was dethroned and exiled. See Kavelin, *Istoricheskoe opisanie*, 7–8.

In the thirteenth of his *Replies*, Nikon explained that Aleksei Mikhailovich himself called the monastery "New Jerusalem." "At the consecration there [at the monastery] of the first Church of Christ's Resurrection, the great hossoudar the *tsar* and grand prince Aleksei Mikhailovich . . . was pleased to be present with all his [Council] and it pleased him, the great hossoudar to call it by the name New Jerusalem, and in his letters so to write and style it with his own hand for more confirmation." Nikon, "Replies," 68.

Two inscriptions at the monastery collaborate this part of Shusherin's account. According to both, Aleksei Mikhailovich indeed named the monastery "New Jerusalem" on October 18, 1657. The first was carved into a stone tablet located near the entrance of the stone Church of the Resurrection. It reads: "In the year 7165 [1657] [his holiness patriarch Nikon] started to build the first wooden church which he finished. While he was still on the patriarchal throne, for he was the head of the holy apostolic church, he made a procession of the cross (*krestnyi khod*) in this Resurrection Monastery and together with him the entire synod of church hierarchs was at the consecration of this wooden church dedicated to the third-day Resurrection. The consecration was in the month of June, on the seventeenth day of that month. And the pious *tsar* was here at the consecration, accompanied by the *boyars* and the entire Council; immediately after the consecration of this church, the *tsar* and his holiness walked around this monastery, rejoicing and praising God for allowing the completion of such an undertaking at this place. His holiness called for the help of Christ our Lord, for he wished to build an even bigger building. And having reached Mount Olive which was to the east of this monastery, across from Zion and seeing the expanse of this place here and there and liking it even more, the pious *tsar* said, the name of this monastery should be the New Jerusalem Resurrection Monastery as in the ancient Jerusalem in Palestine, so be the name of this monastery forever, for this name and the holy city are praiseworthy. He wrote it in his own hand, and so the pious *tsar* reflected the opinion of all, for they said, as Nikon himself foretold: 'This is New Jerusalem, [for so] called it the *tsar*.' The patriarch put this writing in the ark for eternal blessing. This year 7165 [1657] from the creation of the world, October 18." This text is published in Zelenskaia, *Sviatyni Novogo Ierusalima*, 102–103.

The second inscription was carved into a stone cross commemorating the *tsar's* visit. It reads: "Let this holy divine cross of our Lord Jesus Christ be erected on this Mount Olive, to the east across from the Cathedral of the Holy Resurrection, on holy Zion by the blessing of the great sovereign and lord Nikon, his holiness the archbishop of the ruling great city of Moscow and patriarch of all Great, and Little, and White Russias, for the most serene great sovereign and grand prince . . . Aleksei Mikhailovich who was present at the founding of the monastery during the consecration of the wooden church of the holy, life-giving Resurrection of Christ. And walking around the monastery's grounds after the consecration of the church and reaching this place, he ascended it, looked around at the surrounding fields, and taking a liking to it, named the monastery New Jerusalem which he has written with his own honorable hand [in a decree] which the patriarch put into a silver ark and kept it at the Resurrection Monastery for the eternal blessing. In the summer of 7166 (sic!, should be fall of 7165) and 1657 AD, on the eighteenth day of October." This text is published in Kavelin, *Istoricheskoe opisanie*, 6, note 4. See also

Kavelin, *Istoricheskoe opisanie*, 9–10; and Leonid (Kavelin), Archimandrite of the New Jerusalem Monastery, *Kratkoe istoricheskoe skazanie o nachale i ustroenii Voskresenskago, Novyi Ierusalim imenuemago, monastyria* (Moscow, 1872), 6–7.

91. In this case, Shusherin was mistaken. Arsenii made only two trips to the East (1649–1653 and 1654–1655) and could not have brought a model from Jerusalem after 1655. Arsenii did describe the Church of the Holy Sepulcher in Jerusalem and other details of the Holy Land in a commentary titled *Proskinitarii* (1653). See Kavelin, *Istoricheskoe opisanie*, 8–9; and Makarii, *Istoriia*, Vol. 12, 411. Much of Arsenii's *Proskinitarii* is quoted in Zelenskaia, *Sviatyni Novogo Ierusalima*, 15–24. Nikon did receive a model of the Church of the Holy Sepulcher from Paisius, patriarch of Jerusalem, when the latter visited Russia in 1649. In the fourteenth of his *Replies*, Nikon explained that the Church of the Resurrection at the New Jerusalem Monastery "is being built after the pattern of the holy Church of Christ's Resurrection which the pious empress Helena built, a model of which was brought to us by our brother patriarch Paisius of blessed memory, the patriarch of the holy city of Jerusalem, God having sent him hither beforehand for this." Nikon, "Replies," 8. The model exists today and is currently on display at the Art, Architectural and Historical Museum 'New Jerusalem.' See G. M. Zelenskaia, "Model' khrama Groba Gospodnia v Ierusalime," in Iukhimenko, ed., *Patriarkh Nikon. Oblacheniia*, 32–34.

92. Kavelin clarified that the stone church was founded on September 1, 1658. His claim is based on an inscription on a bell cast between 1658 and 1666. It reads: "From the creation of the world 7167, from the incarnation of God's word in the year 1658, on the first day of September, the beginning of creation of this sacred thing, the New Jerusalem Monastery of the Resurrection of Christ." Kavelin, *Istoricheskoe opisanie*, 10–11. If Kavelin's date of September 1, 1658 is accepted as the actual date of the church's founding, Shusherin's account is out of chronological order. The founding of the stone church should follow, not precede the account of Nikon's falling out with Aleksei Mikhailovich in July of 1658 described below, in note 93.

93. Nikon later explained the source of the conflict with the *tsar* in his *Letter to Dionysius*. After noting that Aleksei Mikhailovich did not, as was customary, participate in the festival in honor of the Icon of our Lady of Kazan' (July 8) or appear for the celebration in honor of the Deposition of the Robe (July 10), Nikon recounted that the *tsar* sent his prince Yurii Romodanovskii "to let me know that the *tsar's* majesty was wroth against me, and that on that account he would not be at the morning prayer, and did not desire that I should wait for him at the liturgy. And he, the prince Yurii, said to me in the *tsar's* name: 'Thou despisest and insultest the *tsar's* majesty; and thou hast caused thyself to be styled great hossoudar. But thou art not a great *tsar*. We have only one hossoudar, the *tsar*.' And to that I replied, that for me to be styled great hossoudar was from no desire of my own, but the great hossoudar the *tsar* had been pleased to so style me both by word of mouth and in writing; and of this I have proof in letters written in my own hand. An he, the prince Yurii said: "The *tsar's* majesty honored thee as a father and pastor, and thou didst not know thyself; and now the *tsar's* majesty has commanded me to say to thee, that he forbids thee to style thyself in speaking and in writing great hossoudar, and that he does not want me to honor thee any more.' . . . Seeing the *tsar's* wrath, that same day after the celebration of the divine liturgy, calling to witness the Lord God and our savior Jesus Christ, and the most holy Mother of God, and the holy angels . . . before a great concourse of people and before heaven and earth, we proclaimed the *tsar's* wrath, saying that the *tsar* is wroth against me with unjust cause, and on account of that he abstains from the general assembly." Nikon, "Letter to Dionysius," 385–386. Nikon presented a shorter version of this account in a letter to Paisius Ligarides (written before July 12, 1662), who included the note in his *History*. See Ligarides, 53.

94. Nikon's departure from the patriarchal seat was one of the most controversial actions of his entire patriarchate. It became central in subsequent efforts to remove him from the patriarchal position. The most damning charge was based on a claim that the patriarch voluntarily renounced his throne on July 10, 1658. Those present during Nikon's departure were interrogated in the winter of 1660 as part of the official proceedings against Nikon thereby leaving multiple testimonies. The participants in this event, including Nikon himself however had radically different recollections. Official and eyewitness accounts of Nikon's departure are published in Gibbenet, *Istoricheskoe issledovanie,* Pt. 1, 180–214; and *Delo o patriarkhe Nikone. Izdanie Arkheograficheskoi komissii po dokumentam Moskovskoi Sinodal'noi (byvshei Patriarshei) biblioteki* (St. Petersburg, 1897), Nos. 6–17, 15–52.

In the fifth of his *Replies,* Nikon wrote about the conflict with the *tsar.* "On the tenth of July, having entered into the holy cathedral, it being the anniversary of the bringing to Moscow of the holy and precious Robe of Our Lord God and Savior Jesus Christ . . . and having finished the holy and divine liturgy, and having testified before God and Our Lord Jesus Christ and the all-pure Mother of God, and all the holy angels [etc.] . . . respecting the causeless wrath of the sovereign, and remembering that divine commandment which says 'When they persecute you in this city, flee ye into another' . . . we went away." Nikon, "Replies," 21–22.

Nikon later recounted the same events in his letter to the patriarch of Constantinople. "After these things I put on the worst and humblest dress, and went out from the cathedral to the town lodge of the Voskresenskii Monastery of our own foundation, taking nothing of my personal property with me, but carrying only my personal quality, and taking a single miter and other episcopal vestments, one of each . . . that I might be able to officiate as a bishop but I did not go away as if renouncing the episcopal office, as now they calumniously assert, saying that I of my own self renounced the episcopate; and there I waited, expecting till the *tsar's* majesty should be pacified, [and letting him know] that I wished to go to the monastery which I was founding at Voskresensk." Nikon, "Letter to Dionysius," 387.

Paisius Ligarides also offered an account of the events of July 10. "Nikon had come to the church to celebrate the holy liturgy; and after vesting himself in his patriarchal robes, and ending the whole ceremony of the celebration, he stood in the middle of the church, and began belching forth from his belly publicly, in the presence of all, words of madness, words which it was an absolute duty for him not to utter, if it had been possible for him to be silent . . . And so, after that his stale and rotten and long harangue, he attempted of his own will to divest himself of his patriarchal power, imprecating on himself the greatest curses if he should ever again return to his chair, or take the title of patriarch, or allow himself to be called patriarch by others. And as he spoke, he suited his action to his words. For, taking off his episcopal vestments one by one, he said as he took off each these words, 'I am no longer patriarch,' so that he had all but deposed and degraded himself . . . So then, when he had put all off, Nikon, instead of his white kamilauchion (*kamilavka*), took a black one, and put it on his head as an emblem of penitence. Also he left the pastoral staff, which was the original one of the first metropolitan of Moscow, St. Peter, at the patriarchal chair, and so went forth from the church in humble guise." Ligarides, 41–42.

Early Old Believers treated Nikon's departure from the patriarchal throne as an important proof of patriarch's fallibility. In his *Testimonies,* deacon Fedor Ivanov, aiming to delegitimize Nikon, explained: "When he [Nikon], the defiled one, was expelled from the church by God, he appeared before people and lied that he left the throne in humility. Then he became unreasonably wroth and without serving the liturgy, he tore off his patriarchal dress (because at that time he was out of his mind), put on a simple monk's shirt, and left the church while saying that he is not worthy of being a shepherd and swore before the crowd that: 'I do not wish to be called patriarch. Go ask the *tsar* for a different head of the church!'" Deacon Fedor, "Testimonies," in Titova, 237.

95. In the *Letter to Dionysius*, Nikon explained that "having written with my own hand a letter to the *tsar's* majesty, I sent it by a deacon, letting him [the *tsar*] know that on account of his anger I was going out of the city." Nikon, "Letter to Dionysius," 386. The original letter written by Nikon to the *tsar* is published in *Delo o patriarkhe Nikone,* No. 1, 1–2.

96. Prince Aleksei Trubetskoi later testified that after leaving the patriarchal throne, "[p]atriarch Nikon went to the altar wearing only a tunic (*stikhar'*) and there, in the vestry (*riznitsa*), took off the tunic and put on a black cover (*klobuk*) and mantle (*mantiia*) and took a simple staff (*posokh* or *zhezl*) and as he exited the altar and stood in the middle of the church, the cathedral doors were locked and Nikon, the patriarch, was not allowed out of the church until the great sovereign's decree [arrived], and the dignitaries and metropolitan Mikhailo went to the great sovereign to tell him about the patriarch, that he left the patriarchal throne. And the great sovereign deigned to send to the cathedral his *boyar* prince Aleksei Nikitich Trubetskoi together with the dignitaries and as the *boyar* with the dignitaries came to the church and asked the patriarch for a blessing, the patriarch did not give his blessing to the *boyar*, but said that he is a simple monk, not a patriarch. And the *boyar* asked the patriarch: 'Why are you leaving the hierarchal throne?' And the patriarch told the *boyar*: 'I humbly petition to the great sovereign so that the sovereign will allow me to live in a hermitage near the Resurrection Monastery.' And the *boyar* told the patriarch that he was to stay patriarch as before and not to leave his flock. And the patriarch said: 'I do not wish to be patriarch, I will go to the hermitage.'" Gibbenet, *Istoricheskoe issledovanie,* Pt. 1, 182.

Another official document notes Trubetskoi's conversation with Nikon. "In the last year 7166 on July 10, the great sovereign ordered him, the *boyar*, to go to the cathedral and tell Nikon the patriarch that Pitirim, metropolitan of Krutitsa, came to the great sovereign and said that Nikon, the patriarch, is leaving the patriarchal throne and wanted to go out of the cathedral and on the *tsar's* majesty orders, he, the *boyar*, asked patriarch Nikon why he is leaving the patriarchal throne without asking the great sovereign and from whose persecution and who is expelling him and so that he would not leave the patriarchal throne and remain the patriarch . . . The patriarch also ordered the same *boyar* to humbly petition to the sovereign to give him cells and the *boyar* asked the patriarch for a blessing and he did not bless him, but said: 'How could I bless you? I am not worthy of being a patriarch and, if you need me to, I will confess my sins.' The *boyar* asked the patriarch: 'What business is it of mine to listen to your confession? It is not my place.' And the *boyar* informed the great sovereign about all of this." Gibbenet, *Istoricheskoe issledovanie,* Pt. 1, 182–183. The same account is also published in *Delo o patriarkhe Nikone,* No. 6, 15–16.

Ligarides however offered quite a different interpretation of Nikon's actions and motivations. "The *tsar*, on hearing of these extraordinary and irregular proceedings, was astounded . . . and calling to Aleksei Nikitich Trubetskoi, he sent him out, at the head of other messengers, to attempt to restore a good understanding to Nikon, with many entreaties that he would return to the patriarchate . . . But Nikon purposely worked himself up, and becoming still more fierce, utterly lost himself; and treating the mediatory mission of that nobleman as nothing, and showing no manner of respect or good feeling, he utterly rejected the friendliness expressed, expecting, as it seems, that the potent *tsar* after having first sent others, would come himself to entreat him. And indeed our gentle and pacific sovereign would have gladly done this, if only he had foreseen any prospect of so obtaining the good result which he most greatly desired. However, knowing the exorable and unchanging obstinacy of Nikon, and that he was swollen to a great pitch of arrogance, he let the man go to be quiet for a while, trusting that afterwards, by condescending letters and kind speeches, he should succeed in healing the untimely mortification of Nikon." Ligarides, 42–43.

97. According to the testimony given by Trubetskoi, "the patriarch said: 'I left the patriarchal throne on my own and not on account of anyone's or any persecution, and the sovereign was not wroth with me but I have already humbly petitioned and notified the great sovereign about this before, that I will not be at the patriarchal throne for more than three years' and gave the letter to the *boyar* and ordered to carry it to the great sovereign." Gibbenet, *Istoricheskoe issledovanie*, Pt. 1, 182.

Nikon's version of these events, given much later, in 1665, is radically different from Trubetskoi's account. "And they [Trubetskoi and "certain others"], having come to the church, said to me: 'The *tsar's* majesty has sent us, and has given us command to say from him, 'Wherefore wilt thou go?' And I made the answer: "I give place to the wrath of the *tsar's* majesty; because contrary to justice, the [Council] of the *tsar's* majesty, the *boyars*, and all kinds of people do all manner of wrongs to the ecclesiastical order, and the *tsar's* majesty does not grant any investigation or satisfaction; but when we complain of such things, he is wroth against us. There is nothing more terrible than for any man to incur the *tsar's* wrath." Nikon, "Letter to Dionysius," 386–387.

98. The idea that clergy and people did not allow Nikon to leave is collaborated by several eyewitness accounts. See Gibbenet, *Istoricheskoe issledovanie*, Pt. 1, 180–214, passim.

99. Nikon offered a completely different perspective on this matter, painting the *tsar* as unwilling to reconcile. "I waited, expecting till the *tsar's* majesty should be pacified, and [letting him know] that I wished to go out to the monastery which I was founding at Voskresensk. And the *tsar's* majesty sent again the same *boyars* to desire that I should not go out without having first seen him. And I, after waiting there three days, expecting some message from the *tsar's* majesty, when none came, after those three days went out to the monastery which I was founding at Voskresensk." Nikon, "Letter to Dionysius," 387.

100. The New Maiden Convent, located on the banks of the Moscow River, was founded in 1524 by grand prince Vasilii Ioannovich to commemorate the victory over Lithuania at Smolensk and its incorporation into Muscovy. Historically, the convent housed royal and aristocratic females who took the veil, either voluntarily or involuntarily. It also served as a royal female burial site; *tsarevna* Tatiana Mikhailovna and *tsarina* Evdokiia Lopukhina, Peter the Great's first wife, are buried there. *Tsarevna* Sofiia Alekseevna, Peter the Great's sister and contender for the throne, was imprisoned there under the name of nun Susanna. The monastery enclosed six churches. See Ratshin, 235–237.

101. Aleksei Trubetskoi's efforts to deliver a cart to Nikon on July 12, 1658 are described in *Delo o patriarkhe Nikone*, No. 7, 16–18.

102. See Kavelin, *Istoricheskoe opisanie*, 504–505.

103. For records of Aleksei Mikhailovich's original grants, see Kavelin, *Istoricheskoe opisanie*, 17 and 524. The *tsar* continued to support Nikon and gave him two thousand rubles from the salt mines as late as 1665 or even early 1666. Indeed. the patriarch thanked the *tsar* for his donations, and requested even more support, in a petition dated to that time. See Gibbenet, *Istoricheskoe issledovanie*, Pt. 2, 850–854.

104. In June 1659, Aleksei Mikhailovich learned about a major breech in the Russian borders. An allied force of Ukrainians and Crimean Tartars defeated the Russian army at Konotop inflicting dramatic fatalities. Nearly five thousand men were lost and Moscow was dangerously exposed to the approaching invasion. The *tsar* ordered to fortify Moscow's defense systems, especially given the flood of refugees from the countryside which swelled the capital's population. See Longworth, 137.

105. The difference between the Orthodox "Conception of the Immaculate [Virgin Mary]" and Catholic "the Immaculate Conception" is that the Orthodox do not consider this event as sinless and immaculate, but Catholics do. In other words, the Orthodox accept the immaculate nature of the Virgin, calling her the most pure [*prechistaia*], but not her immaculate conception. The Immaculate Conception of Virgin Mary in the Catholic tradition or the Conception of the Immaculate Virgin Mary by St. Anne in the Orthodox one should not be confused with the Christian doctrine of the Virgin Birth in which Jesus is born to a virgin mother.

Nikon is clearly being sarcastic here, since no such monastery existed at that time in the place specified. Shusherin himself explains that a prison of the same name stood there.

106. Nikon gave two different reasons for his return to Moscow. In his *Replies*, written in 1662, the patriarch described the *tsar's* invitation to prove that Aleksei Mikhailovich's feelings towards him had not changed despite Nikon's not having lived in Moscow for a year. According to this version, Nikon "had been living, after our withdrawal, in the monastery at Voskresensk for a year and more; and the hossoudar the *tsar* had made no question whatever about the patriarchate being vacant, as knowing very well the cause of our withdrawal. Nay, when we were once more at Moscow, it was even told to us that the horde was about to make an irruption (sic!) into the territory of Moscow. And the hossoudar the *tsar*, when we had a personal interview with him, uttered not a word to us of this; and made no allusion whatever to our previous departure; but did all just as he did as if we were still living at Moscow." Reiterating this point, Nikon continued: "And after one year I went again to Moscow; the hossoudar the *tsar* allowed me to see his face; and while I sat with him he made no allusion whatever to anything which had before passed, knowing that I had nothing to answer to him the hossoudar. And he afterwards would have given me orders to send me to the monastery of Koliazin, only I did not choose to go there, but again retired to my own monastery at Voskresensk, conforming myself to the divine commandment which says, 'When they persecute you in this city, flee ye to another." Nikon, "Replies," 101, 105.

Yet three years later Nikon told a different story. In the second, somewhat more skeptical rendition of the events, Nikon appears to be resigned to the prospect that the *tsar's* displeasure with him might indeed be permanent. "And after one year from our retirement to the monastery of Voskresensk, an alarm came upon the *tsar* and all the people of Moscow as an irruption (sic!) of barbarians was at hand. And the *tsar's* majesty sent to me his lord-in-waiting that we might be informed of that; and we said to him: 'Except at Moscow we have no house to which we could go; and to go away to our distant monasteries we have no means; so do thou report to the *tsar*, and ask where it is his pleasure that we should be.' And the same day from other informants we were told that the Tartars were coming upon Moscow. So we, without waiting until the Tartars should come, drove to Moscow, and on arriving there alighted at our own lodge of the monastery of Voskresensk. And there came to from the *tsar's* majesty secretary of the Council Almaz Ivanov, and questioned us thus: 'The *tsar's* majesty has commanded me to ask thee why thou hast come to Moscow?' And we said that we had come in consequence of a message which we had received from the *tsar's* majesty, and on account of invasion of the barbarians. And after that for three days there was no manner of communication made with us: but after three days there came again from the *tsar's* majesty the secretary of the Council Almaz, and said to us: 'The *tsar's* majesty has commanded thee to go to the Koliazin monastery; go, then, and do not be obstinate, lest greater wrath be provoked against thee.' And we said: 'If our coming is disagreeable to the *tsar's* majesty, and peace and blessing are not on his mind, we will go back to our own foundation of the monastery at Voskresensk; but to the Koliazin monastery I will not go.' And so a second time I departed out of Moscow for the monastery of Voskresensk." Nikon, "Letter to Dionysius," 392–393.

107. There is an interesting story behind the title of metropolitan of Krutitsa who is also referred to as metropolitan of Sar and Don. The metropolitanate of Sarai, Sar, and Don was established in 1261 as a bishopric for southern Russian territories under the Tartar control when Sarai was the capital of the Golden Horde. Its resident seat moved to the Krutitsa Monastery outside Moscow in the mid-fifteenth century, becoming a metropolitanate. The metropolitan of Sarai, Sar, and Don served as assistant to the metropolitan of Moscow, and later to the patriarch of Moscow. The metropolitan of Krutitsa/Sarai, Sar, and Don not only supervised church affairs in the south, but was also on occasion designated as overseer of the patriarchal throne in the patriarch's absence or during the transitional period following the death of a patriarch [*locum tenens*]. See Ratshin, 244–246. Pitirim, was metropolitan of Krutitsa (or of Sar and Don) in 1655–1664 and overseer of the patriarchal throne during that period. At least on one occasion in the text Shusherin refers to Pitirim as metropolitan of Sar and Don, not of Krutitsa, making it appear that he meant two different people, but in fact, he described the same person, Pitirim. In 1664, Pitirim was replaced by Pavel (1664–1675), to whom Shusherin usually refers to as "metropolitan of Sar and Don," but who could also be called "metropolitan of Krutitsa." See Makarii, *Istoriia*, Vol. 12, 609–611.

108. Pitirim was one of Nikon's main opponents among the Russian hierarchs. As metropolitan of Krutitsa (Sar and Don), he also was assigned a duty of overseeing the Russian patriarchate in the patriarch's absence (1658–1664). Nikon even anathemized Pitirim for improperly acting as patriarch. In particular, Pitirim took Nikon's place in the Palm Sunday procession. After serving as metropolitan of Novgorod (1664–1673), eventually Pitirim replaced Ioasaf (1667–1672) as patriarch of Moscow and served in this capacity for ten months in 1673. See Gibbenet, *Istoricheskoe issledovanie*, Pt. 2, 535–536; Lebedev, 44; and Lobachev, *Patriarkh Nikon*, 178–179.

109. Nikon arrived at the Iverskii Monastery in September 1659. See Kavelin, *Akty Iverskago monastyria*, 24 and 26. He arrived at the Galilee Hermitage in honor of the Holy Trinity on October 23, 1659. See Sevast'ianova, *Mater'ialy*, 185. Nikon was at the Iverskii monastery until at least December 15, 1659. He arrived at the Cross Monastery by February 3, 1660. See Sevast'ianova, *Mater'ialy*, 186. Nikon arrived at the Resurrection Monastery in mid-September 1660. See Kavelin, *Akty Iverskago monastyria*, 27.

110. Nikon founded the stone church on September 2, 1660. See Kavelin, *Akty Iverskago monastyria*, 27.

111. For example, Nikon founded a wooden church dedicated to All Saints on September 8, 1660. See Kavelin, *Akty Iverskago monastyria*, 27.

112. The Monastery of the Miracles, now extinct, was located within the walls of the Moscow Kremlin. Founded in 1365, it was at one point the seat of the metropolitan of Moscow (until 1817). Aleksei Mikhailovich and his son Piotr, the future Peter the Great, were baptized in the cathedral of St. Aleksei, the monastery's main sanctuary. The sentencing phase of patriarch Nikon's trial was held at the monastery. And on December 12, 1666, in the presence of two ecumenical patriarchs, Nikon was formally divested of his patriarchal status at the monastery's Annunciation Church. See Ratshin, 182–188.

113. Nikon reported Feodosii's confession, including the monk's explanation that he was sent by Pitirim, the metropolitan of Krutitsa (or of Sar and Don), in a letter written to *boyar* Nikita Ziuzin dated June 28, 1660. This missive is published in Gibbenet, *Istoricheskoe issledovanie*, Pt. 1, 95.

114. The official record of Feodosii's interrogation by the *tsar's* officials is published in Gibbenet, *Istoricheskoe issledovanie*, Pt. 2, 497–504. Shusherin's work follows closely the state document.

115. Nikon returned to the New Jerusalem Resurrection Monastery in mid-September 1660. See Kavelin, *Akty Iverskago monastyria*, 27.

116. Nikon himself believed that the royal table attendant Roman Bobarykin was responsible for instigating this accusation. Following a visit to the Resurrection Monastery to resolve a land dispute (see note 121 below), Bobarykin accused Nikon of slandering the *tsar*. "And they drove to the land, in order to mark it off. And while they were about this, the patriarch Nikon went into the holy church of God with the brethren, and sang a prayer service to the holy and life-giving Cross of the Lord, and said holy prayers from the Psalms proper for them who are suffering violence . . . And on the second day the patriarch with the brethren sang again a prayer service after the same manner. And at that time Roman was within the monastery, and present at the prayer service; he said nothing. But after that, having let a long time pass in silence, Roman informed against the patriarch Nikon that he had cursed the *tsar*, with the *tsarina*, and the *tsareviches*, and the *tsarevnas*, and all their house." Nikon, "Replies," 585–586. Nikon also mentioned this charge in his "Letter to Dionysius," 391. Official documents pertaining to Bobarykin's allegations are published in Gibbenet, *Istoricheskoe issledovanie*, Pt. 2, 609–626.

Ligarides offered another interpretation of these charges. "Satan, the enemy of peace, deceiving spirit, instigated Nikon openly to curse the *tsar*, and absolutely to deliver him over to Satan. But that this might not be notorious to all, and manifest to the simpler sort of them that were in the [Resurrection] Monastery, he cunningly veiled his malicious wickedness. He spread out the *tsar's* letters, which were sealed with the great seal . . . and caused to be sung the curses of Psalm 58 (which contains thirty curses against the traitor Judas, who sold the Lord for thirty pieces of silver, . . .), with these words of imprecation, 'Let his children be orphans and his wife be a widow; let his days be few,' with a loud voice so that all should hear." Ligarides, 76.

117. Ligarides, who dates the meeting to July 15–16, 1663, likewise explained that the *tsar* wept. See ibid., 76–77.

118. Ligarides presented his own eyewitness account of this assembly, explaining that Nikon's alleged curse "was reported immediately to the great *tsar*, who, as soon as day dawned, called together all the bishops who were to be found, and related to them, not without tears, what Nikon had done . . . 'Grant,' added the supreme monarch, 'grant that I myself have erred and do err, yet of what sin have my dear children been guilty? And he said in imprecation, "Let his children be destroyed and his posterity clean put out," or wherein, again, has my wife and *tsarina* offended? And yet he has recklessly imprecated curses on all persons, men and women alike, of my court.' We all blushed with shame at the hearing of such things; and with one voice and consent they earnestly besought the *tsar* for a searching and exact investigation of the matter." Ligarides, 76.

119. See ibid., 77–78.

120. Below are competing accounts of the official inquiries conducted at the New Jerusalem Resurrection Monastery in July 1663.

Nikon's version appears in the twenty-sixth of his *Replies*. "In the year 7171, on July 18 (1663), there were sent to the Resurrection [Monastery] *boyar* prince Nikita Odoevskii, and the lord-in-waiting Rodion Streshnev, and the secretary of the Council Almaz Ivanov, and the captain of the *strel'tsy* Vasilii Filosofov, with *strel'tsy*, and with many other people, and with them the metropolitan of Gaza, as he called himself, Paisius commonly called Ligarides . . . And after vespers (*vechernia*) they sent to patriarch Nikon to announce that he the *boyar* prince Nikita Odoevskii, with his colleagues, and the ecclesiastical dignitaries, were sent from the sovereign the *tsar* to me the patriarch Nikon on a matter of state, in the name of the sovereign . . . And when the *boyars* and the ecclesiastical dignitaries were come to the patriarch, into the ante-chamber, the patriarch said, according to the monastic custom, . . . the prayer for the *tsar* and for the *tsarina* and for the *tsareviches* and for the *tsarevnas* . . . And the *boyar* said, 'Where am I to speak to thee the business of the sovereign? Here in the ante-chamber or in thy cell?' And the patriarch said, 'Will you not come into the cell?' And the *boyars* and the church dignitaries went in, and stood in the place of honor, but the church dignitaries at the stove. And the *boyar* said: 'On the petition of Roman Bobarykin there was sent by edict of the sovereign to mark off and award land . . . and when they began to mark off the land thou, with the archimandrite and the brethren, didst sing a prayer service; and in the prayer service thou didst say many prayers with a curse, and didst curse the sovereign the *tsar*, and his *tsar's* children.' And the patriarch said, 'That prayer service I sang, and those psalms I said, according to the form of St. Athanasius the Great, as fit for a time of affliction. But I did not curse the sovereign. For the sovereign I pray to God . . . And against them that were wronging us [I said] such prayers as were composed by David the king and prophet, who prayed in his affliction and persecutions to the Lord God against his enemies. And I said those same prayers. But as to what is written in them, I cannot cut it out . . . But [if you wish to know] how it was, you have only to follow us into the church, and you shall hear yourselves how it was.' And prince Nikita refused the holy Orthodox Church replying, 'Thou didst also place before the cross, and before the icon of the Mother of God, a letter of the sovereign, which thou hadst spread out: and after the prayer service thou didst read that letter of the sovereign. Why didst thou that?' And the patriarch said, 'The letter of the sovereign I placed before the cross and the icon of the most holy Mother of God, and read it after the prayer service, for this reason, because the land about the Resurrection Monastery belongs to the Iverskii Monastery; and that land which they by edict of the sovereign took away and awarded to Roman Bobarykin, was bought and dedicated to the most holy Mother of God and that is my chief monastery. And in the letter of the sovereign it is written thus: "But if any man after us shall in any respect contemn this our *tsar's* perpetual command, and shall in any way or on any pretext infringe this our letter of grant or shall take away from the house of the most holy Mother of God those estates . . . may God judge him as he judged those transgressors of old whom for their great transgression the mercy of God endured not in this life, but destroyed them without mercy" . . . And [I read the letter] because that curse of the sovereign was incurred by that man Roman Bobarykin.' And the prince Nikita with his colleagues began to say, 'We have answers made during his examination by the abbot of the hermitage Aaron, that thou didst curse the sovereign' . . . And the same day in the evening the *boyars* sent to the patriarch that he should send the archimandrite, and the vicar, and the priests, and the deacons, and the brethren to be examined . . . And on the same day, in the evening, late, they sent in different direction about the monastery *strel'tsy*, as in a manner of tyrants and persecutors, to take the archimandrite, and the vicar, and the brethren: and they examined them with the greatest inequity, with the most overbearing heat, threatening them with tortures and distant exiles. And on the nineteenth of July, it being Sunday, they sent during the liturgy into the church *strel'tsy* to take the priests." Nikon, "Replies," 586–589 and 601–602.

Ligarides also offered a first-hand account of the investigations at the New Jerusalem Resurrection Monastery. His narrative focuses largely on Nikon's alleged hostile attitude to him (Ligarides) and does not present the details offered in Shusherin's narrative. According to Ligarides, the *tsar* "called together again both the synod and [the Council], to consult with them as whom he should send. And by common consent the metropolitan of Gaza [Ligarides] was appointed, as being most learned and eloquent, and able both to give him who should ask, and to extort from another, a direct answer . . . We set forth, with full instructions, and escorted and attended by soldiers on all sides, July 17, 1663 AD; and the next day, at the hour of vespers, we arrived at the Monastery of the Resurrection, falsely called by him 'New Jerusalem': and . . . the most illustrious Nikita Odoevskii sent a man to announce us to Nikon, to say there had come certain bishops as commissioners to speak and confer with him. But he was greatly disturbed at hearing there was such an array of soldiers come, and said to them that were about him, being troubled, no doubt, by his own consciousness: 'Their coming bodes no good; they want to send me away to a distance.' . . . We entered, and he began to say the usual prayers, and stood a moment, awaiting our episcopal salutation: but when he saw that we did not go up to him, he looked us in the face and reddened, as, forsooth, being put to shame at our first approaches being so little friendly; and, drawing back abruptly, he entered into his inner chamber, and there awaited us, standing upright, and leaning on a bent-topped and thick staff, and silent as one dumb. Then I, metropolitan of Gaza, began to speak in Latin, looking to Nikon: 'Our most serene *tsar* and autocrat . . . Aleksei Mikhailovich, and all the episcopal synod, sent me to ask thee from what motive or for what cause has thou delivered over to an indissoluble excommunication and most heavy curse, with all his house, our monarch, the most serene *tsarina* . . . and their children and our princes . . . whom the most high has given to us reign upon the earth for the glory of the ecclesiastical firmament, for the increase and happiness of the Christian community?' This was translated into Russian by the *tsar's* interpreter . . . as he translated it, Nikon began to string together words which were nothing to the purpose, never answering to the question . . . After long and patiently waiting, I at length said, 'Answer, I pray, to the question, as the gospel directs, yea, yea, or nay, nay. Didst thou curse or didst thou not curse, our *tsar*?' And Nikon said, 'I make prayers and supplications for the *tsar*, and do not imprecate on him destruction.' 'How does he not imprecate,' I exclaimed, 'who applies the deep and awful curses of the Psalms?' . . . Many words were spoken on this matter by the *boyars*, who took him up with one consent, and disputed with him sharply . . . This discussion was drawn out over the space of many hours; and there was a great tumult among my fellow commissioners and the *boyars*. And Nikon stood there all the time continuously shaking his staff at them; and striking with it violently on the ground, he fluttered them, thundering, confounding, lightening, and answering alone to all of them . . . so that at last we went out from his cell without having done anything, utterly stupefied at his obstinacy and headlong violence, and at the ungovernable rush and ready torrent of his words. But, for fear of tediousness, I have not related here the hundredth part of what the *tsar's* fast-writer took hasty notes of at this time . . . In the meantime however they that lived close to the monastery were summoned and examined, how, and when, and after what fashion Nikon had pronounced against the *tsar* the words of imprecation? And we ascertained many things in agreement with the charges brought against him." Ligarides, 77–81.

For Odoevskii's, Streshnev's, and Ivanov's own versions of the events, see "Otpiski gosudariu tsariu Alekseiu Mikhailovichu boyarina kniazia Nikity Ivanovicha Odoevskago, okol'nichago Rodiona Streshneva i d'iaka Almaza Ivanova, posylannykh v Voskresenskii Novo-Ierusalimskii monastyr', vmeste s dukhovnymi vlastiami, k patriarkhu Nikonu, dlia doprosa ego, po donosu Romana Bobarykina: na kogo on Nikon vo vremia bogosluzheniia proiznios prokliatie i po kakoi prichine zloslovit gosudaria?," in *SGGD*, Vol. 4, Nos. 34–35, 126–131.

121. When Nikon returned to the New Jerusalem Monastery in 1660, he became involved in a controversy over property rights with the neighboring *boyar* Roman Bobarykin. Nikon claimed that Bobarykin had taken control of lands belonging to the monastery and asked the *tsar* to investigate the matter based on the original deeds. When Aleksei Mikhailovich ignored two petitions from the patriarch, Nikon acted on his own, ordering peasants from New Jerusalem to harvest the grain growing on the disputed land and to bring it to the monastery. Following suit, Bobarykin petitioned the *tsar*. Responding to Bobarykin's request, Aleksei Mikhailovich ordered an inquiry into the peasants' actions, and ultimately sided with the *boyar*. See Gibbenet, *Istoricheskoe issledovanie*, Pt. 1, 99–101. Nikon's petition to the *tsar* (December 1661) is published in Gibbenet, *Is-*

toricheskoe issledovanie, Pt. 2, 505–518. See also Kavelin, *Istoricheskoe opisanie*, 119–124.

122. See Kavelin, *Istoricheskoe opisanie*, 525.

123. According to Nikon, these events took place not the next day, July 19, 1663 (a Sunday), but three days later, on July 21, 1663. See Nikon, "Replies," 602.

124. In the twenty-sixth of his *Replies*, Nikon described the commotion at the monastery. "On the twenty-first of July, they sounded the bell that the brethren might hear and come together, to go and clear out a kiln of bricks. And the *boyars* sent to the patriarch the secretary of the Council Almaz and the archimandrite Feodosii . . . And after that he [Almaz] began to say, 'we have heard that thou wishest to go out to the sheds, to bring in bricks; but thou art not to go out of the monastery: thou must remain in thy cell.' And the patriarch said, 'I am ready not only to be confined to my cell, but even to die.' From that time whenever the patriarch went to the church, or to the building work that was going on, to inspect it, there followed a corporal with ten men of the *strel'tsy* with their arms. On the twenty-eighth of the same month there came the *boyar* prince Nikita Odoevskii with his colleagues and the ecclesiastical dignitaries, and said, making a great noise: 'The sovereign the *tsar* and the ecclesiastical authorities ordered thee to live in the Resurrection Monastery, but to keep within thy cell, and except to the church to go out nowhither.' And the patriarch Nikon said to the *boyars*: 'On the edict of the great sovereign I am ready to go even to prison.'" Nikon, "Replies," 602–604.

Ligarides provided a conflicting version of the circumstances surrounding the restrictions placed on Nikon. "Nikon meanwhile, learning that all his conduct was being thus closely investigated, was studying how to make his escape as speedily as possible, and had a very light vehicle got ready, in which, very early in the morning, before it was well day, he was on the point of starting, to escape to certain cunningly concealed hiding places. But his intention of flying was discovered immediately; and so he was prevented, and guards were at the same time set about the monastery." Ligarides, 81.

125. Nikon himself described the final moments before the delegation departed from his monastery in a distinctly negative light. "And they [the delegation], as they were out of their minds, all cried out they themselves knew not what. And at last the *boyar* said, 'The sovereign the *tsar* has made order that a captain of the *strel'tsy* with his men is to be here on guard.' And the patriarch to this said, 'The sovereign's will be done: let it be as the sovereign pleases. We are ready thankfully to suffer for God's sake.' And with that last word they all went out; and getting into their carriages they all drove off from the monastery . . . And on the day of Transfiguration, the captain with his *strel'tsy* went away altogether to Moscow." Nikon, "Replies," 604.

126. Nicholaas Witsen, a seventeenth-century Dutch ambassador to Muscovy, who visited Nikon at the New Jerusalem Resurrection Monastery in early May 1665, observed that most of the building masters and oversees were Poles and Germans. See Nicholaas Witsen, *Moscovische Reyes 1664–1665 Journal En Aentekeningen*. Th. J. G Locher and P. de Buck, eds. (Amsterdam, 1966), 277; and A. M. Loviagin, "Nikolai Vitsen iz Amterdama u patriarkha Nikona," *Istoricheskii vestnik* 9 (1899): 877.

127. Witsen told that during his visit to the New Jerusalem Resurrection Monastery, Nikon mentioned that false accusations, including, for example, the charge that he does not pray for the *tsar*, were made against him. The patriarch was not however in a conciliatory mood. He confided in Witsen that "the *tsar* [was] in a bad position now because he miss[ed] my blessing." Witsen, 288; and Loviagin, 879.

128. In Russia, not unlike in the West, the head of the monastery, let alone the patriarch, usually led a much more comfortable lifestyle than the common monks, enjoying the benefits of his position. Thanks to his authority within the monastery and the donations of secular patrons, he usually had a much more sophisticated diet. So here, in addition to proving the *tsar's* magnanimity and good-will towards Nikon, Shusherin under-

scores the patriarch's generosity, humbleness, and closeness to the monks. Earlier in the text, Shusherin also described Nikon's partaking in monastery's labor activities. These details directly contradict the patriarch's critics who charged him with gluttony and even predatory practices. See, for example, Ligarides, 26; and Borozdin, No. 33, 158.

129. Although referenced by Shusherin only in passing, both Nashchokin and Matveev were such outstanding court officials and statesmen, that they warrant a brief introduction. Afanasii Lavrent'evich Nashchokin (or Ordyn-Nashchokin) (1605–1680) was a head of the Foreign Affairs office under Aleksei Mikhailovich. A well-educated and pro-Western diplomat, he was responsible for the armistice with Poland which ended the 1654–1667 war. Artamon Sergeevich Matveev (1625–July 5, 1682), another pro-Western diplomat who succeeded Nashchokin in the Foreign Affairs office, was connected to the royal family through his niece and ward, Nataliia Naryshkina, who became Aleksei Mikhailovich's second wife (January 22, 1671). In 1671–1676, Matveev was *de facto* a head of Aleksei Mikhailovich's government. After falling out with the *tsar*, Matveev was exiled to Verkhotur'e and then to Pustozersk. In 1682, Peter the Great recalled him from exile, but Matveev came to the capital at a very inopportune time, in the midst of the 1682 *strel'tsy* uprising. He was killed by the *strel'tsy* soon after his arrival. See Kliuchevsky, 130, 294, 369–378; and Solov'ev, Vol. 13, 26–48.

Since both Nashchokin and Matveev were very close to Aleksei Mikhailovich, the reference to their names gave Ziuzin's claim the air of authenticity which would not be lost on Nikon.

130. Nikon presented his version of these events in his letter to the patriarch of Constantinople. "In the year 1665 [actually 1664], one week before the Nativity, a certain man of holy life, named Nikita, who had before been by rank one of the *tsar's boyars*, . . . wrote to us as many as three times (and we know not whether really by the *tsar's* command, or by the instigation of his friends, or of his own piety), wishing to bring about peace and amity between us. The *tsar's* majesty (so he wrote) sent to him certain persons of those about him, whom he regards favorably, and bade him to write to us, the humble Nikon patriarch, that we should come to Moscow before Nativity of Christ uncalled, of ourselves, and that the *tsar's* majesty would be glad of our coming, and would receive us with joy." Nikon, "Letter to Dionysius," 393–394. The official documents pertinent to the Ziuzin affair are included in *SGGD*, Vol. 4, No. 38, 142–143; *Delo o patriarkhe Nikone*, No. 41, 181–210; and Gibbenet, *Istoricheskoe issledovanie*, Pt. 2, 748–755.

131. The patriarch's return to the capital on December 18, 1664 is well documented. Many of those who witnessed the events at the Dormition Cathedral in the Moscow Kremlin were subsequently interrogated. For eyewitness accounts, see Gibbenet, *Istoricheskoe issledovanie*, Pt. 2, 736–759; and *Delo o patriarkhe Nikone*, No. 31, 121; No. 34, 127; Nos. 35–36, 128–137; and No. 40, 147–181. Nikon himself discussed the ill-fated journey in his "Letter to Dionysius" and Paisius Ligarides devoted an entire chapter of his *History* to it. Old Believer authors also sensationalized the event.

Below are the most representative accounts of Nikon's return to Moscow.

Nikon believed that by the time he arrived in the capital the *tsar* has already made up his mind to send him away. "Having come to Moscow, I entered into the holy catholic and apostolic church, and stood at my episcopal place, and sent to let the *tsar's* majesty know. And we, imitating the depth of the humility of God the Word, did all these that we then did. And when we were in the cathedral church we sent thence to the *tsar's* majesty Iona, the metropolitan of Rostov, . . . and the archimandrite of our monastery, and one priest of the cathedral, to announce to the *tsar's* majesty our having come. And the *tsar's* majesty was wroth with the metropolitan, and the archimandrite, and the priest, and sent them out from his presence with dishonor, and gave command to suspend them from performing divine service. And after the *tsar's* majesty sent to us from his highest *boyars* the prince Nikita Odoevskii, with others his colleagues, and asked us: 'Why hast thou come?' And we said: 'To bring peace and blessing to the *tsar's* majesty, and to you, if ye are willing to receive us in the Lord.' And they went with that word to the *tsar's* majesty. And having come again from the *tsar's* majesty to the cathedral, and with them the metropolitan of Gaza and the metropolitan of Krutitsa, and other ecclesiastical dignitaries, they said to us: 'The *tsar's* majesty has commanded us to say to thee: go back to the Resurrection Monastery, and abide there till further orders; and do not delay, that nothing worse be the consequence: and wait for a decree from the ecumenical patriarchs: for they have been written to from the *tsar's* majesty to that end several times; and the *tsar's* majesty is expecting soon to receive a decree from them.' And we, on account of the precept of the gospel, were not inclined to have much more to do with them: for, 'where,' it is said, 'they will not receive you, nor hearken unto your words, when ye go out of that city shake off even the dust of your feet for a testimony to them.' And so, taking the staff which stood in the episcopal place, I went out with it.'" Nikon, "Letter to Dionysius," 394.

Iona, metropolitan of Rostov, the highest ranking hierarch witnessing Nikon's arrival, described this event in a more neutral tone. "Iona, metropolitan of Rostov, reported to the great sovereign and it was written in his report: On the eighteenth of December during the singing of the vigil (*vsenoshchnaia*), at the second proper Psalm (*kafisma*), suddenly a noise occurred and the doors of the cathedral clattered and many people entered the church and behind them a cross was carried, and behind the cross came Nikon, the patriarch, and he stood at the patriarchal stall (*patriarshee mesto*); and his elders were singing "Meet it is in truth to glorify Thee" (*Dosgtoino est'*) and "Many years, your eminence" (*Ispolla eti, Despota,* a greeting sang to announce the entrance of a hierarch); but the patriarch prohibited his sub-deacon from reciting from the Book of Psalms and ordered the cathedral deacon Mikhail to read the litany of supplication (*ektin'ia*). And he himself at that time kissed the icon and the relics of the miracle-workers and after kissing them went up the patriarchal stall and read a prayer and ordered to summon a metropolitan to him to be blessed, and the metropolitan and the archpriest with the brethren came for the blessing. And the patriarch send the metropolitan with the archimandrite to the great sovereign, and ordered to inform him about his arrival, but that the patriarch took the staff of the miracle-worker, that was not known to the metropolitan. And on the order of the great sovereign Iona, metropolitan of Rostov, and the *boyar* prince Odoevskii interrogated the cathedral archpriest, together with the brethren, about the patriarch's arrival and his taking the miracle-working staff." Gibbenet, *Istoricheskoe issledovanie*, Pt. 2, 742.

The Old Believer, Fedor Ivanov, intent on further disgracing the patriarch, explained that "[a]t one point of time, he [Nikon] succeeded in jumping back on the throne. Arriving in the capital city uninvited, he entered the church at night like a criminal. He frightened all who were present at the Sunday all-night service (*vsenoshchnaia*). Upon learning about the thief's presence in church, the *tsar* sent his *boyars* to ask the wolf why he came uninvited and [told him] to go back to where he came from. [Nikon] returned to his Jerusalem in shame, but not without stealing the staff of saint metropolitan Piotr from the patriarchal stall first. Having learned about this, the *tsar* sent Pavel, metropolitan of Sar and Don, and the *tsar's* army to pursue Nikon like a fast dog would pursue a wolf. The *tsar* ordered to take the staff of the saint [Piotr] by force which was done. At this time, the blasphemer tormented many of his servants who were not quick enough to replace his horses while traveling and so he could not escape." Deacon Fedor, "Testimonies," in Titova, 235–236.

132. Nikon actually sent a petition to the *tsar* on December 18, 1664. Explaining his arrival in Moscow, the patriarch wrote: "To the great sovereign . . . [and his family], peace and blessings, today I am in the Cathedral of the Holiest Mother of God. . . . Since I corrected my fault of leaving, which I thought out and realized, I came to see your most

glowing faces and to humbly bow down to the holy glory of your reign . . . so we came
. . . in humbleness and meekness, as our Lord taught us by saying 'learn from me who is
meek and humble in heart.' . . . I wrote this to your majesty not for my own sake, for he
who talks about himself seeks only his glory. . . . But from purity, as from God, and before God I talk about Christ." Throughout the text Nikon compared his return to Moscow to
Christ's appearance to the Disciples after the Resurrection. The full text of this petition is
published in Gibbenet, *Istoricheskoe issledovanie*, Pt. 2, 740–741; and *Delo o patriarkhe
Nikone*, No. 33, 124–126.

133. Ligarides, who was present at this assembly, explained that he himself suggested:
"Let him [Nikon] be asked how he came in hither, and who invited him, that he had with
such confidence mounted suddenly, like a thief and an invader, the patriarchal throne,
certainly before he had been tried, not to say acquitted?" Ligarides, 86. See also *Delo o
patriarkhe Nikone*, No. 31, 121.

134. Ligarides explained that the *tsar* sent Pavel, metropolitan of Krutitsa, to question
Nikon, alleging that the patriarch abused him [Pavel]. "[Pavel], the metropolitan of
Krutitsa, was sent to question him, together with certain lords of the Council. But Nikon,
seeing the aforesaid metropolitan . . . spake thus . . . 'Who are you? You are entirely unknown to me!' But he replied: 'I have been recently consecrated metropolitan . . . But tell
me wherefore, without the will of the sovereign, hast thou thus suddenly come in among
us? For thou hast come in truth not bringing peace, but a sword against the new Israel,
which sees thy exceedingly high mind.' Nikon, in reply, pronounced tragically a multitude of words which were beside the subject." Ligarides, 86. See also *Delo o patriarkhe
Nikone*, No. 31, 121.

135. The urgent message that Nikon tried to pass to the *tsar* was a missive in which
the patriarch described a vision he had at the Resurrection Monastery on December 13,
1664, prior to his arrival in Moscow. It reads: "The story of the humble Nikon, by the
grace of God patriarch, by what reason he returned from the Resurrection Monastery to
his throne in the ruling city of Moscow. Hearing the discord and the great discussion
about the patriarchal throne, some say this and others say different and corrupting things,
but none of it is true, but everyone says whatever they wish; and for this on the fourteenth
day of November of the year 7173 [1664], I left for the hermitage outside the monastery
to pray and fast, so that the Lord God would tell me what should happen. And so I tearfully prayed to the Lord God, but an answer did not come; and so, on the thirteenth day of
December, wounded even more than the first time by God's love, and submitting prayer
after prayer, and tear after tear, and vigil after vigil, and fast after fast before the Lord
God, and fasting even until the seventeenth day, for . . . I started the fast on Tuesday and
fasted until Saturday, not eating anything, nor drinking water, but replacing bread with
prayer, and drink with tears. . . . I sat only for an hour a day, and labored and prayed with
tears, crying out and weeping, until the Lord God told me what must be done and what is
pleasing to His holy will; and praying manifold, I told Jesus Christ our Lord: 'You, Lord,
told me with your most pure unfalse lips: whatever you asked for in prayer will be given
to you in My name.' And again the Lord told me: 'Ask and you shall receive, seek and
you shall find, knock and it will be opened unto you.' And after a while He said: 'He who
asks will receive and it will be opened for he who knocks.' And vexing God's love for
man so much, I sat down in the church on my seat, exhausted, for I did not retire for sleep
[even once] in these four nights and three days; and as I sat down, I drifted into a short
slumber, I sat and saw; I was in the holy cathedral and saw a very great light, yet I did not
see anyone living, but holy hierarchs and priests who died in previous years, who stood
on the sides; I passed the tombs of the holy fathers the metropolitans and patriarchs who
died earlier; however, a certain holy man with gray hair, content and very beautiful, with
a very thick, long beard, dressed in holy hierarchal vestments, stood there. The same
aforesaid holy man was passing all the other holy fathers and was giving all the hierarchs

a charter and cinnabar in a well, and they all were signing the charter; frightened, I approached he who was carrying the charter and the cinnabar well and asked him: 'What are you doing by signing the charter?' He then told me: '[We sign for] your return to the holy throne.' I said: 'Show me, is this the truth?" He showed me, and I saw that it was so. I again asked him: 'Would you sign?' He said: 'I have already signed and showed me his signature.' I looked closely and the following appeared written authentically . . . 'humble Iona, by the grace of God metropolitan, signed by the fear of God.' Inspired, I went to the patriarchal stall and, wanting to go up, I saw a hierarch standing there in honorable hierarchal vestments and I was frightened. He however told me: 'Do not be frightened, oh brother, this is God's will, ascend to your throne and shepherd the sheep of Christ the Word, as God has entrusted you'; and immediately he became invisible. I went up fortified; I thought that it was metropolitan Piotr the miracle-worker who stood there. Yea, yea, God be my witness. Amen." Gibbenet, *Istoricheskoe issledovanie*, Pt. 2, 738–740. The letter is also found in *Delo o patriarkhe Nikone*, No. 32, 122–124; and Solov'ev, Vol. 11, 221–222.

Ligarides not only subverted the text of Nikon's original message to Aleksei Mikhailovich, but also told about the alleged effect the missive had on the *tsar* and his Council. "He produced the note and, holding it in his hand, said: 'Go, and deliver this to the *tsar*, to be read in the presence of all.' And the *tsar,* having with difficulty received this, opened it. The contents of that sealed letter or petition were briefly to this effect: 'After my long absence and fasting, after long continued supplication and earnest prayer, on this now the fortieth day, there appeared to me an angel of the Lord, and said to me: "Go as quickly as possible, O patriarch Nikon, to Moscow, and show thyself personally to thy flock; for all will joyfully receive thee, and install thee in the patriarchal chair." Trusting, therefore, this angelic revelation, that I might not be disobedient to it, or rather to God, low, I am come here of myself, without notice, unannounced. Do ye then choose what it pleases you, and what ye like best, and do, as ye have it now and in your own power, whatever ye deliberately choose.' We were all amazed at this fictitious revelation, and at his fabling, though nothing was said: and all with one accord cried out: 'An angel of Satan has been sent to Nikon, disguised as an angel of light: notwithstanding, let this seer of empty revelations depart from us with all speed: let this buffoon of a man return to his monastery, that there be not any rebellion yea, and needless bloodshed too, among the people.'" Ligarides, 87–88.

136. The circumstances surrounding Nikon's departure from Moscow are described in his letter to the patriarch of Constantinople. "[A]nd as I went out of the city to depart, and at each of the gates of the city, I shook off from my feet the dust, repeating those words of the Gospel: and I came to Chernevo, a village of ours, belonging to our monastery of Voskresensk, twenty *versts* distant from Moscow. And the *tsar's* majesty sent after us those about his person, the lord-in-waiting Rodion Streshnev and the secretary of the Council Almaz Ivanov, and with them six men of the heads of the *strel'tsy* with many soldiers, also the metropolitan of Krutitsa, with other ecclesiastical dignitaries." Nikon, "Letter to Dionysius," 394–395. See also Gibbenet, *Istoricheskoe issledovanie*, Pt. 2, 742, 744 and *Delo o patriarkhe Nikone,* No. 34, 127–129.

The tone of Ligarides' version differs sharply from both Shusherin's and Nikon's interpretation. Ligarides, who explained that he was among those charged with delivering the *tsar's* order, wrote: "After showing his anger against us, and exceedingly indignant, he, I say, at length, being convinced, in spite of himself, that it was so, casting a glance of anger and rage at us three bishops, and having privately ceased hold of the pastoral staff of St. Peter, descended in the utmost wrath from the patriarchal chair, and, scarcely having made his reverence, went out hastily from the church; and having taken his place in a vehicle, as being manifestly detected, he fled off in all haste. And having shaken the dust from his own feet, and having bade his attendants to shake it off likewise from theirs, he had nothing else to congratulate himself upon but having got possession of the pastoral staff, which pleased him vastly; and, as if he had by holy stratagem regained this his standard, he went away with it, and returned towards his monastery, without being seen or hindered, at least by anybody." Ligarides, 88.

137. See *Delo o patriarkhe Nikone*, No. 39, 141–147; and Gibbenet, *Istoricheskoe issledovanie*, Pt. 2, 742, 744.

138. On the dual usage of titles of metropolitan of Sar and Don and metropolitan of Krutitsa, see note 107 above.

139. The *tsar's* decree is published as *Delo o patriarkhe Nikone*, No. 38, 139–140.

140. Shusherin's account is collaborated by *Delo o patriarkhe Nikone*, No. 37, 137–139; No. 39, 141–146; and Gibbenet, *Istoricheskoe issledovanie*, Pt. 2, 742, 744, 748.

Ligarides explained that the *tsar* "immediately sent the metropolitan of Krutitsa and with him two *boyars*, to reprove him both for his desperate audacity and his most imprudent sacrilege; yea, and in the name of piety to demand from him the pastoral staff of the first metropolitan of Moscow. But now, what rhetorical writer could worthily describe his unspeakable and cynical impudence, or relate all the scandalous things he said . . . It is enough to say that he was forced at last to give up the staff, however unwillingly; and that he who had feigned having received an angelic revelation confessed in terms that a certain *boyar* had desired him to come to Moscow; and as he spoke he produced his letter, and delivered it to the commissioners that they might show it to the *tsar*." Ligarides, 88–89.

Nikon also commented on the *tsar's* delegation taking the staff away from him; he tells a much different story. "And they said to us: 'The *tsar's* majesty has commanded us to take from thee the staff.' And I said to them: 'It is not right for the *tsar's* majesty to take from us the staff by force: we did not receive it from him, but from the grace of the Holy Ghost, from above.' And on that account they straitened us much with famine, and with all manner of constraint. And after having endured much, seeing that it was impossible to get away from them with that staff in our hands, I said to them that they were sent from the *tsar's* majesty: 'Before this your coming we called to witness God, heaven and earth, and other holy things, and now we testify before this holy staff that only let the *tsar's* majesty cease to be wroth with us, and then, if our humility is not agreeable to him, to be a patriarch in Moscow, let him do as he pleases. Only let him be in charity again with us and not afflict us. . . . And if the *tsar's* majesty will only observe justice also towards us, then this staff shall be to him for a blessing, and to avenge him of his adversaries. But if there shall be found any injustice on the part of the *tsar's* majesty towards our humble person, then this holy staff shall be to the *tsar's* majesty for a witness against him, and for an exaction of vengeance for all his injustice.'" Nikon, "Letter to Dionysius," 395.

141. These events are likewise recorded in *Delo o patriarkhe Nikone*, No. 39, 146–147. Ziuzin's letters are published in *Delo o patriarkhe Nikone*, No. 41, 181–210; and in Gibbenet, *Istoricheskoe issledovanie*, Pt. 2, 748–755.

142. The official records of the interrogations and sentences of those involved in the Ziuzin affair are published in Gibbenet, *Istoricheskoe issledovanie*, Pt. 2, 755–795; and *Delo o patriarkhe Nikone*, No. 41, 181–210. Nikon himself described the interrogations and subsequent punishments in his letter to patriarch of Constantinople. "Nikita Ziuzin, who was before a *boyar*, was by the *tsar's* wrath deprived of all his property and banished to a distant place; and his wife, a pious women, suddenly departed this life fearing intolerable tortures. The sub-deacon Nikita, who had brought us the letters from him, being cast into prison and into fetters, soon died. The priest Sysoi, who came to us with a letter, was banished, no one knows wither, with all his family . . . And many others whose names we know not: whoever speaks a good word of us, or brings any letters or

information, are banished or tortured." Nikon listed even more people punished in con-
nection with the Ziuzin affair. See Nikon, "Letter to Dionysius," 396.

143. In his travelogue, Witsen provided a contemporary description of the Resurrection Monastery explaining that "the monastery called Jerusalem is perfectly similar to a
Russian fortress from a distance; it has ten or twelve towers. . . . At the gate stands a tall
wooden tower with beautifully carved decorations in the Russian style. Five or six metal
cannons are standing below . . . Before coming to the gate of the tower one has to pass
the building where his holiness receives visitors or everyone of non-monastic rank who
come to him. Next to it are the foundry, bell forgery, brick works, stables and icon shops,
stone quarry, and a building for the workers. When we entered the courtyard, we were
greeted by a service nobleman and secretary to the patriarch Dionisii Ivanovich who was
born in Riga, but captured in Poland, and has now converted." Witsen, 278.

144. On the dual usage of titles of metropolitan of Sar and Don and metropolitan of
Krutitsa, see note 107 above.

145. Nikon explained the reasons why he condemned Pitirim in his letter to patriarch
of Constantinople. "We anathematized Pitirim, the metropolitan of Krutitsa, because after
our departure he ceased in the holy services of the church to name us. And our orders—
whatever it might be that we ordered—he would not at all obey, but began to obey only
the *tsar's* majesty; and whatever he commanded him, though not according to the commandments of God, nor according to the canons of the holy apostles and holy fathers, that
he did. So he consecrated a bishop . . . and the same Pitirim in the holy and divine services . . . stood and sat in those places and seats in which our brethren the former patriarchs
and we used to stand and to sit . . . And we admonished the *tsar's* majesty for that, that
the metropolitan of Krutitsa should not do any such thing, and that he should not order or
permit it: but that admonition was not attended to. And the same Pitirim, by edict (*ukaz*)
of the *tsar's* majesty, assembled repeatedly synods concerning us, and bore false witness
concerning us, that we, departing from Moscow, vowed with an oath that we would be no
more patriarch. But we, when we went forth, anathematized him, whoever he should be,
other than ourselves, who should become patriarch after us so long as we should be living." Nikon, "Letter to Dionysius," 398–399.

146. The visual and verbal records left by foreign visitors to the New Jerusalem Resurrection Monastery provide roughly the same description of Nikon's dress. *Al'bom Mier-
berga* (1661–1662), a seventeenth-century travelogue by the imperial ambassador of the
Holy Roman Empire to Muscovy, featured two drawings of the patriarch. The first image
depicted Nikon in full hierarchal regalia, holding a patriarchal staff. The second picture
showed Nikon wearing a simple frock (*riasa*) and holding a plain walking stick. See *Risunki k puteshestviiu po Rossii rimsko-imperatorskago poslannika barona Meierberga v
1661 i 1662 godakh predstavliaiushchie vidy, narodnye obychai, odeianiia, portrety*,
Fedor Adelung, ed. (St. Petersburg, 1827), lix and lx.

Witsen commented that during his visit to New Jerusalem "the patriarch went up and
took off his clothes: the hat with a pearl cross on it, expensive staff and brocade, striped
liturgical vestment (*riza*) and put on similar, but simpler clothes." Witsen, 877.

147. Kapiton was a monk of peasant extraction from the Kostroma village of
Danilovskoe. He founded his own monastic communities near Kostroma where he lived a
hermit's life. Among his main ideas were the imminent end of the world and the *de facto*
rule of the Antichrist on Earth. Closely related to these notions, was the insistence that
the Russian Church and its clergy should be avoided as complacent in the corruption of
the true faith. Hence, preached the renegade monk, the faithful should enter hermitages
where they were to lead ascetic lifestyle and prepare for the Parousia. In particular, he
insisted on keeping very strict fasts which he himself did not break even on Easter. Kapiton's ascetic deeds attracted followers whose numbers are in dispute. See Michels, *At*

War with the Church, 123–124; Makarii, *Istoriia*, Vol. 12, 309, 526; and Lobachev, *Patriarch Nikon*, 36–37.

148. In the late 1630s, Kapiton's actions drew the attention of church authorities who admonished the monk and his followers about the erroneous nature of their beliefs and practices. In 1651, the Trinity [*Troitskii*] Monastery that Kapiton founded in the village of Danilovskoe in 1634 was destroyed. Rather than submitting to church discipline, Kapitonites fled and took refuge in Kostroma and later, after continued persecution, in Viaz'niki. As late as 1666 there were reports of investigations of Kapiton's Viaz'niki monastic community. There were also reports of self-immolations committed by the monk's followers in defiance of state persecution. See Michels, *At War with the Church*, 23; Smirnov, xxxii–xxxv; and V. S. Romantseva and I. A. Bulygin, eds., *Narodnoe antitserkovnoe dvizhenie v Rossii XVII veka. Dokumenty prikaza tainykh del o raskol'nikakh 1665–1667 gg.* (Moscow, 1986), 87.

Shusherin's reference to Kapiton raises several important questions. First, was the author referring to the actual followers of Kapiton narrowly defined or did he conflate the Kapitonites with the early Old Believers leaders, especially Avvakum, who is conspicuously absent from the rest of Shusherin's narrative? If placed in the chronological context of the seventeenth century, Shusherin appears to mean the actual Kapitonites who were persecuted as late as 1666. Indeed, the author links the state persecution of the monk's followers to the time of Nikon's stay at the New Jerusalem Monastery (July 1658–November 1666). On the other hand, at that time there were no "secret asylums" of Old Believer fathers because they did not flee the authorities until *after* their practices were deemed heretical (1667). In other words, Avvakum and his circle were definitely still visible to the authorities in 1666.

But Shusherin's remark could also be construed as a reference to early Old Believers, Nikon's opponents in church reforms. It is noteworthy that Ligarides too includes commentary on "schismatics" at roughly the same point in his narrative. Moreover, Ligarides highlighted his own role in "zealously attack[ing] and refut[ing] those schismatics who were actively disseminating their mischief in different parts, nominally accusing Nikon, but really holding up reproach against us Romans, as having swerved from Orthodoxy and from traditional faith of our fathers." Ligarides, 110. There are also striking parallels and intellectual links between the Kapitonites and the later Old Believers, including the use of self-immolation as a form of ultimate dissent. The belief of deacon Fedor, one of the early Old Believer writers, that *tsar* Aleksei Mikhailovich was an Antichrist, reportedly came from Kapiton, via the latter's disciple, elder Mikhail. See M. Cherniavsky, "The Old Believer and the New Religion," *Slavic Review* 25, No. 1 (March 1966): 1–39. An important Old Believer father, Kornilii of Vyg, according to his *Zhitie*, reportedly spent time with Kapiton when the latter was weathering the persecution in the Kostroma forests in 1650s. See Smirnov, xxxii–xxxiii.

The second question concerns Shusherin's description of the charges incriminated to Kapiton's followers. As mentioned above, Kapiton directed his criticisms against the Russian Church in general, not necessarily against Nikon *per se* or against his reforms.

149. For the official records of the patriarch's arrival in Moscow, see Gibbenet, *Istoricheskoe issledovanie*, Pt. 2, 997.

150. The business of the sovereign mentioned here probably refers to the accusations that Nikon made two secret trips to Moscow, once by himself, the second time accompanied by Shusherin and Fedor Artsebashev, the stable attendant of the Resurrection Monastery. Allegedly, Nikon used deceit to conceal his movements by telling his associates at the monastery that he was retiring to the hermitage to observe St. Filipp's fast. However, when the stable attendant shared the secret with his wife, and she, in turn, passed the

information to other wives, Nikon ordered the women to be whipped. See Gibbenet, *Istoricheskoe issledovanie*, Pt. 2, 297–298.

151. Nikon discussed his problems with the converts in a letter to the *tsar* written on December 24/25, 1671. "I had at the Resurrection Monastery two newly converted Jews and, forsaking the Orthodox faith, they started to keep their old Judaic faith and to corrupt the young monks; and I, having found the truth about this, ordered to punish Dem'ian and to exile him to the Iverskii Monastery, and Dem'ian told the other convert, Mishka: 'You will not escape trouble either, flee to Moscow and announce that you come on the business of the sovereign'; he did so; and you sent to me the secretary of the Council Dementii Bashmakov to investigate this affair, and, at this time, the young monks, who succumbed to Judaic heresy, stole money and dress from me and helped other converts; they were also helped by the archimandrite of the Monastery of the Miracles." Quoted in Solov'ev, Vol. 11, 359–360. For the full text of the letter, see note 205 below. Official records of the converts' accusations as well as the *tsar's* investigation are published in Gibbenet, *Istoricheskoe issledovanie*, Pt. 2, 964–980.

These events are also covered in the Old Believer *Account about . . . Nikon*. This tale contains additional, quite damning details of Nikon's alleged transgressions, including abuse of the Jewish converts' wives and even murder. As the excerpt below demonstrates, Old Believers were not above further manipulating already controversial aspects of Nikon's life as narrated by Shusherin. Where Shusherin left the end of the affair unexplained, the Old Believers filled in the blanks with salacious and sensationalized details. "Nikon had in his service two converted Jews. . . . One of these converts often visited Moscow and once informed another Jew named Daniil who was the *tsar's* apothecary about all Nikon's lawless imprudence and this Daniil told all of this to the *tsar* and so when Nikon learned about all of this from the Jew who lived with him, he beat him [Daniil] very badly . . . and Nikon ordered to imprison him [Daniil]. The other Jew, who saw this persecution and imprisonment, ran away to Moscow and cried: 'I came on the business of the sovereign!' And he was delivered to the *tsar* at once and when the *tsar* questioned him about Nikon's lawlessness and imprudence, he also told about Nikon and his sin with their wives. And these wives were nearly beaten to death. Hearing this, the *tsar* ordered the Jews with their wives and children to be brought to Moscow and to be held at the Monastery of the Miracles, to be used as eyewitnesses of Nikon's terrible lawlessness . . . and all the Jews who were held were killed and some thought that Nikon's accomplices killed them." Borozdin, No. 33, 162–163.

152. Messengers were sent to Nikon three times. See Gibbenet, *Istoricheskoe issledovanie*, Pt. 2, 308–319. Official reports by the members of the delegation sent to Nikon are published in *Delo o patriarkhe Nikone*, No. 58, 286–287 and No. 60, 288–289; and Gibbenet, *Istoricheskoe issledovanie*, Pt. 2, 994–1091.

According to Ligarides, who was not a member of the *tsar's* delegation, the council's resolution read: "The most blessed patriarchs, Kyr Paisius . . . and Kyr Macarius . . . and all the most sacred synod of the bishops, call thee to come to this great capital city of Moscow without delay, and to appear personally before us respecting certain spiritual matters. Be not disobedient to this summons; but come in a humble manner. Thus we charge thee to do." Ligarides, 167–168.

For useful discussions of Nikon's summons to the council of the synod, see N. Subbotin, *Delo patriarkha Nikona. Istoricheskoe issledovanie po povodu XI T. "Istorii Rossii," prof. Solov'eva* (Moscow, 1862), 169–171; Gibbenet, *Istoricheskoe issledovanie*, Pt. 2, 308–319; Makarii, *Istoriia*, Vol. 12, 341–345; and Lobachev, *Patriarkh Nikon*, 223–224.

153. Ligarides offers a slightly different account explaining that when the delegation arrived, "Nikon, having insolently shut the doors, not only did not receive them that were

sent, but also, as highly indignant, sent them away, saying: 'I will not come voluntarily, but by imperial compulsion perhaps I may. . . . So they that had been sent departed without any success from the monastery and drove straight back to Moscow." Ligarides, 168. See also *Delo o patriarkhe Nikone*, No. 58, 286–287.

154. The last of these works refers to Nikon's *Replies*.

155. Ligarides mentioned that Nikon was anointed with oil at the service. See Ligarides, 168.

156. Official records of this event can be found in *Delo o patriarkhe Nikone*, No. 60, 288.

157. For official accounts of Nikon's departure from the New Jerusalem Resurrection Monastery and his journey to Moscow, see *Delo o patriarkhe Nikone,* Nos. 59–60, 287–289; Gibbenet, *Istoricheskoe issledovanie*, Pt. 2, 994–1091; and Ligarides, 168.

158. Throughout the text, we see Nikon's obsession with the proprieties of rank. He appears to be less concerned with personal matters and more worried about the insults to the institution of the patriarchate. In this case, Nikon is making a valid claim since only a bishop or a hierarch of even greater rank could summon a patriarch (or another bishop) to a clerical trial. See note 167 below. However, as our glossary points out, an archimandrite could be the highest ceremonial rank of a town or region in the absence of a bishop or metropolitan. For example, Filaret of the Monastery of the Nativity in the town of Vladimir represented the entire holy synod and the *tsar* during the initial greeting of the ecumenical patriarchs when they arrived to the 1666 council of the synod. See Makarii, *Istoriia*, Vol. 12, 260.

There is another reason for Nikon's displeasure with the emissaries. On November 29, 1666, Filaret was sent to New Jerusalem on the *tsar's* orders commanding Nikon to depart immediately and so when the archimandrite's path crossed with Nikon's in Chernevo, Filaret presented him with a document which was no longer relevant, since the patriarch has already left. Nikon's irritation at hearing the old order is almost palpable. See *Delo o patriarkhe Nikone*, No. 60, 288 and No. 61, 289.

159. State records of this segment of Nikon's journey to Moscow are published as *Delo o patriarkhe Nikone*, No. 61, 289–290.

160. For official accounts of the emissaries' mission to Nikon, see ibid., No. 61, 289–290 and No. 62, 290–291. According to these sources, Nikon was directed to arrive on December 2, not December 3.

161. Metropolitan Filipp was secretly murdered by Ivan IV's order in 1568. See note 37 above.

162. The *tsar's* order prescribed the time and route of Nikon's entrance into the capital. It also stated that Nikon should be accompanied by ten or less people. See *Delo o patriarkhe Nikone*, No. 61, 290.

163. On December 1, 1666, Aleksei Mikhailovich recounted a different version of this event to the ecumenical patriarchs presiding over Nikon's trial. "The great sovereign told their holinesses the patriarchs that patriarch Nikon came to Moscow and is placing his fate in the sovereign's hands because their holinesses the patriarchs and the entire holy synod ordered him, Nikon, to come to Moscow without a large entourage. [And he also told] how Nikon was traveling to Moscow and how, by the order of the sovereign, the youth [Shusherin] was taken from Nikon because he [Shusherin] was bringing various messages to Nikon for nine years and caused many quarrels and Nikon tried to dishonor the sovereign on the account of that youth, by saying: 'The *tsar* is tormenting me; he ordered to take this youth from under the cross.' And should patriarch Nikon start talking about this during the council, the patriarchs would know about it as well as that Nikon, [being] at the Resurrection Monastery confessed before his trip to Moscow, took holy

communion and anointed himself with holy oil." Gibbenet, *Istoricheskoe issledovanie*, Pt. 2, 1043.

164. Ligarides confirms the close guarding of Nikon, but claims that the patriarch was not separated from his entourage. "He remained with all his attendants under strict guard of soldiers, for greater security and for safe custody." Ligarides, 168.

165. There was no Aleksandr, bishop of Viatka and Suzdal', only Aleksandr, bishop of Viatka and Velikaia Perm' (1657–1674), a remote outpost established by Nikon very far from Suzdal', so Shusherin is obviously mistaken here. Initially, Aleksandr was one of Nikon's major allies and a supporter of his reforms, but became dissatisfied after loosing a powerful position as a bishop of Kolomna. As bishop of Viatka and Velikaia Perm', a disenchanted Aleksandr turned against his former patron during the latter's trial. The compiler of two influential collections of dogmatic writings, he was eventually recognized as an important early Old Believer figure. Aleksandr died in 1679. See Michels, *At War with the Church*, 80–85.

166. According to the official documents, Nikon's first appearance before the council of the synod took place on December 1, not December 2, 1666, as Shusherin described. For records of the proceedings against Nikon on December 1, 1666, see Gibbenet, *Istoricheskoe issledovanie*, Pt. 2, 1042–1080; and Ligarides, 168–177. A complete list of those present at the trial on December 1, 1666 is included in Ligarides, 168–169.

167. The trial transcripts described the *tsar's* instructions on how Nikon should proceed to the council. "And the great sovereign asked who is to be sent to summon Nikon to the council, for Nikon wants to come to the council with a cross and a Bible, and is it fitting for him to come in such a way, or should he come in a humble manner, and when he comes, should he be seated and where should he be seated, and should he not sit down or, should he not come to the council at all, what should be done with him? And the patriarchs said: 'There should be a hierarch and two archimandrites sent for Nikon, and he can come to the council with whatever he wants and when he comes, he should sit for a short period and then stand, and he should sit on a bench to the right of the *tsar's* place, and should Nikon not sit down, or if Nikon would not come to the council when summoned, then their holinesses the patriarchs would start Nikon's trial in his absence." Gibbenet, *Istoricheskoe issledovanie*, Pt. 2, 1044.

The same record also clarified that "archimandrite Iosif returned to the council of the synod and said that patriarch Nikon told bishop Mefodii . . . that he will take the life-giving cross with him because the cross protects Christians. And their holinesses the ecumenical patriarchs ordered bishop Mefodii together with archimandrite Iosif to allow patriarch Nikon to come with the cross." Gibbenet, *Istoricheskoe issledovanie*, Pt. 2, 1044.

168. Ligarides explained only that Nikon arrived at the meeting, "sitting in a sleigh with a cross borne before him and his episcopal staff borne aloft, as he himself had directed." Ligarides, 169.

169. Official records described the physical setting of the trial much the same way as Shusherin did. "For the council, the refectory is arranged [in the following manner]: His majesty's place is adorned with silver and gold, and next to his majesty's place, to the left, are two places for their holinesses the ecumenical patriarchs, upholstered with velvet, and cherry-colored cloth, and in front of those patriarchal stalls is a table, covered with a golden fabric and golden Persian rug; and where the ecclesiastical dignitaries and the *boyars* are to sit, benches are placed on both sides of his majesty's place, the ecclesiastical dignitaries to the right, the *boyars,* and lords-in-waiting, and nobles of the Council to the left. And the great sovereign deigned to go to the refectory with the *boyars,* and the lords-in-waiting, and nobles of the Council, and chamberlains, and his entire Council on that day [December 1, 1666], at the third hour; and in front of his majesty they carried an

ark covered with silver . . . with two parchments signed by their holinesses the four ecumenical patriarchs, that they, the patriarchs, sent to him, the great sovereign, with deacon Miletius, and translations bound in velvet, and patriarch Nikon's letters covered with taffeta. After the great sovereign entered the refectory, he ordered the ark with parchments to be put on the table which stood in front of the patriarchal places, and after taking the parchments from the ark, to place them on the table." Gibbenet, *Istoricheskoe issledovanie*, Pt. 2, 1042.

170. The trial transcripts noted that "Patriarch Nikon came to the council and the life-creating cross was carried in front of him. And after coming to the council he said: 'Meet it is in truth to glorify Thee o birth-giver of God, ever blessed . . . Glory to Thee now and forever [and other prayers]. And having finished he bowed to the great sovereign three times. He bowed to their holinesses the ecumenical patriarchs twice." Gibbenet, *Istoricheskoe issledovanie*, Pt. 2, 1044.

171. The official documents also note Nikon's decision to stand rather than sit in a place that he considered unsuitable. "And their holinesses the ecumenical patriarchs ordered him, patriarch Nikon, to sit down. And Nikon did not sit down, but said: 'I do not see a place where I may be seated and I did not bring my own seat with me, I came to learn why I was summoned. And the great sovereign deigned to come down from his place and stood at the table in front of the ecumenical patriarchs. And patriarch Nikon came to the same table." Gibbenet, *Istoricheskoe issledovanie*, Pt. 2, 1044–1045. See also Gibbenet, *Istoricheskoe issledovanie*, Pt. 2, 1062.

Ligarides gave a conflicting report in this case. "A sign was made to him [Nikon] to sit in his usual place. But he demanded a seat like those of the two patriarchs, considering himself to be a judge, and by no means a man under condemnation. And he gravely blamed the *tsar* about the seat, saying: 'Though for myself I am not come hither to sit in honor, but to answer, as has been notified to me, to your questions, still thou oughtest, O Christian *tsar* Aleksei, to have honored the patriarchal rank and to have revered it, as it is decent and just.' Then both the patriarchs said: 'Is this, then, Nikon on account of whom for eight years and more all Muscovy has been in commotion, and the Eastern Church has suffered intolerable evils, and the four patriarchates have been in danger, and on account of his single person have all but been overthrown and desolated? And doest thou demand a chair? Rememberest thou not that to sit is reserved to a judge, and belongs not to a man who is being condemned? . . . It is not therefore for thee to sit now, being under accusation, and in the act of being condemned, but to stand upright on thy feet, and to answer for thyself.' . . . Nikon was persuaded by these words, and so standing in the midst, heard the questions which were put to him." Ligarides, 169–170.

172. The trial transcripts explain that the *tsar* said something quite different. "The great sovereign told their holiness the ecumenical patriarchs: 'Since the beginning of the Muscovy no one committed so many disgraces as patriarch Nikon did, he dishonored the holy catholic and apostolic church and left the patriarchal throne for no reason, persecuted by no one, and from that many disturbances and rebellions were committed and the holy catholic and apostolic church is to this day a widow without a shepherd." Gibbenet, *Istoricheskoe issledovanie*, Pt. 2, 1045.

The abridged records of the trial simply explain that "the great sovereign, *tsar* and grand prince Aleksei Mikhailovich . . . told their holinesses the ecumenical patriarchs to interrogate patriarch Nikon. Why did he leave the patriarchal throne and go to the Resurrection Monastery? And the ecumenical patriarchs asked Nikon: 'Why did you leave the patriarchal throne?'" Gibbenet, *Istoricheskoe issledovanie*, Pt. 2, 1062. See also Ligarides, 170–172.

173. According to the official court records, "patriarch Nikon said he left the patriarchal throne because the lord-in-waiting and the master-at-arms Bogdan Matveevich Khitrovo beat his man at the time when the Georgian prince was at the table of the great sov-

ereign and that this man introduced himself as the patriarch's man and that the lord-in-waiting Bogdan Matveevich told him: 'Do not be so proud of yourself and the patriarch,' and Nikon, the patriarch, asked the great sovereign for protection against the lord-in-waiting and the great sovereign did not deign to grant him [Nikon] protection against the lord-in-waiting in this matter and the great sovereign wrote to Nikon, the patriarch, that the great sovereign wishes to see and talk to Nikon about this; and Nikon waited for three days and the great sovereign saw Nikon, the patriarch, during the holiday of the holiest Mother of God of Kazan', during the procession, but on the day of the healing Robe of Our Lord and Savior Jesus Christ did not deign to come to the cathedral during the all-night vigil and the liturgy, but the table attendant, prince Yurii Ivanovich Romoda-novskii, came from the great sovereign to Nikon and told him: 'The great sovereign is wroth with you, patriarch Nikon. Why do you sign as great sovereign?' And so he was not to sign this way in the future; but Nikon [said that he] so signed on the orders of the great sovereign the *tsar* and he left the throne because of the *tsar's* wrath and waited three days for the delegation at the lodge of the Resurrection Monastery, but the delegation did not come and he went to the Resurrection Monastery where he recited the Psalm 'Judge, Lord, those who offend me.' And after that he said: 'It is written nowhere that the patriarchs should listen to the *tsars*, but the Holy Gospel says: He who listens to you, hears Me.'" Gibbenet, *Istoricheskoe issledovanie*, Pt. 2, 1045–1046. According to Li-garides, Nikon repeated the position he expressed earlier in his *Replies* and his letter to patriarch of Constantinople. See Ligarides, 170–172.

174. The missive mentioned here refers to Nikon's *Letter to Dionysius*. The trial transcripts explain that "the great sovereign told their holinesses the patriarchs that patriarch Nikon sent a letter written in Greek to the patriarch of Constantinople in which he wrote many dishonorable and reproachful things about him, the sovereign, but the great sovereign wrote to the ecumenical patriarchs and asked them to come to judge, but he did not write anything about Nikon's affairs to them, so that their holinesses the patriarchs would interrogate him. [The *tsar* told them to ask Nikon] what did he truthfully write in his letter, did he protect the church and its dogmas, and did he consider patriarch Iosif a brother and a saint, and does he have any sins, and whether or not the church possessions were moved? And Nikon, the former patriarch, described what was written in his letter, and [said] that he wrote the whole truth in that letter, and he considers patriarch Iosif to be a patriarch, and whether he is a saint, that he does not know, and he did not say anything more about him. And the great sovereign ordered to read the translation of Nikon's letter point by point to the council of the synod and that translation was read." Gibbenet, *Istoricheskoe issledovanie*, Pt. 2, 1048–1049. See also Gibbenet, *Istoricheskoe issledo-vanie*, Pt. 2, 1065; and Ligarides, 172–176.

In a letter to Aleksei Mikhailovich, dated December 25, 1671, Nikon commented on the circumstances that compelled him to confront the *tsar*. "At the council, having ap-proached me you [the *tsar*] said: 'We summoned you honorably and you are making noise!' and I asked you to order not to read my decree at the council, but to speak pri-vately, and I would have done everything according to your will; but you did not deign it, and I, against my will, taking into account my written words, contradicted you and spoke vexingly; for this I ask your forgiveness." Quoted in Solov'ev, Vol. 11, 360.

175. While Shusherin presented Nikon as responding with decorum, Ligarides de-scribed much more contemptuous behavior. The two authors also stipulated completely different motivations behind Nikon's writing the letter to the patriarch of Constantinople. If Shusherin viewed Nikon as deferring to a senior patriarch, Ligarides commented on Nikon's human fallibility, namely uncontrolled passion. According to Ligarides, "Nikon said that in point of fact he had belched out this calumnious imputation at that time through human passion." Ligarides, 173.

176. Shusherin's account of the proceedings against Nikon is abbreviated and does not mention the various charges raised against Nikon, or the patriarch's responses to those charges. Shusherin also confused the chronology of the trial's events. In reality, Nikon's letter to ecumenical patriarch Dionysius of Constantinople was read on December 1. Following the reading of the letter, the *tsar* and the council of the synod countered the accusations mentioned in Nikon's letter and raised additional charges, including the Ziuzin affair, Nikon's return to Moscow in December 1664, his taking metropolitan Piotr's staff from the Dormition Cathedral, his alleged reading of the Psalms against the *tsar*, and his actions at the New Jerusalem Resurrection Monastery during the resulting investigations. Nikon responded to the charges put against him with his own version of the events in question. See Gibbenet, *Istoricheskoe issledovanie*, Pt. 2, 1049–1061 and 1065–1068; and Ligarides, 171–177.

177. The *tsar* informed the visiting patriarchs of Nikon's refusal to accept the food and drink at the next meeting of the council of the synod on December 3. Aleksei Mikhailovich had previously sent victuals to Nikon and his men on December 2. "The great sovereign announced to the ecumenical patriarchs that the great sovereign sent him, patriarch Nikon, food and drink on the second of December, and that patriarch Nikon did not accept it, and said that he has enough of his own and that he never asked the great sovereign for it." Gibbenet, *Istoricheskoe issledovanie*, Pt. 2, 1081. Nikon later commented on the food delivery, striking a more apologetic note. In his letter to Aleksei Mikhailovich, dated December 25, 1671, Nikon wrote: "You sent to me at the Lykov Court provisions equal to that of the patriarchs, but I refused your charity and by doing so dishonored you; forgive, for the sake of the Lord. You also sent with Rodion Matveevich Streshnev money and furs, and I, sinful, did not accept them either; forgive, for the sake of Christ's Birth." Quoted in Solov'ev, Vol. 11, 360.

178. Official records of the second day of the trial, December 3, 1666, are included in Gibbenet, *Istoricheskoe issledovanie*, Pt. 2, 1080–1084 and 1080–1086; and Ligarides, 168–177. Ligarides however explained that the events of December 3, 1666 transpired on December 5.

179. According to other documents, the events described here, i.e. the reading of the letter and the discussion about Athanasius, transpired on the first day of the trial, December 1, not on December 3, as Shusherin wrote. See Gibbenet, *Istoricheskoe issledovanie*, Pt. 2, 1048–1056, and Ligarides, 172–176. See also "Perepiska sviateishago patriarkha Nikona s mitropolitom Ikoniiskim Afanasiem i gramotonostsem ierusalimskago patriarkha Nektariia Sevast'ianom ili Savvoiu Dmitrievym," *Russkii Arkhiv* 51 (1873): 1602–1640. Nikon also discussed Athanasius in his *Letter to Dionysius*. See Nikon, "Letter to Dionysius," 369.

180. This discussion between Aleksei Mikhailovich and Nikon is not recorded in the trial transcripts. Shusherin's qualification that this dialogue was heard only by the monks explains its absence from the official accounts of the proceedings. It is noteworthy that in a letter written in the early summer of 1667 Nikon himself complained to Aleksei Mikhailovich that there was no record of conversations they had during the trial. The relevant section of Nikon's complaint reads: "During the trial they should write down the speeches, of both the defendant and the accused, and read them back to both. Was it what the defendant and the accused said? And then each should verify his speech with his signature and then their speeches should be discussed and judged against your majesty's laws. Here nothing was according to the law; me and you, great sovereign the *tsar*, were talking, but they did not write our speeches down and he who has little experience in interpretation himself knows little. And all the judges were asleep or half asleep and nobody knows who was writing down your majesty's orders. And what he has written, that nobody heard." Sevast'ianova, "Pis'ma patriarkha Nikona," 270–271.

181. The events discussed here actually happened on December 5, not December 3, as Shusherin wrote. Contemporary accounts of the proceedings on December 5 are recorded in Gibbenet, *Istoricheskoe issledovanie*, Pt. 2, 1086–1092; and Ligarides, 178–190.

The taking of the cross from Nikon was likewise highlighted in the official trial transcripts. "And the patriarchs were accusing him [Nikon] that he denounced his throne and so it was not suitable for him, Nikon, to come in such a manner, with a cross carried in front of him, and they ordered to take the cross away from his deacon." Gibbenet, *Istoricheskoe issledovanie*, Pt. 2, 1090.

Ligarides also describes the cross being taken from Nikon, but in a completely different context. "Kyr Macarius of Antioch questioned Nikon, saying: 'Thou O Nikon, wast not used in time past to have the sign of the cross in silver carried before thee: whence then hast thou now learned to have this brought in before thee, inconsiderately?' Nikon replied that 'the sign of the venerable cross is the standard of all Christians, and our weapon of victory, which routs and puts to flight all enemies visible and invisible.' 'Yes,' said the patriarch; 'but if in the time when thou wast patriarch this was not customary, how hast thou dared now to lift up this standard, when thou comest to trial, and after the abdication completed by thee with so much emphasis and solemnity?' Nikon answered nothing, but, as being justly confuted, held his tongue. Then therefore, both the patriarchs gave order that the cross should be taken away from him. And thereupon Anastasius, the archdeacon of the patriarch of Alexandria, having first made his reverence, went up to and took the cross out of the hands of Nikon's deacon, and held it before the two patriarchs to the end [of the session], preceding them also with it as far as to the door of the new patriarchal palace." Ligarides, 185. On the cross, see E. A. Morshakova, "Krest prednosnyi (pokhodnyi)," in Iukhimenko, ed., *Patriarch Nikon. Oblacheniia*, 42.

182. The knife with which Demetrius stabbed himself to death was supposedly left in his cell by the repairmen working there. On Demetrius' suicide, see Gibbenet, *Istoricheskoe issledovanie*, Pt. 2, 362–365.

183. During this time the patriarchs composed the "Council Resolution by the Patriarchs of Alexandria and Antioch about the Deposition of Nikon Patriarch of Moscow from the Patriarchal Throne" which summarized the charges against Nikon. This document is published as "Sobornoe postanovlenie patriarkhov aleksandriiskago i antiokhiiskago o nizlozhenii patriarkha moskovskago Nikona s patriarshago prestola," in Gibbenet, *Istoricheskoe issledovanie*, Pt. 2, 1093–1097. A later version of the same proclamation is published in *SGGD*, Vol. 4, No. 53, 182–186. Ligarides quoted the document in his *History*, 191–195. See also E. M. Iukhimenko, "Prigovor sobora 1666 g. o nizlozhenii patriarkha Nikona," in Iukhimenko, ed., *Patriarch Nikon. Oblacheniia*, 132–133.

184. Ferapontov Monastery in the Vologda region was founded in 1397 by the reverend Ferapont, a pupil of St. Sergius of Radonezh. This minor monastery consisted of two churches. It is best known for being a place of exile for deposed patriarch Nikon who spent almost ten years (December 21, 1666–June 4, 1676) there. See Ratshin, 348. For classic treatments of the Ferapontov Monastery's history, see I. Brilliantov, *Ferapontov Belozerskii monastyr', mesto zatocheniia patriarkha Nikona* (St. Petersburg, 1899); and Murav'ev, *Russkaia Fivaida*, 372–384.

185. The official sources on the final act of Nikon's deposition include "Ob'iavlenie patriarkhu Nikonu patriarshago postanovleniia o nizlozhenii ego s patriarshago prestola (12 dekabria 1666 goda)," in Gibbenet, *Istoricheskoe issledovanie*, Pt. 2, 1098–1099. This document reads:

"On the twelfth day of December, in the Cross Chamber of their holinesses the ecumenical patriarchs, the [council of] the holy synod was held and at that council were present the Muscovite and Greek metropolitans and archbishops, and bishops, archimandrites and abbots. And as the metropolitans and other hierarchs arrived at the council,

their holinesses the ecumenical patriarchs sent the table-attendant, prince Piotr Pro-
zorovskii to inform the great sovereign so that the great sovereign would deign to send to
them, at the council, those from the *tsar's* Council whom the great sovereign would des-
ignate. And to the former patriarch Nikon they sent Mefodii, bishop of Mstislavl' and
Orsha, and with him two archimandrites, and they ordered them to tell him that he is to
go to the council. And the great sovereign sent *boyars* prince Nikita Ivanovich Odoevskii,
Piotr Mikhailovich Saltykov, service nobleman of the Council Prokofii Kuz'mich
Elizarov, and the secretary of the Council Almaz Ivanov to their holinesses the ecumenical patriarchs. And as the *boyars* and the noble of the Council and the secretary of the
Council came to the Cross Chamber, their holinesses the patriarchs, having blessed them,
ordered them to sit down on a bench. And they sent the battalion commander of the
strel'tsy (*polugolova*) Luka Iz'edinov to former patriarch Nikon to tell him to go to the
council of the synod at once. And as former patriarch Nikon came to inner porch of the
Cross Chamber, their holinesses the ecumenical patriarchs went to the church . . . at the
Miracles Gate and ordered all the ecclesiastical dignitaries to go with them and put on
their chasubles and stood at their patriarchal stalls and ordered the hierarchs to put on
their chasubles (*sakkos*) and to stand according to rank. And as the former patriarch
Nikon entered the church and having prayed to the holy icons, he bowed twice to their
holinesses the patriarchs and stood to the left of the western doors. And their holinesses
the patriarchs ordered their presbyter (*presviter*) Ioanis to read excerpts from the council's resolution about Nikon's degradation in Greek. And as the presbyter read the excerpts, their holinesses the patriarchs ordered Illarion, archbishop of Riazan', to read the
charges against Nikon from the same resolution. And when this archbishop read the excerpts and the charges, their holinesses the patriarchs went down from their patriarchal
stalls and stood at the royal doors (*tsarskie vrata*) and summoned the former patriarch
Nikon and, having announced the charges to him, they themselves took off his black
monastic hood (*klobuk*) and the patriarch of Alexandria took the medallion (*panagiia*)
from him and told Nikon that he was not to be called or sign 'patriarch' in the future, but
to be called and sign 'simple monk Nikon' and he was to live quietly and serenely in a
monastery and he is to pray to the all-merciful God for his sins. And the former patriarch
Nikon told their holinesses the patriarchs: 'I know how to live without your instructions,'
and as for the black monastic hood and medallion being taken from him, [he said that]
they should divide the pearls from the hood and medallion amongst themselves so that
each would receive five or six *zolotniks* [about 25 grams] of pearls and ten or more *zolotniks* [about 43 grams] of gold. And having instructed former patriarch Nikon, their holinesses the patriarchs released him to his temporary residence."

Ligarides included the full text of the official summary of charges against Nikon. See
Ligarides, 191–195. He also reported that while Illarion, archbishop of Riazan', read the
charges in Slavonic, "at times Nikon muttered something while it was being read, as if to
show that he was not willing so much as to listen to it. Wherefore he often murmured his
objections, and denying, reviled in return . . . And he continued gainsaying to no purpose,
pouring out weak washy nonsense." Ligarides, 195.

The metropolitan of Gaza offered quite a different account of Nikon's being stripped
of the patriarchal authority. "Then the patriarchs, standing in the middle of that holy
chapel, declared his perfect degradation in the usual form, saying both of them that he
must also be stripped of the customary insignia of the episcopate, viz. of the pectoral
(*panagiia*) and of the mandya (*riasa*). But none dared take from him, from some reverence to the highest rank of the priesthood. At length, therefore, the patriarch of Alexandria, approaching him gently and quietly, took off the black monastic hood from the head
of Nikon. And Nikon said, 'Take also my mandya, if thou wilt; for now thou hast the
power.' 'Well, we ought indeed to do so,' said the patriarchs; 'but in consideration of the
urgent request and entreaty of our long-lived *tsar* Aleksei, we allow thee to retain the

episcopal mandya which thou art wearing until thou be come to the monastery appointed for thy place of banishment; for then thou must be finally stripped of it, in token of thou being only a simple monk, and no longer a bishop.' So they left it on him, and also the pectoral, which was set all over with pearls. But Nikon said sarcastically, "I know that, as ye are poor, ye will be glad to have some pearls, so you had better take my pectoral.' But the patriarchs answered him, 'Take back this, and keep it to thine own confounded perdition.'" Ligarides, 195–196.

Other contemporary accounts of the final act of Nikon's deposition on December 12, 1666, include *SGGD*, Vol. 4, No. 53, 182–186; and *DAI*, Vol. 5, No. 26, 105.

186. This is a prime example of Shusherin's weaving homiletic threads into the *Account*.

187. On December 11, 1666, Aleksei Mikhailovich decreed that Athanasius be exiled. See Gibbenet *Istoricheskoe issledovanie*, Pt. 2, 113.

188. Ligarides gave a different version of the events explaining that "the bishops were indignant at what had been said [by Nikon], and smarting under it, they were exceedingly annoyed about the pectoral. Wherefore they all desired that this same ornament might be taken back immediately. So two of the *boyars* being sent, as if from the patriarchs, regained it, stripping it off from him [Nikon], and hanging it up in the great church with triumph, where the patriarchs also gave up of their own accord the cross of silver gilt [taken from Nikon at the trial on December 3], as if shaking off from themselves all imputation of covetousness." Ligarides, 196. See also *Delo o patriarkhe Nikone*, No. 74, 310–311.

189. For an official account of the first stage of Nikon's journey to the Ferapontov Monastery, the place of his exile, see *Delo o patriarkhe Nikone*, No. 74, 310–311.

190. On December 14, 1666, Aleksei Mikhailovich ordered the first Iosif, actually mentioned by Shusherin, to be replaced by the second and decreed that Nikon be taken to the Ferapontov Monastery, traveling through the towns of Dmitrov and Uglich. See *Delo o patriarkhe Nikone*, No. 75, 311–312.

191. Nikon's surrender of his staff and mantle on December 21, 1666 are documented in *Delo o patriarkhe Nikone*, No. 77, 313. The actual order to take Nikon's regalia was proclaimed by patriarchs Paisius of Alexandria and Macarius of Antioch. See *Delo o patriarkhe Nikone*, No. 74, 310–311.

192. In late December 1666, archimandrite Iosif described Nikon's living conditions to the ecumenical patriarchs and Russian holy synod asking them if it was possible to give Nikon more freedom. See *Delo o patriarkhe Nikone*, No. 77, 313–314.

193. This date is given in both archimandrite Varlaam, *O prebyvanii patriarkha Nikona v zatochenii v Ferapontove i Kirillove monastyriakh* (Moscow, 1858), No. 1, 21; and Sevast'ianova, *Mater'ialy*, 250–251.

194. The text of the original letter was recently published as "Gramota patriarkha Nikona tsariu Alekseiu Mikhailovichu i vsem chlenam tsarskago semeistva (posle 7 sentiabria 1667 g.)," in Sevast'ianova, "Pis'ma patriarkha Nikona," 266–267.

195. This section of Shusherin's narrative is out of chronological order. The events involving Obraztsov's visit actually happened earlier, in 1667. Ioann Obraztsov arrived at the Ferapontov Monastery with new orders regarding Nikon's treatment on June 20, 1667. See Sevast'ianova, *Mater'ialy*, 254. According to Nikon's letter to Aleksei Mikhailovich (December 25, 1671), "You [the *tsar*] sent Ioann Obraztsov with a merciful edict; he released us, but did not dispense any punishment for Stefan, as was ordered; he only kept him in the bread chamber for two hours and Stefan, shortly thereafter, started to torment me even worse than before: my servant went to him ten times on the account of one matter, but he had no time! And when he looks out the window, he yells: 'I wrote to the monasteries to send supplies, but they did not listen, and I do not have an edict to

force them; it is time to abandon your caprices, eat what you are given.'" Quoted in So-lov'ev, Vol. 11, 361.

196. Contrary to Shusherin's account, the reasons for Nikon's deprivation were not his voluntary refusal of food sent from Moscow, but the failure of the abbot of the Kirillov Monastery, to whom the packages were first delivered, to pass them to the imprisoned patriarch at the Ferapontov Monastery. Nikon's warden Stefan Naumov reported to the *tsar* on March 1, 1668: "And the former patriarch, elder Nikon, told me that you, great sovereign, should show mercy towards him and order to give him and his brethren bread and food, and candles, and wheat for liturgical breads, and other supplies monthly; and so deign, oh sovereign, to pronounce an edict about this." According to this letter, Nikon, far from the refusing, actually asked the *tsar* for food. See P. Nikolaevskii, *Zhizn' patriarkha Nikona v ssylke i zakluchenii posle osuzhdeniia ego na Moskovskom sobore 1666 goda* (St. Petersburg, 1666), 25.

197. The *tsar's* edict carried by Obraztsov permitted Nikon to fish in Lake Boro-davskii. See Sevast'ianova, *Mater'ialy*, 254.

198. It appears that Nikon's message to the *tsar* had a positive effect. On April 9, 1668 at [the council of] the holy synod in Moscow, the ecumenical patriarchs declared that Nikon should be transferred to a different monastery and confined under harsher condi-tions. The *tsar*, at least at this time, refused. For the council's declaration, see *Delo o patriarkhe Nikone*, No. 87, 331; and Nikolaevskii, *Zhizn'*, 26–27.

199. The fate of the monks mentioned by Shusherin is documented in *Delo o pa-triarkhe Nikone,* No. 77, 313–314. See also Nikolaevskii, *Zhizn'*, 23, 27–30.

200. By introducing these details Shusherin attempts to prove that Nikon was isolated from the general populace during his time at the Ferapontov Monastery. But, in 1673–1676 alone, the patriarch reportedly healed one hundred and thirty-two visitors afflicted by physical ailments and demonic possessions. Ironically, records of these visits and healings were often appended to Shusherin's *Account* by subsequent copiers, who unwit-tingly cast doubt on the patriarch's alleged isolation. See Belokurov, *Dela sviateishago Nikona*, 86–100; and Michels, *At War with the Church*, 214–215. This is a prime exam-ple of Shusherin's conscious decision to avoid a more hagiographical slant by omitting important and well-known details of Nikon's life. The reasons for Shusherin's purposeful omission are quite telling. In May 1676, Nikon was charged with receiving a host of un-authorized visitors including the rebel Sten'ka Razin and numerous women and girls. Nikon denied the charges, but was nonetheless transferred to the Kirillov Monastery to halt his interaction with the outside world. Thus, it appears that although the healings could be considered as proofs of Nikon's status as a holy man, the fact that Nikon himself denied having contact with those he allegedly healed was more important to Shusherin. See also notes 209, 215, and 216 below.

201. On Nikon's gardening practices, see *Delo o patriarkhe Nikone,* Nos. 102–103, 380–383.

202. Another description of the island and the cross appeared in the records of the in-terrogation of Stefan Naumov, Nikon's warden, carried out by Iu. P. Lutokhin, captain of the *strel'tsy*: "On Lake Borodavskii across from the Ferapontov Monastery and across from elder Nikon's cells, . . . large wild stones were loaded into the water in the middle of the lake for half a *sazhen'* [a meter]. These stones were brought from the shores by his cell companions and by people of various ranks hired by elder Nikon. The stones are elevated from the water for half a *sazhen'* [a meter]. The stone [island] measures nine *sazhens* [about twenty meters] in length and seven *sazhens* [about fifteen meters] in width. On the stones there stands a wooden frame . . . and inside the frame, on a stone, stands a wooden cross which is two *sazhen'* and a *lokot'* [about five meters] in height, and on the upper beam there is an inscription in Greek, as it is written on the crosses used

for blessing, on the middle beam it is written 'Jesus Christ,' on the lower beam it is written "NIKA" and below, on the lowest beam, it is written 'Nikon, by the grace of God patriarch, erected this cross of Christ being imprisoned at the Ferapontov Monastery in the year 7176 [1668] on the fifteenth day of May.'" Sevast'ianova, *Mater'ialy*, 258–259.

203. On Ioakim, the ninth patriarch of Moscow (1674–1690), see Lebedev, 44–49.

204. Iona's "rumors" were ultimately appropriated by the dissenting writers and can be found in the Old Believer *Account about . . . Nikon*. "This spiteful false prophet acted like a diligent worshiper of the Lord's cross and crucified Christ, and images of the Holy Virgin; in reality, he was the wicked enemy of these. And I will describe his reasons for erecting this cross. My explanation is that when he was in the monastery under the supervision of the archimandrite and the colonel of the *strel'tsy*, it was not easy for him to communicate apostasy with bad spirits and that is why he decided to create this island and to erect a cross there and under the veil and protection of this cross, he liked going there for adoration, and was free to visit this island at any time; and he visited this island very often after sunset with Iona, the monk from the Resurrection Monastery, who was very cunning and practiced evil magic. There they appealed for the devil's appearance and this devil appeared in the form of a dreadful great snake and Nikon hugged and kissed him on his deadly and poison-bearing lips and while kissing, he asked him: 'What is the talk about me among the people and what is happening?' And this snake informed him and talked with him as is they were best friends and after that Nikon went away to his residence. And this malicious monk Iona wrote about this magic and meeting with the snake to colonel Shepelev as many as three hundred times, and this Shepelev made a report about this to *tsar* Fedor Alekseevich and patriarch Ioakim and when the *tsar* and the patriarch found out about this, they sent Pavel, archimandrite of the Monastery of the Miracles, and nobleman Ioan . . . to the Ferapontov Monastery to investigate whether or not it was true. And when they both arrived, they investigated . . . and it was confirmed to be true. That is why, by the edicts of the *tsar* and the patriarch, on June 2, 7184 [1676], Nikon was sent to the Kirillov Monastery." Borozdin, No. 33, 166.

205. Nikon himself wrote about his prayers for the deceased *tsarina* in a letter to Aleksei Mikhailovich, dated December 25, 1671. "When you sent Rodion Matveevich Streshnev with news about the demise of the *tsarina* and the charitable donation for her and asked that I should forgive her and remember her in my prayers forever, I told Rodion that the Lord God will forgive her, and I would be happy to remember her majesty in prayers for her past charity, but I did not take the money because I am not the hireling of your majesties, and must pray to God, as I do, for your charity; Rodion told me: 'Now, take the renumeration from the sovereign, and you will receive a large delivery and then everything will be good.' I told him: 'If his majesty will be charitable, then the money would not dry up, and you will be a intercessor in this good deed. And [as far as] the other [accusation is concerned], yea, out of the great sorrow for her majesty the *tsarina* and your children, I lost my mind and for this, I ask forgiveness, but I read the Book of Psalms and the canon for her majesty the *tsarina* throughout great Lent and continue to remember her in prayers to this day without failing." Quoted in Solov'ev, Vol. 11, 361.

206. For the end of the feud between the *tsar* and patriarch Nikon, see Nikolaevskii, *Zhizn'*, 37–38.

207. Nikon's letter to the *tsar*, dated December 24/25, 1671, is published in its entirety in Solov'ev, Vol. 11, 359–361. An abridged version of the same letter appears in Nikolaevskii, *Zhizn'*, 38–39. The relevant sections of the letter read: "In the year 7160 [1652], by the will of God and your grace, great sovereign, and by the choice of the entire holy synod, I was installed as patriarch, not by my own will; I, knowing my wickedness and scarcity of mind, petitioned to you many times that I am not suitable for such great-

ness, but your speeches prevailed. After three years passed, I petitioned to you to release me to go to the monastery, but you retained me for another three years; after the passing of another three years, I again petitioned to you to release me to the monastery, and you did not pronounce a merciful edict. I, seeing that I cannot leave you through petitions, started to pester and annoy you and left the patriarchal throne for the Resurrection Monastery. You, following the heavenly father in your generosity, did not forget me in your charity even in the Resurrection Monastery, you sent bread on the days of your patron saint and charitable donations, and I received your charity with contempt, and did all this deliberately so you would forget me. Once I happened to become sick at the Resurrection Monastery, and you, having learned about this, sent to me Afanasii Matiushkin with promises and conciliatory words that you would not forsake me until death; I did not much rejoice in that charity, and then, by the slander of my enemies, Roman Bobarykin, Ioann Sytin and others, great discord grew between us; they offended me and slandered me to you. . . . For all my transgressions I sit rejected at the Ferapontov Monastery for the sixth year, and I am imprisoned in a cell for the fourth year. Now I am sick, naked, and barefoot, and I do not wear a cross for the third year, I am ashamed to go to the next cell where they bake bread and prepare food, because many of my shameful parts are not covered; I developed scurvy from various deprivations in my cell, my arms hurt, I cannot raise the left one, I have sores on both eyes from smoke and fumes, stinking blood oozes from my teeth and they tolerate neither hot, nor cold, nor sour [food or drink], my feet are swollen, this is why I cannot observe the church rituals and there is only one priest, but even he is blind, and says that he does not see the books; the wardens allow me neither to sell nor to buy anything, no one comes to me, and there is no one to ask for charity. And all this Stefan Naumov did to me because I spoke both directly and behind his back about his injustices, that he beat, tormented, and took bribes from many elders, servants, and peasants; I called him a tormentor and a usurer, and a daylight rascal, and for this, he locked me up in a cell from the ninth of May to St. Elijah's Day [in August] and ordered not to give me any supplies; I carried water and cut wood by myself. . . . When Stefan received the news that your son, *tsarevich* Aleksei had expired, his girl came to another chamber and said: 'Now Moscow is aggrieved, but our *boyar* is rejoicing,' she said, 'now our prisoner lost all hope, the one on whom he was relying, has passed away, he will be meeker now.' And now prince Samoila Shaisupov [Yusupov] does everything as Stefan did. I beg you, ease up on me a little, and if I do not die before this, I ask to live in the house of the Lord during all the days of my life." Solov'ev, Vol. 11, 359–361.

208. In this case, Shusherin confused two members of the Lopukhin family. See also note 210 below. In January 1672, the *tsar* sent Illarion, not Koz'ma, Lopukhin to the Ferapontov Monastery. Illarion Lopukhin arrived on January 18, 1672 and brought Nikon money, furs, and fish. Aleksei Mikhailovich also sent a message to Nikon with Illarion Lopukhin. It reads: "From the time that you left the patriarchal throne to your trial by the eastern patriarchs, the *tsar* always wished to reconcile with you, but it did not happen because you wanted to change the state, contrary to the custom of the ecumenical patriarchs, who left their thrones. Now, after your letter, the sovereign wants to end the enmity with you more than ever, he happily wishes to reconcile with you in everything and he himself asks for your forgiveness. . . . You were sent to the Ferapontov Monastery by the ecumenical patriarchs and the council of the synod, and not the sovereign; the service nobles and the *strel'tsy* were sent to protect you and not to persecute you; if warden Naumov committed any persecution towards you, he did it on his own accord and not according to the edict of the sovereign, and we are now ordered to find out [what happened]. Rodion Matveevich, sent to you with gifts after the death of *tsarina* Mariia Il'inichna, was interrogated and swore that he was trying incessantly to persuade you to accept the gifts and to remember the *tsarina* in prayers and that he did not say any other words or make any other promises described by you in the letter. You told warden Shai-

supov [Yusupov] that Don Cossacks visited you during Naumov's [tenure]; reveal who wanted to start the bloodshed in Vologda; . . . moreover, the brigand Sten'ka Razin, while interrogated under torture and with fire, testified that one of your elders met him at Simbirsk and invited him [Razin] to go up the Volga, and that you, on your part, will come to him, because you are sick of the *boyars* [who] waste the sovereign's seeds; and that you have five thousand people ready for this at Beloozero; that the elder was even in the battle and Razin witnessed how he stabbed a junior *boyar* to death with his own hands and then left Simbirsk. All the prophecies about the revolt that you related to Shaisupov [Yusupov], as if God's word to you, you learned not from the Lord our God but from the brigands who came to you; one must think that the revolt and bloodshed came through them. If you wanted to do well according to Christ's commandments, you would not have concealed such a great affair and would have ordered to capture and bring to the sovereign those thieving Cossacks who came to you; you could have captured three people, the sovereign's service men were always near you to protect you. Do tell the truth about all this; otherwise you ask the sovereign for various charities and forgiveness, but you, yourself, do not tell him the truth." Nikolaevskii, *Zhizn'*, 39–41. See also Solov'ev, Vol. 11, 362–363.

209. In this part of the narrative, Shusherin omits almost four years of Nikon's captivity. Importantly, during the time that Shusherin skips, Nikon's plight improved dramatically to the point that he had numerous servants, traveled, accepted visitors, and interacted with guests unhindered. See Nikolaevskii, *Zhizn'*, 48–117; and Brilliantov, 171–206. Clearly, Shusherin opted to disregard information which contradicted his intent to paint Nikon as suffering under harsh conditions and in isolation. See also note 200 above.

210. Shusherin was mistaken in this case. Aleksei Mikhailovich died on January 29, 1676. Koz'ma Lopukhin, a crown agent (*striapchii*) in the *tsar's* service, arrived at the Ferapontov Monastery first, having been dispatched on January 26, 1676 by Aleksei Mikhailovich. "Illarion" Lopukhin arrived at the Ferapontov Monastery in February with news of the *tsar's* death. Koz'ma and Illarion, who both happened to be at the monastery at the same time, asked Nikon to pardon Aleksei Mikhailovich. See Nikolaevskii, *Zhizn'*, 88–89.

211. Samuil Nikitich Shaisupov [Yusupov], who replaced Naumov as Nikon's primary warden, actually arrived at the Ferapontov Monastery on July 12, 1671. Ioann Ivanovich Adadurov replaced Shaisupov [Yusupov] on March 29, 1676. Patriarch Ioakim ordered Adadurov to keep Nikon under strict guard. See *Delo o patriarkhe Nikone*, No. 94, 344.

212. The Kirillov Monastery is located on the shores of the lake Odol'skoe in the Novgorod the Great region. It was founded in 1391 by the reverend Kirill, formerly of Moscow's St. Simon Monastery. One of the most powerful Russian monasteries, by the eighteenth century Kirillov had in its possession twenty-one thousand peasants and was designated as a township. It was surrounded by a fortified two-storey wall with defense towers. The Kirillov Monastery consisted of two parts, the Major Monastery enclosing ten sanctuaries and the smaller, St. John Monastery which included only two churches. The treasury of the monastery was considered one of the richest in Russia, rivaling that of the Monastery of Trinity and St. Sergius. It also served as a place of imprisonment and exile; among its famous prisoners were prince Shuiskii, Simeon Bekbulatovich, Kirill Naryshkin, grandfather of Peter the Great, and of course patriarch Nikon who spent the last five years of his life in the monastery (June 4, 1676–August 1681). See Ratshin, 339–341. For a classic treatment of the monastery's founding and history, see Murav'ev, *Russkaia Fivaida*, 150–224.

213. See *Delo o patriarkhe Nikone*, No. 94, 341; No. 95, 361–363; No. 96, 363–364; and No. 97, 364.

214. For archimandrite Pavel's account of these events, see *Delo o patriarkhe Nikone*, No. 100, 268–369.

215. The official charges against Nikon are recorded in *Delo o patriarkhe Nikone*, No. 94, 343–357 and No. 100, 368–374. The charges ranged from meetings with Sten'ka Razin to performing non-consensual marriages and receiving unauthorized visitors, specifically women and girls.

216. Not surprisingly, Nikon denied the charges, including healings that occurred during the alleged "unauthorized meetings." The patriarch's responses during the interrogations by the *tsar's* delegation are recorded in *Delo o patriarkhe Nikone*, No. 100, 369–375. This would explain why Shusherin left this aspect of Nikon life in exile out of the *Account*. See also note 200 above.

217. See *Delo o patriarkhe Nikone*, No. 94, 357–358.

218. The punishments for Nikon's cell companions are described in *Delo o patriarkhe Nikone*, No. 94, 360–361 and No. 100, 375–376. Importantly, Varlaam and Mardarii testified about Nikon's healings, noting that women and infants were among those healed. See *Delo o patriarkhe Nikone*, No. 100, 376–378.

219. On June 7, 1676, monks at the Ferapontov Monastery compiled a list of church utensils that Aleksei Mikhailovich had donated to Nikon. See *Delo o patriarkhe Nikone*, No. 101, 378–379. Patriarch Ioakim eventually ordered to keep the valuables at the Ferapontov Monastery. On December 16, 1676, he wrote: "From the great sovereign, his holiness Ioakim, patriarch of Moscow and all Russia, to Afanasii, abbot of the Ferapontov Monastery in Belozerskii district, to Isaiia, the abbot of the hermitage (*starets-stroitel'*), and the brethren. In this year 7185 [1676], you wrote to us, our holiness the patriarch, and attached to your letter was a petition about the church utensils which were catalogued at your Ferapontov Monastery in the gateway Church of the Holy Epiphany [*Bogoiavlenskaia*] which were left after monk Nikon was transferred; the said utensils were donated by the great sovereign, *tsar* and grand prince of all Great, and Little, and White Russias, Aleksei Mikhailovich, let his memory be blessed, on the request of monk Nikon, to the Ferapontov Monastery, to the aforesaid Church of the Holy Epiphany: and we, our holiness the patriarch, order to keep these church utensils in the Ferapontov Monastery in the Church of the Holy Epiphany. When this, our decree, reaches you, you are to do with the church utensils according to our edict. Written in Moscow on the sixteenth day of December in the year 7185 [1676]." *DAI*, Vol. 4, No. 217, 303. On June 8, 1676, a list describing Nikon's gardens, barns, and fishing-related supplies was compiling. See *Delo o patriarkhe Nikone*, No. 102, 380–382. The same day Pavel, archimandrite of the Monastery of the Miracles, prepared a list of things in Nikon's cell which were to be transferred to the Ferapontov Monastery. See *Delo o patriarkhe Nikone*, No. 106, 404–405. For an inventory of the supplies transferred from Nikon's stores in the Ferapontov to the Kirillov Monastery, see *Delo o patriarkhe Nikone*, No. 103, 382–383. These records clearly show that Nikon was not in need of food or other supplies at the time of his relocation to the Kirillov Monastery.

220. Comparative analysis strongly suggests that Shusherin's account of Nikon's transfer from the Ferapontov to the Kirillov Monastery is based on the official reports filed by Pavel, archimandrite of the Monastery of the Miracles, and his companions. See *Delo o patriarkhe Nikone*, No. 94, 341–361.

221. In June 1676, the monastery's superiors wrote to patriarch Ioakim, explaining that the furnaces in the cells where Nikon lived bellowed smoke. The patriarch responded by issuing a decree on July 5, 1676. The decree arrived at the Kirillov Monastery on July 22, 1676. See Nikolaevskii, *Zhizn'*, 118; and Varlaam, No. 13, 37. In this document, patriarch Ioakim proclaimed: "We, our holiness the patriarch, learned that you at the Kirillov Monastery have brick furnaces in the cells in which monk Nikon is ordered to

live and that they produce poisonous fumes: and we, our holiness the patriarch, order to build in those cells tile furnaces so that there will not be poisonous fumes, and behind those cells, where appropriate, . . . build him a personal stone cookery with chimney for his, Nikon's, needs and the chimney should be built higher than the wooden building so that it will not cause a fire. . . . And as this decree of ours . . . shall reach you, you are to act according to our edict without delay and to order to make a plan of these his cells and of all old and new buildings and to write to us . . . about this, and to submit the letter and the plan. . . . Written in Moscow on the fifth day of July of the year 7185 [1676]." *DAI*, Vol. 4, No. 213, 290. See also Apollos, 154; and Nikolaevskii, *Zhizn'*, 118–119.

Ironically, in this letter, Ioakim calls himself "great sovereign," precisely the same self-address for which Nikon was criticized and condemned at the 1666 council of the synod. See the summary of official charges against Nikon in Ligarides, 162–163. Nikon, of course, always claimed that *tsar* Aleksei Mikhailovich insisted on this title. See Nikon, "Replies," 261–270.

On July 27, 1676, the hierarchs of the Kirillov Monastery wrote to patriarch Ioakim explaining that Nikon's cells were repaired. See Nikolaevskii, *Zhizn'*, 119 and Varlaam, No. 13, 37. The exact repairs made are described in *Delo o patriarkhe Nikone*, No. 107, 406.

222. There is a mistake in new style dating (AD) in the original. It should be 1679.

223. Fedor first visited the New Jerusalem Resurrection Monastery together with the royal family on September 5–8, 1678. See Kavelin, *Istoricheskoe opisanie*, 32; and *Vykhody gosudarei tsarei i velikikh kniazei*, 690.

224. Fedor went to the New Jerusalem Resurrection Monastery on December 5, 1678 and then again on November 25, 1679, staying until December 1, 1679. Fedor returned to the monastery for the fourth time on September 18, 1680 and finally on December 2, 1680. See Kavelin, *Istoricheskoe opisanie*, 32–39; and idem., *Kratkoe istoricheskoe skazanie*, 11. Examples of Fedor's gifts are found in Kavelin, *Istoricheskoe opisanie*, 31, 33, and 35.

225. This letter was published in Apollos, 155–158; and Kavelin, *Istoricheskoe opisanie*, 38–41.

226. The names of all brethren who signed the plea to the *tsar* were published in Kavelin, *Istoricheskoe opisanie*, 42–43; and Apollos, 157–158.

227. The letter cited by Shusherin reads: "To our father in the Holy Spirit, Nikon the patriarch, the sinful Fedor with his spouse bows to the ground and I announce to your honor that, if God deigns for this letter to be handed to you . . . that, trusting God, your transfer is forthcoming and you yourself are to live in New Jerusalem and it will be completed after receiving you. And for this, I sinful *tsar* Fedor and my wife wish to receive your blessing when we meet and through letters. Amen." Quoted in Nikolaevskii, *Zhizn'*, 128; and Brilliantov, 232.

228. On the monks' release, see Kavelin, *Istoricheskoe opisanie*, 43 and 59.

229. See note 227 above.

230. See Kavelin, *Istoricheskoe opisanie*, 37 and 39.

231. Nikon composed this letter in June 1681. The text of this missive is published in Kavelin, *Istoricheskoe opisanie*, 45; and Nikolaevskii, *Zhizn'*, 129.

232. Fedor sent his requests to the ecumenical patriarchs earlier, on June 26, 1681. See Nikolaevskii, *Zhizn'*, 127; and Sevast'ianova, *Mater'ialy*, 324.

233. The text of the inscription is published in Kavelin, *Istoricheskoe opisanie*, 6, note 4.

234. Kavelin published two slightly different accounts of Nikon's funeral at the New Jerusalem Resurrection Monastery. The first was included in the monastery's book of donations (*vkladnaia kniga*). "In the year 7139 (1681) on the twenty-fifth day of August,

in the thirteenth hour of daylight [6 PM], grand prince Fedor Alekseevich . . . her majesty *tsarina* . . . Nataliia Kirillovna, . . . and grand prince Piotr Alekseevich [the future Peter the Great] and . . . *tsarevnas* . . . Tatiana Mikhailovna, Evdokiia Alekseevna, Marfa Alekse-evna, Sofiia Alekseevna, Ekaterina Alekseevna, Mariia Alekseevna, Feodosiia Alekseevna, and Nataliia Alekseevna arrived. . . . And on that day, the great sovereign listened to evening services near the cross which is called Golgotha. And on the twenty-sixth day of August, in the second hour of daylight, by the edict of the great sovereign, they started to ring the bells according to the church custom, and an hour later, they started to ring the same bells, each bell three times without a break, and the great sovereign deigned to go to the church, and at the church, Kornilii, metropolitan of Novgorod, Nikita, archimandrite of the Kirillov Monastery, Sil'vestr, archimandrite of the St. Savva Monastery, German, archimandrite of the Resurrection Monastery, together with priests and deacons in vestments, holding icons, walked in a procession to the cross which is erected across from the Resurrection Monastery. And the great sovereign deigned to take part in the procession and during the procession, he ordered the members of his choir to sing the hymn (*stikhira*) 'Today we are assembled by the Grace of the Holy Spirit.' And at the cross, the great sovereign met Vikentii, archimandrite of the Trinity and St. Sergius Monastery, in full vestments together with priests and deacons, and he also stood next to the body of patriarch Nikon and they sang at the cross: 'With the souls of the righteous.' And afterwards, the great sovereign ordered the priests and deacons to carry the body to the monastery . . . and so walking, they sang: 'Holy God,' and having come to the monastery, they put the body of patriarch Nikon in the stone Church of Dormition of the Holiest Mother of God, and in this church, the great sovereign and the pious *tsarina* and the pious *tsarevich*, and *tsarevnas* deigned to listen to the divine liturgy, and after the liturgy ended, the great sovereign ordered everyone to go ask patriarch Nikon for forgiveness and to kiss his hand. And after that, they read the memorial service (*panikhida*)) for him, according to the custom, and buried him in the church near St. John the Baptist on the same day (August 26), in the ninth hour of daylight . . . And in the stone church, near St. John the Baptist, the noble *tsarevnas* deigned to listen to morning prayers, and after the morning prayers, deigned to read a burial service (*zaupokoinaia sluzhba*) for patriarch Nikon, and the noble *tsarevna* and grand princess Tatiana Mikhailovna, on her righteous oath, granted the church many utensils and liturgical vestments. The same day the great sovereign deigned to listen to the holy liturgy at the stone church near the honorable cross together with the pious *tsarina* and *tsarevich* at the Church of the Dormition of the Holiest Mother of God and the noble *tsarevnas* at the Church of St. John the Baptist." Kavelin, *Istoricheskoe opisanie*, 50–52. Interestingly, Ioann Alekseevich was notably absent from the ceremony and only one of the future co-rulers, Piotr Alekseevich, also known as Peter the Great, attended.

Another version of these events appeared in the "Forward to the Book of Church Canons of the Resurrection Monastery" which inserts the following passage after the phrase "with the souls of the righteous" cited above: "And so having reached the honorable cross which is in front of the monastery, on the road to Moscow, and where the body of his holiness patriarch Nikon lay, and having come, they lit the large black candles prepared for this and his eminence Kornilii, metropolitan of Novgorod the Great, gave out the candles according to rank, first to the *tsar*, then to the entire clergy, and the *tsar's* Council, and the archimandrite of the Trinity Monastery gave out [candles] to numerous people, men and women; because these candles were paid for by the *tsar's* treasury; some of the candles were large, a *sazhen* long [almost two meters], and members of the *tsar's* choir walked with these candles near the deathbed of his holiness patriarch Nikon in patterned vestments (frocks similar to tunic made of Chinese silk . . .), made for this occasion; and so having taken the honorable body of his holiness patriarch Nikon and having priests carry it to the monastery." The rest of the second passage is identical to the first one after the phrase "and so walking, they sang: 'Holy God.'" Quoted in Kavelin, *Istoricheskoe opisanie*, 51.

The second account also ends on the following note: "And at the end of singing, the pious great sovereign . . . Fedor Alekseevich, . . . although he did not see patriarch Nikon alive, touched him with love from his entire heart, and, crying, deigned to commit his body to the coffin and the earth with his own hands to the wonderment of all people present here who saw the pious great sovereign the *tsar* doing this from such a heartfelt love for his holiness patriarch Nikon, as was unheard in today's generations. And the memory of this will amaze the generations to come." Kavelin, *Istoricheskoe opisanie*, 52.

235. The New Jerusalem Resurrection Monastery inventory of 1685 lists many of these items. See Kavelin, *Istoricheskoe opisanie*, 272–273.

236. The New Jerusalem Resurrection Monastery inventory of 1685 described several of these items, including Nikon's medallions (*panagiia*), frocks (*riasa*), pectoral crosses (*napersnyi krest*), etc. See Kavelin, *Istoricheskoe opisanie*, 290–293.

237. In the 1930s, Nikon's tomb was opened by the Soviet authorities, who discovered the patriarchal regalia which Shusherin describes. See Zelenskaia, *Sviatyni Novogo Ierusalima*, 276–277.

238. On the date, see Nikolaevskii, *Zhizn'*, 127 and 134.

239. Fedor made his seventh and final visit to the New Jerusalem Resurrection Monastery on November 30, 1681. The *tsar's* activities during this visit were recorded in the monastery's book of donations. It states: "On the thirtieth of November in the year 7190 (1681), there was a visit by the great sovereign, *tsar* and grand prince of all Russia, Fedor Alekseevich to the monastery of the holy life-giving Resurrection of Christ. During the fifth hour of night, in the first quarter, archimandrite German, priests, deacons, and the entire brethren met him, the great sovereign, at the holy gates of the monastery, according to custom, and after entering the monastery, the great sovereign deigned to go to the stone church, called Golgotha, and being at Golgotha, deigned to go to the Church of John the Baptist, where his holiness patriarch Nikon was buried, and sang earnest entreaties. And on the first day of December, the great sovereign donated fifty rubles for charity to archimandrite German and the abbot of the hermitage Sergii and the entire brethren, and to the hospital brethren [he donated] three rubles, and one *altyn* [three *kopeks*], and two *den'gas* [one *kopek*], and [he also gave] one hundred rubles to the monastery treasury." Kavelin, *Istoricheskoe opisanie*, 61.

Fedor's direct participation in the construction of the Resurrection Monastery and its main sanctuary in 1679–1682 is outlined in Kavelin, *Istoricheskoe opisanie*, 56–61.

240. For descriptions of the treasures Fedor gave the monastery, see ibid., 289, 292 and 307.

241. The monasteries, estates, and peasants Fedor granted to the Resurrection Monastery between 1673 and 1682 are listed in Kavelin, *Istoricheskoe opisanie*, 524–525.

242. On Fedor's grant of the village of Troitskoe and surrounding areas to the monastery, see ibid., 525.

243. For the decrees rehabilitating patriarch Nikon issued by Dositheus, patriarch of Jerusalem; Iakov, patriarch of Constantinople; Parthenius, patriarch of Alexandria; Neofyte, former patriarch of Antioch; Cyril, newly installed patriarch of Antioch, see *SGGD*, Vol. 4, Nos. 135–140, 417–432.

244. Ioann Alekseevich, also known as Ivan V, ruled Russia in 1682–1696; his half brother Piotr Alekseevich, also known as Peter the Great, first co-ruled with Ioann in 1682–1696 and then ruled autonomously in 1696–1725. The death of their older brother Fedor Alekseevich (an issue from Aleksei Mikhailovich's first marriage to Mariia Il'inichna Miloslavskaia) unleashed a succession crisis between the descendants of Aleksei Mikhailovich's first marriage, which included Fedor, Sofiia (Sophia), and Ioann, and his

progeny from the second marriage to Nataliia Kirillovna Naryshkina, including Piotr, a struggle which continued well into the eighteenth century. If it was not for Ioann's feeble physique and questionable mental faculties, he would have been the first in line for the Muscovite throne and would have ruled alone. So, Miloslavskiis' opponents supported Piotr as a co-ruler, despite the established order of succession. This unusual move sparked intense opposition culminating in 1682 *strel'tsy* uprising. After the issue was settled, at least temporarily, Sofiia was named regent for both adolescent co-rulers (1682–1689).

245. This heated exchange and open defiance as well as Ioakim's earlier obstinacy in refusing to attend Nikon's funeral despite impassioned pleas from *tsar* Fedor Alekseevich, which Shusherin dutifully records, add new perspectives to our understanding of the tensions between the secular and ecclesiastical authorities that culminated in Peter the Great's abolition of the Moscow patriarchate in 1712.

246. A seventeenth-century document published by Nikolaevskii explains that "on February 13, 1683, on Tuesday, during the cheese-fare Sunday, before the liturgy, the patriarch conducted a memorial service for patriarchs Ioasaf, Nikon, and the metropolitans. The liturgy was conducted by the metropolitan of Krutitsa, and a memorial meal was held at the Cross Chamber; the next day, on the fourteenth of February, after the morning prayer, the patriarch left for the Resurrection Monastery, and arrived there in the third hour of night; on the fifteenth, before the liturgy, he conducted a memorial service near Nikon's tomb; he also served the liturgy in the Golgotha Church. And at the Church of John the Baptist, where Nikon is buried, the archimandrite of the Epiphany Cathedral served the liturgy with the clergy; the memorial meal was served in the monastery's refectory, the patriarch dined together with the brethren and after the meal gave charitable donations to them." Quoted in Nikolaevskii, *Zhizn'*, 139. Patriarch Ioakim also visited the New Jerusalem Resurrection Monastery on August 19–23, 1684, January 18, 1685, and August 22–23, 1685. See Nikolaevskii, *Zhizn'*, 139; and Sevast'ianova, *Mater'ialy*, 328.

247. The royal family continued to visit the New Jerusalem Resurrection Monastery in the years following Nikon's death. Tatiana Mikhailovna and Sofiia Alekseevna were there on September 11, 1682, while Ioann Alekseevich visited on December 4–6, 1683. Tatiana Mikhailovna's and Sofiia Alekseevna's activities at the New Jerusalem Resurrection Monastery on September 11, 1682 are recorded in the monastery's book of donations. "In the year 7191 (1682), on the eleventh day of September, in the third hour of daylight, in the second quarter, there was a visit by noble *tsarevnas* and grand princesses Tatiana Mikhailovna and Sofiia Alekseevna and archimandrite German, priests, and deacons in vestments met them with the cross and holy water at the holy gates of the monastery, and after entering the monastery, their highnesses deigned to go to the stone church called Golgotha and deigned to listen to the holy divine liturgy there; after the dismissal prayer (*otpust*), they deigned to go to the Church of St. John the Baptist, where his holiness patriarch Nikon is buried and sang a memorial service and, after the dismissal prayer, they deigned to eat at the archimandrite's cells, and after dining, they deigned to go to the hospital, and from the hospital they went to the church near patriarch Nikon's tomb and from the tomb, at eight o'clock at night they deigned to go to the village of Pavlovskoe . . . and archimandrite, priests, deacons, and all the brethren presented them with an icon of the Resurrection of Christ and bread at the holy gates of the monastery." Kavelin, *Istoricheskoe opisanie*, 63. Records of Nikon's belongings being transferred from the Kirillov Monastery to the New Jerusalem Resurrection Monastery are published in Varlaam, No. 16, 38–39.

248. In 1685, Ioann Alekseevich and Piotr Alekseevich, the future Peter the Great, ordered to officially describe the church. This record details the exact measurements, appearance, ornamentation, etc. of the church, drawing repeated comparisons with the

Church of the Holy Sepulcher in Jerusalem. This document is published in Kavelin, *Is-toricheskoe opisanie*, 70–81.

249. Examples of Tatiana Mikhailovna's donations of books, vestments, and church utensils were duly recorded in the monastery's inventory of 1685. See Kavelin, *Is-toricheskoe opisanie*, 226, 264–267, 289, 294, 301, and 311. For an important recent study of extant artifacts originally donated by Tatiana Mikhailovna, see E. I. Rogozhkina, "Tsarskie vklady iz dragotsennykh metallov i kamnei v Voskresenskii Novo-Ierusalims-kii monastyr' v XVII veke," in G. M. Zelenskaia, ed. *Nikonovskie chteniia v muzee 'Novyi Ierusalim.' Sbornik statei* (Moscow, 2005), 190–198.

250. On the dual usage of titles of metropolitan of Sar and Don and metropolitan of Krutitsa, see note 107 above. Varsonofii served as metropolitan of Sar and Don/Krutitsa in 1676–1688. See Makarii, *Istoriia*, Vol. 12, 611.

251. On Afanasii of Kholmogory, see G. Michels, "Rescuing the Orthodox: The Church Policies of Archbishop Afanasii of Kholmogory, 1682–1702," in Robert Geraci and Michael Khodarkovsky, eds., *Of Religion and Empire. Missions, Conversion, and Tolerance in Tsarist Russia* (Ithaca and London, 2001), 19–37. Afanasii (Lubimov, d. 1701), was a former Old Believer who converted to the official church, eventually rising to the rank of archbishop of Kholmogory (1682). He was a major anti-Old Believer po-lemicist, penning widely-circulated *Spiritual Exhortation* (1682). See also Michels, *At War with the Church*, 114, 118, 170–171, and 186.

252. A more detailed account of the consecration ceremonies, written before 1686, was published by Kavelin. "On the eighteenth day of January, in the first half hour of daylight, the main bells were rung as was customary during processions and the consecra-tion of churches. The archimandrite of the Resurrection Monastery, priests, and deacons prepared holy water at the great church during the first hour of daylight and, after sancti-fying the water, during the second hour of daylight, his holiness patriarch Ioakim with ecclesiastical dignitaries, archimandrites, abbots, and the entire holy synod came to the great church and, upon entering, made the sign of the cross near the holy icons. And at his patriarchal stall, he put on vestments fit for the consecration of the holy church, as was customary; and at that time, the pious *tsarinas* and the noble *tsarevnas* and grand princesses came to the holy church, and stood at their places behind the taffeta sanctuary screen [dividing male and female parishioners]; and his holiness patriarch Ioakim ordered the archdeacon to start the consecration of the church and to start the holy sacraments inside the altar; doing so, his holiness the patriarch and the ecclesiastical dignitaries la-bored and during this service there was a visit to the church by the great sovereign. And after the service, his holiness the patriarch went to the holy relics at the wooden Church of the Resurrection with the entire holy synod and the pious sovereign the *tsar* and his Council, and a multitude of people, walking with holy banners and crosses and praying. And having taken the holy relics from that church, they walked back by the same route to the southern church doors and, from the southern doors to the new great stone church near the wall. And from the very beginning of the procession, his holiness patriarch Ioakim carried the relics on a paten; behind him his eminence Gavriil, archbishop of Vo-lotsk and Beloozero [sic!, should be 'of Vologda and Beloozero'], carried holy water and a holy water sprinkler (*kropilo*) on a silver platter. And having entered the southern doors, they walked to the left, behind the pillar, passing the church yard, and stood by the western pillars where the Lord's Sepulcher is depicted, following to the service as was customary in the holy church. After the *tsarevnas* dined, they visited the hermitage . . . where his holiness patriarch Nikon lived. . . . On the nineteenth day of January, the noble *tsarevnas* and the noble *tsarinas,* and his holiness the patriarch listened to the morning services in the newly consecrated great stone church, and the patriarch deigned to sing a memorial service for his holiness patriarch Nikon and after the memorial service, having

given peace and blessing, as was customary, to the great sovereigns and having thanked the sovereigns for their charity and having praised God, his holiness the patriarch went to Moscow." Quoted in Kavelin, *Istoricheskoe opisanie*, 65–69.

253. The *tsar* and his entourage arrived at the monastery on January 15, 1685. See Kavelin, *Istoricheskoe opisanie*, 65.

254. Shusherin or his copiers made a mistake here. The year was 1685, not 1687.

255. Nikifor served as archimandrite of the New Jerusalem Resurrection Monastery from July 1683 to January 1686. He wrote a description of the church's consecration in January 1685, shortly after the event transpired. See *Istoricheskoe opisanie stavropigial'nago Voskresenskago, Novyi Ierusalim imenuemago, monastyria* (Moscow, 1886), 72.

256. On Sergii Turchaninov and the casting of the bells, see Zelenskaia, *Sviatyni Novogo Ierusalima*, 79–94.

257. Here Shusherin appears to make a grammatical mistake by using the plural form instead of the singular. In 1678, Fedor Alekseevich was the only ruler of Russia, and thus should have been referred to as great sovereign and pious *tsar*. By using the plural address of "great sovereigns and pious *tsars*," Shusherin makes it sound as if he means Piotr (the future Peter the Great) and Ioann, but they were still in line for the Muscovite throne. For the proof of the salt mine and monetary donations by Fedor Alekseevich and their correct attributions, see Kavelin, *Istoricheskoe opisanie*, 35 and 524. However, in 1685, Ioann and Piotr, then actually the *tsars* of Russia, did make a major donation to the Resurrection Monastery, which included numerous villages, forests, meadows, and salt mines with all the usage rights thereto. Just a short time later, on March 1, 1686, Ioann and Piotr made another major grant of lands, villages, and peasants. So, indeed, Shusherin or his later copiers might have confused the dates referring to 1685/1686 royal donations, not to 1678 bequests. On Ioann and Piotr's donations, see Kavelin, *Istoricheskoe opisanie*, 106–108 and 526. The end of Shusherin's account in general is confusing, with frequent mistakes in dates and non-chronological sequence of events. It is not clear who is to blame here, the original author or his later copiers who interjected new style dating into the seventeenth-century narrative.

258. For instance, Ioann, Tatiana, Sofiia and other members of the royal family returned to the monastery on May 15, 1685. There they visited Nikon's grave, made donations, and ordered the construction of a new church which was completed and dedicated to St. Tatiana in 1692. See Kavelin, *Istoricheskoe opisanie*, 102–103.

Tatiana Mikhailovna was perhaps the most devoted royal patron of the Resurrection Monastery. She commissioned several churches, including the Church of Nativity (consecrated December 13, 1692) and the Church of St. Basil the Great, Gregory the Theologian, and John Chrysostom (1698). The *tsarevna* also funded the refurbishment of several churches, for example the Church of John the Baptist (1690), and paid to decorate a side altar in honor of St. Nicholas in the main sanctuary, the Church of the Resurrection (1682). See Zelenskaia, *Sviatyni Novogo Ierusalima*, 379, 382, 387, and 390. Tatiana Mikhailovna also commissioned a stone hospital consecrated on April 18, 1698. See Kavelin, *Istoricheskoe opisanie*, 104 and 288. Tatiana's other noteworthy gifts to the monastery included the relics (hand) of St. Tatiana in a silver reliquary (January 7, 1691). See Kavelin, *Istoricheskoe opisanie*, 104; and Zelenskaia, *Sviatyni Novogo Ierusalima*, 256–259. For a concise overview of Tatiana's patronage of the monastery, see Kavelin, *Istoricheskoe opisanie*, 113–114. Her generosity to the monastery is immortalized in various commemorative stone tablets dating to the late seventeenth century. See Zelenskaia, *Sviatyni Novogo Ierusalima*, 105.

Other Romanovs supported the monastery too. On May 6, 1690, Ioann and Piotr, the future Peter the Great, issued a decree commissioning a major improvement, the construction of a new stone wall around the monastery. Piotr apparently wanted to use the monastery as a fortress. The project was finished in 1694. See Kavelin, *Istoricheskoe opisanie*, 104. Piotr's daughter, empress Elizabeth I became a major patron of the monastery. See, for example, Zelenskaia, *Sviatyni Novogo Ierusalima*, 343–345, 379, and 381.

Indeed continued royal patronage made the Resurrection Monastery one of the most economically powerful. In 1674, it already had 16,287 adult males assigned to it; in 1710, this number grew to 17,319. For a complete overview of the history of the monastery's holdings, see Kavelin, *Istoricheskoe opisanie*, 504, and 540–543.

259. The book to which Shusherin refers here is his *Keleinaia letopis'*. On this lesser known work, see N. Iu. Bubnov and A. V. Lavrent'ev, "Ioann Kornil'ev Shusherin-Ripatov," in D. M. Bulanin and A. A. Turilov, eds. *Slovar' knizhnikov i knizhnosti drevnei Rusi (XVII vek)*, Issue 3, Pt. 2 (St. Petersburg, 1993), 70.

260. Shusherin signs with the pseudonym Ripatov, not his real name, perhaps because the Russian letter "sh" (μ) as well as soft and hard signs do not have equivalents in the numerological system. But in this case he counts the letters incorrectly; it should be 561, not 563. R(100)+i(8)+p(80)+a(1)+t(300)+o(70)+v(2)=561. Converting the last name "Shusherin" into a numerological system however gives the correct number of 563: sh(no number)+u(400)+sh(no number)+e(5)+r(100)+i(8)+n(50)=563.

Bibliography

Published Primary Sources

Akty istoricheskie, sobrannye Arkheograficheskoiu komissieiu. Vols. 4–5. St. Petersburg: V Tipografii II-go Otdeleniia sobstvennoi Ego Imperatorskago Velichestva Kantseliarii, 1842.

Akty Moskovskago gosudarstva, izdannye Imperatorskoiu Akademiei Nauk. Ed. N. A. Popov. Vol. 2. St. Petersburg: Tipografiia Imperatorskoi Akademii Nauk, 1894.

Akty sobrannye v bibliotekakh i arkhivakh rossiiskoi imperii arkheograficheskoi ekspeditsiei Imperatorskoi Akademii Nauk. Vol. 4. St. Petersburg: V Tipografii II-go Otdeleniia sobstvennoi Ego Imperatorskago Velichestva Kantseliarii, 1842.

Arkheograficheskaia Komissiia. *Delo o patriarkhe Nikone.* St. Petersburg, 1897.

Avvakum, archpriest. "The Life of Archpriest Avvakum by Himself." In *Medieval Russia's Epics, Chronicles and Tales.* Ed. S. A. Zenkovsky. Revised and enlarged edition. New York: Meridian, 1974, 399–448.

Bachmiester, J. *Beytraege zur lebensgeschichte des Patriarchen Nikon.* Riga: Johann Friedrich Hartknosh, 1788.

Belokurov, S.A. *Dela sviateishago Nikona patriarkha, pache zhe rechi dela vrachebnye. Materialy dlia russkoi istorii.* Moscow: Universitetskaia Tipografiia, 1888.

Borozdin, A. K. *Protopop Avvakum. Ocherk iz istorii umstvennoi zhizni russkago obshchestva v XVII veke.* 2nd ed. St. Petersburg: A. S. Suvorin, 1900.

Denisov, Simeon. *Istoriia o ottsekh i stradal'tsekh Solovetskikh.* Eds. N.V. Ponyrko, and E. M. Iukhimenko. Moscow: Iazyki Slavianskoi Kultury, 2002.

Dopolneniia k aktam istoricheskim, sobrannye i izdannye Arkheograficheskoiu komissieiu. Vol. 3–4. St. Petersburg: Tipografiia Eduarda Pratsa, 1848–1851.

Drevnosti Rossiiskago gosudarstva. 6 Vols. Moscow, 1849–1853.

Epiphanius the Wise, "The Life, Acts, and Miracles of Our Blessed and Holy Father Sergius of Radonezh." In *Medieval Russia's Epics, Chronicles and Tales.* Ed. S. A. Zenkovsky. Revised and enlarged edition. New York: Meridian, 1974, 262–290.

Gibbenet, N. I. *Istoricheskoe issledovanie dela patriarkha Nikona.* 2 Vols. St. Petersburg: Tipografiia Ministerstva Vnutrennikh Del, 1882–1884.

Izvestie o rozhdenii i vospitanii i o zhitii sviateishago Nikona patriarkha moskovskago i vseia Rossii, napisannoe klirikom ego Ioannom Shusherinym. Moscow, 1908.

Izvestie o rozhdenii i vospitanii i o zhitii sviateishago Nikona patriarkha moskovskago i vseia Rossii, napisannoe klirikom ego Ioannom Shusherinym. Moscow: Universitet-skaia Tipografiia, 1906.

Lavrentii, archimandrite. *Kratkoe izvestie o Krestnom Onezhskom, arkhangel'skoi eparkhii, monastyre.* Moscow: Synodal'naia Tipografiia, 1805.

Leonid (Kavelin), archimandrite, ed. *Akty Iverskago Sviatoozerskago monastyria (1582–1706).* St. Petersburg, 1878.

————. *D'iakon Lugovskoi po Tatishchevu pisatel' xvii veka i ego sochinenie o sude nad patriarkhom Nikonom.* St. Petersburg, 1885.

————. *Istoricheskoe opisanie stavropigial'nago Voskresenskago, Novyi Ierusalim ime-nuemago, monastyria.* Moscow, 1876.

Nikon, patriarch. *Rai Myslennyi.* Ed. V. S. Belenko. St. Petersburg: Zhurnal "Neva," 1999.

Opisanie staropechatnykh knig slavianskikh, sluzhashchie dopolneniem k opisaniiam bib-liotek grafa F. A. Tolstova i kuptsa I. N. Tsarskago. Ed. P. M. Stroev. Moscow: Ti-pografiia Selivanovskago, 1841.

Palmer, William. *The Patriarch and the Tsar.* 6 Vols. London: Trubner, 1871–1876.

Peretz, V. N. *Slukhi i tolki o patriarkhe Nikone v literaturnoi obrabotke pisatelei XVII–XVIII vv.* St. Petersburg, 1900.

Polnoe sobranie rossiiskikh letopisei. Vol. 3. St. Petersburg: Tipografiia Eduarda Pratsa, 1841.

Povest' o rozhdenii, vospitanii i zhizni sviateischego Nikona, patriarkha Moskovskago i vseia Rossii, napisannaia ego klirikom Ioannom Shusherinym. Reprint of 2nd ed. Mos-cow, 1908. Moscow: Pravoslavnaia Entsiklopediia, 1997.

Risunki k puteshestviiu po Rossii rimsko-imperatorskago poslannika Barona Meierberga v 1661 i 1662 godakh, predstavliaiushchie vidy, narodnye obychai, portrety. St. Peters-burg: Fedor Adalung, 1827.

Romantseva, V.S., and I. A. Bulygin, eds. *Narodnoe antitserkovnoe dvizhenie v Rossii XVII veka. Dokumenty prikaza tainykh del o raskol'nikakh 1665–1667 gg.* Moscow: Nauka, 1986.

Shmidt, V. V. *Patriarkh Nikon. Trudy.* Moscow: MGU, 2004.

Sobranie gosudarstvennykh gramot i dogovorov. Vols. 3 and 4. Moscow: Tipografiia Se-livanovskago, 1822–1828.

Tikhomirov, M. N. "Dokumenty o Novgorodskom vosstanii 1650 g.," In *Novgorod. K stoletiiu goroda.* Moscow, 1964, 286–296.

Titova, L. V. "Skazanie o patriarkhe Nikone: Publitsisticheskii traktat pustozerskikh uz-nikov." In *Istoriia russkoi dukhuvnoi kul'tury v rukopisnom nasledii XVI–XX vv.* Ed. E. K. Romodanovskaia. Novosibirsk: Nauka, 1998, 232–237.

Vernadsky, G., and A. A. Tumins, eds. *Patriarch Nikon on Church and State, Nikon's Refutation.* The Hague: Walter de Gruyter & Co., 1982.

Vremennik Moskovskago obshchestva istorii i drevnostei Rossiiskikh. St. Petersburg, 1852.

Vykhody gosudarei tsarei i velikikh kniazei, Mikhaila Feodorovicha, Alekseia Mikhai-lovicha, Feodora Alekseevicha, vseia Rossii samoderzhtsev. Bk. 18. Ed. P. M. Stroev. Moscow: Tipografiia Avgusta Semena, 1844.

Witsen, Nicholaas. *Moscovische Reyes 1664–1665 Journal En Aentekeningen.* Eds. Th. J. G. Locher, and P. de Buck. Amsterdam: Martinus Nijhoff, 1966.

Zapiski Russkago Arkheologicheskago Obshchestva. Vol. 2. St. Petersburg, 1861.

"Zhitie i chudesa prepodobnago otsa nashego Eleazara chudotvortsa, nachal'nika Anzer-skago skita. Sobrano ot mnogikh i vernykh skazatelei i spisano vkratse." *Pravoslavnyi sobesednik* January 1860: 108–120.

"Zhitie sviateishago patriarkha Nikona, pisannoe nekotorym byvshim pri nem klirikom." *Russkii Arkhiv* 1909 (9): 109–144.

Zhitie sviateishago patriarkha Nikona, pisannoe nekotorym byvshim pri nem klirikom. St. Petersburg: Tipografiia Imperatorskoi Akademii Nauk, 1817.

Zhitie sviateishago patriarkha Nikona, pisannoe nekotorym byvshim pri nem klirikom. St. Petersburg, 1784.

Ziolkowski, M., trans. *Tale of Boiarynia Morozova: A Seventeenth-Century Religious Life.* Lanham: Lexington Books, 2000.

Secondary Sources

Altaev, A. *V debriakh Mordvy. Detstvo patriarkha Nikona.* Moscow: Izdatel'stvo zhurnala "Iunaia Rossiia," 1912.

Andreev, V. V. *Raskol i ego znachenie v narodnoi russkoi istorii.* St. Petersburg, 1870.

Apollos, archimandrite. *Kratkoe nachertanie zhizni i deianii Nikona, patriarkha moskovskago i vseia Rusi, s portretom ego.* 2nd ed. Moscow: Universitetskaia Tipografiia, 1836.

———. *Nachertanie zhitiia i deianii Nikona, patriarkha moskovskago i vseia Rusi. Sochinenie Novospaskago pervoklassnago stavropigial'nago monastyria.* Moscow, 1845/6.

———. *Nachertanie zhitiia i deianii Nikona, patriarkha moskovskago i vseia Rusi, vnov' ispravlennoe i dopolnennoe s prilozheniem perepisok Nikona s tsarem Alekseem Mikhailovichem i vazhneishikh gramot.* Moscow, 1859.

Baron, S. H., and N. S. Kollmann, eds. *Religion and Culture in Early Modern Russia and Ukraine.* DeKalb: Northern Illinois Press, 1997.

Batalov, A., and A. Lidov, eds. *Ierusalim v russkoi kul'ture.* Moscow: Nauka, 1994.

Belokurov, S. A. *Arsenii Sukhanov.* 2 Vols. Moscow: Universitetskaia Tipografiia, 1891–1893.

———. "Sobiranie patriarkhom Nikonom knig s vostoka," *Khristianskoe Chtenie* 1882 (2): 444–494.

Bezgodov, A. A. "Liutaia godina." In *Kalendar' Drevlepravoslavnoi pomorskoi tserkvi na 2002 god.* Moscow, 2002, 65–71.

Bobrovnitskaia, I. A. "Tsar' Aleksei Mikhailovich i patriarch Nikon. 'Premudraia dvoitsa.'" In *Tsar' Aleksei Mikhailovich i patriarkh Nikon.* Moscow: Khudozhnik i kniga, 2005, 8–15.

Botsianovskii, V. P. Patriarkh Nikon: tragediia v 5 deistviiakh i 6 kartinakh. Petrograd: Teatr i Iskusstvo, 1923.

Breshchinskii, D. H. "Zhitie Korniliia Vygovskogo kak literaturnyi pamiatnik i ego literaturnye sviazi na Vygu." In *Trudy otdela drevnerusskoi literatury Akademii Nauk SSSR.* Vol. XXXIII. Leningrad: Nauka, 1979, 127–141.

Brilliantov, I. *Ferapontov Belozerskii monastyr', mesto zatocheniia patriarkha Nikona.* St. Petersburg: Tipografiia A. P. Lopukhina, 1899.

Brumfield, William Craft. *A History of Russian Architecture.* New York: Cambridge University Press, 1993.

Bubnov, N. Yu. "Litsevye rukopisi staroobriadcheskoi knigopisnoi masterskoi vologodskikh krest'ian Kalikinykh." In *Staroobriadchestvo: Istoriia i sovremennost', mestnye traditsii, russkie i zarubezhnye sviazi.* Ulan-Ude: BNTs SO RAN, 2001.

———. "Skazaniia i povesti o patriarkhe Nikone." In *Trudy otdela drevnerusskoi literatury Akademii Nauk SSSR.* Vol. XLI. Leningrad: Nauka, 1988.

———. *Staroobriadcheskaia kniga v Rossii vo vtoroi polovine XVII v.* (St. Petersburg: BAN, 1995.

Bulanin, D. M., and A. A. Turilov, eds. *Slovar' knizhnikov i knizhnosti drevnei Rusi (XVII vek)*, Issue 3, Pt. 2. St. Petersburg: Dmitrii Bulanin, 1993.

Bunina, P. *Nikon i velikii raskol*. Moscow: Knigoizdatel'stvo "Delo," 1912.

Bury, J. B. "Iveron and Our Lady of the Gate." *Hermathena* 1899 (10): 71–99.

Bushkovitch, Paul. *Religion and Society in Russia: The Sixteenth and Seventeenth Centuries*. New York: Oxford University Press, 1992.

Bychkov, A. A. *Patriarkh Nikon. Biograficheskii ocherk*. St. Petersburg: Tipografiia Obshchestva "Obshchestvennaia Pol'za," 1891.

Cherniavsky, Michael. "The Old Believer and the New Religion." *Slavic Review* March 1966 (25:1): 1–39.

Chiretskii, S. F. *Patriarkh Nikon, ego zhizn' i deiatel'nost'. Biograficheskii ocherk*. St. Petersburg: Tipografiia "Gerol'd," 1908.

Cracraft, James. *The Petrine Revolution in Russian Imagery*. Chicago: The University of Chicago Press, 1997.

Crummey, Robert O. *The Old Believers & the World of the Antichrist: The Vyg Community & the Russian State 1694–1855*. Madison: The University of Wisconsin Press, 1970.

Dmitreevskii, M. *Puteshestvie v Novyi Ierusalim ili kratkoe istoricheskoe, khronologicheskoe i topograficheskoe opisanie stavropigial'nago Voskresenskago monastyria*. Moscow, 1808.

Flier, Michael S. "Court Ceremony in an Age of Reform. Patriarch Nikon and the Palm Sunday Ritual." In *Religion and Culture in Early Modern Russia and Ukraine*. Eds. S. H. Baron and N. S. Kollmann. DeKalb: Northern Illinois University Press, 1997.

Fal'kovskii, V. N. *Konchina patriarkha Nikona*. Kiev: F. D. Dubovika, 1913.

Fedotov, G.P. *Sviatoi Filipp mitropolit Moskovskii*. Reprint Moscow: Strizhev-Tsentr, 1991.

Filippov, M. A. *Patriarkh Nikon*. St. Petersburg: V. V. Komarov, 1885.

Flier, M., and D. Rowland, eds. *Medieval Russian Culture*. Vol. 2. Berkeley: University of California Press, 1994.

Fonkich, B. L. *Grechesko-russkie kulturnye sviazi v XV–XVII vv*. Moscow, 1977.

Fuhrman, Joseph. *Tsar Alexis: His Reign and His Russia*. Gulf Breeze: Academic International Press, 1981.

Georgievskii, G. *Nikon sviateishii patriarkh vserossiiskii i osnovannyi im Novyi Ierusalim*. 3rd ed. St. Petersburg, 1902.

Gorchakova, E. *Poezdka v Novyi Ierusalim, Savvino-Storozhevskii monastyr' i gorod Dmitrov*. Moscow: Tip. L. F. Snegireva, 1886.

Gosudarstvennyi khudozhestvenno-istoricheskii kraevoi muzei v gorode Voskresenske Moskovskoi gubernii. Putevoditel' po muzeiu. Voskresensk: Izdatel'stvo Gosudarstvennyi khudozhestvenno-istoricheskii kraevoi muzei, 1925.

Gosudarstvennyi khudozhestvenno-istoricheskii kraevoi muzei v g. Voskresenske, Moskovskoi gubernii. Kratkii putevoditel'. Moscow: Tip. Kooperativa "Nauka i Prosveshchenie," 1928.

Grechushkin, S. I. *Iz russkoi istorii. Patriarkh Nikon*. Moscow: V. V. Dumnov, 1910.

Gunn, G. P. "Patriarkh Nikon i Eleazar Anzerskii." In *Drevnerusskaia knizhnost' po materialam Pushkinskogo Doma*. Ed. A. M. Panchenko. Leningrad: Nauka, 1985, 230–242.

Hemer, Christiane. *Herrschaft und Legitimation im Russland des 17 Jahrhunderts: Staat u. Kirsche zur Zeit d. Patriarchen Nikon*. Frankfurt: Haag und Herchen, 1979.

Hionides, Harry T. *Paisius Ligarides*. New York: Twain Publishers, Inc. 1972.

Hughes, Lindsey. *Sophia Regent of Russia 1657–1704*. New Haven: Yale University Press, 1990.

Ikonnikov, V. S. *Novye materialy i trudy o patriarkhe Nikone.* Kiev: V Tipografii Imperatorskago universiteta sv. Vladimira, 1888.

Il'in, M. A. *Kamennaia letopis' Moskovskoi Rusi.* Moscow: Izdatel'stvo Moskovskogo Universiteta, 1966.

Istoricheskoe opisanie stavropigial'nago Voskresenskago, Novyi Ierusalim imenuemago, monastyria. Moscow: Tipografiia I. Efimova, 1886.

Istoricheskoe opisanie stavropigial'nago Voskresenskago, Novyi Ierusalim imenuemago, monastyria. 6th ed. Moscow: Tipografiia I. A. Morozova, 1914.

Iukhimenko, E. M., ed. *Patriarkh Nikon i ego vremia.* Moscow: GIM, 2004

———. *Patriarch Nikon. Oblacheniia, lichnye veshchi, avtografy, vklady, portrety.* Moscow: GIM, 2002.

Kapterev, N.F. *Patriarkh Nikon i tsar' Aleksei Mikhailovich.* 2 Vols. Sergiev Posad: Tipografiia Sviato-Troitskago monastyria, 1909–1912.

———. "Ispravlenie tserkovno-bogosluzhebnykh knig pri patriarkhe Nikone." *Bogoslovskii Vestnik* 1908 (3): 538–559; 1909 (1): 24–44.

———. *Patriarkh Nikon i ego protivniki v dele ispravleniia tserkovnykh obriadov.* 2nd ed. Sergiev Posad: Tipografiia Sviato-Troitskago monastyria, 1887.

Kliuchevsky, V. O. *A Course in Russian History: The Seventeenth Century.* Trans. N. Duddington. Chicago: Quadrangle Books, 1968.

Kol'tsova, T. M. "'Krestovyi obraz' Kiiskogo Krestnogo monastyria." In *Nauchno-issledovatel'skaia rabota v khudozhestvennom muzee.* Archangelsk, 1998, 14–30.

Konstantinova, T. "N. F. Kapterev o patriarkhe Nikone i tsare Aleksee Mikhailoviche." In *Kalendar' Drevlepravoslavnoi pomorskoi tserkvi na 2004 god* (Moscow, 2004), 71–75.

Kratkoe istoricheskoe opisanie stavropigial'nago Voskresenskago, Novyi Ierusalim imenuemago, monastyria. Moscow: Tipografiia V. Got'e, 1852.

Kratkoe skazanie o iavlenii chudotvornoi ikony Bozhei Materi Iverskoi ob ustroenii Valdaiskoi Iverskoi obiteli i prazdnestva. St. Petersburg, 1861.

Krestnyi Monastyr' osnovannyi patriarkhom Nikonom. St. Petersburg, 1894.

Lebedev, Lev. *Moskva Patriarshaia.* Moscow: Stolitsa, 1995.

Likhachev, D. S., ed. *Slovar' knizhnikov i knizhnosti drevnei Rusi.* Leningrad/St. Petersburg, 1988–1998.

Lindt, A. *Nikon i Avvakum.* Moscow: Tipografiia D. P. Efimova, 1906.

Lobachev, S. V. "K voprosu o rannei biografii patriarkha Nikona," In *Srednevekovaia Rus'.* St. Petersburg, 1995, 52–69.

———. *Patriarkh Nikon.* St. Petersburg: Iskusstvo, 2003.

Longworth, Philip. *Alexis Tsar of All Russias.* New York: Franklin Watts. 1984.

Lupinin, N. B. *Religious Revolt in the Seventeenth-Century: The Schism of the Russian Church.* Princeton: Princeton University Press, 1985.

Makarii (Bulgakov), metropolitan. *Istoriia Russkoi tserkvi.* Vol. 11. St. Petersburg, 1882.

Makarii (Bulgakov), metropolitan. *Istoriia Russkoi tserkvi.* Bk. 7. Vol. 12 [St. Petersburg, 1883] Reprint Moscow: Izdatel'stvo Spaso-preobrazhenskogo Valaamskogo monastyria, 1996.

———. *Istoriia russkago raskola, izvestnago pod imenem staroobriadchestva.* St. Petersburg, 1855.

Matthes-Hohlfeld, E. *Der Brief des Moskauer Patriarchen Nikon an Dionysios patriarch Konstantinopel.* Amsterdam: Verlag Aldolf M. Hakkert, 1970.

Metallov, M.V. *Ocherk istorii pravoslavnago tserkovnago peniia v Rossii.* Moscow, 1896.

Meyendorff, Paul. *Russia: Ritual & Reform.* Crestwood: St. Vladimir's Seminary Press, 1991.

Michels, G. "Rescuing the Orthodox: The Church Policies of Archbishop Afanasii of Kholmogory, 1682–1702." In *Of Religion and Empire. Missions, Conversion, and Tolerance in Tsarist Russia.* Eds. Robert Geraci, and Michael Khodarkovsky. Ithaca and London: Cornell University Press, 2001, 19–37.

———. *At War with the Church.* Stanford: Stanford University Press, 1999.

———. "The Solovki Uprising: Religion and Revolt in Modern Russia." *The Russian Review* 1992 (51:2): 1–15.

Mikhailovskii, S.V. *Zhizn' sviateishago Nikona patriarkha vserossiiskago.* Moscow: Stavropigial'nyi Voskresenskii Novo-Ierusalimskii Monastyr', 1887.

Mirsky, D. S. *A History of Russian Literature.* Ed. F. J. Whitfield. New York: Alfred A. Knopf, 1949.

Mordovtsev, D. L. *Velikii raskol.* St. Petersburg: Tipografiia Ministerstva putei soobshcheniia, 1881.

Murav'ev, A. N. *Russkaia Fivaida na Severe.* Reprint Moscow: Palomnik, 1998.

———. *Puteshestvie po sviatym mestam russkim.* St. Petersburg, 1836.

Nikolaevskii, F. *Obstoiatel'stva i prichiny udaleniia patriarkha Nikona s prestola.* St. Petersburg, 1883.

———. *Puteshestvie Novgorodskago mitropolita Nikona v Solovetskii monastyr' za moshchami sviatitelia Filipa.* St Petersburg, 1885.

———. *Zhizn' patriarkha Nikona v ssylke i zakluchenii posle osuzhdeniia ego na moskovskom sobore 1666 goda.* St. Petersburg: Tipografiia F. Elkonsa, 1886.

Opisanie sobornago khrama Voskreseniia Khristova, postroennago po Ierusalimskomu obraztsu sv. patriarkhom Nikonom v Voskresenskom, Novyi Ierusalim imenuemom, monastyre. Moscow, 1870.

Paert, I. K. *Old Believers, Religious Dissent and Gender in Russia, 1760–1850.* Manchester: Manchester University Press, 2003.

Pasternak, O. P. "Ikonografiia 'Kiiskogo kresta' i ego povtoreniia." In *Original i povtorenie v zhivopisi.* Moscow, 1988, 47–60.

Patriarkh Nikon. Moscow, 1879.

Patriarkh Nikon s portretom pervosviatitelia. St. Petersburg: Izdanie redaktsii zhurnala "Mirskoi Vestnik," 1869.

Piotr, archimandrite. *Opisanie pervoklassnago Iverskago Bogoroditskago monastyria, Novgorodskoi eparkhii (izvlecheno iz Istorii Rossiiskoi Ierarkhii, iz knigi Rai Myslennyi i Zhizneopisaniia patriarkha Nikona).* 2nd ed. St. Petersburg: Tipografiia III-go Otdeleniia Sobstvennoi Ego Imperatorskago Velichestva Kantseliarii, 1850.

Postoiannaia komissiia po ustroistvu narodnykh chtenii pri Ministerstve Narodnago Prosveshcheniia. *Novyi Ierusalim (Voskresenskii monastyr').* St. Petersburg: Tipografiia F. Eleonskago i Ko., 1887.

Ratshin, A. *Polnoe sobranie istoricheskikh svedenii o vsekh byvshikh v drevnosti i nyne sushchestvuiushchikh monastyriakh i primechatel'nykh tserkvakh v Rossii.* Reprint Moscow: Knizhnaia Palata, 2000.

Robson, R. R. *Solovki: The Story of Russia Told Through Its Most Remarkable Islands.* New Haven: Yale University Press, 2004.

———. *Old Believers in Modern Russia.* DeKalb: Northern Illinois Press, 1995.

Rowland, D. B. "Moscow—The Third Rome or the New Israel?" *The Russian Review* October 1996 (55): 591–614.

Sergeev, N. *Kratkoe zhizneopisanie sviateishago patriarkha Nikona.* Viatka: Tipografiia Kuklina, 1888.

Sergeevskii, N. *Sviateishii vserossiiskii patriarkh Nikon. Ego zhizn', deiatel'nost', zatochenie i konchina.* Moscow: Tipografiia I. Ia. Poliakova, 1894.

Sevast'ianova, S. K. *Mater'ialy k 'Letopisi zhizni i literaturnoi deiatel'nosti patriarkha Nikona'*. St. Petersburg: Dmitrii Bulanin, 2003.

———. *Prepodobnyi Eleazar, osnovatel' Sviato-Troitskogo Anzerskogo skita*. St. Petersburg, 2001.

Shchedrina, K. A. *Tsarei derzhava*. Moscow, 2000.

Sheerson, N. A. *Antireligioznaia propaganda v kraevedcheskikh muzeiakh*. Istra, 1930.

Shevelkin, I. "Slovo v den' torzhestvennago otkrytiia . . . bratstva sviatago Petra mitropolita." In *Dushepoleznoe Chtenie*. Pt. 1. Moscow, 1873, 13–57.

"Skazanie o zhitii i stradanii sviatago sviashchennomuchennika i ispovednika Pavla, episkopa Kolomenskago." In *Tserkovnyi Kalendar' na 2002 god*. Moscow, 2002, 107–114.

Smirnov, P. S. *Vnutrennie voprosy v raskole XVII veka*. St. Petersburg: Tovarishchestvo "Pechatnia S. P. Iakovleva," 1898.

Solov'ev, S. M. *Istoriia Rossii s drevneishikh vremen*. Bk. 5, Vols. 9–10, Bk. 6, Vols. 11–12, and Bk. 7, Vol. 13. Reprint Moscow: AST, 2001.

Solov'ev, S. M. *History of Russia from Earliest Times*. Vol. 18. *Religious Struggle in Poland-Lithuania. Tsar Alexis' Reign Begins, 1654–1676*. Ed. and trans. Marian J. Rubchak. Gulf Breeze, FL: Academic International Press, 2002.

———. Vol. 21. *The Tsar and the Patriarch*. Ed. and trans. T. Allan Smith. Gulf Breeze, FL: Academic International Press, 2000.

———. Vol. 22. *The Reign of Tsar Alexis. Poland, Turkey, and Ukrainian Cossacks, 1667–1674*. Ed. and trans. Cathy J. Potter. Gulf Breeze, FL: Academic International Press, 2002.

———. Vol. 23. *Tsar Alexis. A Reign Ends*. Ed. and trans. Martha L. Lahana. Gulf Breeze, FL: Academic International Press, 1998

Subbotin, N.I., *Delo patriarkha Nikona*. Moscow: Tipografiia V. Grachev i Ko., 1862.

Suvorin, A. S. *Patriarkh Nikon. Rasskaz*. St. Petersburg: Izdanie A. S. Suvorina, 1893.

———. *Zamechatel'nye liudi: patriarkh Nikon, Ermak—pokoritel' Sibiri, boyarin Artamon Sergeevich Matveev*. St. Petersburg: Atranelia, 1874.

Sviateishii Nikon-patriarkh vserossiiskii i osnovannyi im Voskresenskii monastyr'. Moscow: Tipografiia Vil'de, 1909.

Sviateishii patriarkh vserossiiskii Nikon. Moscow: Tipografiia Tovarishchestva I. D. Sytina, 1904.

Tikhomirov, M. N. *Novgorodskii khronograf XVII v*. Moscow, 1979.

———. "Novgorodskoe vosstaniie 1650 goda." *Istoricheskie zapiski*, 1940 (7): 91–114.

Varlaam, archimandrite. *Istoriko-arkheologicheskoe opisanie drevnostei i redkikh veshchei, nakhodiashchikhsia v Kirillo-Belozerskom monastyre*. Moscow: Universitetskaia Tipografiia, 1859.

———. *O prebyvanii patriarkha Nikona v zatochenii v Ferapontove i Kirillo-Belozerskom monastyriakh, po aktam poslednego i opisanie sikh aktov*. Moscow, 1858.

Wortman, R. *Scenarios of Power. Myth and Ceremony in Russian Monarchy*, Vol. 1 Princeton: Princeton University Press, 1995.

Zelenskaia, G. M. *Sviatyni Novogo Ierusalima*. Moscow: Severnyi Palomnik, 2003.

———, ed. *Nikonovskie chteniia v muzee 'Novyi Ierusalim.' Sbornik statei*. Moscow: Leto, 2005.

———, ed. *Nikonovskie chteniia v muzee 'Novyi Ierusalim.' Sbornik statei*. Moscow: Severnyi Palomnik, 2002.

Zhivov, V. M. "Religious Reform and the Emrgence of the Individual in Russian Seventeenth-Century Literature." In *Religion and Culture in Early Modern Russia and Ukraine*. Eds. S. H. Baron and N. S. Kollmann. DeKalb: Northern Illinois University Press, 1997.

Zhiznevskii, A. K. *Pokhod velikago gosudaria sviateishago Nikona patriarkha moskovskago i vseia Velikiia i Malyia i Belyia Rossii v 1656 g. v Tver', Viaz'mu i Iverskii
monastyr'.* Tver', 1889.
Zhizn' sviateishago Nikona patriarkha vserossiiskago. Moscow: Tipo-Litografiia I. Efimova, 1878.
Zhizn' sviateishago Nikona patriarkha vserossiiskago. Moscow: Tipo-Litografiia I. Efimova, 1907.
Zyzykin, V. M. *Patriarkh Nikon. Ego gosudarstvennye i kanonicheskie idei.* Warsaw:
Sinodal'naia Tipografiia, 1931–1938.

Glossary of Russian Terms

I. Religious Descriptors, Titles, and Ranks of the Russian Orthodox Church

Apostol'skaia tserkov' – apostolic church; church which preserves the apostolic traditions and succession.

Avtokefal'naia tserkov' – autocephalic church; in Eastern Christian Church, an autonomous national church, not directly accountable to a patriarch and supervised by a national or local hierarch. Today, there are sixteen autocephalic Eastern Christian Churches.

Edinaia, sviataia, sobornaia i apostol'skaia tserkov' – one holy, catholic, and apostolic church; a common description of the Orthodox Church.

Sobornaia tserkov' – catholic church, conciliary church; in Eastern Christianity a church that practices consiliarism, conciliarity, i.e., unity and voluntary association of church body/family through collective participation in the divine liturgy; a name used when referring to the Russian Orthodox Church.

Black Clergy (celibate)

Arkhiepiskop – archbishop; in the Russian Orthodox Church, one of the upper ranks of the black clergy. An archbishop wears a black *klobuk* with cross and a *panagiia*.

Arkhierei – hierarch, eparch, chief hierarch; the term used to denote a member of the church hierarchy, usually a bishop or a archbishop in charge of a region, a province, or a large territory as well as a metropolitan or the patriarch.

Arkhiereiskii keleinik – servant to a hierarch; cell companion of a hierarch.

Archimandrit – archimandrite, head of a large monastery, also ceremonial doyen of the local or regional clergy in the absence of a bishop; member of the middle rank clergy, usually directly below bishop.

Bliustitel' – overseer, supervisor. *Bliustitel'* (*mestobliustitel'*) *patriarshego prestola* – locum tenens; in Eastern Christianity, a hierarch in charge of a particular patriarchate in the absence of the patriarch.

Bogomolets – God-entreater, pilgrim; self-identification of monks or higher ranking black clergy in communications with a *tsar;* usually used to justify royal patronage and material support of the clergy.

Episkop – bishop; in the Russian Orthodox Church, one of the upper ranks of the black clergy. A bishop's regalia include a black *klobuk* and a *panagiia.*

Ierod'iakon or ***chernyi d'iakon*** – monastic deacon; deacon who also accepted monastic vows.

Ieromonakh, or ***sviashchennoinok,*** or ***sviashchennomonakh*** – monastic priest, *ieromonk,* black priest, ordained monk, monk-presbyter; a priest who also pledged monastic vows, or a monk who was previously ordained as a priest. Monastic priests usually conduct liturgies at a monastery.

Igumen – abbot, *hegumen*; religious title usually given to the head of a monastery or the rector/dean of the cathedral, if he is a monk; a ceremonial rank below archimandrite.

Kelar' – cellarer, bursar, sacristan, procurator; a monastic novice serving another monk or hierarch or the monastic steward of a monastery, senior logistics manager in a monastery.

Keleinik – cell monk, cell companion, cell mate, lay brother; a monastic servant of a hierarch sharing the latter's cells.

Keleinyi starets – monastery elder; cell companion, or servant of a high ranking black clergyman at a monastery.

Mitropolit – metropolitan; one of the highest hierarchs in Russian Christianity just below patriarch, an archbishop in charge of a large diocese, a practice that dates to the sixteenth century. A metropolitan's regalia include a white *klobuk* and a *panagiia.*

Monakh, or ***chernets,*** or ***inok*** – a monk; a man who denounced secular life to serve God, the main inhabitant of a monastery.

Monakhinia, or ***inokinia,*** or ***naselnitsa*** – a nun; a woman who denounced secular life to serve God, the main inhabitant of a nunnery.

Otshelnik – solitary, religious recluse, ascetic hermit, solitudinarian; a monk who renounced communications with the world and retired to a remote place to live a solitary existence.

Patriarkh – patriarch; in Eastern Christianity, the highest religious rank, the head of an autocephalous church.

Postrig – monastic tonsure; the rite of taking monastic vows (for monks) or the rite of taking the veil (for nuns). In Eastern Christianity, during this ritual four strands of hair are cut in a shape of a cross, a symbolic initiation in the black clergy.

Pustynnik – anchorite, hermit; a monk living in a remote hermitage or monastery.

Skhima – schema; a term used for the two highest ranks of monastic orders which observe stricter vows. *Velikaia skhima* – great schema; extreme mortifications of a monk, final vows. *Malaia skhima* – lesser schema; also the habit of a monk who has taken the vows of *skhima.*

Skhiarkhimandrit – archimandrite, who has taken vows of the great schema.

Skhiigumen – abbot, who has taken vows of the great schema.

Skhimnik, skhimonakh – monk who has taken the vows of the schema, ascetic; the second highest monastic rank.

Starets – elder, monastic mentor; a monk who advises other inhabitants of a monastery.

Staritsa – an aged and venerable nun.

Sviatitel' – hierarch, prelate; a celebratory title given to church hierarchs. In the Russian Orthodox Church, *sviatitel'* means a sainted hierarch, holy hierarch, i.e., a hierarch who has been canonized as a saint.

Starets-stroitel' – abbot of the hermitage, prior; rank of a monastery superior below an archimandrite, usually selected from the monastic priests. This honorary title was also given to a clergyman who supervised the construction of a monastery.

Stroitel' – steward; an unordained clergyman in charge of a monastery's household.

Velikoskhimnik – monk who has taken vows of the great schema, a great ascetic; the highest monastic rank.

White Clergy (non-celibate)

Altarnik – sexton, sacristian; a person responsible for cleaning the altar, lightening candles, and preparing censers.

Arkhid'iakon or *protod'iakon* – archdeacon; in Eastern Christianity, the main deacon assisting a bishop.

Chtets – reader, lector, anagnost; member of the clergy or a secular person who reads the Gospel and other religious texts during the liturgy.

D'iachok – sexton, reader; a member of the lower clergy in Eastern Christianity who is responsible for reading psalms.

D'iakon – deacon; clergy of the lower rank responsible for assisting bishops and priests in conducting sacraments and religious services.

Dukhovnyi otets, or *dukhovnik*, or *ispovednik* – confessor, spiritual father; a priest who hears confession.

Ierei or *sviashchennik* – priest; a clergyman assigned to a church who conducts, by the power of divine grace, all sacraments, except the sacrament of ordination, both in the church (liturgy and other public services) and out, in the fields and homes of parishioners (prayer services, extreme unction, etc.), i.e., wherever there is a need in prayer and sacraments.

Ipod'iakon – sub-deacon; in Eastern Christianity, clergy of the lower rank assisting church hierarchs during the services, and especially the liturgy, the rank between a reader and a deacon.

Klir – the clergy of a parish or a church, including lectors and choir-members.

Klirik – a clergyman; in Russian Orthodoxy, a priest or a deacon.

Klirosnyi or *kliroshanin* – choir brother; member of the lower clergy responsible for singing during religious services.

Krestovaia sluzhba – service in the private patriarchal church, usually entrusted to a deacon.

Pevchii – member of a choir. *Pevchii d'iak* – a cantor.

Ponomar' – sexton; in Eastern Christianity, a member of the lower clergy in charge of ringing bells, lighting candles and icon-lamps, and assisting with the liturgy; the position of *ponomar'* was abolished in the nineteenth century.

Pop – priest; reverend. *Pop* is a colloquial term used for a more proper *ierei* or *sviashchennik*.

Pricht – the actual clergy of a parish or a church appointed by a hierarch according to the number of parishioners.

Prichetnik – junior deacon, psalm reader, lector; member of the clergy of a parish, common title given to all members of clergy, with the exception of priests and deacons, including lectors, sextons, choir members, etc., i.e., those who are responsible for reading liturgical books, church singing and participation in all religious services.

Protopop or ***protoierei*** – archpriest, senior priest in charge of a church; member of the middle ranks of the white clergy. Already in the nineteenth century, the term *protopop* was replaced by *protoierei*.

Psalomshchik – psalmist, psalm singer, psalm reader, sexton, acolyte; member of the lower clergy, whose responsibilities include singing psalms, accompanying a priest during his parochial visits, and keeping all church correspondence.

Raspop – former priest; member of the white clergy who leaves the church service.

Rasstriga – renegade monk, defrocked monk or priest; a member of the black or white clergy who rejects his vows.

Riznichii – sacristan, sexton, vestiary; a member of the lower clergy in charge of church possessions.

Starets sobornyi – synodal elder, church council's elder; also a member of the monastery's council.

Sveshchenosets – a candle bearer; a member of the lower clergy, usually sexton carrying a tall candle holder with a lit candle during the reading of the Gospel or during the entrance procession.

Znamenshchik – a notary priest.

II. Religious Architecture and Decorations of the Russian Orthodox Church

Amvon – ambo; in the Russian Orthodox Church, a central part located across the church from *tsarskie vrata*, the place where a priest recites supplications, delivers homilies and a deacon reads the Gospel.

Analoi – altar stand, lectern, reading stand, *analogion*; in the Eastern Christian Church, a tall desk covered with cloth on which icons and liturgical books are placed during the service.

Kel'ia – monastic cell, reclusory, cabin; a residential room or a house in a monastery intended as a dwelling for one or several monks.

Kliros – choir place, choir gallery; in the Russian Orthodox Church, an elevated place in front of the *iconostasis* on which the choir, readers, and non-participating clergy stand during the liturgy to assist in its conduct by singing and reading. Usually a church has two *kliroses*, a southern one and a northern one.

Lavra – in the Russian Orthodoxy, a large and exceptionally significant monastery; a monastery of the highest rank; a chief monastery which is officially governed by a high ranking hierarch, including a patriarch.

Monastyr' – monastery (for monks), convent, nunnery (for nuns); in Eastern Christianity, a community of monks or nuns who accepted certain rules of communal living with its own church hierarchy and economic structures, also, several buildings designed for such communities. *Stavropigial'nyi monastyr'* – monastery directly accountable to the patriarch or synod.

Pripisnoi monastyr' – dependent monastery, monastery assigned to a larger and more important one.

Navershie – roofing; cupola and tent roof of a church.

Papert' – church outer porch; an elevated entrance to the church preceded by a small staircase.

Patriarshee mesto – patriarchal stall, throne, chair, bench, or pew; ornately decorated place in a cathedral with a canopy roof, designated for a patriarch

Prestol – the holy communion table, the holy throne, the holy altar table; the main part of an Orthodox church, rectangular table standing in the middle of the altar used in the sacrament of the Eucharist.

Pritvor – ante-church, fore-church, vestibule; the western part of church which leads to the middle of the church. Services of *litiia* and *oglashenie* are conducted exclusively in an ante-church. It is also used by the newly converted, non-Orthodox Christians and non-Christians as well as the anathemized. Many monasteries use ante-church as a refectory for monks.

Pustyn' – hermitage, remote monastery, hermitage monastery, isolated cell of a hermit in a large monastery.

Riznitsa – vestry, sacristy; a room in the church were liturgical vestments and utensils are kept.

Skit – hermitage; austere monastic building, hostel, or cabin-like cells located away from the main monastery's territory or in a desolated place in which a monk or a group of monks live devoting their lives to prayer, meditation, and labor. Administratively, a hermitage could be directly ruled by an abbot or an archimandrite of a monastery or be independent of any monastery, provided that it had an *ieromonk* alongside with an authoritative elder.

Sobor – cathedral, cathedral church; the main church in a town or monastery, intended for a services conducted by a hierarch together with a large number of clergy.

Trapeznaia – refectory; a building or a room in a monastery where the monastic orders are assembled to eat.

Tserkov' – church; religious building with altar and space for prayer and liturgy.

Tsraskie vrata – sanctuary royal doors, sanctuary holy doors; in the Eastern Christian church, a central entrance to the altar, part of the *iconostasis*. The shutters flanking *tsarskie vrata* usually depict the four Evangelists and the Annunciation.

III. Religious Books, Rituals, and Services of the Russian Orthodox Church

Antidor – the *Antidoron* Bread, the *eulogia*, the holy bread; parts of the altar bread from which the Holy Lamb is removed during the office of preparation and given to the faithful who did not partake in holy communion

Apostol – Book of Acts and Epistles of the Apostles; theological book containing parts of the New Testament as well as the annual church calendar.

Blagovest – ringing of the church bell; ringing of a single bell before the liturgy and the Eucharist when the words "it is meet and right" are uttered.

Chasoslov or *chasy* – Book of Hours; religious and liturgical book which includes psalms, prayers, songs, and other elements of the daily liturgical services as well as texts of the most common books of prayers. *Ustavnye chasy molitv* – canonical hours; *zautrenia i chasy pered obednei* – matins with lauds; *sluzhba 1-ogo chasa* – prime; *sluzhba 3 chasa* – tierce, *sluzhba 6-ogo chasa* – sext; *sluzhba 9-ogo chasa* – nones; *vechernia i bogosluzhenie v vechernie chasy* – vespers and complin.

Chasy – the daily canonical hours, offices of the hours; daily religious services, an established order of daily religious activities divided by an hour.

Ektin'ia – litany of supplication, aitesis; communal prayer during the liturgy which consists of several brief petitions accompanied by exclamations "Lord, have mercy" and "Lord, hear our prayer." In contemporary Eastern Christianity, there are great, little, double (fervent), and soliciting *ektin'ias* which differ in length and the exclamations being uttered. *Ektin'ia ob usopshikh* – the litany for the departed; *ektin'ia ob oglashennykh* – the litany for the catuchumens.

Epitim'ia – penance, discipline; penalty assigned by a spiritual father or confessor to a repentant sinner, spiritual exercise to conquer sinful habits, including fasting, praying, reading of the Bible, pilgrimages, etc.

Evkharistiia – the Eucharist, holy communion, the sacramental communion, the sacrament of communion; one of the major sacraments of the Christian Church when the faithful partake of bread of wine which represent the true Blood and Body of Christ. In Eastern Christianity, the Eucharist is conducted after the liturgy, during the Eucharistic canon.

Glas – tone, mode, tune, melody in church music. Together, tones form the eight ecclesiastical modes used in Eastern Christianity to sing prayers during a liturgy. Modes change every week and every ninth week, a new round of eight ecclesiastical modes begins.

Edinoglasie, edinoglasnoe penie – monophonic singing, unison singing when only one text is read or sung.

Kafisma – proper psalm, *cathisma*; one of twenty divisions in the Book of Psalms. When *cathismas* are read, one is allowed to sit. According to the church rules, the Book of Psalms is read once a week during the regular periods and twice a week during Lent.

Kanon – (1) canon; collection of rules and exemplars of dogmatic nature.

Kanon – (2) canon; together with *kondak* and *tropar'*, one of the forms in Orthodox hymnography.

Kanonik – Book of Canons, the Canon; in Eastern Christianity, liturgical book containing canons to Jesus Christ, the Mother of God, and guardian angel, as well as morning and evening prayers and prayers recited before communion.

Khomovoe penie – singing of a text which substitutes soft and hard signs with the letter "o" at the end of verbs and nouns.

Kondak – *contakion*; short song which briefly describes the life of a saint or a history of a sacred event/holiday.

Krestnyi khod – procession of the cross, religious procession with the crosses and banners, icon bearing procession; procession of the clergy and the faithful with crosses, banners, icons, and other sacred subjects, usually performed during Easter, the Epiphany, or a local religious holiday.

Litiia – earnest entreaties, utia, a short prayer for the dead; public prayer, part of the vigil on the eve of important church observances. *Zaupokoinaia litiia* – earnest entreaties for the dead; short burial service.

Liturgiia – the liturgy; the main Christian service during which the sacrament of communion is being offered

Maslenitsa or ***syrnaia nedelia*** – Shrovetide, pancake week; in Eastern Christianity, the week before great Lent during which meat consumption is prohibited, but consumption of dairy, eggs, and fish are still allowed. *Syropust* or *syropustnaia nedelia* – cheese-fare Sunday; the last day of Shrovetide, the Sunday before great Lent when the faithful are still allowed to eat dairy products.

Mesiatseslov or ***sviatsy*** – Menology; the book of saints with a church calendar, list of saints revered by the Russian Orthodox Church arranged according to months and days.

Mnogoglasie, mnogolosoe penie – polyphonic singing when several texts are being recited at once.

Moleben – prayer service, public supplicatory or thanksgiving service; religious service conducted either in gratitude when the faithful thank Jesus Christ, Virgin Mary or a saint, or in times of duress when the faithful ask for protection. Prayer service can be conducted in a church, at home, or in the open (e.g., when blessing a new crop), but it is always a public, collective service facilitated by a priest.

Molitvennik – prayer book, primer, book of devotions, processional, synopsis, missal.

Molitvennoe pravilo – prayer rule, set of one's daily prayers; in the Eastern Christianity, morning and evening prayers read daily by the faithful as well as pre-communion prayers. It also includes the four canons that every Orthodox monk must read during the day.

Molitvoslov – Book of Prayer, prayer manual; a book used in private devotions, includes morning and evening prayers, recited by the faithful daily, as well as communion prayers. It may also include personal prayers, penance canons, and hymns.

Narechnoe penie – religious singing of a text which omits soft and hard signs.

Obednia – the liturgy, afternoon services, day offices, the office of the Mass, the Mass; a Eucharistic service usually conducted in the afternoon.

Oglashenie – *catechumenation*; a ritual preceding the baptism which familiarizes future Christians with the essence of the Christian creed. *Oglashennyi* – audient, catechumen; a person preparing for the sacrament of baptism.

Otpust – the final dismissal after the liturgy, dismissal prayer "May the blessing of the Lord, through His Divine Grace and love, towards mankind, be upon you always, now and ever, and unto ages of ages," read by a priest at the end of the liturgy.

Panikhida – memorial service, office of the dead, dirge, the burial service for a deceased.

Polunoshchnitsa – the midnight prayer, the night office of vigils, matins; service conducted at midnight and every hour of the night in memory of the Lord's midnight prayer in the Garden of Gethsemane. The midnight prayer is usually recited in Orthodox monasteries and does not have an equivalent in Western Christianity.

Poluustav – the book containing rituals performed during the Church Slavonic liturgy.

Pominovenie usopshikh – prayer for the dead, remembrance of the dead in prayers.

Povecher'e – night prayer, small vespers; a service conducted in monasteries after the evening meal which consists of prayers read before going to sleep asking for forgiveness of sins and protection from evil.

Prosfora – altar bread, *prosphora*; white round liturgical bread used in the sacrament of the Eucharist and for remembering the living and the dead during the office of preparation. Altar bread is made of unleavened wheat dough and bears a cross and letters for Jesus Christ and Victor.

Proskomidiia – the office of preparation, the preface of the mass, offertory, service of oblation, service of preparation; the preface to the liturgy of John the Chrysostom and Basil the Great, during which priests and black clergy hierarchs prepare bread and wine for the Eucharist. In contemporary Russian Orthodox Church, five altar breads are used in the office of preparation, while Old Believers still use seven.

Psalom – psalm; prayer singing.

Psaltyr' – (1) Book of Psalms; collection of psalms, part of Old Testament; (2) Book of Psalms; liturgical book which consists of 151 psalms divided into twenty *cathismas* and supplemented by prayers and *troparions* (stanzas) recited after the *cathismas*. The Book of Hours and Menology with a church calendar are sometimes appended at the end of the Book of Psalms.

Raspevy – chants; a round of religious melodies, which usually include all eight ecclesiastical modes. *Znamennyi raspev* – the Byzantine plain chant, the first Russian liturgical chant, common in eleventh through seventeenth centuries. Initially monophonic, it evolved into polyphonic singing. *Znamennyi* chant used eight tones and special notations, also known as *kruki*. *Grecheskii raspev* – Greek chant, the ancient monophonic chant of the Greek Church; in seventeenth-century Russia, Greek chants gained greater popularity than their predecessor, *Znamennyi* chants. Seventeenth-century Greek chants were more closely connected to the non-Greek Orthodox Church, including Romanian and Bulgarian ones, than the Greek monosonic originals. Greek chants are characterized by melodic symmetry, repetition of syllabic melodic structure. *Kievskii raspev* – Kievan chant, one of liturgical chants of the Russian Orthodox Church which originated in the present-day Ukraine as a simplified variation of *Znamennyi* chant and became wide-spread in the seventeen century. Kievskii chant is shorter and simpler than the *Znamennyi* chant, and it uses repetition of certain phrases of the hymn's text.

Razreshitel'naia molitva – the Absolution; a prayer read by the priest at the end of the burial service in which he asks for forgiveness of sins committed by the deceased. After the service, the paper with a prayer is folded and put in the right hand of the deceased.

Sinodik – book of the deceased and sick to be prayed for, *synodicon*, death bill, bead roll, obituary; a book, in which the names of the deceased are written by those grieving them to be permanently remembered in church services.

Sluzhebnik – Service Book, Ritual Book, Euchology, the Book of Communion Service; liturgical book containing texts recited by a priest or a deacon.

Soborovat' or *prichishchat' umiraiushchego* – to administer extreme unction, to administer last sacraments; one of the Christian sacraments.

Soborovat'sia – to receive extreme unction.

Stikhira – hymn, *sticheron*, from Greek word for multiple verses; a brief religious song or hymn celebrating a holiday or a saint, sung after a verse from one of the psalms.

Sviatki – Christmastide, Yuletide; the days of rejoicing after Christmas, in Eastern Christianity, twelve days between Christmas and the Epiphany (January 7–19) commemorating both events.

Treba – service of prayers celebrated on occasion of personal significance, occasional religious rite (Christening, marriage, funeral, etc.).

Trebnik – Book of Devotions, Book of Needs, Breviary, Eucology; liturgical book containing descriptions of observances and prayers.

Tropar' – stanza for a religious holiday or a saint's day, *troparion*; in Orthodox liturgical services, a short song explaining the essence of the holiday or event being celebrated, occasionally *tropar'* may also list deeds of the saint being celebrated.

Ustav – Book of Church Canons; a compendium consisting of the rules regulating the life of a monastery or a monastic order.

Utrenia – morning prayer, orthron; public liturgy conducted in the morning or on the eve of the previous day which consists of the midnight prayer, morning prayer, and the prime.

Vechernia – evening service, vespers; public liturgy, celebrated in the evening before sunset because the church daily cycle begins in the evening and always refers to the next day of a secular calendar. *Velikaia vechernia* – great vespers, complin(e); public liturgy on the eve of important religious observance, especially Easter, and Sundays.

Vsenoshchnaia – all-night vigil, night service, night office, vespers and matins; public service conducted on the eve of religious holy days and Sundays, which consisted of the midnight prayer, great vespers, and the morning prayer.

Zaupokoinaia sluzhba or ***otpevanie*** – burial service, service of burial, office of the dead.

Zautrenia – morning prayer, prime, matins; the start of the daily religious service, usually conducted on the eve of the previous day or at night. *Paskhal'naia zautrenia* – the Easter Vigil.

IV. Liturgical Vestments and Utensils of the Russian Orthodox Church

Chiotki – rosary beads, prayer beads; a string with knots or beads which assists in counting prayers. *Chiotki-lestvitsa* – narrow leather string with nine large dividing beads and ninety-one smaller beads. The ends of the string are bound together with two triangles. Currently, only Old Believers use this type of the prayer beads.

Diskos – paten; a liturgical vessel, a platter depicting Baby Jesus on which Eucharistic Lamb taken from the middle of altar bread is placed prior to holy communion.

Epitrakhil' – priestly stole, scarf, *epitracheleon*; one of the liturgical vestments of the priesthood, a broad band worn around the neck and extended to the ground. In the front, two ends of the stole are sewn together and are usually decorated with seven crosses. It symbolizes the perfect grace of the Holy Spirit descending on a priest. No liturgy can be conducted without it.

Felon' – cloak, mantle; long, loose sleeveless outer dress of a priest usually decorated with a cross on the back which symbolizes the purple mantle of Jesus Christ placed on Him by Roman soldiers in jest.

Istochniki – sources, fountains; narrow ribbons of different colors, usually red or white, sewn onto the mantle of a hierarch. Sources symbolize grace, wisdom, and knowledge emanating from a hierarch in the exercise of his pastoral duties.

Kadilo – incensory, censor; a metal vessel hung on chain, in which incense is heated.

Kaftan – man's long outer garment, similar to contemporary overcoat.

Kamilavka – biretta, *kamilauchion*; monastic headdress usually of black or dark violet color, in the shape of inverted cylinder with a small brim, worn by the three orders of the white (non-celibate) clergy. Black clergy usually cover this hat with the *klobuk*.

Khorugv' – holy banner; icon made of fabric or metal and attached to a tall pole depicting Jesus Christ, the Mother of God, or saints, which is carried in the front during the religious processions.

Klobuk – monastic hood, veil; a black cover or veil worn by the monastic ranks over the *kamilavka*, or black hat. A patriarch wears a white *klobuk* with an elevated cross on top.

Kropilo – holy water sprinkler, aspergill; a thick brush used for sprinkling the holy water.

Mantiia – mantle, gown, cloak; wide and loose outer dress, a black sleeveless cape symbolizing disdain for riches worn, by the black clergy. Hierarchs of the Russian Orthodox Church wear light blue, green, or purple mantles.

Mitra – miter, crown; the gilded headdress decorated with a mounted cross worn by the highest ranks of black clergy during the liturgy.

Napersnyi krest – pectoral cross; cross worn by a clergyman over his dress, a sign of honor, dignity, or a high rank. A pectoral cross is worn by both priests and black clergy hierarchs, but the latter wear it together with *panagiia*.

Omofor – bishop's scarf, amice, *omophorion*, *pallium*; a liturgical vestment worn by bishops in the Eastern Church, a wide band worn on the shoulders of a hierarch, decorated with crosses. It symbolizes a lost and found sheep carried by the Good Shepard. The great *omofor* is a long and wide band decorated with crosses, worn around the neck with its ends hanging in the front and back. The small *omofor* is a wide band worn around the neck and fastened in the front by buttons. Small *omofor* is worn by a hierarch over *sakkos* exclusively for conducting the liturgy.

Orar' – deacon's stole, *orarion*; a long narrow band of fabric worn on the left shoulder by a sub-deacon, archdeacon, or deacon.

Orlets – eagle's rug; a small oval or circular rug embroidered with a soaring eagle, placed over the throne or hierarchical ambo on which hierarchs stand during the liturgy. Eagle's rug symbolizes the governance of a local church or a diocese.

Palitsa – part of the liturgical dress of a priest, archimandrite, or hierarch; a diamond shaped piece of cardboard covered with fabric hanging by a cord from the left thigh. It symbolizes the spiritual sword, or a word of God, which a priest always carries with him.

Panagiia – medallion, pectoral image, pectoral plate, encolpion; small, usually round icon depicting God or the Mother of God that a church hierarch wears on his chest.

Panikadilo – church chandelier, hanging from the ceiling which consists of several tiers of candles; church lamp containing twelve or more candles.

Podriasnik – inner rason; the everyday wear of both the black and the white clergy, long, ankle-length dress with tight collar and narrow sleeves, worn underneath the frock or outer rason.

Podriznik – under-tunic, alb, inner rason; liturgical dress, inner wear of priests and hierarchs made of light-colored fabric and symbolizing chastity and purity of heart required of the clergy.

Poias – a sash, zone, girdle, belt; part of the liturgical vestment worn by a priest or a hierarch, used to bind a stole and an alb/inner tunic.

Poruchi – liturgical cuffs; part of liturgical dress worn by a deacon, priest, or a hierarch during liturgical services, broad bands with strings and buttons used to fasten the sleeves of a tunic. Liturgical cuffs symbolize the chains binding Jesus Christ during His trial.

Potir – chalice, calyx, the communion cup; a chalice containing wine which symbolizes the blood of Jesus Christ used in holy communion.

Riasa – frock, cassock, outer rason; outer dress of the Orthodox black and white clergy worn in between liturgical services, loose long dress with wide sleeves, usually made of dark-colored fabric.

Riza – liturgical vestment, chasuble, cape, similar to *mantle*; outer liturgical dress with arm slits, worn by a priest or a bishop.

Sakkos – bishop's chasuble, dalmatic; outer liturgical dress, an alb-like, cross-ornamented vestment made of satin or silk, worn by the hierarchs of the Eastern Christian Church.

Skrizhali – pomata, Tables of the Law; four squares sewn onto the hierarchal mantle.

Stikhar' – tunic, surplice, alb, *sticharion*; a clerical robe usually made of white linen, sometimes richly ornamented. In the Eastern Christianity, an outer long dress made of light-colored fabric with opening for the head and wide sleeves, worn over inner rason by priests and deacons, i.e., those serving in the altar.

Trikirii and *dikirii* – triple and double candlesticks or candelabra used by a bishop to give solemn blessings. *Dikirii* holds two candles, symbolizing the dual nature of Christ as God and Man; *trikirii* holds three candles, symbolizing the Trinity.

Vozdukh – paten and chalice veil, chalice and paten cloth covering; an embroidered veil which covers the Eucharistic bread and wine; paten and chalice are first covered by small, individual veils and then, together, by a bigger one.

Zhezl or *posokh* – staff, crosier. When carried by a bishop or an abbot, staff is a symbol of spiritual power.

V. Russian Measures of Length, Weight, and Money

Altyn – a small coin used in Muscovite Russia whose value equaled three *kopeks*.

Arshin – measurement of length used in Muscovite Russia, about seventy-one centimeters.

Chetvert' – measurement of length used in Muscovite Russia, about 17.8 centimeters.

Chetvert' – measurement of dry substances (including grain, flour, sand) used in Muscovite Russia, about two hundred and ten kilograms.

Den'ga – a small coin used in Muscovite Russia whose value equaled one-two-hundredth of a *ruble* or half a *kopek*.

Grivna – a silver coin used in Muscovite Russia whose value equaled ten *kopeks*, or one-tenth of a *ruble*.

Lokot' – cubit, ell; measurement of length used in Muscovite Russia, about half a meter.

Poltina – a silver coin used in Muscovite Russia whose value equaled fifty *kopeks*, or half a *ruble*.

Poprishche – measurement of length used in Muscovite Russia, about 1.473 kilometers. *Poprishche* can also mean an equivalent of the Greek *stadion* or *milia* (185 meters), or a Russian measure of two-thirds of *versta*.

Sazhen' – fathom; measurement of length used in Muscovite Russia, about 2.133 meters.

Vershok – measurement of length used in Muscovite Russia, about 4.4 centimeters.

Versta – measurement of length used in Muscovite Russian, about 1.06 kilometer.

Yefimok – Russian term for *Joachimstalers*, German silver coins re-stamped in Russia; Russia was importing coinage at the time.

Zolotnik – measurement of weight used in the Muscovite Russia, about 4.25 grams.

VI. Russian Secular Titles and Governmental Offices

Boyarin or ***boyar*** – highest social rank in Muscovite Russia, aristocracy, upper nobility; member of the Council of *Boyars* [*Duma*]. The group of Russian *boyars* consisted of (1) *bol'shie* (great), also known as *blizhnie*, or *vvedennye boyars* – privy councilors, who served as the *tsar's* advisers and (2) *malye*, or *putnye* – administrative *boyars* who served as special envoys and received compensation for their travel expenses.

Boyarskii syn, boyarskie deti – junior *boyar(s)*, member(s) of the lower nobility, *boyar* descendants who did not inherit a title and who usually served the *tsar* as special envoys and/or trusted cadets. *Arkhiereiskie deti boyarskie* – junior *boyars* assigned to an archbishop. *Patriarshie deti boyarskie* – junior *boyars* assigned to a patriarch.

Chinovnik – state functionary, secular functionary, official, civil servant.

D'iak – chancellery or chamber secretary; high ranking government official or chancellor in charge of local government office or chancellery.

Dumnyi d'iak – secretary of the Council [of *Boyars*], Council secretary, *Duma* chancellor; in Muscovite Russia, a high ranking state official, supervising regular *d'iaks* (clerks). While regular clerks working in the Council of *Boyars* were responsible for drafting official documents, the secretary of the Council was in charge of forwarding documents to be considered by the Council of *Boyars*. He was also entrusted to sign the sovereign's name on decrees and official documents, which was later verified by an official royal seal. There could be more than one *dumnyi d'iak* at a time.

Dvorets – housekeeping building of the court, including *kormovoi* and *sytnyi dvorets* (food keeping building) which contained food and beverages.

Dvoretskii – butler, majordomo, usually selected from the *boyars* or junior *boyars*. His responsibilities included supervision of the lower ranks of court servants. He was also in charge of *dvorest* or housekeeping office, its possessions and income derived from *dvorets* economy.

Dvoriane – the highest ranking servitors below the *boyars* and other courtiers, the middle-upper rank of the Muscovite nobility.

Duma of boyars or ***synclete***[i] – in Muscovite Russia, the *tsar's* Council consisting of the highest ranking boyars.

Dumnye dvoriane – service gentry of the Council [of *Boyars*]. *Dumnyi dvorianin* – conciliar noble, state servitor.

Kaznachei – treasurer, household treasurer.

Kluchnik – steward, keeper of keys; a court official responsible for food and wine cellars.

---

[i] *Synclete* is a Byzantine equivalent of the Russian term *Duma*.

Konushii – master of the horse, stable attendant; one of the highest ranks of the *boyars*.

Okol'nichii – lord-in-waiting; in Muscovite Russia, a *boyar* of the second highest rank. Lords-in-waiting were usually selected as governors, chancellors, or ambassadors. *Blizhnii okolnichii* – privy lord-in-waiting.

Pod'iachii – clerk, undersecretary, scribe, scrivener, chancellery official.

Polugolova – battalion commander of the *strel'tsy*.

Postel'nik or **postel'nichii** – chamberlain, gentleman of the bedchamber; one of the highest court ranks.

Prikaz – chancellery, office, department, bureau; part of an administrative structure in Muscovite Russia. *Dvortsovyi prikaz* was in charge of all crown and patriarchal possessions, including servants and serfs. It supervised realization of the *tsar's* and the patriarch's orders. In 1649, another office, *Monastyrskii prikaz*, was established within *dvortsovyi prikaz* to supervise all secular proceedings involving the clergy. Peter the Great established his own *monastyrskii prikaz* (also known as *raspravnyi prikaz*) in 1701. *Kazennyi prikaz* or treasury was in charge of collecting taxes and levies and other sources of income, including revenues from monasteries and church possessions. *Sudnyi prikaz* was in charge of all trials and court proceedings. *Patriarshii prikaz* was entrusted with internal church affairs and administration. *Prikaz tainykh del* was Aleksei Mikhailovich's Privy Chancellery or Private Office; in Peter the Great's reign, *Tainyi prikaz* or the chancery of secret affairs denoted a security office.

Prikaznye liudi – chancellery officials. *Prikaznyi dvorianin* – chancellery courtier, member of the nobility serving at a chancellery, a servant assigned to a dignitary and responsible for executing orders of his master.

Pristav – warden, bailiff.

Sokol'nik or **sokol'nichii** – a falconer, master of the falcons; one of the highest court ranks.

Sotnik – lieutenant or captain of the *strel'tsy*, company commander, centurion; a military rank of the officer in charge of a hundred men. *Sotnik streletskii* – captain of the *strel'tsy*.

Stol'nik – royal table attendant, one of the highest ranks of the *boyars;* a high official at the *tsar's* court or the civil administration.

Streletskii golova – captain of the *strel'tsy*, military commander, head of the *strel'tsy* regiment; each town usually employed several such regiments.

Strel'tsy – palace guard, musketeers, professional infantrymen; members of the military in Muscovite Russia.

Striapchii – crown agent in *tsar's* service, *boyar* responsible for the *tsar's* wardrobe and grooming; an official rank in Muscovite Russia. Crown agents were usually selected from the upper nobility to serve the *tsar* and to run a variety of errands for him, including dressing. They held the *tsar's striapnia*, i.e., hat, gloves, scarves, and staff, while the *tsar* was attending church services or official business inside.

Tamozhennaia izba – customs, tax, and levies office in Muscovite Russia.

Tsar – Russian title of a royal male crown bearer, derived from Caesar.

Tsarevna – title given to the female descendants of a *tsar*, daughter of a *tsar*, or an unmarried female member of the royal household.

Tsarevich – title given to the male descendants of a tsar, son of a *tsar;* a male heir to the throne.

Tsarina – Russian title for married royal females, *tsar's* mother or wife, or a royal female crown bearer.

Tsarskii d'iak – secretary to the *tsar,* a court rank.

Voevoda – a town's military commander and governor; often the most important governmental position in Muscovite Russia's towns, a high ranking officer either in the civil administration or in the army equal in rank to the general or governor. *Bol'shoi voevoda* – commander in chief of a large military unit, army. *Blizhnii voevoda* – privy commander.

Zemskaia izba – town hall, judicial chamber, district or provincial office, city government office in Muscovite Russia; office of local authorities, an elected office of local self-government established as a result of the local government reforms of Ivan IV (the Terrible). *The zemskaia izba* was headed by a *starosta* (elder, prefect) who was often directly accountable to a town's military commander and governor.

VII. Russian Official Documents

Chelobitnaia – petition, a document which contained the plea of a subordinate to his superior.

Gramota – decree, letter missive, charter, deed, issued by a *tsar* or a patriarch. *Zhalovannaia gramota* – letter patent; a document issued by the tsar to legalize granting of a title or land holdings.

Opisi – inventory, catalog, description of monastery possessions and holdings.

Otpiska – a short note, letter; a less formal form of official correspondence.

Ukaz – edict, order.

Index

195